WOMEN IN AFRICAN CINEMA

Women in African Cinema: Beyond the Body Politic showcases the very prolific but often marginalised presence of women in African cinema, both on the screen and behind the camera.

This study provides the first in-depth and sustained study of women in African cinema. Films by women from different geographical regions are discussed in case studies that are framed by feminist theoretical and historical themes, and seen through an anti-colonial, philosophical, political and socio-cultural cinematic lens. A historical and theoretical introduction provides the context for thematic chapters exploring topics ranging from female identities, female friendships, women in revolutionary cinema, motherhood and daughterhood, women's bodies, sexuality, and spirituality. Each chapter serves up a theoretical-historical discussion of the chosen theme, followed by two in-depth case studies that provide contextual and transnational readings of the films as well as outlining production, distribution and exhibition contexts. This book contributes to the feminist anti-racist revision of the canon by placing African women filmmakers squarely at the centre of African film culture.

Demonstrating the depth and diversity of the feminine or female aesthetic in African cinema, this book will be of great interest to students and scholars of African cinema, media studies and African studies.

Lizelle Bisschoff is a researcher and curator of African film and founder of the Africa in Motion (AiM) Film Festival, an annual African film festival taking place in Scotland. She is currently Senior Lecturer in Film and Television Studies at the University of Glasgow.

Stefanie Van de Peer is researcher and programmer of African and Arab cinema. Her award-winning collection *Animation in the Middle East* came out in 2017. She programmes for film festivals worldwide and works for Africa in Motion. She is Research Fellow at the University of Exeter and Lecturer in Film and Media at Queen Margaret University in Edinburgh.

This book is dedicated to female friendship

CONTENTS

FOREWORD

On a warm night in July 2003, I sat by the edge of the Indian Ocean on the fragrant island of Zanzibar mentally preparing for an interview with a journalist. I was nervous. I had just screened my first feature-length film, *Dangerous Affair*, to a live audience in a packed Ngome Kongwe, the Old Fort, Zanzibar's oldest building, built by Omani Arabs in Stone Town in 1699. The journalist, a Frenchman whose name I have long since forgotten, crouched himself at my feet in the sand, seemingly agitated. He pressed a button on his recorder and held it closer to me, to ensure he captured my responses over the sound of the crashing waves behind us, and asked the question I will never forget:

"Your film is not African. It's Western. Why didn't you make a real African film?"

Dangerous Affair is a story about modern relationships set in middle-class Nairobi, the capital of Kenya. Nairobi's nightlife, which features heavily in the film, is like many of my wonderful and diverse female friends: loud and lively. It was an unusual homage to a version of Africa that I knew well, as the city I had lived in for most of my life but had never seen on the silver screen. It offers a version of Africa that my producer Njeri Karago and I felt was necessary – and missing in the film narratives we had so far seen of "us." But for the French journalist, who had never lived in my city, never met women like those in my film, it was an aberration. Perhaps he believed that a true African film could only be one in which all problems were economic and solved under trees by a cluster of desperate people waiting for rain, or better leadership, or some form of economic emancipation. As an African woman, I had offended his sensibilities by daring to suggest that there were other truths and realities on my continent. He didn't understand my film's portrayal of an African city where women worked in finance and marketing and danced and drank the night away to unwind. He couldn't conceive that the women who drove fast cars and fell in and out of love could possibly exist outside of the West. An African film by a female filmmaker couldn't be *this thing* I had made, populated by cliché-defying, multi-dimensional females whose families accepted dowry but who also traded stories about dating disasters with sharp-witted, feminist girlfriends over large glasses of chilled white wine. Where in this film was my dry, famine-struck village and why did my characters not tremble and heed the advice and directive of village elders? Where were the corrupt leaders or the market women? Why did some of my film's female characters go clubbing, smoke cigarettes, talk back to and cheat on their husbands? And most importantly, why was there an absence of anyone standing in silhouette against a fiery orange African sunset?

The answer lay in my past.

My foray into film had begun decades earlier, when I struggled to find my calling. I felt cursed as a female with artistic tendencies at a time where many parents wanted their children to be lawyers, doctors or engineers. I didn't even dare to imagine I could call myself an "artist" or a "storyteller" because it just was not done. Still, I had an ambition that would lead me to be a partner or director of some important organisation. And that important "Director-Thing" did not include being a film director. That was inconceivable – even to me.

As a young woman, I had witnessed my famous maternal uncles Sam, David and Leonard Kibera pen novel after novel – one of which, *Potent Ash* (a collection of short stories) went on to become an East African classic. And so, I knew that whilst storytelling might fill my soul, it wasn't guaranteed to keep my belly full. Film directing was not something I even considered – directors were white men who flew into Nairobi from England, Portugal or Italy to direct adverts: infallible, mysterious, well-paid males allowed to shout or whisper at everyone from a chair that had the word DIRECTOR on the back.

One day, aged 19 and home from school in the United Kingdom, I walked in to visit a Kenya High School girlfriend, Mary Wakaba, at work. I had just finished my A-Levels and had applied to do a business course, certain that no career for storytellers or artists existed in Kenya. Mary was a stunningly beautiful girl with a huge heart and quick wit, who had landed a job as a receptionist in Kenya's largest advertising agency, McCann Erickson. As I sat with her at the reception, I observed how fast everyone walked, talked and worked and was mesmerised.

In 1980s Nairobi, everything outside this strange space I had wandered into appeared to move fairly slowly. The political climate was fearful – this was a dictatorship under Daniel arap Moi after all. We were only 25 years into an independent Kenya and even though I did not know it at the time, I was part of the first generation living under the leadership of the first generation of African leaders. We had no idea that we were in the midst of building a nation. This place I had wandered into was one where employees worked and played hard and seemed to have a healthy disrespect for everything I had thus far regarded as "normal." They dressed however they wanted and still earned good money, telling stories about brands. So, when my friend Mary told me that the agency was looking for a copywriter – I had no idea what that was – I found myself in a quick interview with a handsome English creative director who nonchalantly handed me some briefs, which I wrote a pile of copy for overnight.

The next day, Mary told me, he rushed in, clutching my pile of scribbles shouting, "Where is she? Can she start tomorrow?"

Yes. This was my kind of place.

I spent my entire holiday there, coming in early and leaving so late on most days that I was given a key to lock up after just a few weeks. After two months, I was offered a permanent job, but didn't take up the offer – I needed to finish college. A few years later I was back and started developing my writing, art directing and storyboarding skills in a space I soon regarded as home.

Ten years on, aged 31, with accolades and the fancy title of Creative Director (the first non-white, non-male to hold this title in an international agency in the region), I had grown weary. I simply could not find it in me to write another Coca Cola or margarine advert. So, I quit. I wanted to make films, because I had realised as the years unfolded, that there was no one on television, outside commercials, who looked or sounded or lived like me or the people I knew. In leaving advertising, I found a new challenge: I didn't realise how quickly all the things I had imagined I would retain fell away like dry leaves – a comfortable escalating salary, a fancy car, insurance benefits, status, friends, parties. The sense of belonging in a space I understood. Even though advertising had been a kind of mini-film school, I didn't really know how to produce a film. I knew how to write and storyboard and oversee low and high budget 30 or 60-second radio and TV commercials, to write the mood, write jingle lyrics, brief a composer, sit in a post-production house and oversee an edit, but I didn't know how to really make a film. I didn't understand the hierarchy of film. I did not go back to this comfort, because confining myself to creating adverts was strangling my soul. But how would I become a filmmaker if travelling abroad to go to film school was financially out of reach? My pension plan for my decade of work gave me about six months of breathing space and bought me a shiny new Mac and a soul-searching trip to India, but that was all.

I survived by taking up just about any brief that came my way, as long as it presented me with an opportunity to learn something new about storytelling for the screen. A neighbour's fiancée asked me to make a corporate video for his organisation. And then another and another. The word spread – there was a girl who could make stuff. I made more NGO films than I can reliably count – and learned to love this much-demeaned genre. Slowly, I came to appreciate that this too was a kind of film school. After years of being cooped up in a Nairobi office reading research and marketing briefs on which I based commercials, these "boring little films" gave me wings and a bird's eye vision of my continent, and a chance to reassess and better understand who I was and where I lived. I was soon traversing the continent and gaining invaluable film lessons: How to edit a story on a small budget. How to parachute into a new country and find a crew. How to gain access to characters who spoke a different language or lived a different life from me. Where to find stories. I learned that everyone had a story, that everything had the potential to *be* a story worth seeing. And best of all, I began to meet the strong women of my continent that would inspire and propel me forward from that moment on.

At first, the shock of travel was enormous. I thought I alone had been blinded by my decade in the corporate world. And then, I came to realise we were all blindfolded, all ignorant of each other's countries and cultures. And more power-fully, it dawned on me that we were even sheltered from each other's neighbour-hoods, hiding fearfully within our own individual cultures and tribes. I lost friends: many of my close friends felt I was suddenly too angry and too aggressively vocal about the things I was making films about – land rights, gender justice, poverty, inequality. But for me, even though I was making some fiction – my first love – it was as though being an NGO filmmaker had given me a superpower to observe the entire continent from a micro and macro level. And on this journey, I began to observe and deeply respect the women of our continent.

In St Louis, Senegal, I sat under a tree with a group of women in colourful cloths, scooping up balls of jollof rice from a communal platter and spooning them into my mouth (after licking their fingers), discussing female genital mutilation whilst cracking loud, raucous jokes. With a jolt, I understood that being victimised had not turned them into lifelong victims and that there were multiple definitions and realities of poverty. I travelled deep into the rocky, infertile farmlands of South Africa in KwaZulu-Natal and filmed a village of women harvesting maize, singing traditional harvest songs in strong melodious tones despite the fact that their com-munity had, through apartheid, been consigned to farming on near-barren land just a few kilometres away from some of the most fertile commercial farms and forests on the continent, owned by white men. In Mozambique, I was empowered by schoolgirls stretching condoms over carved wooden phalluses in an initiative that taught them that they had choices. I sat silenced, part of a ring of early teen schoolgirls in a city council school in Nairobi, listening as these fragile, traumatised youths described their battle with drugs and predators – and I learned how some overcame and others fell. I met a feisty young woman who had arrived in Nairobi in the dead of night from a small rural town, expecting its streets to be paved with gold only to find muddy paths and arrogant middle-class families who expected her to eat their left-overs. In the slums of Nairobi, I met an aged grandmother, sole provider to scores of grandchildren after her son and daughter had been lost to HIV, paying school fees by washing clothes and worrying about how her grand-children would have to suffer to buy her a coffin. I had to stop the camera rolling when my cameraman and I found ourselves sobbing, horrified, as a woman in Burnt Forest Kenya emotionally described now her neighbour and fellow Christian and friend participated in decapitating her sons and husband during post-election violence in 2007 just because they were from different tribes. "Today," her friend had told her, "today we won't say praise to God. Today, today is war." I spent nearly three hours with Wangari Maathai, Kenya's fierce, forest-protecting Nobel Prize winner who described her journey to me – to me! I *adored* these women. They made me cry, they made me laugh, made me angry, made me sad. They made me realise I had been living a life more dead than awake. My love for these women of different incomes, realities and situations deepened, as I delved deeper and deeper and I began to transition into the marvellous world of independent documentary making, my soul reverberating with the power, beauty, strength and resilience of my African sisters, aunties, mothers and grannies.

I also deeply struggled with my own privileged background, inadequate language skills, and many other insufficiencies as a storyteller in my journey to become a film director. But somewhere along the way, accepted by these women of all backgrounds and nations, I realised that my experience was also important and unique, and that I too, was enough. I too was worthy, and had stories that I should tell loudly and proudly without shame. My parents, Jane and Leonard Kibinge, grew up in humble rural homesteads. My father recalls being so poor and hungry as a child that in a moment of desperation, he tried to sate his hunger by eating salt. At 35, he was appointed first resident Ambassador to the United States in 1969, just 15 years after segregation. I spent my earliest years in America, but never experienced discrimination, thanks to my parents who must have sheltered us. To be embarrassed as an adult of what I was and how I was would be to deny the sacrifices that they and their parents and forefathers and mothers had made in order to produce me: a storyteller. I *had* to tell these stories: whether the Frenchman on that beach in Zanzibar thought they were authentically African or not.

Who is anyone to tell me, or anyone else, that our stories are not African enough? That I am not African enough?

In the space of about six years, in which I directed three dramatic features, a couple of independent documentary features and a few fictional and documentary shorts, nothing taught me more about my continent than those early excursions documenting villages and towns through simple videos. As my film language slowly and painfully formed, so did my understanding of how colonial borders had separated me from my sisters, and I realised how modern African patriarchy was reducing traditionally strong womenfolk to second-class citizens, maintaining oppressive cultural practices whilst simultaneously stripping away the respect and esteem that past generations had accorded us.

At the same time, it slowly dawned on me that hard work and accolades did not make creating or raising the money for the next film job any easier. Colonialisation has forced us Africans to shed who we are and adopt new customs and beliefs leaving artists kneeling in the dust, begging the Western world for the next fistful of dollars to tell our own stories. No post-colonial African governments have followed the visionary philosophy of Thomas Sankara, first President of Burkina Faso, and his belief that film can inform a new post-colonial identity, therefore, almost no local film funds existed for us and public broadcasters paid little for indigenous content. Each completed film sent me spiralling into panic, clueless as to where my next film financing would come from. A highly unstable film industry made it nearly impossible to create local films that would provoke and inspire much needed self-reflection among African citizens. We needed our own film funds.

Urged by Joyce Nyairo at the Ford Foundation, who became both a friend and mentor, I began to research the viability of the region's first Documentary Film Fund, to try and build a stronger ecosystem to provide filmmakers like me with the support and community we need to tell our stories well. I was terrified at the mere thought of starting a film fund – something I knew nothing about. So when I returned to Joyce to excitedly share that a European NGO would not only match-fund the grant she had raised at Ford, but also house and benchmark it to European film fund ideals, she did not hide her disappointment that I was not brave enough to trust my own instincts as an African filmmaker intimately acquainted with the issues local filmmakers face. Seeing that disappointment in her eyes lit a fire in my heart and I determined that although seed money might not initially be from an African country, the philosophy, employees and inspirations for funding would be entirely homegrown. I was fortunate that a strong woman such as Joyce would strongly guide and urge me not to fear the power that I, and all women like me, had in our grasp to reinvent not just ourselves but the world as we saw it. I'm eternally grateful to her for pushing me way past my comfort zone.

When the first film applications to Docubox in 2013 were selected by a panel of acclaimed filmmakers from around the world, five out of our first six $22,500 production grants were won by phenomenal female filmmakers – Philippa Ndisi-Herrmann, Maia von Lekow (co-directing with her husband Chris King), Ng'endo Mukii, Zippy Kimundu and Zippy Nyaruri. This first batch of films were brave and bold, giving new female-driven perspectives on what it means to be an African woman. I was ecstatic that my 70-year-old mother, Jane Kibinge, was present to witness our grant-giving ceremony. The production and completion of these films has not been easy. We had much to learn, with the filmmakers and fund teaching and urging each other forward. It was made all the harder by not being able to raise pan-African funding, as co-production treaties do not exist between our nations. And yet, despite the slow progress, many of these films, and the ones that followed, are near completion as I write this. The first to finish, *New Moon* by Philippa Ndisi-Herrmann, won the Best Documentary prize at the extremely competitive Durban International Film Festival and the Creative Excellence Award from Luxor in Egypt. I was disappointed that the European funds that supported her film did not understand our struggle as the first Africa-initiated film fund and the excellence and bravery of her film enough to award it. More recently, in 2018, The Box (a Docubox offshoot) awarded our first two short fiction grants, and once again, the two first prizes selected by a diverse, mixed gender panel were awarded to films written and directed by two very different women, Lydia Matata and Neha Shah.

Over the years, I have witnessed the prolific, resilient, persistent and courageous nature of female filmmakers, standing ground in an industry globally dominated by men. But with the benefit of being located in Kenya, with its unique track record of pioneering female producers and directors, I stand proud of the powerful matriarchs and daughters of film I have encountered past, present and undoubtedly, future.

I remain hopeful that the future will give birth to a multiplicity of films that reflect who we are as Africans, through more female African eyes.

There's one thing left on my plate which I struggle with, which I have yet to determine a path for: local philanthropy and funding. I want to inspire Africans to find a way to support culture, art and their own African stories. With so few governments (South Africa, Senegal and the North African countries being the only ones supporting the production of films), I feel we have a real battle on our hands. Part of the problem is that African governments and African citizens do not seem to acknowledge that without telling our own stories, we will never rise. We are the stories we tell ourselves, so if we do not make excellent films about where we came from, who our forefathers were, what colonialism was, and more, we are lost.

Our first and only private local philanthropist at Docubox has been a strong, accomplished female – Njeri Karago, who conceived and produced my first film *Dangerous Affair*. She supported one of our Box short fictional films and as the new Consul General to Los Angeles has pledged to continue to find ways to support East African film.

It's a great start, but not enough.

The inaugural Good Pitch was hosted by Docubox in 2013 with great support from the Doc Society, a British organisation founded by indomitable women whom we are proud to call our Big Sisters. Government, philanthropists and local corporate organisations attended our inaugural Good Pitch and the six films we showcased in that single day raised over \$112,400. A year earlier though, I attended the Good Pitch in Sydney where the films raised nearly \$7 million dollars. We must get there – and local philanthropy is key.

Raising the profile of women in African cinema is another huge leap towards documenting with great sensitivity and passion the little-known world of films made by strong, talented African women. When I first read the manuscript for the book you are holding in your hands, *Women in African Cinema: Beyond the Body Politic* by Lizelle Bisschoff and Stefanie Van de Peer, I was surprised by how emotional it made me feel. While I always felt I was part of a far larger jigsaw puzzle than I knew, these meticulously researched, thoughtfully constructed, succinctly written eight chapters took me by the hand and connected me to the S/heroines I have been longing to meet throughout my whole film-life. This book is a map, and with it, I am now able to truly see and better understand the world in which I am situated. It has given me a path through which to locate my long-lost sisters in cinema. We have been scattered and separated by language, generations and colonial boundaries, and here, within the pages and chapters of this wonderful book, we are connected for the very first time.

If asked to look back and reflect on life lessons, my first would be that it's all story: even we are the stories we tell ourselves.

I am a strong woman with a loving father, supportive husband, inspirational brothers and a little boy who holds my heart in the palm of his hand. Some of my most loved friends and collaborators are men. But none of this makes me any less of a feminist, or any less of a female filmmaker. I am, in fact, more. My version of the world is so because of – not despite – these layers. My personal journey has been shaped and informed by all genders and continents and the stories that I've heard along the way have become an intrinsic part of whom I am. And so, an

African filmmaker meandering through an increasingly unequal world, I simply reflect what I see and feel back at the world. I am not, and will never be, apologetic for any of it.

Complex as I am, complex as the women in this book are, we are as African as it gets. And in this complexity, borne largely by women, lies the future of African film.

Judy Kibinge
Nairobi, 30 June 2019

ACKNOWLEDGEMENTS

One chilly evening in Brussels in 2016, Lizelle gave a public lecture on women in sub-Saharan African cinema to a mixed group of scholars, filmmakers and festival organisers interested in this topic. We had not seen each other for over a year, and though we had been in touch regularly, we had missed talking about and working together on our shared passion. We had done our PhDs together at the University of Stirling and met during the second Africa in Motion Film Festival in Edinburgh in 2007, after which we went to FESPACO film festival together in 2009. This was Stefanie's first time at the festival, while Lizelle had been twice before. FESPACO is where we really bonded and realised how much we had in common – in particular, of course, our passion for, and research interest in, women in African cinema. So, on that evening in Brussels in 2016, after a few drinks, we agreed to finally make good our long-held ambition to write a book together on women in African cinema. As Lizelle had pointed out during the lecture, there was no such book yet, and everyone in the room agreed it was a matter of urgency to right/ write this wrong. Here we are, three years later, and we have done it. We have really enjoyed the process, not only because we love working together, but also, more importantly, because both of us strongly believe in the importance and quality of African cinema and in cinema's ability to affect social change. What we hope to achieve with this book is to bring more attention to the remarkable and talented women working in African cinema and to foster a more sustained scholarship that recognises the importance of continuing the legacy and acknowledging the contemporary work of women making films in Africa.

Writing partnerships are special, especially the kind that become stronger and more productive as time goes on. We appreciate each other's specialised knowledge and dedication, and support one another when times are tough and insecurities come to the surface, as they often do during ambitious projects like this one. Our complementarity is unique, and so our first acknowledgement as well as the dedication of this book go to our friendship and our intellectual partnership. Throughout the writing of the book we supported and encouraged one another, and had endless fascinating and challenging conversations, and we hope that the heightened self-awareness created through our constant interaction shines through in our writing. Any gaps, shortcomings or mistakes are entirely our own and we welcome feedback that can help us to continue to address issues of emancipation for all women creative practitioners everywhere.

We did the research for and wrote this book at a time of growing interest in, and an ongoing global conversation on, the presences and absences of women and people of colour in the film industry, which provided great inspiration. But we also became increasingly aware of our own positionality as White women of great privilege working in the UK academy, a position and location enabling us to write this book in the first place. This awareness was a source of insecurity, White guilt, and sometimes even writer's block. But it also led to enlightening discussions with friends, colleagues and audience members at the public and academic events and film festivals we organised and attended. We are therefore immensely grateful to friends and colleagues, in particular Justine Atkinson, Nene Jayne Camara, Myriam Mouflih and Sara Shaarawi – the organising team behind Africa in Motion at the time of writing the book – for challenging and lively discussions on creative practice, race and privilege; to inspiring women such as Fatma Alloo, Sara Blecher, Firdoze Bulbulia, June Givanni, Wanuri Kahiu, Judy Kibinge, and to Lara Preston and Edima Otuokon from the Ladima Foundation, whose exemplary work as activists, writers and filmmakers has been invaluable for us; and to female scholars of African cinema like Lindiwe Dovey, Beti Ellerson, Jacqueline Maingard, Lesley Marks and Melissa Thackway, whose pioneering work has led the way. Stefanie would like to thank Will Higbee, her supportive and encouraging manager at the University of Exeter, for allowing her time and space to write and for productive feedback and assurances on some chapters. Both of us would like to thank critical friends and colleagues Justine Atkinson, Becky Bartlett, Kaya Davies Hayon, Amy Holdsworth, David Martin-Jones and David Murphy for providing productive feedback on chapters in the late stages of finalising the manuscript. We are also immensely grateful to Judy Kibinge, who wrote the heart-felt foreword for this book. Her generosity has been remarkable over the years, and we feel privileged that she has been willing to share her thoughts and experiences with us.

We are, most of all, immensely grateful to the women working in African cinema. To the many filmmakers and actors we have met, the film festival organisers we admire, the producers, editors, production managers, writers, artists, camera women, photographers, runners, extras and every woman active in Africa's great film cultures. We are deeply appreciative of your willingness to share your work with us at the Africa in Motion Film Festival and for this book. African films are not always easy to discover because of inhibitively biased canons and journalism, and getting hold of the films is often a case of real detective work. We acknowledge your brilliance and your generosity.

Lastly, we have the good fortune of having life-partners who understand and encourage our commitment to women, Africa and cinema. They helped us with the emotional and practical hurdles of writing a book such as this one. We thank them for nourishment, for music and silences, and for journeys and discussions that have kept our minds sane and bodies healthy.

INTRODUCTION

Women in African cinema

African women are the central figures in this book. Despite their beauty, wealth and diversity, and their exceptional past, present and future, they have been neglected and oppressed throughout history. Their global image has suffered because of this general disregard. Here, though, they take centre stage. Although underrepresentation and especially *mis*representation have been detrimental to the image of African women, they have spoken to the imagination of artists around the globe and through time. One of the most iconic African women, represented in film since the beginning of the twentieth century, is Cleopatra. One could even write the history of Hollywood cinema itself by tracing the depictions of this African queen. The biggest stars have portrayed her, from Jehanne d'Alcy (1899), Helen Gardner (1912), Theda Bara (1917), Claudette Colbert (1934) and Vivien Leigh (1945) to Elizabeth Taylor (1963). What these depictions have in common though is their portrayal of her as White, romantic and while strong politically, she seems fickle in her relationships with men. Seeing Cleopatra portrayed consistently as a White[1] woman not only robs African history of one of its most powerful leaders, it also perpetuates the Western appropriation of the erotic, sexualised African woman. Moreover, the fact that these White Cleopatras are depicted as "sirens of the Nile,"[2] accompanied by symbols of an exotic nature, such as elephants, snakes, golden headbands and translucent veils, appropriates the harem aesthetic as popularised by European Orientalists. Seeing the queen repeatedly depicted as White, sexual and exotic influences assumptions about what Cleopatra really looked like, something which is in itself a matter of much contestation. She was a transnational African queen of mixed Greek and African heritage who, most importantly, became one of the most powerful African rulers of her era (Roller 2011). Her character and *her*story represent the immense diversity of women on the African continent. The Whitewashing of history is an unsavoury aspect of Hollywood at large, and makes it all the more necessary for global audiences to watch and listen to African stories as they are owned and told by African women.

This book addresses the prolific but marginalised presence of women in African filmmaking. As is the case for female film practitioners everywhere, women are underrepresented in the male-dominated African film industries as well as the male-dominated scholarly work on African cinema. And yet, even a cursory glance at the landscape of African cinema rapidly reveals that an ever-increasing number of women are using the audio-visual medium as a way to tell stories, reveal important issues, express identities and subjectivities, and reflect on traditions, histories and cultures. It is this wealth of work that has existed historically, is being produced continuously and is emerging from the continent, that is the main focus of this book. In very different contexts, both women and film have been essentialised as representing the postcolonial nation, and those women and films that have veered away from this essentialised view have often been dismissed as unrepresentative or inauthentic. Independence or anti-colonial discourses no longer define filmmaking from the African continent, just as women are no longer the embodiment of the gendered nation or the motherland. As the title suggests, this book engages with, but moves beyond, the anti-colonial filmmaking that has received most attention in scholarly publications. Instead we highlight the wide variety of subjects, approaches, aesthetics, genres, forms and politics that have been woven into the fabric of African women's filmmaking practices, by filmmakers from all periods in cinema history and all areas of the continent. At the same time, we recognise our own and the book's limitations: we cannot possibly cover every historically significant film from every country. Every process of inclusion unavoidably also involves exclusion. The films we have included are representative as a sample of filmmaking by African women. Some of the films are stylistically and thematically representative, others have been selected exactly because they are unique within a consideration of female filmmaking practices. Selections were also made on the basis of uncovering films on which little work has been done analytically and theoretically. We prefer a transnational approach, looking beyond (though also recognising) individual nations' specific outlook on and history of filmmaking. Even the term "Africa" conjures up emotions, images and responses as diverse as the continent itself. Importantly, we recognise that this book is a reflection of our own privileged, subjective experience and knowledge. As a White South African and a Belgian woman, working in the UK academic context, we also recognise our lack of lived experience of African women in film. We received our training as film scholars in the Western academic context, and this context, which also informs the films we have access to, inevitably shapes and influences the lens through which we view these films. We believe that access, representation and privilege are issues that should be central to academic enquiries, as we are fully aware that any claims of objectivity in academic research is merely a smokescreen for Eurocentric bias. The most we can hope for is that, as informed and passionate scholars, our work will make a valuable contribution to African film studies and prise open the door for further studies on women in African cinema.

Mahen Sophia Bonetti, founder and director of the New York African Film Festival and originally from Sierra Leone, stated: "No aspect of African cinema is more miraculous than the most unbidden emergence of female filmmakers on the continent" (Ellerson 2000, 73). It is this miraculous emergence that will be unlocked in this book. Inevitably, this book is celebratory to an extent as we are attempting to bring to light works that are not widely known internationally and we wish to highlight the best of what these films have to offer the viewer. While we cannot be exhaustive, we do aim to contribute to opening up the canon in order to start to address, in more depth, the diverse and significant roles and representations of women in African cinema.

Approach

The writing of this book came at a time of self-assessment, introspection and perhaps an increased opportunity for equality in the global film industry. While we have been researching women in African cinema for more than a decade, it was not until 2017 that the global film industry started to seriously assess its institutionalised racism and sexism. Of course, this did not happen in a vacuum, as initiatives such as the Bechdel test, F-Rating and #OscarsSoWhite have been calling out the industry's White male privilege for some time. Female directors are underrepresented and marginalised all over the world, including Africa. However, it is not only imperative to look at women's work in filmmaking, we also need to look into White privilege and racism, and the intersection between racism and sexism. In our view, being a feminist inherently requires one to be anti-racist, yet international movements such as #MeToo and Time's Up often forget or marginalise women of colour, because they are driven by the Global North's priorities, which are taken as the "norm" (with mouthpieces such as social media and other media channels). It is thus unsurprising, in our view, that the most effective criticism of the #MeToo movement has come from Black women. Indeed, in 2007 – 10 years before Alyssa Milano popularised the hashtag – African American civil rights activist Tarana Burke came up with the phrase to raise awareness of issues in health and well-being affecting young women of colour. The fact that it became co-opted by a privileged White feminist movement which all but ignored its roots in Black women's activism has become increasingly problematic as the inequalities between White and Black women in the global film industry, such as the pay gap, are now openly discussed.

Likewise, in the global film industry, African cinema remains almost completely ignored, except for the occasional film that appears on the shortlist of a Cannes, Toronto, Berlin or Oscars line-up. Almost no attention is paid in the media of the Global North to Africa-based (or indeed Arab, Asian or Latin American) film festivals, where a different, parallel circuit of cinema thrives. We cannot ignore the calls for more diversity on screens, but even within global movements, African voices are still marginalised. Africa has also had its own responses to the global movement. One example is Sisters Working in Film and Television (SWIFT), an agency for advocacy in South Africa that aims to protect women in the entertainment industry, conceptualised during the 2016 Durban International Film Festival. SWIFT initiated a campaign against gender inequality in the screen industries around the hashtag #ThatsNotOk (Blignaut 2018), which highlights instances of unacceptable workplace behaviour affecting women in the South African screen industries. According to SWIFT's first Sexual Harassment and Discrimination Survey, which ran from January to April 2017, 66.7% of women in the South African film industry feel unsafe in the workplace, 65% have witnessed sexual harassment, 23.7% indicated they had been unwillingly touched and 71% felt they did not have a platform or strong support structure where they could address these issues (SWIFT 2017). As a result, SWIFT established an industry-wide code of conduct entitled "Respectful Workplace Policy and Code of Conduct" endorsed by the National Film and Video Foundation (NFVF) of South Africa (De Groot 2017). It was also acknowledged by the IBFC (Independent Black Filmmakers Collective) in May 2018, which released a strongly worded statement entitled "Filmmakers condemn sexual harassment and violence, and pledge to take action including educational campaigns, ensuring support for victims and naming and shaming perpetrators" in response to the lack of response from the industry (Blignaut and Marshall 2018). Endorsed by the NFVF and IBFC, SWIFT has widened its network and its sphere of influence by championing women's rights not only in South Africa, but more widely on the African continent as well. Likewise, the Ladima Foundation works on the basis of a collaborative pan-African vision for the future of women's filmmaking on the continent, with the intention to correct the imbalances within the industry. The Foundation celebrates tolerance, diversity and Afro-positivity through filmmaking (Ladima Foundation). Our work aims to add a scholarly dimension to these industry initiatives. In what follows we discuss the three main topics of our book: women, Africa and cinema, as our approach to these intersecting categories will explain our preoccupations and methodologies.

Women

We wrote this book because we identified a lacuna in scholarship on African cinema. We follow the values of SWIFT and Ladima in that we are passionate and optimistic about films by African women, and our approach and methodology are therefore rooted in seeing as many films as possible, as researchers, film festival organisers and audience or jury members at festivals. We educate ourselves by viewing historically significant as well as new, innovative work. Alongside studying the context within which they were made we are committed to close readings of the artworks: we combine a textual with a contextual approach. We are not only interested in the films' narratives, themes, genres, aesthetics and styles, but we also place these elements of the films within their wider, gendered political, social and economic contexts.

We acknowledge the challenges inherent in using "woman" as an analytical category. As both a biological and a social category, we understand "woman" both as a gender *and* as a sexual identity. A strictly binary understanding of categories of either gender or sexuality is no longer advisable: our concept of women includes non-cisgender females, transgender females and non-heteronormative categories of gender (specifically because these have been even less visible than women in

African cinema). We regard as "female" those who self-identify as such. While we look across eras and areas, we aim to bring new analytical and theoretical configurations into our thinking about African cinema and about women. We are especially interested in transnational readings of production and distribution, in new genres and forms, and in new ways of thinking about global and African feminisms, beyond the "bread, butter and power" preoccupations of the most prominent era of African feminism in the 1990s. This book aims to make creative women more visible, historically, politically and practically. In this sense, we are interested in how African women filmmakers reach their intended audiences, how they "shoot back" at the global north, and how they navigate the increasingly divided and contested yet "global" film industry.

Cinematic representations of women have primarily been created by male filmmakers. Many filmmakers and historians argue that these representations will always be flawed, partial and incomplete, and need to be complemented by women making films. But to say that only women can tell stories about women, or men about men, or Africans about Africa is also reductive. In addition to being transnational, we need to be transcultural and value men's representations of women for their strengths as well. However, as long as the agency of representation remains imbalanced, i.e. if many more men make films than women; or if much more attention is paid to the work of male filmmakers in research than to the work of female filmmakers; or if the canon remains overwhelmingly male, there is a problem. Stories in general, including women's stories, have predominantly been told by men, and African stories have principally been told by non-Africans.

As anywhere else in the world, we see many more male protagonists on screen than female, and the African character in non-African cinema is more often than not reduced to a stereotype or peripheral presence. The fact that women have directed far fewer films than men results in an imbalanced representation of socio-cultural complexities, and disproportionate representations of individual and collective subjectivities and identities. This is a problematic reality of the underrepresentation of women and of Africans, an imbalance and marginalisation that this book aims to redress. As such, we are not disregarding the fact that many male African filmmakers have tackled women's issues and have created alternative visions for (female) emancipation and change. We maintain, however, that it remains essential for these representations to be complemented by women filmmakers in order to enable an increasingly fair and balanced point of view. Women need to get the opportunities to tell their own stories, from perspectives and in forms, styles and ways that offer alternatives to men's films. Much has been written on the work of male African filmmakers, including on their representations of African women and their handling of women's issues, while comparatively little has been published on the work of female African directors, due to their marginalisation and underrepresentation.

In this respect, we recognise that gender is a more fluid category than sex, since one needs to acknowledge that male filmmakers can also portray a "feminine" sensibility in their filmic representations of women (and vice versa). Certain male West African directors in particular – such as Ousmane Sembène from Senegal,

Med Hondo from Mauritania, Désiré Ecaré from Ivory Coast, and Cheick Oumar Sissoko from Mali have – through their depictions of female characters and the gender critiques embedded in their films – put forward a vision of female emancipation inextricably linked to development in the postcolonial era. As Lindiwe Dovey has shown:

> From the earliest days of non-commercial, expressive, African-authored film production on the continent in the 1960s, to the present moment, there has been a consistent stream of films that focus on strong women characters, powerful and positive matriarchal cultures, and a critique of tyrannical, patriarchal cultures – whether colonial, neo-colonial or postcolonial.
>
> *(2012, 18)*

This postcolonial, emancipated view is certainly shared by many African intellectuals and writers, even though it has not yet fully resulted in transformations in the socio-political and economic realities of African cinema. Although the work of these male directors has been crucial in challenging Western colonialist ideologies which typically evoked the African woman as either an exotic being or silent victim, female film theorists and practitioners claim that a male vision can never fully represent the female experience. Farida Ayari, for example, states:

> [T]he image of African women in African cinema remains essentially that created by men. Of course, African films, however modest, do present us with a fairly representative kaleidoscope of female figures. However, these are women fabricated within the imaginary of the men who make the films, regardless of how close to reality this imaginary at times may be. The image of women in African cinema is the result of a male gaze and a mostly male society.
>
> *(1996, 181)*

Ayari uses the Peulh proverb, "a man cannot imagine what a woman can do," to support her conviction that representations of women by male filmmakers will always be incomplete, partial and flawed. Cameroonian writer Werewere Liking goes even further in her critique of male directors' cinematographic representations of African women in an article entitled "An African Woman Speaks out against African Filmmakers," published in 1996, in which she criticises male directors for internalising, reproducing and disseminating the negative image of the African woman created and perpetuated in Western media. In terms of the underrepresentation of women in public spheres, and the importance of women taking part in opening up society to alternative views, Grace Alele-Williams writes: "[I]f these roles are so few, so long will the values of society continue to be formulated to the disadvantage of women" (Eboh 1998, 35).

Likewise, in *Caméra d'Afrique* (1983) and *Caméra arabe* (1987), Tunisian filmmaker Férid Boughedir's two-part documentary on Arab and African cinema, Tunisian Néjia Ben Mabrouk makes this point exactly, when she says that men cannot represent women the way women can. In an interview with one of the authors of this book, Selma Baccar, one of the first feminist filmmakers from North Africa, equally asserted that men do not and cannot understand the complex psychology of women, and therefore cannot tell women's stories, even if they can include women in their stories. Mary Kolawole (Amfred 2004, 27) argues that many female African writers and critics have emerged as gender theorists, and notes that theorists who are attempting to reconceptualise gender in Africa do so through the double approach of creative as well as theoretical writing. We add to this argument the creative endeavours of female African filmmakers. These writers and filmmakers often reconceptualise myths, proverbs, anecdotes and folktales through a gendered lens, contesting patriarchal interpretations and offering feminist understandings of culture and history. Even progressive representations of women in films by men need to be complemented by representations created and directed by a female vision and sensibility. This is the central reason why a book on this topic is necessary today.

By focusing on African women making films, we want to bust the canon of male directors and contribute to the formation of a new canon that includes and prioritises women. With this, we mean that both the canon of films and the canon of scholarship need to be challenged, as they both focus on the male "auteurs" of African cinema such as Ousmane Sembène, Djibril Diop Mambéty, Gaston Kaboré, Idrissa Ouédraogo, Youssef Chahine, Nouri Bouzid et al. Simultaneously, instead of focusing on the same *token* women filmmakers who are usually highlighted briefly in books on African cinema (for example pioneering Tunisian director Moufida Tlatli, Algerian filmmaker and writer Assia Djebar, Senegalese director Safi Faye, and Togolese director Anne-Laure Folly), this book offers a sustained effort to focus on women filmmakers and auteurs that may have been neglected globally *because* of their gender. Creating a concerted vision that considers films both by established and emergent filmmakers, we offer a long view of the female presence in African cinema, debunking the myth that there are no women except for the canonised ones: there are many outstanding women filmmakers and they have been telling their own stories for decades. We have arrived at a time where we can confront our own ignorance, really listen to their stories, watch their films, and recognise their combined and individual brilliance.

Africa

Geographically, this book focuses entirely on the African continent, but we also look beyond it, as we recognise that history, politics and economies have resulted in exilic, diasporic and transnational filmmaking practices that position Africa as a global "place." However, we are particularly interested in filmmakers with continued and personal links with the continent, and thus we do not include filmmakers who, for instance, identify as African American or Black British. We agree that it is not possible or advisable to set up strict categories. Identity is fluid, heterogeneous and complex, and people of African descent are scattered throughout the world, often because of painful histories of slavery and colonisation. But we do have to set parameters for this book, and have chosen to concern ourselves and our research with those women who maintain a continued lived experience in Africa and see it as the "home" they tell stories about. As such we include those women who have experienced voluntary or involuntary exile, with which we recognise that African directors also sometimes choose to live, work, and train away from the continent. We also, perhaps controversially, include White African women in our study, and Maghrebi or Arab women (even though they are excluded from other studies on African cinema), as Africa as a place has always been and will continue to be a multicultural and multi-ethnic space. We argue that Africa should not be sealed off as a geographical or ideological entity or unity. Yet we aim to retain a pan-African vision of the continent that recognises a geographical unity, as well as shared historical experiences and trajectories.

Increasingly, African film studies is acknowledged as an academic field of study, and this book is contributing to this field, while enriching it with a focus on women and emphasising its internal diversity. As Sylvia Tamale (2011, 1) argues, studying "Africa" is at times a political strategy that calls attention to some of the commonalities and shared historical legacies inscribed in cultures within the regions by the forces of colonialism, imperialism, globalisation and fundamentalism. Being "African" highlights those aspects of cultural ideology, "the ethos of community, solidarity and ubuntu[3] - that are widely shared among the vast majority of people within the geographical entity baptised 'Africa' by the colonial map-makers" (ibid.).

As is evident from our understanding of African cinema, this book takes as its starting point the assumption that no female director works within a monolithic framework, nor that there is a group of women who have in common an approach or aesthetic that could be called "African." We emphasise first and foremost the diversity on the continent; secondly, the diversity within the selection of women directors; and thirdly, the diversity of filmmaking practices, forms, genres and stories. But we also want to acknowledge that affinities do exist between films, approaches and experiences. The different political, thematic and aesthetic approaches of directors is often dependent on funding, production and national contexts and opportunities, and so the works under consideration in this book are explored through theoretical, historical, political and socio-economic contexts from across the continent, to illustrate differences between as well as similarities across the work.

While we cannot include all women filmmakers, let alone all films made by women, the selection process was dependent on our knowledge of films, and inevitably limited to their availability, and to films that lend themselves readily to certain themes. While we recognise that many African films are hard to come by, we have been privileged to see a great amount of women's films due to our affiliations with African and international film festivals. Equally, we are very aware of films being made, more and more, by young African women: with the inauguration of more festivals, film funds, schools and other training initiatives, as well as the growing prevalence of accessible digital filmmaking technology. The growth in the number of films being made professionally is exponential, boding very well for the future of African filmmaking but also confronting us with our own limitations, in that we cannot possibly see or discuss all films. In this context, we have at the very least endeavoured to move beyond the usual suspects, while still acknowledging the hugely significant female pioneers, in order to consider films by both those filmmakers whom we have all heard about, as well as those filmmakers who are less well-known.

In order to accommodate this diversity, in the chapters and structure of the book we have opted for a thematic rather than a geographic or historical approach. This is not to say that we do not pay attention to geography, history and politics: each chapter and each film is contextualised for analysis precisely through these aspects. A thematic focus, devoted to diversity, has allowed us to select some of the most representative films by both older and younger directors, rather than addressing the same films, the same directors, as part of a "parallel canon." In fact, as we want to make a departure from the canon (if there is such a thing for women filmmakers) and avoid repeating what other scholars have focused on in their analyses of directors like Tlatli, Djebar and Faye; we engage mostly with younger filmmakers, and recent films by established women of African cinema. This is because we live in a historical moment that has changed the outlook on women in history, specifically their presences and absences in the history of film. We accept that a canon is perhaps needed to establish African film studies as an academic discipline and to create a basis of knowledge for a potentially wider audience, but then a critique of this canon becomes equally necessary in order to start to understand the simplified version of history that a canon offers.

While respecting and celebrating diversity on the African continent, we recognise that regionality is a strength in understanding aspects of history and politics that continue to define and shape filmmaking today, like colonial structures, postcolonial moments and linguistic dominance. A regional, transnational, pan-African approach provides a way to underscore our attempts to be representative and expansive. This is inherent to previous collaborations the two authors of this book have worked on, and influenced by personal factors as well: Bisschoff specialises in Francophone West African and South African cinema, and has developed knowledge and experience of East African cinema as well. This is due in part to her identity as South African, and her focus on women from Francophone West African cinema in the majority of her research. Van de Peer is an expert in North African cinema and as a Belgian national has developed an interest in films from the Democratic Republic of the Congo. Nollywood has become a side-project for both authors due to the huge growth of this industry and the authors' continued engagement with film festivals devoted to African cinema around the world. Likewise, a regional focus allows us to keep in mind the way in which colonialism has had an undeniable influence on the socio-political, economic, and also cultural production of the majority of African cinemas. Even if we do not want to take a nationalist approach, we do have to take into account the historical reality of colonialism and its impact on the African film industries, especially its continuing influence on production and distribution.

A very brief overview of how we approach the different regions in Africa is necessary at this point. In the majority of African studies, and thus also in African film studies, it has been francophone West Africa and South Africa that have received most attention. Indeed, francophone West African cinema is often seen as the cradle of African filmmaking *tout court*, with Sembène being recognised as "the father of African cinema." This is due in some part to France's continued support of, and influence on, co-productions and its dominance over the European distribution of African films. South African cinema is often seen as something that has more recently, since the end of apartheid in the 1990s, become emancipated and grown very fast to become included in Western cinema, on a par with Hollywood, and indeed sometimes working in collaboration with Hollywood. South African films have been nominated for Oscars and South African directors have crossed over into Hollywood filmmaking, while Hollywood as well as European actors have performed in South African films and a handful of South African actors have made their names in Hollywood.

In contrast, Nollywood, despite its denomination, is seen as something entirely separate from any other (African) cinema, due to its specific development as a local, hugely successful and lucrative form of filmmaking that does not travel well, except in the African continent and the Nigerian diasporas around the world. As Yaba Badoe, Amina Mama and Salem Mekuria argue in their introduction to the special issue of *Feminist Africa* on film in 2012, Nollywood takes up "an inordinate amount" of contemporary discussions of African cinema, and so does its "endless pandering to misogynistic fantasies about evil women getting their comeuppance" (2012, 2). As such, in many cases, Nollywood has become a topic of curiosity rather than of genuine interest. Meanwhile, East Africa, living with the legacy of British colonialism, has been a comparatively late arrival in African cinema history, and scholarship has likewise been delayed. In spite of these delays, Kenyan film-making for example, and in particular women in Kenyan cinema, are now at the forefront of innovative film genres and addressing daring themes in their work. Cinema from the DRC is also catching up due to an increased self-confidence and a few outstanding dissident voices in filmmaking, again, especially coming from young women. Due to its particularly brutal colonial and postcolonial history, Congolese filmmaking has been late to appear on the scene, as Belgian colonialists were not interested in enabling infrastructure or storytelling.

Lastly, in our pan-African scope, North Africa, including Egypt, is an inherent and indeed very powerful contributor to African film culture. This region is often wholly neglected in the context of African studies, which regularly limits itself to sub-Saharan Africa, and also because it is presumed to be an intrinsic part of the Arab world rather than a contributor to the ideas of pan-Africanism. And yet we include it as one of the most productive, challenging and female-centred regions for cinema on the continent, travelling easily across the Sahara to other regions' festivals, often winning the main prizes at these events. While Egypt was one of the first industries to start to develop an anti-colonial national cinema, and has since been seen as the hinge (rather than the fringe) of Arab film culture, it is also an important contributor to the ideals of pan-Africanism and the socio-cultural history of the African continent. The Maghreb (consisting of Algeria, Morocco, Tunisia) has received much attention in francophone film studies, but is not usually seen as either part of Africa or of the Arab world. Here, we recognise its influence across the Sahara, as a crossroads for film circuits and an increasingly fertile space for co-production and exhibition through collaborations with sub-Saharan film professionals.

Cinema

In our use of the term "cinema" we refer to the entire business of the film industry, not only the films themselves, but also the making of the films (training, production and funding) as well as the life of the film beyond the studio (distribution, exhibition and reception). The diversity on and of the continent and its filmmaking is also recognised in our selection of genres and forms. Female-identified filmmakers in Africa make films about any topic that speaks to them and any style that fits their creative vision, and while they often focus on "women's issues" and put female protagonists at the centre of their narratives, this is by no means exclusively the case. We want to show that a feminine/female/feminist aesthetic in African cinema is just as multiple and diverse as approaches to filmmaking and ways of fitting into the industry at large. African women make short films, documentaries and fiction feature films in countless different themes, styles and formats. They are entrepreneurs and active agents in the film industry, as producers, funders, directors, actors, editors, camera people, sound engineers and DOPs. While most of our longer analyses focus on fiction feature films, we also reference documentaries, shorts, animation and experimental films as well as commercial, activist and educational work. Many more female directors work in television and documentary than in fiction feature filmmaking, and a lot more shorts than feature films are being made.

While our book does not include work on television productions, we are aware that media convergence is increasingly taking place, specifically as cinema attendance falls, online viewing platforms expand and TV continues to feed into film production, as is the case in Morocco, Nigeria and South Africa, for instance. Again, then, it is not advisable to set up strict categories of genre or form, but we do preserve a preference for cinematic works in this study, by which we mean films that mostly start their exhibition journeys in film festivals and on theatrical release, viewed on the big screen. Despite the rapid growth of online viewing platforms and other alternative exhibition avenues, at the present moment film festivals still remain one of the primary spaces to view African women's films.

We do, however, have to bear in mind that many African fiction feature films, while they may receive funding or co-production support from abroad and from several African nations, do not make it to wider theatrical distribution. If they do gain theatrical distribution often it will be limited to those countries that have been involved in the production. As such, for many films, screenings can be confined to one-off events at specific African or other international film festivals or within special seasons or retrospectives. This means that our knowledge of films may be limited to those films we have had access to at festivals we have visited, or through the festivals we organise. This, again, forces us to rethink categories of origin, identity, genre and style in a loose and inclusive sense. This study is therefore not intended to be complete or encyclopaedic in scope – rather we hope to contribute to a reshaping of the "canon" of women making films in Africa by reflecting on what we have seen and what we know.

Naturally, it comes down to a subjective selection and choice, but we have constructed a thematic structure and a geographical scope that will provide readers with a confident overview of that which is beyond only the most readily available, so that we can start to discern trends, strengths and highlights. In our recognition of the wealth, depth and breadth of African women's filmmaking, we cover a lot of ground and hope to inspire further research, awaken an interest in the films and develop a wider appreciation of the diversity of the continent, its filmmakers, and in particular, its women. This book is intended for researchers, students, cinephiles, audiences, cinema and festival programmers, archivists and all those who are interested in opening their eyes and listening more intently to African women's stories.

Presences and absences

African women in scholarship

In our experience as researchers of African cinema, we have noticed a glaring absence. In women's or feminist film studies, African women have been and continue to be ignored, while in African film studies, women's work has been neglected. We want to address these conspicuous gaps in our work, balancing proximity with critical distance. Working intersectionally, this book contributes to and expands the well-established work of women's/feminist film studies scholars such as Laura Mulvey, Annette Kuhn, Teresa de Lauretis, E. Ann Kaplan, B. Ruby Rich, Barbara Creed, Ella Shohat, Kaja Silverman, Patricia White, and many others. Thus far, seminal work in the field of feminist film studies has ignored African women's films (with the exception of a few edited collections that include a reference to Maghrebi women's cinema). Likewise, we hope to broaden the scope of the field of transnational women's studies. Work that claims to represent "global" women's cultural work still usually ignores African women, for example in studies like *Women's Cinema, World Cinema: Projecting Contemporary Feminisms* (White 2015) or *Contemporary Women's Cinema: Global Scenarios, Transnational Contexts* (Pravadelli 2017). In that respect we aim for this book to become a starting point of establishing a field of African feminist film studies. Furthermore, part of the motivation for and the initiative to start work on this book is based on our acute awareness that existing books and publications on African cinema rarely focus in detail on women filmmakers from the continent. This absence is partly due to the fact that, until quite recently, it has been very difficult to access African films, in particular women's films, and this inaccessibility has affected the ability of critics and scholars to engage with this work. With increased visibility in film festivals, and broader access through DVDs and online streaming, there is now much wider availability of a whole body of previously unknown filmmaking (see the Epilogue). At a time of important changes and developments in film distribution worldwide, this book aims to rectify this imbalance in the academic study of African cinema. An overview of available studies of African cinema will illustrate the gaps and shortcomings that we address.

Women in African cinema have been the subject of discussion in work by scholars including Françoise Pfaff, Kenneth Harrow, Sheila Petty, Maureen Ngozi Eke, Melissa Thackway, Lesley Marks, Florence Martin, Roy Armes, Lindiwe Dovey, Jyoti Mistry, and others. Most importantly, we value the ground-breaking work of Beti Ellerson, whose research has contributed immensely to the visibility of women in African cinema. The particular strength of Ellerson's work comes from interviews and first-hand reviews of films at film festivals, and the presence of African women at festivals internationally. Her pioneering work has been invaluable in shaping our enquiries into this field, both through her publications and through her bilingual African Women in Cinema blog (http://africanwomenci nema.blogspot.co.uk/). Ellerson's work is based on the histories of an impressive and comprehensive catalogue of films directed by African women, and complemented by an abundance of first-hand interviews she has conducted with female filmmakers. She published her research in an early book, *Sisters of the Screen* (2000), as well as various other publications on the topic, and a documentary film of the same title. Her work initiated a new field of critical and theoretical study that she terms African Women Cinema Studies. Rooted in in-depth knowledge of these women and their films, Ellerson's work is not primarily analytical, and we therefore see her work as a foundation for further analytical work that we hope to offer. Ellerson's research aside, scholarly work devoted to African women's cinema is few and far between.

Neither of the two key foundational texts of African cinema studies, Manthia Diawara's *African Cinema: Politics and Culture* (1992) and N. Frank Ukadike's *Black African Cinema* (1994), pays much attention to women directors. One of the first feminist approaches to films by women of colour was *Women Filmmakers of the African and Asian Diaspora: Decolonizing the Gaze, Locating Subjectivity* by Gwendolyn Audrey Foster (1997). This book focuses on the practice of six women of colour, with roots in both the African and the Asian diaspora, in American cinema. While the book is exemplary in its critical feminist approach to cinema by women of colour, our focus is rather on women with a strong emphasis on Africa as their home continent, and who see themselves as an inherent part of filmmaking of the African continent. Olivier Barlet's *African Cinemas: Decolonising the Gaze* (1996) mentions one female filmmaker (Safi Faye) and rather focuses, when he writes about women, on their socio-economic roles in African societies, on their roles as audience members, and on how they are portrayed on the screen by male filmmakers. Kenneth Harrow's edited collections *With Open Eyes: Women and African Cinema* (1997) and *African Cinema: Postcolonial and Feminist Readings* (1999), with Beti Ellerson's *Sisters of the Screen* (2000) were the first engaged studies on women and women's issues in African film. While the sub-title of *African Cinema:*

Postcolonial and Feminist Readings (1999) by Kenneth Harrow centralises feminism, the majority of films discussed in the book are by men, and part of the "canon" of African cinema, primarily due to the early publication date of the book. In our book we move well beyond this initial research, building on these scholars' groundwork, as most of the films we discuss were made in the twenty-first century.

Similarly to Foster's book, *African American Women and Sexuality in the Cinema*, by Norma Manatu (2002), looks specifically at African American women film-makers living in the USA. Melissa Thackway's book *Africa Shoots Back: Alternative Perspectives in Sub-Saharan Francophone African Film* (2003) has a chapter entitled "On Screen and Behind the Camera: African Women and Film." However, because it is one of the first gender-inclusive works on African cinema in addition to Harrow's and Ellerson's work described above, Thackway spends some time on covering the basics of politics, history and socio-economic issues in filmmaking and only deals with women making films in this one albeit very insightful chapter. Likewise, Françoise Pfaff's book *Focus on African Films* (2004) features one chapter on a female filmmaker, "Africa through a Woman's Eyes: Safi Faye's Cinema" which consists of a collection of materials including an interview, a transcript of a press conference, and a chronology of Faye's career, all with a focus on *Mossane*. As such we see the same scholars returning to the same filmmakers (and films), and while these are critical contributions to the field, our book engages on a broader and more in-depth level with both those filmmakers who have enjoyed recognition but also, crucially, with those that have remained in the margins.

In *Contact Zones: Memory, Origin, and Discourses in Black Diasporic Cinema* (2008), Sheila Petty explores a variety of African American, Caribbean, Black British, and African Canadian perspectives, including women's perspectives, and *Black Women Film and Video Artists* by Jacqueline Bobo (2013) also looks at African American women making a specific type of art film, while our book delves more deeply into films made on the African continent, consistently dealing with women's issues in a range of themes and styles. In 2012, *Feminist Africa* released a special issue entitled "African Feminist Engagements with Film," edited by female African filmmakers/scholars Yaba Badoe, Amina Mama and Salem Mekuria, discussing issues of representation, ownership, historical difficulties in the production of films and the recent change in attitudes towards women in African cinema. The journal challenges European and White perspectives on African cinema and leads the way for an African feminist approach to cinema, an agenda-setting manifesto from which we have drawn ideas. A year later, a special issue of the *Journal of African Cinemas* (2013), dedicated to forty years of filmmaking by African women, to which both authors contributed, opened up avenues towards a more historical approach to women making films on the African continent, which our book seeks to consolidate and bring to fruition.

A more recent work by Patrick E. Okon, *Women's Representation in African Cinema: A Study of the Postcolonial Films of Burkina Faso and Senegal* (2016), focuses on the representation of women in four successful films from West Africa: *La nuit de la vérité/The Night of Truth* (Fanta Régina Nacro, 2004), *Samba Traoré* (Idrissa

Ouédraogo, 1992), *Madame Brouette* (Moussa Sène Absa, 2002), and *Faat Kiné* (Ousmane Sembène, 2001). Aside from *The Night of Truth*, these films were all directed by men. The same is true for *Gender Terrains in Africa Cinema*, a recent work by Dominica Dipio (2016). Though the division of Dipio's book into chapters is innovative, structured along the lines of the different stages in a woman's life, from the girl child, to the young adult woman, to the elderly woman, the scope of the study is limited to films made by men from Francophone West Africa and describes these as canonical in nature. Azodo and Eke's edited volume, *Gender & Sexuality in African Literature and Film* (2007) contains a section on African film exploring masculinity and femininity, but there is only one chapter on a female-directed film, *The Season of Men* (2000) by Moufida Tlatli. Most of the other chapters discuss representations of gender in male-directed films. While we cannot deny that the canon is overwhelmingly male, we must break with this tendency to only regard films by male directors as worthy of canonisation or analysis, especially if the scholar is concerned with the representation of women on the screen.

Gaze Regimes: Film and Feminisms and Africa, edited by Jyoti Mistry and Antje Schuhmann (2015) comes closest in scope to our project. It is a collection of essays primarily based on first-hand interviews, showcasing the experiences of women working in film, either as practitioners or in other areas such as curators, festival programme directors or fundraisers. While its innovative and diverse approach includes the voices of male directors, and analyses of female representations in male-directed films, our sole focus on female-directed films differentiates it from this edited collection.

In summary, past publications on women in African cinema show that where there are studies focusing on the topic, they are either limited in cohesion because they consist of single chapters in edited collections or articles in special issues of journals. Where a book is entirely dedicated to women in African cinema, as is the case with Ellerson's work, it might be limited to primary research through interviews or encyclopaedic work, or it might be devoted to a specific country, region or form/ genre of filmmaking. What we offer here is a monograph with a specific approach and style, combining our strengths as regular collaborators with a constructive, critical vision that stems from deep subjective knowledge of our respective specialities with a critical distance. This allows us to offer sustained scholarly analyses and an optimistic vision of cinema by African women. We aim to establish a considerate, sustained and consistent approach to the diversity of films made by women across the African continent. What *Women in African Cinema: Beyond the Body Politic* does differently is to offer not only critical readings of women's positions in front of and behind the camera, but also a painstaking study that brings together an attentive look at women in African cinema from different geographical regions, with a diversity of styles and themes, as seen through an historical as well as socio-political and cultural cinematic lens. By looking at commercial as well as more independent, artistic and experi- mental work from the African continent, including both new and emerging talent and more recent films by established filmmakers, it embraces a considerable number of female filmmakers and their views on filmmaking.

Women in African cinema

Senegalese director Safi Faye is generally credited as the pioneering Black African female filmmaker from sub-Saharan Africa. She made her first short film, *La passante* in 1972, and also directed the first commercially distributed feature fiction film by a sub-Saharan woman, *Kaddu Beykat,* in 1976. Cameroonian film director Thérèse Sita-Bella's documentary *Tam-tam à Paris,* made in 1963, is regarded as the first film made by an African woman (Schmidt 1999, 279). Sita-Bella started her career in journalism in the 1950s and moved into filmmaking in the 1960s. Her documentary was screened at the first Week of African Cinema in 1969, a festival which later became the Pan-African Film and Television Festival of Ouagadougou, FESPACO, in Burkina Faso. Sita-Bella was a trailblazer not only in film, but also as Cameroon's first female pilot, a writer, musician, model and politician. She passed away at a hospital in Yaoundé in 2006, apparently forgotten, in poverty, and her death sparked a debate on how national icons are treated by the state and by society (Taylor, 2018). Although her pioneering role in African women's filmmaking is recognised in many histories of African cinema, references are brief because little is known about her and as far as we are aware her documentary has not been preserved and is thus not available for analysis. This neglect is to the detriment of African film history and scholarship as a whole.

Ousmane Sembène, known as the father of African cinema, made his first film in 1963: it is clear then that African women started making films at the same time, and were certainly part of the industry almost from its inception, in roles as varied as script writers, producers and actresses. Despite the fact that more African women have made films than might generally be believed or known, women remain hugely underrepresented in the African film industries as directors. Indeed, even Safi Faye's films remain largely unseen, and while many scholars mention her films, they are not readily available for viewing. Her first feature made in Senegal, *Kaddu Beykat,* appeared in 1976, produced with funding from the French Ministry of Cooperation. While it was the first commercially distributed feature film directed by a Black woman from sub-Saharan Africa, on its release the film was banned in Senegal because of its critique of government agricultural policies. It is important, then, to recognise that Faye as a pioneer and being among the most significant representatives of African cinema, is on a par with her compatriots Ousmane Sembène and Djibril Diop Mambéty. If Sembène is called the father of African cinema, Faye really should be known much more widely as the mother of African cinema. Yet, very few scholars of women's cinema and cinephiles worldwide are aware of her work.

In 1983 Farida Ayari (Bakari and Cham 1996, 181) claims that cinema is "men's business," with the technical matters of filmmaking as well as directing regarded as a male preserve. While exact statistics on the presence of women in the African film industries do not exist, the Center for the Study of Women in Television and Film in San Diego found that, in 2018, women comprised 20% of all directors, writers, producers, executive producers, editors, and cinematographers working on the top 250 grossing films in the US, and accounted for 8% of directors (https://wom enintvfilm.sdsu.edu/research/). It seems probable that the picture would not be much different in African film industries. Thus, despite a growing awareness of global gender imbalances existing in the film industries through 2017's #MeToo campaign, we could ask whether much has really changed since Ayari made the statement quoted above. Ayari names Sarah Maldoror and Safi Faye as two examples of a handful exceptions.

This underrepresentation is reflected in African film directories, which also tend to exclude television and video work, usually listing a very small number of female filmmakers compared to men. Keith Shiri's *Directory of African Filmmakers and Films* (1992), for example, lists 259 filmmakers of whom only eight are women. Even a cursory glance at Roy Armes's *Dictionary of African Filmmakers* (2008), which includes only feature films and filmmakers, confirms this domination of male directors. For a great but necessarily selective work that includes North African women, Rebecca Hillauer's *Encyclopedia of Arab Women Filmmakers* (2005) is exemplary, but where her focus is on Arab filmmakers, we include North Africa in our pan-African treatment of the African continent. David Murphy and Patrick Williams's book *Postcolonial African Cinema: Ten Directors* (2007) includes one chapter on a female director, Moufida Tlatli. N. Frank Ukadike's *Questioning African Cinema: Conversations with Filmmakers* (2002) does no better: out of 20 chapters only one focuses on a female director, Safi Faye. Thus, Tlati and Faye reappear in these books as the usual lone female figures who are supposed to be seen as representative of female filmmaking from an entire continent. Directories focusing specifically on women show that there are many more; Emilie Ngo-Nguidjol lists 100 women in her filmography of sub-Saharan African women filmmakers (1999, 320–328) and Beti Ellerson's book *Sisters of the Screen* (2000) lists 123 African female directors of film, television and video, some from the African diaspora. Ellerson's blog *African Women in Cinema* contains hundreds of posts on individual female directors, with more constantly being added. These film historians contend that the number of female African directors at international film festivals does not provide a full picture of female participation in the film industry, since African women produce more work in documentary and television than in feature fiction filmmaking. More and more young African women are also making short films, some of whom will continue to feature filmmaking. A particularly innovative initiative is the A-List, a database of women professionals working in film, television and digital content across Africa, launched by the Ladima Foundation in 2018. Their aim is for this list to become the most comprehensive database of professional women working in the screen industries in Africa (Preston 2018).

Viewing the presence of women in African cinema historically, Ellerson cites the creation of African Women for Research and Development (AAWORD), in Senegal in 1977 as a turning point (Ellerson 2015, 3). AAWORD understood the importance of women working at the intersection of media and African development. In the 1980s, films by African women drew on the themes highlighted by the United Nations first Decade for Women, which ran from 1976 to 1985.

Ellerson states that during and after the UN Decade there was a surge in female African filmmaking with more international visibility for the filmmakers and their films, many of which focussed on themes of women's empowerment in social, economic and cultural spheres (ibid). By the 1990s, increasingly important conversations were taking place about the presence of women in African cinema.

One central event in the 1990s was when African women professionals of cinema, television and video came together for a workshop at the 1991 FESPACO festival, in an attempt to address the silences and omissions left by their virtual invisibility in the audio-visual industries. They released a statement that outlined their most urgent questions and needs. In it they asked, after forty years of cinematographic production and twenty-five years of televisual production on the African continent, how many women were involved, what roles they fulfilled and which images of African women were shown to women of the African continent (Bakari and Cham 1996, 35). Their discussions during the workshop emphasised the unsatisfactory number of women working in audio-visual professions and the problems women face in gaining access to training and funding. They put forward their vision of the world that aimed to achieve space for women to gain a decision-making position in the audio-visual sector. A working group and a programme of action were set up that were needed to lead to an increase in the number of women working in the profession.

The importance of African women taking part in the production of cultural products intended to challenge perceptions and change attitudes was emphasised in their statement:

> if pictures produced by African women do not give another view on African women's reality, then there is a great risk that women themselves, because they are the main educators of children – the citizens of tomorrow – will not be able to show an alternative vision of the world.
>
> *(ibid.)*

Ellerson describes the important agendas of strengthening networks through organising, outreach and advocacy throughout the 1990s (2015, 4). The roots of this organised movement in African women's cinema established at the 1991 FESPACO can be found at the "Colloque Images de Femmes" – the women's film forum at Vues d'Afrique, held in Montreal in 1989, where women started to develop a framework for action. The 1991 discussions led to the establishment of the Pan-African Union of Women in the Image Industry, which still exists today.

Claire Andrade-Watkins states that in the long run the workshop was a catalyst for understanding and growth (1995, 149). Patterns in terms of the presence of women in the audio-visual industries were identified. For example, women work in documentary, television and video more often than they do in film, and most women working in cinema do so as actresses, or are steered towards distribution or editing. If women are underrepresented in the director's chair, they do doubtlessly work in various roles in the film industries; the actresses and star system of African cinema, for instance, could easily warrant their own book. While our focus in this book is on female directors, there is huge scope for further research on the whole range of roles that women fulfil in the African film industries.

Fast-forwarding several years, at FESPACO in 2005, when the authors of this book started to attend the festival, the number of women working in the audio-visual medium had certainly increased, but still only three female directors were included in the official competition for feature fiction films. These included the debuts of Burkinabe filmmakers Fanta Régina Nacro and Apolline Traoré as well as a feature film by German-Nigerian director Branwen Okpako. Looking back now, the 2005 FESPACO was in fact a good year for women. At FESPACO 2007 and 2009 no sub-Saharan women had films in competition, though North African female directors were represented, and Leïla Kilani from Morocco won with her documentary *Nos lieux interdits/Our Forbidden Places* in 2008 (she had also won the documentary prize in 2003 for her film *Tanger, le rêve des brûleurs/Tangier, the Burners' Dream*). It is in fact primarily in documentary that women have been recognised for their work at FESPACO. In 2011 *Oh whites* by Ivorian director Fatima Ouattara won in that category and in 2013 Tunisian Nadia El Fani won with *Même pas mal!* It is only the Algerian film *Yema* by Djamila Sahraoui that has gone so far as to win second prize for best feature in 2013. Alongside Sahraoui, Burkinabe director Apolline Traoré's feature film *Moi Zaphira* was also in competition in 2013. The feature film competition of FESPACO 2015 included two female-directed films, Senegalese director Dyana Gaye's *Des étoiles/Under the Starry Sky* and Tunisian director Raja Amari's *Printemps tunisien/Tunisian Spring*. FESPACO 2017 also featured two female-directed films in the main competition, another film by Apolline Traoré, *Frontières/Borders*, as well as Nigerien director Rahmatou Keïta's *Zin'naariya!/The Wedding Ring*. FESPACO 2019 pleasingly had four female-directed films in competition, the prolific Apolline Traoré presented her fourth feature film, *Desrances*, and Algerian director Yasmine Chouikh's *Ila Akher Ezaman/Until the End of the Time*, Kenyan director Wanuri Kahiu's *Rafiki*, and Moroccan director Selma Bargach's *Indigo* also featured. The importance of continuing discussions about the presence of women in film was underscored by a roundtable entitled "The place of women in the film industry in Africa and the diaspora" that took place at FESPACO 2019, in which a large number of women journalists, actors, directors and curators took part. The roundtable was organised by a collective, Non-Aligned Cineastes, an association of women filmmakers supporting diversity, parity and increased representation of women in the film industries internationally, founded in 2016. In 2019, in light of two years of intense attention paid to the representation and presence of women in the global film industry, the roundtable focused on the role of women in the African industries, distribution and exhibition.

The roundtable also considered that, although the figure of the grand prize for feature films at FESPACO is the bronze statuette of Princess Yennenga, a legendary princess and warrior from the Mossi people in Burkina Faso, it has not yet borne witness to the recognition of more African women working in film. Despite the statuette's symbolic allusion to the important roles women have played in

African histories and cultures, no female director has yet won the prize for Best Feature since the first FESPACO was held in 1969 (although women have been awarded in the categories noted above as well as in best short film, best cinematography and various special prizes). Burkinabe director Franceline Oubda stated in an interview with Beti Ellerson:

> [The Étalon de Yennenga] demonstrates the importance of women in society. And I think to have this prize is a crowning achievement. And we women must fight so that women will achieve this. If we succeed in obtaining the Étalon de Yennenga, the efforts of women will be crowned and we will have reached a certain objective. Princess Yennenga was the proof of courage and bravery, the proof of endurance, and she was a woman who did a great deal in Burkina history. I think to fight for a woman to obtain the Yennenga is truly a step forward, and it will be for the greater welfare and improved standard of women in general.
>
> *(2000, 238)*

Looking back over the past three decades, the vision set out by female film practitioners at FESPACO in 1991 is far from fulfilled, and there is an acute awareness that the struggle continues. There have been various other, more recent attempts to bring together female African filmmakers. An event at the 2008 Cannes Film Festival, entitled "L'Engagement de femmes cinéastes," included a roundtable organised by the now-defunct Cinemas of the South Pavilion. Another gathering of female African filmmakers took place in Johannesburg in 2010 at the Goethe-Institut.[4] The African Women in Film Forum (AWIFF) took place in Accra, Ghana in 2012 and 2013, and the African Women Filmmakers Hub was launched in Harare, Zimbabwe, in 2016. As we describe above, South Africa's SWIFT and the Ladima Foundation are two of the most significant currently active organisations intended to bring together women working in the African screen industries, through offering support structures; discussing common problems, challenges and barriers; and offering training, networking and other development opportunities for female African filmmakers. In Chapter 3 we reflect further upon the importance of female affiliations and networks in film.

While women are underrepresented as directors in almost all film industries worldwide – for cultural, structural and systemic reasons – often due to the prevalence of patriarchal career structures and a lack of true gender equality in the workplace, women in the African screen industries are underrepresented for a complex variety of context-specific reasons, described by Beti Ellerson as the "triple challenges" suffered by African women filmmakers (1997). Firstly, there are myriad production and distribution difficulties that confront all directors working in Africa; add to that the obstacles women face because of their gender; and lastly, women filmmakers' face additional challenges in their expected mothering/motherhood and family roles. It is indisputable that both male and female African filmmakers generally encounter immense challenges in making films, often working against all odds in their attempts to gain access to training, funding, distribution and exhibition. However, it is clear that female filmmakers face additional barriers when taking on the challenge of making films, in Africa and elsewhere. Burkinabe director Fanta Régina Nacro stated in an interview with Melissa Thackway that there is a certain "veiled mentality" when potential funders or distributors are dealing with women (2003, 197). Well-known Burkinabe filmmaker Gaston Kaboré stated in an interview with Kimani Wa Wanjiru: "The question of insufficient funds is a perennial one for African filmmakers and it is more pronounced where women filmmakers are concerned" (Wa Wanjiru 2003). African women who desire to establish independent careers regularly have to face up to the challenges posed by societal and neo-colonial norms which perpetuate and maintain women's confinement to the domestic sphere.

Some female filmmakers have expressed the prejudices they have endured from a society or culture that might not regard filmmaking as an honourable career for a woman. Where women have managed to gain access to the film industry, their presence and participation typically follow familiar patterns of gender relations in African societies and elsewhere, with women working "behind the scenes" while it is the (mostly male) directors who are publicly acclaimed. Furthermore, to direct a film means in most cases to direct a largely male crew, which can be problematic in patriarchal societies where the authority of women is often undermined. The majority of women who work in the African film industry – and this is true internationally – stay within the "traditionally" female roles like production manager, wardrobe and make-up assistant, casting, editing and continuity. Directing and technical roles, including cinematography, are conventionally regarded as a male preserve. Women typically enter the industry through one of these conventionally female roles, and the handful of women who do eventually direct feature films mostly achieve this well after first focusing on the more "women-friendly" short fictions and documentaries. It should be noted here that the accessibility and affordability of digital technology is rapidly changing the landscape of African filmmaking, as epitomised by Nigeria's prolific Nollywood industry. Digital technology makes filmmaking vastly more accessible than expensive celluloid film production, and this has led to an explosion of filmmaking on the African continent over the last decade or so, including an increase in female directors.

In many cases, female African filmmakers have ended up directing projects sponsored by international organisations and NGOs, where they do not have a lot of control over the narrative and style of the film. Often female directors receive specific funding or are encouraged to make films addressing specifically "female themes" like polygamy, domestic abuse or female genital mutilation. This exposes how, on the one hand, women are being cornered into making development films on "women's issues," and how, on the other hand, women often choose to address specific issues that affect African women. Burkinabe filmmaker Valerie Kaboré stated in an interview with Ellerson that making only institutional films is limiting, since being forced to work with precise terms and references required by the funders, one cannot really measure one's creative capacity as a director (2000, 129). Short films, documentaries and audio-visual development work for television on non-theatrical distribution are commonly viewed as stepping stones towards directing fiction feature films, still the ultimate career ambition for most filmmakers. In addition, many African women filmmakers do not start their careers in the film industry, but end up in the industry through other career paths, usually juggling their filmmaking with another career, as well as with motherhood. This is the case, for example, for Kenyan director Judy Kibinge, who started her creative career in advertising.

Training and funding are the two main barriers to African women's entry into the film industries as directors. Access to film schools needs to be increased for women, and commissioning bodies should prioritise the work of female directors, as was done by the South African National Film and Video Foundation's Female Filmmaker Project 2017/18, which aimed to provide ten women, particularly those from historically disadvantaged backgrounds, with an opportunity to make a film in collaboration with other women. Similarly, Sisters in Film – MENA is a development programme announced in 2019 and supported by UNESCO to build the capacity of women film professionals in the MENA (Middle East and North Africa) region. Given the lack of dedicated government-awarded film funds in most African countries (South Africa being an exception), the answer to funding and distribution problems might lie in the private sector. The media and tele-communication industries in Africa are fast-growing in many regions, and invest-ment in audio-visual production could be allocated from these channels.

There is a greater need for production support for women's films, in particular for mid-career directors who are often locked out of viable funding options. Funding and alternative distribution should be put in place to support independent filmmaking in particular, and this might be done through a pan-African circuit for developing and distributing film projects. While support for independent film-making is crucial to develop unique creative voices, NGO and donor-funded projects also play an important role in helping filmmakers to gain skills and as a platform for female filmmakers to cut their teeth. The mentorship model could be a successful way to nurture the talents of female African filmmakers and providing them with safe spaces to learn and experiment. Importantly, space should be assigned, through ratios in and privileging of women in training, funding, pro-duction and distribution projects, to ensure their participation in a male-dominated environment. Finally, where formal training and education are not available, digital technologies could increase the participation of women in the African film indus-tries by making more information available online, participating actively in digital forums, innovating digital projects, training in seminars and open Skype sessions, and launching crowdsourcing platforms and digital distribution for women's films.

Structure of the book

The first chapter outlines the histories and theories we regard as most relevant to the positions and roles of women in African cinema. We move through brief histories of filmmaking on the continent in a chronological and regional manner, highlighting the contributions and achievements of women in particular. This is followed by an outline of different configurations of and approaches to African feminisms, which serves as the analytical framework of the book. The remainder of the book contains eight chapters, each dealing with a thematic challenge, which allows us to approach the topic of women in African cinema with geographic breadth and analytical depth.

In Chapter 2, the multiple individual and collective identities represented in women's films are explored. The image of the African woman has often been stereotyped by two polar opposites: the image of the strong, resourceful woman as backbone of her community and "mother of the nation" on the one hand, and the African woman as silent victim bearing the burden of her society, on the other hand. However, in between these two opposites there is a spectrum of subject positionings, and the films by African women depict the diversity of identities that form part of African womanhood. The multiple roles that African women fulfil in their societies, and the different but often intersecting spheres of race, class, nationality, ethnicity, sexuality and gender that inform their subjectivity, mean that female identity in Africa is fluid and plural. The films discussed in this chapter show how individual and personal identities exist alongside social, cultural and communal identities, with a special focus on transnational female identities in the contemporary era.

In Chapter 3 we explore female friendships, affinities and affiliations, and the multiple societal, cultural and activist ties and networks of African women. African women's identities are not only dependent on the formation of the self, or on the relationship with a man or other partner, and as such we want to move beyond the dominant heteropatriarchal view of interpersonal relations. The chapter positions female friendship as foundational to feminism, apparent as much in theory as in practice. We are interested here in a sense of community, in the professional film world as well as in the women-only communities we see on screen. The main themes in this chapter are friendships and alliances, female activism, communities and transnational connections, themes that are further explored in our chosen case studies.

Many African countries have undergone prolonged traumatic periods of oppression, revolution, division, war and conflict, events that have particularly complex effects on the emancipation of women. Chapter 4 examines the experiences of conflict, trauma and reconciliation represented in film, addressing topics such as rape as a weapon of war and women's roles in liberation struggles and revolutions. Filling gaps left in official historiography, women's films offer alternative, complementary vistas of history. Historiography is too often cynically detached from colonial atrocities, and cinema has the power to address these gaps and "his"tories. Indeed, as Ramanathan tells us: "it is not sufficient to fill in gaps, to do the crucial elemental work of acknowledging women's existence and participation, but it is equally vital to relate patriarchal ideology to the contemporary lived conditions of women" (2006, 89). The films under discussion show that women have never only been passive victims of war and conflict. Quite on the contrary, we see active contributors to wars, resistance, conflict resolution and post-war reconciliation. These portrayals by women serve as "corrections" of male-dominated historiography, highlighting the everyday experience of resistance and war time, and their resilience.

Chapter 5 asserts that while motherhood remains a fundamental part of many African women's lives and has been depicted extensively in African cinema, the complexities of daughterhood have not been addressed in enough detail in African film scholarship. African womanhood and the motherhood of sons are typically invoked as symbolic and allegorical representations of the nation, with nationalist discourse employing archetypes such as "Mother Africa," where women become a trope in idealising national identity. A European construct of Africa as "Other" includes incomplete and fixed ideas regarding the role of mothers in communities rather than roles that vary depending on time, space and circumstance. However, as we show through the films discussed in this chapter, female filmmakers tend to focus on affirmative cross-generational relationships between mothers and daughters. Often these relationships are complex and antagonistic, but ultimately the understanding between mothers and daughters returns *if* the breakdown in communication is overcome.

Chapter 6 examines the power and beauty of the female African body. Through an exploration of the body as an experience, we turn to an imagined growth from physical and psychological "object," to a philosophical "subject." Finding inspiration in film philosophy's recent turn to world cinema and its exploration of inter-subjectivity in art across borders, we look into the subjective experience and the body's interaction with other subjectivities. An awareness of the other's and one's own existence in a shared phenomenological world serves to make possible a different appreciation of the female body, beyond gender, beauty or class. The subject's being in the world has meaning mainly through a consistent self-awareness of her presence in front of the others. We ask then how women experience one another and get acquainted with one another through physical manifestations and psychological processes. In the case studies we look specifically at the skin and its colour, at the body and its attendant identity's outer border, and at the complex identity development through the experience and expression of the body.

African cinema has at times been described as "prudish," due to its relatively rare depictions of overt and explicit representations of sexuality, but in Chapter 7 our analyses of the depictions of sexualities reveal that sexuality has indeed been explored by women in African cinema, often in daring and courageous ways. We argue that female sexuality in Africa in particular has been subject to too much anthropological speculation and misapprehension. African cultures are generally regarded as more closed than Western cultures with regard to public displays of a sexual or erotic nature, as the result of a different perspective on intimacy and privacy. Despite the fact that these societal norms have, historically, led to a dearth of explicit displays of sexuality or nudity in African cinema, there is an increasing amount of films by female directors that explore sexuality and desire more overtly. We spend some time in this chapter reflecting on non-heteronormative sexualities in Africa, in particular lesbianism, as many African scholars, activists and cultural practitioners have made great strides in disputing pervading homophobia, as also indicated in our case studies.

Chapter 8, on spirituality, looks at the diverse ways in which spirituality has contributed to the socio-political and economic history of African cinema, and at the role of spirituality in women's lives, be it traditional belief systems, Christianity, Islam, Judaism or other minority spiritualities. The chapter outlines some of the most important and influential spiritual philosophies from different parts of the continent, both in historical and contemporary terms. A discussion of how cinema depicts or performs various spiritualities is followed by an analysis of how spiritualities can serve both as limiting forces and as productive tools on the journey to emancipation. We engage with the ways in which women are changing strained spiritual experiences, and ultimately find alternative ways to express their agencies and make life choices that reveal how gender inequalities can lead to drastic action.

★★★★

In this introduction we have detailed our approach to our topic, women in African cinema, describing in some depth our approach to *women* and *cinema* as analytical and critical categories, and our understanding of *Africa* as geopolitical place and space. The content of the book reveals a broad interest in, and a necessary reworking of, the study of filmmaking on the African continent through women's films. Having been neglected in women's film studies and in studies of African cinema, these filmmakers and their films reshape cinematic historiography, and writing about them is an attempt to make more complete the histories of African cinemas. The inspiration for writing the book came out of many years of research and a deep awareness of the neglect of African cinema in film studies more broadly, and the neglect of African women's cinema in women's film studies. As such, we hope that this work will enrich both fields and contribute to the nascent field of African feminist film studies, since we regard our approach as candidly feminist, as we describe in the first chapter. We conclude this book with a final section on where to find African women's films, as we do hope that this book will not only be of interest to African studies and film studies scholars, but can also inspire general readers to engage with more African women's films. We want to present a challenge to our readers, and argue that you do not know world cinema if you do not know African cinema, and you do not know women's film if you don't know the work of the female African directors we discuss in this book.

Notes

1 In this book we have capitalised White and Black, as we employ these terms as proper nouns describing an ethnic origin or ancestry, similar to Arab or Asian.
2 See the marketing materials for the Elizabeth Taylor film *Cleopatra* (1963) by Joseph L. Mankiewicz.
3 Ubuntu, originating from Southern Africa, is the now widely used philosophical concept of a shared humanity, a belief that a shared universal bond connects all humanity.
4 This event became the origin and inspiration for Mistry and Schuhmann's book *Gaze Regimes*.

Bibliography

Andrade-Watkins, Claire (1995) "A mirage in the desert?: African women directors at FESPACO." In Michael T. Martin (ed.) *Cinemas of the Black Diaspora: Diversity, Dependence, and Oppositionality.* Detroit, MI: Wayne State University Press, pp. 145–152.

Armes, Roy (2008) *Dictionary of African Filmmakers.* Bloomington: Indiana University Press.

Arnfred, Signe (2004) "Re-thinking sexualities in Africa: Introduction." In Signe Arnfred (ed.) *Rethinking Sexualities in Africa.* Uppsala: Almqvist and Wiksell Tryckeri, pp. 7–34.

Ayari, Farida (1996) "Images of women." In Imruh Bakari and Mbye Cham (eds) *African Experiences of Cinema.* London: British Film Institute, pp. 181–184.

Azodo, Ada Uzoamaka and Maureen Ngozi Eke (eds) (2007) *Gender & Sexuality in African Literature and Film.* Trenton: Africa World Press.

Badoe, Yaba, Amina Mama and Salem Mekuria (2012) "African feminist engagements with film," *Feminist Africa,* 16, pp. 1–7.

Bakari, Imruh and Mbye Cham (eds) (1996) *African Experiences of Cinema.* London: British Film Institute.

Bakari, Imruh and Mbye Cham (eds) (1996) "Statement of African women professionals of cinema, television and video, Ouagadougou, Burkina Faso, 1991." In *African Experiences of Cinema.* London: British Film Institute, pp. 35–38.

Barlet, Olivier (1996) *African Cinemas: Decolonising the Gaze.* London: Zed Books.

Blignaut, Charl (2018) "SA film and television industry responds to #MeToo claims," *City Press* (29 April). Available online: https://city-press.news24.com/News/sa-film-and-television-industry-responds-to-metoo-claims-20180429 [Accessed June 2018].

Blignaut, Charl and Rhodé Marshall (2018) "Women speak out," *City Press* (29 April). Available online: https://city-press.news24.com/News/khalo-matabane-women-speak-out-20180429 [Accessed June 2018].

Bobo, Jacqueline (2013) *Black Women Film and Video Artists.* Abingdon-on-Thames: Routledge.

De Groot, Sue (2017) "Time for a close-up, sisters," *Sunday Times* (26 November).

Diawara, Manthia (1992) *African Cinema: Politics and Culture.* Bloomington: Indiana University Press.

Dipio, Dominica (2016) *Gender Terrains in Africa Cinema.* Grahamstown: NISC (Pty) Ltd.

Dovey, Lindiwe (2012) "New looks: The rise of African women filmmakers," *Feminist Africa,* 16. Available online: www.agi.ac.za/agi/feminist-africa/16/ [Accessed April 2018].

Eboh, Marie Pauline (1998) "The woman question: African and western perspectives." In Emmanuel Chukwudi Eze (ed.) *African Philosophy: An Anthology.* Oxford: Blackwell.

Ellerson, Beti (1997) "Visualizing herstories: Towards an introduction to African women cinema studies." Available online: www.africanwomenincinema.org/AFWC/Visualizing_Herstories.html [Accessed May 2018].

Ellerson, Beti (2000) *Sisters of the Screen: Women of Africa on Film, Video and Television.* Trenton and Asmara: Africa World Press Inc.

Ellerson, Beti (2015) "African women in cinema: An overview." In Jyoti Mistry and Antje Schuhmann (eds) *Gaze Regimes: Film and Feminisms in Africa.* Johannesburg: Wits University Press, pp. 1–9.

Foster, Gwendolyn Audrey (1997) *Women Filmmakers of the African and Asian Diaspora: Decolonizing the Gaze, Locating Subjectivity.* Carbondale: Southern Illinois University Press.

Harrow, Kenneth (ed.) (1999) *African Cinema: Postcolonial and Feminist Readings.* Trenton, NJ: Africa World Press.

Hillauer, Rebecca (2005) *Encyclopedia of Arab Women Filmmakers.* Cairo: American University of Cairo Press.

Ladima Foundation (2018) "African women have stories to tell. Let's watch them." Available online: www.ladima.africa [Accessed June 2018].

Manatu, Norma (2002) *African American Women and Sexuality in the Cinema*. Jefferson: McFarland & Co.

Mistry, Jyoti and Antje Schuhmann (eds) (2015) *Gaze Regimes: Film and Feminisms in Africa*. Johannesburg: Wits University Press.

Murphy, David and Patrick Williams (2007) *Postcolonial African Cinema: Ten Directors*. Manchester: Manchester University Press.

Ngo-Nguidjol, Emilie (1999) "Women in African cinema: An annotated bibliography." In Kenneth W. Harrow (ed.) *African Cinema: Postcolonial and Feminist Readings*. Trenton and Asmara: Africa World Press Inc., pp. 305–338.

Okon, Patrick E. (2016) *Women's Representation in African Cinema: A Study of the Postcolonial Films of Burkina Faso and Senegal*. Ota: Livingproof.

Petty, Sheila (2008) *Contact Zones: Memory, Origin, and Discourses in Black Diasporic Cinema*. Detroit: Wayne State University Press.

Pfaff, Françoise (2004) *Focus on African Films*. Bloomington: Indiana University Press.

Pravadelli, Veronica (2017) *Contemporary Women's Cinema: Global Scenarios, Transnational Contexts*. Milan: Mimesis International.

Preston, Lara (2018) "The Ladima Foundation launches the A-list," *Screen Africa*. Available online: www.screenafrica.com/2018/08/07/film/business/the-ladima-foundation-launches-the-a-list/ [Accessed January 2019].

Ramanathan, Geetha (2006) *Feminist Auteurs: Reading Women's Films*. London: Wallflower Press.

Roller, Duane W. (2011) *Cleopatra, A Biography*. Oxon: Oxford University Press.

Shiri, Keith (ed.) (1992) *Directory of African Film-Makers and Films*. Westport: Greenwood Press.

Schmidt, Nancy J. (1999) "Sub-Saharan African women filmmakers: Agendas for research." In Kenneth W. Harrow (ed.) *African Cinema: Postcolonial and Feminist Readings*. Trenton: Africa World Press.

SWIFT (2017) "Sisters working in film and television launch #ThatsNotOk campaign," *Sex Rights Africa Network*, 19 October. Available online: www.sexrightsafrica.net/swift-sisters-working-film-television-launch-thatsnotok-campaign/ [Accessed June 2018].

Tamale, Sylvia (2011) "Introduction." In Sylvia Tamale (ed.) *African Sexualities: A Reader*. Cape Town: Pambazuka Press, pp. 1–8.

Taylor, Mildred Europa (2018) "The sad and lonely final days of Sita Bella, Africa's first woman filmmaker." Available online: https://face2faceafrica.com/article/the-sad-and-lonely-final-days-of-sita-bella-africas-first-woman-filmmaker [Accessed 11 January 2019].

Thackway, Melissa (2003) *Africa Shoots Back: Alternative Perspectives in Sub-Saharan Francophone African Film*. Oxford: James Currey.

Ukadike, Frank N. (1994) *Black African Cinema*. Oakland: University of California Press.

Ukadike, Frank N. (2002) *Questioning African Cinema: Conversations with Filmmakers*. Minneapolis: University of Minnesota Press.

White, Patricia (2015) *Women's Cinema, World Cinema: Projecting Contemporary Feminisms*. Durham: Duke University Press.

Wa Wanjiru, K. (2003) "Women and cinema at ZIFF." Available online: www.africanfilmny.org/2001/women-and-cinema-at-ziff/ [Accessed 20 September 2019].

Filmography

Caméra arabe, Dir. Férid Boughedir, Tunisia, 1987

Caméra d'Afrique / Twenty Years of African Cinema, Dir. Férid Boughedir, Tunisia/France, 1983

Des étoiles / Under the Starry Sky, Dir. Dyana Gaye, France/Belgium/Senegal, 2013

Desrances, Dir. Apolline Traoré, Burkina Faso, 2019

Faat Kiné, Dir. Ousmane Sembène, Senegal, 2001

Frontières / Borders, Dir. Apolline Traoré, Burkina Faso/France, 2017

Ila Akher Ezaman / Until the End of the Time, Dir. Yasmine Chouikh, Algeria/United Arab Emirates, 2017

Indigo, Dir. Selma Bargach, Morocco, 2018

Kaddu Beykat, Dir. Safi Faye, Senegal, 1976

La nuit de la vérité / The Night of Truth, Dir. Fanta Régina Nacro, Burkina Faso/France, 2004

La passante, Dir. Safi Faye, Senegal, 1972

Madame Brouette, Dir. Moussa Sene Absa, Canada/Senegal/France, 2002

Même pas mal!, Dir. Nadia El Fani, France, 2012

Moi Zaphira, Dir. Apolline Traoré, Burkina Faso, 2013

Nos lieux interdits / Our Forbidden Places, Dir. Leïla Kilani, Morocco/France, 2008

Oh whites, Dir. Fatima Ouattara, Ivory Coast, 2011

Printemps tunisien / Tunisian Spring, Dir. Raja Amari, France/Tunisia, 2014

Rafiki, Dir. Wanuri Kahiu, Kenya/South Africa/Germany/Netherlands/France/Norway/Lebanon, 2018

Sisters of the Screen: African Women in the Cinema, Dir. Beti Ellerson, US, 2002

Samba Traoré, Dir. Idrissa Ouédraogo, Burkina Faso/France/Switzerland, 1992

Tam-tam à Paris, Dir. Thérèse Sita-Bella, Cameroon, 1963

Tanger, le rêve des brûleurs / Tangier, the Burners' Dream, Dir. Leïla Kilani, France, 2003

Yema, Dir. Djamila Sahraoui, Algeria/France/United Arab Emirates, 2012

Zin'naariya! / The Wedding Ring, Dir. Rahmatou Keïta, Burkina Faso/Niger/France, 2016

1

HISTORIES AND THEORIES

The moving image arrived on the African continent not long after its invention in Europe at the end of the nineteenth century, with Egypt on the continent's northernmost point, and South Africa at its southern tip, boasting the first and second oldest African industries respectively. While South Africa, due to its long history of Black oppression and White domination, has a more complex history, women were active in Egyptian cinema, in front of and behind the camera, from the early twentieth century onwards. With indigenous sub-Saharan African cinema emerging after independence, from the late 1950s onwards, women also made their mark early on in those industries. Nevertheless, women's presence as central protagonists on screen and creative driving forces off-screen remains underexplored. African histories boast matriarchies, queens and female warriors, and male-directed African films have created representations of such strong and emancipated female characters. But without the central creative presence of women, our cinematic understandings of the continent will continue to be shaped by an incomplete vision. In what follows we focus on specific geographic regions of the African continent, in order to describe an imagined feminist chronology and historiography of African film history.

It is well-known how the Lumière Brothers sent out their camera men to capture "*vues*" or "views" of exotic African places to include in their earliest films. As such, moving images *of* Africa have existed since the very beginning of cinema. These image-making views and their capturers influenced the development of perceptions of Africa and its peoples. But these views and screenings also awakened a spirit of defiance by people *from* Africa, to set right the way Africa and Africans were being portrayed. This was the case for young Tunisian entrepreneur Albert Samama Chikly, who – after having seen the "views," which in Tunisia were shot by Félix Mesguich – made his own short film clips from 1909 onwards. In 1922 and 1924 Chikly made the first two films with entirely African (Tunisian) crews: respectively

Zohra and *The Girl from Carthage*. The reason Chikly is interesting to our study is that the scripts for these two films were written by his daughter, Haydée Samama Chikly Tamzali, who also portrayed the protagonists. She is likely the first actress and screenwriter on the African continent. The films reveal an interest in defying social expectations by a lack of respect for power and financial privilege in favour of love and romance. The earliest film made in Africa by an entirely African crew, in 1924, was therefore a political statement of intent.

Around the same time in the Alexandria expat community, Stephan Rosti made *Laila* in 1927. Because of its nationalist fervour, spurred on by a patriotic drive, like *The Girl from Carthage, Laila* is still regarded as the first truly Egyptian film, specifically because it was produced, written and acted by Egypt's first superstar actress Aziza Amir. Talaat Harb, a banker and investor in cinema who had voiced his pessimism for a homegrown Egyptian cinema, expressed his surprise, saying "Aziza Amir has accomplished what no man was able to" (Hillauer 2005, 102). As such, from the very beginning, Egyptian cinema was defined by a woman able to tell her story, defining early developments in a national cinema where women were and remained in charge for a very long time.

By and large, African cinema is a postcolonial endeavour. There is a (limited) national cinema in most countries. Although observers generally agree that regional and continental collaboration is beneficial to developing national cinemas, the notion of an "African cinema" is hugely complex and problematic. Africa is a vast, heterogeneous continent with diverse cultural traditions and different colonial experiences, which have left distinct aesthetic baggage in terms of filmmaking. However, one approach that is, at least partially, shared by film practitioners in these countries, particularly by the early pioneers on the continent, is a view of cinema that recognises the potential of film to address socio-cultural issues of contemporary importance. Likewise, the commercial possibilities of popular African cinema, spearheaded by Nigeria's Nollywood industry, are increasingly embraced by entrepreneurial filmmakers across the continent intent on shaking off the shackles of colonialism in order to construct a homegrown aesthetic approach to storytelling through film. African cinema inevitably has to be understood as a plural term, with a diversity in aesthetic styles, genres and themes as well as in professional and industry conditions.

The way the African continent was colonised differed greatly depending on the colonising power. France's colonial endeavours were different from those of Britain or Portugal, which in turn influenced the manner in which film was offered to the colonised peoples and the way in which the freshly independent nations then turned to filmmaking in the 1960s. While filmmaking was a prohibited activity for francophone Africans under colonial rule, in post-colonial times France became a key funder of filmmaking in its ex-colonies. The infrastructure left behind after independence influenced postcolonial film practices. While Francophone cinema remains hugely influenced by fictional explorations, Britain established a legacy of documentary film, influenced by its colonial film practices. The Bantu Educational Kinema Experiment (BEKE) was set up in 1935, and the Colonial Film Unit was set up in 1939, both producing colonialist instructional and educational films that adhered to British colonial policies. These films had straightforward educational purposes, for example addressing issues of health and sanitation, and formed part of Britain's "civilising" mission (Rice 2019). In the postcolonial era, they are regarded as simplistic, paternalistic and inherently racist films.

The lusophone African countries (Angola, Mozambique, Cape Verde, Guinea-Bissau, and São Tomé and Príncipe) share a legacy of a harsh Portuguese colonial reign, extreme poverty and a revolutionary movement for independence (Andrade-Watkins 1999, 178). Portugal produced a series of highly propagandist documentaries and did not establish any production or training facilities for Africans (Diawara 1992, 88). The development of home-grown cinema in lusophone Africa is often aligned with the Third Cinema movement of Latin America (more about this in Chapter 4). Film production was regarded as a powerful tool in the liberation struggle and a vital component in the documentation, education and dissemination of information about the war. Film production was supported by the international community, especially the USSR, with the concept of "guerrilla filmmaking" developing out of the Marxist ideals of Third Cinema.

Homegrown African filmmaking has endeavoured for decades to rectify the exoticised and limited image of Africa perpetuated by the West.[1] In what follows we outline, in broad terms, some of the main developments in African film history as they pertain to women's and feminist cinema. We deal with regional and national cinemas, in order to show an acute awareness of the wide diversity but also to point out productive regional/transnational similarities and impacts. This is followed by an overview of the main theories we espouse in our analyses of films in the thematic chapters that follow.

North Africa

Cinema in North Africa can be divided into two, or even three, regions that influence one another to a certain extent. First, there is Egypt, the centre of Arab filmmaking with a Golden Age in the 1940s and 1950s, but also characterised in North Africa as the industry *against* which Algerian, Moroccan and Tunisian filmmakers made their films. Second, we have the Maghreb, with Morocco, Algeria and Tunisia as three variably productive filmmaking countries, under the continued sphere of influence of France. Independence came to Morocco and Tunisia in 1956, but not to Algeria until 1962 and after a brutal war. In the 1960s and 1970s Algerian cinema was dominated by revolutionary films in the service of independence. Tunisian cinema experienced its real blossoming with a Golden Age in the late 1980s and early 1990s, and Morocco, delayed by the dictatorial repression under King Hassan II and the Years of Lead, suffered from a very late cinematic awakening in the 1990s. Third, there is Libya, which under Gaddafi produced only two films, entirely based on the dictator's life and his interpretation of the Quran. Libyan cinema has recently made some strides, in particular in non-mainstream cinema, notably through the efforts of young women like Naziha Arebi, whose films *Granny's Flags* (2012) and *Freedom Fields* (2018) assert a strong, individual voice.

As mentioned above, Egypt had a unique experience of cinematic emancipation. Long before independence in the Maghreb, it had firmly established a women-centred national film industry to rival Hollywood. There were six particularly prominent female pioneers in early Egyptian cinema: Aziza Amir, Assia Dagher, Behidja Hafez, Fatma Rouchdi, Amina Mohamed and Mary Queeny. What sets them apart from other actresses of the time is that they did not limit themselves to their roles as starlet actresses. A feminist movement was active in Egypt during the 1920s. In that feminist spirit, these women developed their professional careers in film as directors and producers, mostly during the 1940s and 1950s. With them, the Egyptian film industry began to thrive and became a feasible area of employment for women. The fading popularity and success of Egyptian cinema came at a time when increasing socio-economic and cultural oppression prevented women from taking on public lives, and increased Islamist attitudes towards the veil and women's roles in the household dominated discourse. After an early feminist wave and the opportunities afforded to women during the World Wars, the return to the private sphere for women was also to the detriment of national cinema in Egypt. Since then, women's roles in Egyptian cinema have fluctuated. So, although our overall position is that there are not enough women in the (African) film industries, Egypt is the exception that proves the rule as it boasts almost too many to mention. Here, we will focus on a few who have defined the perception of women in cinema, by tackling taboos or with their notable contributions to the history of Egyptian women in cinema.

Some very powerful filmmakers have made films, but the fluctuating attitudes towards women's roles in public define cinema's treatment of women as well. Inas El-Degheidy is a good example of those who bridged the period between the Golden Age and the current "new wave" of female filmmakers post-Revolution. She was the first female student at the Cairo Higher Film Institute and has become a controversial, confrontational filmmaker. Her films deal with taboo subjects like homosexuality, premarital pregnancy and virginity. Her 1985 drama *Sorry, Mr. Law* exposes the Egyptian law's double standards in dealing with men and women. In spite or perhaps precisely because of her controversial stances, El-Degheidy is one of the most successful female film directors and producers ever in Egyptian cinema. Mona Abu El-Nasr (1952–2003) returned to Egypt after studying animation at the California Academy for Arts during 1987–1988, where she produced her first animated short. She established her own studio, Cairo Cartoon, in 1990 and started projects in cooperation with Egyptian TV, the aim being to produce cartoon series for children, the most famous one being *Bakar* (El-Nasr, 2001). Abu El-Nasr's work is inspired by local folklore stories and Arabian Nights fairy tales. More recently, since the 2011 Revolution in Egypt, audiences have come to expect different things from Egyptian film. The (past) grand narratives of Egyptian cinema can be summed up in expectations regarding stars, gender roles and fast paced narrative constructions. Now, a malaise has set in, especially among women revolutionaries who have been used and abused by the systems of the past, by the anti-revolutionaries, and by the newly self-appointed regime. As a result, women's films defy expectations in the sense that they are often revolutionary films in understated ways: their pace is slow and they are aesthetically challenging rather than politically clear. More insights on this topic are offered in Chapter 4.

Where Egypt's cinema is currently revolutionary in nature, historically Algerian films have played a central role in global Third Cinema. France's brutal role in Algerian history has defined its post-colonial struggle with cultural expression. During the War of Independence, filmmakers used guerrilla practices and made cinema a way to raise awareness of injustice and to inspire nationalist fervour in its audiences. Film became a tool in the fight for self-rule. While this particular history puts Algeria at the forefront of Third Cinema, Algeria now lacks filmmakers, particularly female filmmakers. There are large lacunae in Algerian film history, but those films that are made are often very powerful statements of resilience and power in young women, whose strength comes from an inner youthful naivety as well as a socially constructed pragmatism. In contemporary women's films, it is often the older generations that function as commemorators on a particularly painful history.

As Guy Austin shows, "gender is one of the most vexed questions in modern Algeria," and there is, in film, "a genuine loss caused by the segregation of the sexes and the patriarchal nature of Algerian familial and social relations" (2012, 61). Scholars usually refer to Assia Djebar, author and filmmaker, in studies of Algerian women and feminism, as her work engages very deeply with the way in which gendered bodies function in a rigidly organised and state-endorsed patriarchal structure. Her two films, *La Nouba des femmes du Mont Chenoua* (1979) and *La Zerda, ou les chants de l'oubli* (1983) are cited as examples of feminist revisionist filmmaking. Her experimental films were the first feminist films made in Algeria, dealing with how women's roles in history have been erased. Yamina Bachir-Chouikh, Djamila Sahraoui, Yamina Benguigui, Rayhana Obermeyer followed.

Theorists and historians of Algerian cultural life have shown how "women have taken in hand traumatised society" (Austin 2012, 149). *Rachida* by Yamina Bachir-Chouikh is the most well-known of Algerian films by women, and its director has been involved in a multitude of the best and most well-known films from Algeria by men (her husband included). She is the scriptwriter, editor and producer of a dozen films. Djamila Sahraoui's oeuvre is equally impressive under the circumstances, with a number of documentaries, and she has made two very strong feature length films, *Barakat!* (2006) and *Yema* (2012). Both deal with intergenerational relationships, the legacy of the Algerian Civil War on women, and the roles of mothers in transmitting the stories of the past to the younger generation. Yamina Benguigui is likewise very active, mostly as a documentary maker, and her well-known film *Inch'Allah Dimanche* (2001) received numerous awards. Being an immigrant shapes all Benguigui's films, and the difficulties of integration are at the centre of her work.

One of the young new talents in Algerian cinema is Rayhana Obermeyer, whose *À mon âge je me cache encore pour fumer/I Still Hide to Smoke* (2016) (discussed in more detail in Chapter 3), starring transnational Palestinian superstar Hiam

Abbass, portrays a small community of women of all generations gathered in a bath house, as outside tensions increase in an Algerian city subject to terrorism. In spite of its isolated status and its lack of support for film, the country thus boasts some outstanding female filmmakers who need more attention paid to them as part of a distinct filmmaking culture.

Tunisia, known as the land of fictions, has struggled with serious censorship issues. Post-colonial cinema in Tunisia is known throughout the world for popular films like Férid Boughedir's *Asfour Stah/Halfaouine: Boy of the Terraces* (1990), Nouri Bouzid's *Bezness* (1992), and Moufida Tlatli's *Les Silences du palais/The Silences of the Palace* (1994) from the so-called Golden Age in the 1990s. It has become known as a cinema that deals with women's sensuality and the magic and beauty of the old Tunis. In most historians' eyes, like Hédi Khelil and Férid Boughedir, Tunisian cinema is a cinema of the mythical feminine. However, there is a much more problematic gendered positionality going on in Tunisian cinema than these commentators care to illustrate. The identity politics in Golden Age films foreground women as the bearers of the nation's troubles. Both Bouzid and Boughedir emphasise that the theme of the defeated Arab man runs through men's films in post-independence cinema, giving some space to women protagonists, but after independence it took until 1975 before a woman, Selma Baccar, made a feature-length film. Selma Baccar was active in the cine-club movement, preoccupied with films in which criticisms of the government, the state of the nation and women's status was expressed. This criticism increased as the government repression of the clubs grew, and inspired more outspoken and political commentary. Baccar's first short, a 1966 silent black-and-white titled *L'Éveil/The Awakening* was made collaboratively with other women at her cine-club. After this she worked as assistant director on several films with Moufida Tlatli, Nouri Bouzid and Férid Boughedir. Her first feature-length film *Fatma 75* came out in 1975. It was an openly feminist film, made in the spirit of the UN International Year for Women. With *Fatma 75* she wanted to show that women had contributed significantly to the most important stages of the country's ancient and modern history. The historical context of women's ongoing activism needed to be addressed as well. But the film was banned for thirty years, and never shown in commercial cinemas.

Women who have followed in Baccar's footsteps are Néjia Ben Mabrouk, whose *The Trace* (1988) was the first to portray an emancipated young woman who wants to study in higher education but who is limited in her experiences by every man in her life. Moufida Tlatli made *Les Silences du palais/Silences of the Palace* (1994) and *La saison des hommes/The Season of Men* (2000), both focusing on communities of lower-class women who find strength in solidarity and fight the patriarchal nature of the society in which they live. Tlatli also played a very important role in the establishment of Bouzid and Boughedir as the most well-known filmmakers in Tunisia, as she scripted some of their films, and edited most of them. Of the younger female generation, Nadia El Fani is perhaps best known. She made her first short films in the early 1990s. Her features, both fiction and documentary, include *Bedwin Hacker* (2003), *Ouled Lénine/The Children of Lenin* (2007), *Laïcité, Inch'Allah!* (2011), *Même pas mal* (2012) and *Nos Seins, Nos*

Armes (2013). Her style combines reportage with combative activism. Raja Amari made a name for herself with *Satin rouge/Red Satin* (2002), *Anonymes/Buried Secrets* (2009) and *Corps étranger/Foreign Body* (2016), which is discussed in Chapter 7. Her strong feminist films show independent women with a touch of defiance about them, who develop a sensual confidence and face their oppressive world alone. In her turn, Amari inspired Kaouther Ben Hania and Leyla Bouzid, the prize-winning Tunisian women of the current era. The 2010s and Ben Ali's removal from power allowed Tunisian women directors to offer powerful challenges to the status-quo. Ben Hania's mockumentary *Le challat de Tunis/Challat of Tunis* (2013), her documentary *Zaineb takrahou ethelj/Zaineb Hates the Snow* (2016), and her narrative feature *Aala Kaf Ifrit/ Beauty and the Dogs* (2017) are all rooted in real-life events and, on their own terms, offer an indictment of the hypocritical attitudes towards women's freedoms in con- temporary Tunisian society. *Beauty and the Dogs* in particular explores women's rights to be heard and to see justice served while Leyla Bouzid's *A peine j'ouvre les yeux/As I Open My Eyes* (2015), discussed in Chapter 5, explores through family melodrama the power of state control over personal liberty and freedom of expression that led to the Revolution of 2011.

The history of cinema in Morocco delineates the struggle with national and cultural identity, mainly due to the country's colonial experience as a Protectorate of France and Spain, but also due to post-colonial circumstances dependent on the monarchy and religion. Likewise, women's positions have become more precarious again with increased political uncertainty and religious fundamentalism. The country's position as a crossroads nation has perpetuated a duality of identity: Morocco occupies a unique position between the Arab World, Africa and Europe and as such, its national identity has never been settled or homogeneous. Indeed, many films depict the struggle in migrants' experiences, whether these are Mor- occans migrating to Europe, or migrants transferring through Morocco. As such, a developing transcultural identity is finding full expression in the country's cinema; while for most of the twentieth century, Morocco had by far the lowest film production levels in the Maghreb, since the late 1990s, production levels have surged as Moroccan cinema found its domestic audience, ushering in a true revolution in filmmaking.

Reflecting the country's struggles with conflicting visions of its national identity, the representation and presence of women in the Moroccan film industry has his- torically been unbalanced. Very few women had any significant role in Moroccan cinema until the 1970s. In that decade, Farida Bourquia took on a variety of roles in administration and production (scriptwriter, assistant director, production man- ager), but she has become especially prolific as a television producer. In 1975, the UN International Year of Women, she developed a ground-breaking television series about the history of women in Morocco. In 1989, following a successful career as a screenwriter, Farida Benlyazid became the first Moroccan woman to direct her own feature film: *Bab Al-Sama Maftuh/A Door to the Sky* (see Chapter 8). Subsequently she has made, among others, *Keïd Ensa* (1998), *La vida perra de Juanita Narboni/Juanita from Tangier* (2005) and *Frontieras/Borders* (2013). These two women long dominated the documentary scene in Morocco, with Benlyazid having directed *Casa Nayda* and Bourquia *Deux femmes sur la route/Two Women on the Road*, both in 2007. In the 2000s, Laila Marrakchi (*Marock,* 2005 and *Rock the Casbah*, 2013 – *Marock* is discussed in detail in Chapter 8), Narjiss Nejjar (*Les yeux secs/Cry No More*, 2003; *L'amante du rif,* 2011; *Apatride/Stateless*, 2018), and Leila Kilani (*Tanger, le rêve des brûleurs/Tangier, the Dream of the Burners,* 2003; *Nos lieux interdits/Our Forbidden Places*, 2008; *Sur la planche/On the Edge*, 2011; *Indivision/Joint Possession*, 2018) joined their ranks with their significant documentaries and feature films, confronting political and economic inequalities. These young women's prize-winning oeuvres are becoming more and more representative of the urban, realist trend in recent Moroccan cinema.

Southern Africa

British colonial rule and its approach to educational and instructional filmmaking in its colonies have resulted in documentary films being much more common, at least initially, in anglophone African countries like Zimbabwe, Tanzania and Kenya. Many NGOs in these countries supported didactic documentary films to the detriment of feature film production (Ukadike 1994, 109). Tafataona Mahoso critiques the proliferation of documentaries in Southern Africa that address "development themes" (2001, 211). He calls this phenomenon a relationship of "centralised distance" between the Global North and the Global South, claiming that these development films, rather than depicting the lived experiences and responses of Southern Africans, mostly reflect the donors' determination to convey singular messages in line with what he calls "a predetermined logomonic system" (ibid.). This system is a continuation of the paternalistic agenda of the British Colonial Film Unit. Development films present themselves as text ignoring context, Mahoso argues, and the effect of these colonial and neo-colonial obstacles is that those purporting to "develop" African communities hold on to predetermined positions that prevent any meaningful representation of reality. This context of filmmaking has changed, or at least expanded, over the last two decades, with many Southern African countries and ex-British colonies developing homegrown filmmaking industries and individual filmmaking voices, including those of women.

Zimbabwe gained independence from Britain in 1980, after a brutal liberation struggle. The new government of Zimbabwe saw the economic potential in promoting the country as a location for foreign film production, leading to the production of films such as *King Solomon's Mines* (J. Lee Thompson, 1985), *Cry Freedom* (Richard Attenborough, 1987) and *A World Apart* (Chris Menges, 1988). Nyasha Mboti calls the 1990s "the decade of the NGO film" (2014, 153), a type of film primarily funded by foreign non-governmental organisations, of which the Media for Development Trust, an American NGO established in 1989, was central. Tsitsi Dangarembga, Zimbabwe's most prominent female filmmaker and also an award-winning author, commenced her filmmaking career in this period.

Her first feature, *Everyone's Child* (1996), was funded by the American NGO Media for Development and tells the story of a brother and sister who must take responsibility for their younger siblings when they lose both their parents to HIV/AIDS. These types of development films, produced through the NGO model, could be regarded as a neocolonialist continuation of the filmmaking practices established under colonialism but it did not last, as audiences grew tired of the films' linear and simplistic messages. Media for Development permanently relocated to Tanzania in the early 2000s due to Zimbabwe's land redistribution programme that exiled White farmers and created an unstable environment for the American NGO to continue its work. Dangarembga has since criticised this type of filmmaking and denounced her involvement in *Everyone's Child*. Some of her other work, in particular the remarkable short film *Kare kare zvako: Mother's Day* (2005), an innovative and experimental interpretation of a Shona folktale, show a sharp departure from the development films she directed previously.

We find instances of independent filmmaking in Zimbabwe during the 1990s as well, including *Jit* (1990), directed by White Zimbabwean filmmaker Michael Raeburn, regarded as Zimbabwe's first local fiction feature film. The work of the production company Zimmedia, formed by Zimbabwean producer Simon Bright and British filmmaker Ingrid Sinclair, is of particular interest to our study. Bright and Sinclair made the feature film *Flame* in 1996, the first fiction feature film that deals with Zimbabwe's liberation struggle from the perspective of women. The film traces the journeys of two young women, Flame and Liberty, who decide to join the liberation struggle and travel to Mozambique to train as guerrilla soldiers. Sinclair interviewed female ex-combatants to inform the story, and the film's narrative, controversially, includes a scene of one the women being raped by her male comrade. The film was criticised by the government for tainting the legacy of the veterans who fought for Zimbabwe's independence, but what it really reveals is that nationalist ideologies, promoted during the liberation struggles of African countries, betrayed women – as patriarchal structures were not dismantled post-independence. Zimmedia also produced the Mama Africa series in 2001, six 26-minute short films produced by female directors from across the continent. The series includes *A Close-up on Bintou* by Fanta Régina Nacro (Burkina Faso), *Hang Time* by Ngozi Onwurah (Nigeria), *One Evening in July* by Raja Amari (Tunisia), *Raya* by Zulfah Otto-Sallies (South Africa), *Riches* by Ingrid Sinclair (Zimbabwe) and *Uno's World* by Bridget Pickering (Namibia). Together they form a collection of diverse and dynamic portraits of female African storytelling.

The 2000s saw Zimbabwe move to digital filmmaking, as was the case all over the continent, even though fiction feature film production has been scarce. Importantly, Tsitsi Dangarembga founded the International Images Film Festival for Women (IIFF) in Harare in 2002, one of the earliest Africa-based feminist film festivals with a mission to strengthen gender equality in Zimbabwean society by depicting women's stories and experiences through film. The festival has, since 2007, presented the Distinguished Woman of African Cinema Award. In fact, Zimbabwe has been a model of good practice in its support of female filmmakers.

Its Institute of Creative Arts for Progress in Africa (ICAPA) runs Women Film-makers of Zimbabwe (WFOZ), Zimbabwe's leading women filmmakers' organi-sation, founded in 1996, with a remit to increase the participation and production capacity of women in the screen industries, locally and regionally. Dangarembga wrote that a survey undertaken by the organisation found that in the period from 2013 to 2017, only 17% of feature-length documentaries and only 14% of feature fiction films were made by women (Dangarembga 2019). ICAPA also runs the African Women Filmmakers Hub, a Pan-African platform initiated at the 2016 IIFF, designed to increase African women's production capacity and presence in film. As a result of these and many other initiatives, women's involvement in the screen industries in Zimbabwe in various capacities has flourished.

As noted above, the lusophone countries have entirely different histories to anglophone Southern Africa, which is also reflected in their film industries. Gua-deloupean-born filmmaker Sarah Maldoror, who was married to the Angolan revolutionary Mário Pinto de Andrade, made a huge contribution to the film cul-tures of Angola and Mozambique, often focusing on the role of women in the liberation struggles in these countries. Maldoror, who studied film in the ex-Soviet Union with Senegalese director Ousmane Sembène, started her career in film-making during the years of African independence struggles and reveals in her films a deep commitment to the history of the liberation struggles, a strand of revolu-tionary filmmaking we discuss further in Chapter 4. Before *Sambizanga*, her main feature film completed in 1972, she made the short film *Monangambé* in 1968 in Algeria. Both *Monangambé* and *Sambizanga* were adapted from stories by the Angolan novelist Luandino Vieira. *Sambizanga*, which deals with women's partici-pation in the liberation struggle through the journey of the female protagonist, is a classic African film that has been widely taught, discussed and analysed, and is central to the development of African cinema.

Given Maldoror's Caribbean background, she was caught in the crossfire that erupted at the 1991 FESPACO women's gathering when women from the African diaspora were asked to leave the meeting. Maldoror stated the following about the event in an interview with Ellerson: "We were told to leave because we were not considered African. We are in Africa, of course I am African. Certainly, my parents were Africans. Why am I Guadeloupean? Because my parents were sold into slav-ery. I am part of the group of Africans who were enslaved and deported" (Ellerson 2000, 165). Today she is regarded as one of the most important female African filmmaking pioneers.

The governments of lusophone countries played an important role in forming national cinemas after the countries gained independence simultaneously in 1975. In Mozambique, President Samora Machel had a strong awareness of the power of the moving image and was committed to developing cinema in Mozambique through setting up the National Institute of Cinema (INC) and inviting Jean-Luc Godard, Jean Rouch and Ruy Guerra to Mozambique to help develop a national industry. Hopes for flourishing national cinemas with socialist tenets were dashed by the civil wars that broke out in Angola and Mozambique shortly after independence. The film industries in these countries are now slowly growing and in recent years a few prominent female filmmakers have emerged, notably Teresa Prata with *Terra Sonâmbula/Sleepwalking Land* (2007), about a young boy's journey in war-torn Mozambique. Margarida Cardoso started directing films in 1995, mostly exploring themes related to her personal and social history, such as Portugal's colonial history in Mozambique, and the anti-colonial struggle. *A Costa dos Murmúrios/The Murmuring Coast* (2004) in particular addresses the White European experience in an unnamed African country in the 1960s, against the backdrop of civil war and conflict. Pocas Pascoal was Angola's first female camera operator, and directed her first feature film, *Alda and Maria*, about two sisters escaping the Angolan war by fleeing to Lisbon in the 1980s, in 2012. It is significant then, that these lusophone female directors all deal with the colonial and postcolonial histories and circumstances of their countries, thematic choices that are closely linked to the principles of Third Cinema and a continuation of the work of Sarah Maldoror.

Angola and Mozambique were part of a regional coalition of African countries from the 1960s to the 1990s called the Frontline States, which worked with Namibia, Botswana, Zimbabwe, Swaziland, Lesotho, Zambia, Malawi and Tanzania to bring about the end of apartheid and White minority rule in South Africa. Film was used as part of their strategy, as is evident in the anti-apartheid narratives of films such as *Cry Freedom* and *A World Apart*, both produced in Zimbabwe, and it is even clearer in the ideological approach to filmmaking of the lusophone Southern African countries.

As democracy and freedom came to South Africa only in 1994, the history of filmmaking in South Africa has a problematic and complex legacy full of omissions and silences left by the absent voices of those oppressed, first during a rule of foreign colonial powers, followed by White minority rule. Under the White, patriarchal rule of the Afrikaner Nationalist Party, women's voices, the voices of mixed-race people and the Asian diaspora, and the voices of all the various Black ethnic groups remained absent from audio-visual representation during the oppressive regimes that constituted South Africa's official history before the end of apartheid. Although a number of early book-length studies on South African cinema (Gutsche 1972, Tomaselli 1989, Hees 1991, Blignaut and Botha 1992, Botha and Van Aswegen 1992, Davis 1996) have been published, Isabel Balseiro and Ntongela Masilela (2003, 1) claim that none of the earlier studies constitutes a serious consideration of South African cinema in its own right, nor do they offer a systematic approach to film history that problematises the absence of Black voices in South African cinema. It was not until the mid-2000s that a number of additional volumes on South African cinema appeared that more fully address the issues pointed out by Balseiro and Masilela (see for example Keyan Tomaselli 2006, Jacqueline Maingard 2007, Martin Botha 2004 & 2012, Lucia Saks 2010, and Litheko Modisane 2013).

Botha and Van Aswegen (1992) show that ideology and capital came together through the South African government's subsidy system under apartheid to create a national cinema representative of the dominant ideologies of the apartheid regime under Verwoerd. This idealistic conservatism was characterised by an attachment to the past, to ideals of linguistic purity and to religious and moral norms (Botha 2004). As such, a substantial tradition of radical activist Black filmmaking, as in Angola and Mozambique, failed to develop in South Africa during apartheid. A few films made by South Africans in exile (for example Lionel Ngakane's London-set *Jemima and Johnny*, 1966) and by foreigners (for example Lionel Rogosin's *Come Back, Africa*, 1959; Sven Persson's *Land Apart*, 1974; Richard Attenborough's *Cry Freedom*, 1987; Chris Menges's *A World Apart*, 1988; and Euzhan Palcy's *A Dry White Season*, 1989) served to alert the rest of the world to the conditions of the oppressed under apartheid. Although they played an important role in international consciousness-raising on the conditions under apartheid, the films' problematic notion of a foreign gaze onto the South African situation – resulting in stereo-typical, romanticised or simplified representations – problematise postcolonial ana-lyses of these films. On the whole, film was not used as an activist tool in the country to the extent that it was used to depict, document and support anti-colo-nialist struggles in other southern African countries. Although a long tradition of activist theatre and consciousness-raising music can be traced in locations like Hillbrow, Sophiatown and Newtown in Johannesburg, the medium of film – expensive and inaccessible to most Black South Africans during apartheid – was not taken up as a weapon in the struggle against apartheid.

In the post-apartheid era South African film is gradually being reintegrated into African cinema at large. The last three decades have seen massive policy and structural changes as well as a transformation in the country's national, regional and international relationships. The processes of regional, continental and international reintegration that South Africa is going through have implications for the film industry, not least because the South African government as well as industry and commercial players are committed to encouraging film production and exhibition for its commercial, cultural and educational benefits. Over the last few years, the films produced in South Africa show that multiple genres and themes are being explored – from post-apartheid dramas and struggle stories to popular comedies, musicals and Westerns.

The first White woman to make a short fiction film in South Africa was Anna Neethling-Pohl in 1959, and it took two decades for three more White female directors to make feature films: Elaine Proctor, the Mozambican-born Helena Nogueira and Afrikaans director Katinka Heyns. Harriet Gavshon (1992, 251) states that of the approximately 605 feature films made in the country between 1985 and 1989, only two – *Quest for Love* (1988) and *Fiela se Kind* (1988) – were directed by women, Helena Nogueira and Katinka Heyns respectively. Palesa Letlaka-Nkosi was the first Black woman to make a short drama, *Mamlambo*, in 1997. The first feature film by a Black South African woman, Maganthrie Pillay, who is of Indian heritage, was released only in 2005. Her film *34 South* deals with issues of rural–urban migration, race and identity. As elsewhere on the continent, women have more often directed short films and documentaries, or work in tele-vision, while the number of women who have directed fiction feature films remains small. In addition to the three pioneering White directors and Pillay's feature film from 2005, other female-directed fiction features have been made by Black directors Lwazi Mvusi, Nosipho Dumisa and Stephina Zwane – whose debut features all came out as late as 2018. Lwazi Mvusi's *Farewell Ella Bella* is the story of a young White woman finding her way after the death of her alcoholic father, aided by her father's best friend, a Black jazz musician. Nosipho Dumisa's *Number 37* is a thriller that reinterprets Hitchcock's famous *Rear Window* (1954) as a paraplegic witnesses a mob killing through the window of his apartment and attempts to blackmail the killer. Zwane's *Baby Mamas* is a populist film closer in aesthetic and theme to Nollywood, as it depicts the lives of four female friends sharing the joys and challenges of being single mums. The distinct approaches of these three films, in style and narrative, are indicative of the prolific and diverse contemporary South African film industry where no single genre dominates.

Female directors of Muslim or Asian heritage have also produced fiction feature films, including Zulfah Otto-Sallies, Rayda Jacobs, Jyoti Mistry, Shamim Sarif, Judy Naidoo, Jayan Moodley and Biana Isaac. Their films often address the role and position of South African Muslim women, and reveal an interest in Islamic feminism, a topic we explore further in Chapter 8. White women who have directed fiction features include Claire Angelique, Sara Blecher, Jenna Bass, Jann Turner, Minky Schlesinger, Catherine Stewart, Meg Rickards and others. It should also be noted that there many South African female documentary filmmakers, working across film and television. The continuing underrepresentation of Black female directors helming fiction feature productions is a troubling legacy of the structural inequalities left by the apartheid era. At a roundtable during the 2018 Durban International Film Festival, filmmaker Zamo Mkhwanazi powerfully stated: "There isn't a single space where I feel that we've been treated fairly, we've been represented, whether it's because of our gender or because of our race. We are black and we are women all the time" (Vourlias 2018b). A representative of SWIFT (Sisters Working in Film and Television), Zoe Ramushu, also acknowledges that the plight of Black women in the industry is

> an intersectional issue that needs to be dealt with as such […] Although we are fighting for the same thing as women, we have to understand that women are not starting from the same starting point. There are different struggles for women.
>
> *(ibid.)*

On the upside, many hugely talented young Black female directors are emerging in short and documentary filmmaking and some will, no doubt, go on to make feature fiction films.

Lesley Marx (Blignaut and Botha 1992) cited the films of Proctor, Nogueira and Heyns as what should have been the vanguard of female, and possibly feminist, work in South African cinema. Although female themes and a questioning of patriarchal norms are central to their films and are also stylistically reinforced in their work, the notion of a South African feminist film aesthetic in the absence of any Black female voices is deeply problematic. Although Nogueira and Proctor's films in particular display a deeper engagement with the realities of Black people in apartheid South Africa, on the whole the films by these three White directors portray the personal perspectives of the lives and experiences of White women, and could as such only count as part of a *White* South African feminist aesthetic. The consequences of complete racial segregation under the apartheid state mean that the search for a common sisterhood between all the women in South Africa, Black and White, is an impossible quest. As such, their films do not constitute bodies of work that emerging Black South African female directors could build upon or draw inspiration from. Instead, Black women directors look rather towards the rest of Africa when seeking inspiration for their careers, as is clear from regional networks and the presence of African female filmmakers at festivals all over the continent. Despite the important roles that women played in the anti-apartheid struggle, explored further in Chapter 4, these contributions have not yet resulted in equal representation for women, and particularly Black women, in post-apartheid South Africa.

Francophone West Africa

Filmmaking by Africans in francophone West Africa started after countries in the region (including Benin, Burkina Faso, Cameroon, Guinea, Ivory Coast, Mali, Mauritania, Niger, Senegal and Togo) gained independence in 1960 (1958 in the case of Guinea). Under French colonial rule Africans were denied the right to film their own countries, and the Laval Decree of 1934 attempted to control the content of films and to minimise the creative role of Africans in production (Diawara 1992, 22). Colonial powers preferred to import Western, mostly French films and actively discouraged the development of any African filmmaking activity (Thackway 2003, 7). It was only after colonies gained their independence that France started to develop African film, with the creation of the Consortium Audiovisuel International (CAI). The film distribution and exhibition networks left by the French colonial administration after the independence of African countries as well as institutionalised support for African cinema, contributed to the development of national film production in African francophone countries from the 1960s. In the 1980s, the socialist government of the Mitterrand era supported African directors, with this support still continuing today, and France (and various funding schemes within the European Union) remaining one of the main financiers of West African film. France did not develop local cinema units like the British, with aid centralised in Paris. West African filmmakers often criticise the paternalistic nature of French aid to francophone African countries; Ousmane Sembène, for example, stopped using French funding in the late 1960s. Nevertheless, it is mainly France's support of the cultural endeavours in its ex-colonies that has ensured that francophone countries were at the forefront of the development of cinema in sub-Saharan Africa. The history and development of francophone West African filmmaking has been well documented by scholars and historians.[2]

Although economic difficulties, as elsewhere on the continent, make filmmaking a challenging career choice, most internationally significant African filmmakers have emerged from this region. Of the first generation of West African filmmakers, Senegalese Ousmane Sembène is undoubtedly the best known. Sembène was the first black sub-Saharan African to direct a film in Africa, thus earning him the honorary title of father of African cinema. Sembène gained international recognition in the 1960s with his third film *La Noire de…/Black Girl* (1966), the story of a young Senegalese woman who travels to France to work as maid for a French couple, only for her hopes of a better life to be dashed by the mistreatment she suffers under her employers. *La Noire de…*, with its central female protagonist, initiated Sembène's career-long commitment to the social, cultural and economic status of women in Africa. He addressed issues affecting women, such as polygamy, economic emancipation, colonisation and Islamisation in many of his films and was outspoken about his belief that progress in Africa lies in the advancement of women's roles and positions. Sembène was devoted to political and social issues, and his last film *Moolaadé* (2004) is a masterful and profoundly humane condemnation of female genital mutilation.

As typified by Sembène's work, the socially and politically committed films from francophone West Africa have incorporated progressive representations of African women for decades. These dynamic depictions of African women are not surprising if one considers, as Andrea Cornwall does (2005, 1), that West Africa created the foundational images of women's power and autonomy in Africa, and some of the most influential critiques of Western stereotypes and assumptions about Africa. Finding alternatives to the stereotypical cinematic portrayal of African women as exotic beings or silent victims has been an inherent part of cinematic representation in francophone West Africa since the birth of homegrown filmmaking. In addition to Sembène, this is also the case with the work of Mauritanian director Med Hondo, Ivorian Desiré Ecaré, and Mahama Johnson Traoré from Senegal. Indeed, film scholars and historians such as Lindiwe Dovey (2012, 18) argue that films from this region constitute a male-authored feminist cinema. Female characters in these films are often progressive forces for change, raging against an established patriarchal order. Despite their continuing underrepresentation in West African filmmaking, the region has seen the gradual emergence of female directors. An increasing number of women are directing their own films, building on the work of the pioneering (though mostly male) West African filmmakers.

Sembène's compatriot, Safi Faye, is the female pioneer of sub-Saharan African cinema, as we outlined in the introduction, and was one of the only female filmmakers active in francophone West Africa during the 1970s. Faye studied ethnology and film in France, eventually gaining a doctorate degree in ethnology. Her initiation into cinema came with acting experiences with French ethnographic filmmaker Jean Rouch. Informed by her educational background and her work with Rouch, Faye's films are in-depth studies of African cultural, political and economic life, often set in rural Africa, combining elements of fiction and documentary filmmaking styles. Faye has made more than ten documentaries drawing on African cultural, economic and political life, and three feature films (*Kaddu Beykat*, 1976; *Fad'jal*, 1979 and *Mossane*, 1996). The findings of her ethnological research on her own ethnic group, the Serer people, inspired *Kaddu Beykat* and *Fad'jal*. Faye's films mostly address a rural milieu, and emphasise the central role that women play in traditional village societies. The fact that she entered filmmaking through ethnology, anthropology and teaching is indicative of the interdisciplinarity that many female African filmmakers bring to cinema, as many female filmmakers also work in other areas. Most of Faye's films, including the documentary *Selbé et tant d'autres/Selbe: One Among Many* (1983) and fiction film *Mossane* (discussed in Chapter 5), place women at the centre of the narrative and focus on the day-to-day realities of women's lives. However, Faye has stated in numerous interviews that being a female director is not necessarily key to shaping subjectivities and sensibilities in her films. She maintains that her films are about the whole of society since male and female roles are complementary:

> [W]omen alone cannot live in Africa. Women live in a community, and I cannot eliminate the community. [...] This is typical of African cultures. You cannot live alone; you can't do it because a big family, a big community, is all around you.
>
> (Ukadike 2002, 34).

Faye emphasises that male and female African filmmakers face the same problems in gaining access to the film industry. In fact, she said in her interview with N. Frank Ukadike that it has probably been easier for her to enter the film industry, as being one of the first African female filmmakers afforded her attention and possibilities others since have not received. However, her decision to foreground the role women play in village communities suggests that Faye draws on her female sensibilities for her films, a position not irreconcilable with the notion of gender complementarity. According to Thackway: "Faye combines women's concerns and a powerful female voice with her own cultural sensibilities, creating a distinctive and highly personal style that reflects both her dual female and African perspectives" (2003, 156). This duality is part of two interrelated perspectives that position her firmly as a female African director conscious of the importance of complementary gender roles in African society.

The second generation of West African filmmakers who emerged from the 1980s onwards firmly believe that African film can be competitive and profitable, while maintaining its artistic integrity (Ukadike, 2002). Senegal and Burkina Faso are the powerhouses of francophone West African filmmaking, with the region's male and female pioneers hailing from Senegal, while Burkina Faso has created a prolific film industry with some of the best developed training, production, distribution and exhibition facilities in Africa. The Burkinabe government funded a film school, Institut Africain d'Education Cinématographique (INAFEC), which was set up in 1977 and grew out of the Pan African Federation of Filmmakers (FEPACI), where many female Burkinabe filmmakers trained. While the school closed its doors in 1987, well-known Burkinabe filmmaker Gaston Kaboré now runs a film school in Ouagadougou, Institut Imagine. Burkina Faso's capital of course also hosts the largest and most important African film festival, FESPACO, since 1969, with the government following a cultural policy that supports cinema and promotes the centralisation of diverse components of the audio-visual field. With these educational, cultural and political support systems, Burkina Faso has delivered some of the most prominent filmmakers from francophone West Africa, including the female filmmakers Fanta Régina Nacro and Apolline Traoré (whose film, *Frontières* is discussed in Chapter 4).

Burkinabe director Fanta Régina Nacro is part of the second generation of African filmmakers and one of the best-known female filmmakers in Africa. She studied filmmaking at the Burkinabe film school INAFEC, worked as a television announcer at the National Television Centre, and as an editor on Idrissa Ouédraogo's first feature film. Although she entered the film industry through editing and continuity work, she has said in interview that she knew from the beginning that she wanted to direct. Nacro's fictional short films are made in a realist style, often employing humour and parody. Her first short *Un certain matin* (1991), a glimpse of Burkinabe peasant life, received several international prizes. Nacro says that she was "an out and out feminist militant" (Verschueren 2002) when she made her first short and made a conscious decision to employ a wholly female crew in rebellion against film schools that tend to channel women towards so-called "women's jobs" like editing and continuity. After the success of her first short, Nacro received several offers to make films on subjects specific to women, such as female genital mutilation, but she has stated that she did not enter filmmaking to take part in the fight for women's freedom. Rather, she makes films out of a desire to tell stories, with storytelling gatherings being a fond memory from her childhood. Nacro's feature debut, *La nuit de la vérité/ The Night of Truth* was completed in 2004 and presented in competition at the 2005 FESPACO (Bisschoff 2012). She has not presented any high-profile cinematic work since, but is very active in the Burkinabe television industry.

In addition to Nacro and Traoré, French/Burkinabe director Sarah Bouyain, Senegalese Dyana Gaye and Burkinabe Eléonore Yaméogo, among others, have also directed fiction feature films. French/Senegalese filmmaker Mati Diop was widely acclaimed as the first Black woman with a feature film in competition at Cannes in 2019. Her debut feature, *Atlantique*, a love story about African migrants with magic realist elements, won the Grand Prix Award at the festival. Nigerien director Rahmatou Keïta's prize-winning *Zin'naariya!/The Wedding Ring* (2016) is set in a rural Sahelian village in Niger and tells the story of Tiyaa, a beautiful young woman of aristocratic birth on the verge of marriage. It has been screened internationally to high acclaim, and was the first film to be submitted by Niger in the Foreign Language Oscar category. Keïta is particularly proud of the film's transnationally African provenance, as it was funded entirely by African sources, unusual for high-profile features films from this region. She says:

This film is 100% African. I gathered Africa around this film. It is an African Union film. It was entirely funded by African countries, including Algeria, Niger, Congo Brazzaville, Rwanda, Morocco and Uganda. In all, it took me eight years to find funding, one month for the shooting, the budget being limited, and a year to do the editing and all post-production.

(Baldé 2016).

The work of German/Burkinabe filmmaker Cilia Sawadogo is also of great interest to us, as she is one of the most accomplished female animators from the region. With a Burkinabe father and German mother, Sawadogo's childhood was divided between Germany and Burkina Faso, and she studied for a degree in communications from Quebec. She has directed animations for the American children's television series *Sesame Street*, as well as award-winning animation shorts infused with African traditions, cultures and folktales, including *La femme mariée à trois hommes/The Woman with Three Husbands* (1993) and *L'arbre aux esprits/The Tree Spirit* (2005) about two young children who must find a way to save a centuries-old baobab tree. Ivorian writer Marguerite Abouet also made a great contribution to animation filmmaking with the feature animation film *Aya de Yopougon/Aya of Yop City* (2013), which she co-directed with Clément Oubrerie and was based on the graphic novel of the same title, written by Abouet and drawn by Oubrerie.

As elsewhere on the continent, the documentary form lends itself more easily to women filmmakers, including celebrated work by filmmakers such as Senegalese Angèle Diabang Brener, Dyana Gaye, Rama Thiaw and Katy Léna N'diaye; Cameroonian Florence Ayisi, Osvalde Lewat and Rosine Mbakam; Nigerien Rahmatou Keïta; French/Ivorian Isabelle Boni-Claverie; Giovannia Atodjinou-zinsou from Benin, Swedish/Burkinabe Theresa Traoré Dahlberg; and French/Gabonese Samantha Biffot. Togolese Anne-Laure Folly deserves a prominent place in the genealogy of West African documentary filmmaking, as a pioneering film-maker who started making films in the early 1990s. An international lawyer and filmmaker, Folly's documentaries feature women in real-life situations recounting their experiences, and touch upon themes such as war, female circumcision and spirituality. One of her best-known films, *Femmes aux yeux ouverts/Women with Open Eyes* (1994) consists of interviews with women from Benin, Burkina Faso, Mali and Senegal, exploring how various societal issues affect them. Her first film, *Le gardien des forces/The Guardian of the Forces* (1992) deals with fetish practices in her native Togolese village, and *Femmes de Niger/Women of Niger* (1993) focuses on how issues such as polygamy and Muslim fundamentalism affect Nigerien women. *Les oubliées/The Forgotten Women* (1997) deals with the struggles of Angolan women in a war-torn society. This film was inspired by Guadeloupean director Sarah Maldoror's feature film *Sambizanga* (1972), and this cross-fertilisation by the work of women across the continent is something we find greatly interesting and encouraging.

Female directors are increasingly central to francophone West Africa, working transnationally with some living and working on the continent, some in Europe, the US and other countries internationally. Different backgrounds and experiences influence their stylistic and thematic filmmaking choices, and while not all the works by female directors from this region are overtly feminist, and some film-makers openly resist the label, the centralising of female characters, subjects and topics is a recurrent tendency throughout all the work.

East Africa

The East African region has been underrepresented in historical film scholarship. Indigenous film cultures in this region emerged later than in other parts of the continent, not least because of the lingering effects of British colonialism. How-ever, over the past two decades various types of homegrown filmmakers and film industries have developed quickly: filmmaking practices in East Africa show excit-ing innovation in themes, genres, styles, approaches, techniques and distribution and exhibition methods (Bisschoff 2015, 71). At the same time, the region as a whole is no stranger to the moving image, exploited as it is not only for tourism but also for location-shooting for foreign productions. The breath-taking natural environment of countries like Kenya and Tanzania have been used as the backdrop of a multitude of foreign films – mostly classic British adventure films – such as *Trader Horn* (1931), *King Solomon's Mines* (1950), *Simba* (1955), *Born Free* (1966), and *Out of Africa* (1985). The other prevalent type of filmmaking before indepen-dence was that established by the Bantu Educational Kinema Experiment (BEKE), a project of the International Missionary Council in collaboration with the British colonial governments of Tanganyika (now Tanzania), Kenya, Uganda, Northern Rhodesia (now Zambia) and Nyasaland (now Malawi). The BEKE was a short-lived but highly influential experiment in filmmaking for African audiences that produced 35 films between March 1935 and May 1937, exhibited to the colonial subjects by mobile cinema van. The films covered a wide range of genres and topics, roughly aligned along the common theme of "progress versus African methods". Productions focused predominantly on agriculture and health, teaching new farming methods and promoting Western medicine and ways of life. Both of these historical examples of filmmaking in East Africa – the sweeping dramas and hair-raising adventures that used the unspoilt landscape as a backdrop, as well as the didactic, paternalistic and simplistic films of the BEKE – are deeply problematic when viewed from a post-colonial vantage point. They additionally highlight the urgency of indigenous, local and homegrown industries to be nurtured and devel-oped. As outlined in the case of Zimbabwe, the legacy of the British colonial film policy meant that many donor-funded NGO films were produced in the anglo-phone African region, and this is still the case, if to a lesser extent than in the 1990s, through the work of Media for Development and other NGOs.

On the whole, scholarship on Tanzanian film and in particular its booming video film industry known as Bongowood, is probably the best-developed, largely because of the work of German anthropologist Matthias Krings and others such as Claudia Böhme. Historian Laura Fair has written extensively on the development of popular culture in Tanzania, including film. Scholarship on Kenyan cinema is growing, partly motivated by the establishment of Kenya as the technological hub of the East African region and the attendant use of digital technologies in games design, animation, short film production, music videos and so on. There is a relative dearth of scholarship on film from other East African countries – including Malawi, Uganda, Burundi, Eritrea, Somalia and Djibouti – primarily because filmic output has been modest, in some instances due to ongoing unrest and civil conflicts.

Despite a lack of filmmaking activity in some East African countries, innovative developments and creative filmmaking trends can be observed, with contemporary fiction films that address locally relevant themes and stories, exploring the recent past and current socio-political situations. In Kenya, artist collectives such as The Nest Collective – which produces films, television content and web series – and production companies such as One Fine Day Films, set-up with German funding and operating on a mentoring and workshop format, have contributed significantly to the growth of the creative and audio-visual industries. Of great interest to our study is the fact that Kenya boasts a substantial number of female directors, with more well-known women than men working in the screen industries, and more and more young female directors emerging with impressive work that is increasingly screened internationally. Anne Mungai became the pioneering female Kenyan director in the 1980s, and directed her first fiction feature film, *Saikati* in 1992, about a young Maasai girl's quest to gain an education. Alongside Mungai, there is the work of women directors including Jane Lusabe, Dommie Yambo-Odotte, Jane Murago-Munene and Wanjiru Kinyanjui, who formed part of the first wave of Kenyan filmmaking in 1980s and 1990s (Ellerson 2018b). Many of them received their training in film at the Kenya Institute of Mass Communication.

In the contemporary era, we include the work of Wanuri Kahiu, Judy Kibinge, Wanjiru Kairu, Hawa Essuman, Zipporah Nyaruri, Jinna Mutune, Ng'endo Mukii, Philippa Ndisi-Herrmann, Zippy Kimundu and many other Kenyan women who direct features, documentaries and short films. Wanuri Kahiu in particular has gained international recognition with her short film *Pumzi* (2009), a futuristic science fiction short film with a female protagonist, her feature film *From a Whisper* (2008), which retells the tragedy of the 1998 bombing of the US embassy in Nairobi through the eyes of a young woman, and her most recent feature *Rafiki* (2018), a lesbian love story set in Nairobi (discussed in Chapter 7). As in Kahiu's *From a Whisper*, the aftermath of traumatic violence is the topic of Judy Kibinge's *Something Necessary* (2013), discussed in Chapter 4, set in the immediate post-conflict period after the inter-ethnic violence that erupted during Kenya's 2008 elections. In Uganda, Caroline Kamya directed the acclaimed *Imani* in 2010, also a post-conflict tale and featuring Rehema Nanfuka, a prolific actress who has started to direct her own films. Judith Lucy Adong, Kemiyondo Coutinho and Evelyn Cindy Magara have also developed successful careers in the film and television industries in Uganda. Highly acclaimed Indian-American filmmaker Mira Nair, who teaches at Media for Development in Uganda, directed *Queen of Katwe* (2016), featuring Lupita Nyong'o as the mother of 10-year-old Phiona Mutesi, a Ugandan girl living in a slum in Katwe who became a world-class chess player.

Contemporary homegrown East African filmmaking has thus allowed film-makers to find a voice, tell their own stories, and reflect on their cultures and his-tories, and this has been embraced by women in particular. Exploring new genres, like science fiction and fantasy, is an important development because it allows filmmakers to speculate about possible futures for Africa, and these genres com-pletely subvert the "media for development" agenda of NGO-funded films. In addition, some East African countries have been through turbulent periods of political and social instability, and film has become a tool in dealing with the traumatic aftermath of conflict and opening up a space for telling previously untold or suppressed stories. This is perhaps nowhere more so than in Rwanda, where the spate of foreign films made about the 1994 genocide (*Hotel Rwanda*, 2004; *Shooting Dogs*, 2005; *Sometimes in April*, 2005, and others) contributed to the development of a local film industry in direct and indirect ways. Rwanda boasts a growing number of female filmmakers, including Marie-Clémentine Dusabejambo, Anisia Uzeyman, Cynthia Butare, Jacqueline Kalimunda, Apolline Uwimana, Poupoune Kamikazi Sesonga, Kantarama Gahigiri and Ndimbira Shenge. Often their stories reflect on the effects of the genocide and its aftermath on women, as well as the central participation of women in post-conflict efforts in Rwanda. Decades of civil war and conflict left the country with a skewed gender distribution, with women making up 70% of the population after 1994. Rwanda has been a model of good practice in terms of women's positions and rights, with many women taking on leadership positions, the highest percentage of women in parliament compared to any other country in the world, and a government that prioritises girls' education. It follows that the creative industries would also see a rise in female practitioners.

Ethiopian film culture is booming as well, and female directors are central to it (see Kassahun, 2018). Kidist Yilma's films have been very well received in Ethiopia and she has won many local film awards for best director, most recently with her film *Taza* (2017). Her first really successful film was *Rebuni* (2015), followed by the equally successful *Meba* (2015) and *Keletat* (2015). Since 2016, when more televi-sion stations started operating, there has been a high demand for local content and Kidist, like other filmmakers, is now in the process of producing television content. Mekdes Tsegaye is another influential player who has produced and starred in successful TV drama *Mogachoch* and has starred in and produced a number of films. The one female filmmaker to have made films that have been well received locally and internationally is Hermon Hailay. Her films *Balageru* (2012) and *Yaltasebew* (2013) were very popular in Ethiopia and her most recent film *Yefikir Wagaw* (2015) featured in many international film festivals. Her films regularly tackle cur-rent social issues such as poverty and the perils of rural-urban migration. While *Yefikir Wagaw* wasn't a commercial success in Ethiopia it was recognised at the Gumma Film Awards 2016, winning the best director award.

There is also a number of female Ethiopian filmmakers working in the diaspora, including Salem Mekuria and Lucy Gebre-Egziabher, both based in the US. Mekuria is a video artist and filmmaker who produces films and video installations related to her Ethiopian heritage, with her work having been exhibited at the Venice Biennale and various galleries and film festivals internationally. Gebre-Egziabher is a scholar and filmmaker. She has actively worked towards gender parity in the classroom and was invited by the US Embassy in Addis Ababa to lead a screenwriting workshop for Ethiopian women journalists and filmmakers (Ellerson 2018b). Her screenwriting workshop was entitled "Telling Herstory" around the theme of gender-based violence, and each of the three scriptwriting finalists produced a five-minute film funded by the US Embassy. Her goal is to set up the Ethiopian Women Filmmakers Association (EWFA) to provide support and training opportunities to young and upcoming Ethiopian women filmmakers in Ethiopia. Ethiopia has also developed a very successful popular, low-budget Amharic-language industry in the Nollywood mould, as Nollywood continues to serve as an inspiration and an example of commercial viability for younger local filmmaking cultures and industries.

Anglophone West Africa: Nollywood

Nollywood cinema is a hugely popular strand of cinema in Nigeria based on Yoruba theatre and on Nigerian television drama. Early Nigerian films on celluloid were made from the 1970s onwards, but it was with the introduction of video and home movies that the Nollywood industry really took off. What started as a grassroots initiative in response to the rising prices of celluloid filmmaking, has become an increasingly professional, ambitious international industry dominated by online and alternative distribution corporations (Haynes 2016). Oluyinka Esan (2018) emphasises that Nollywood takes great pride in telling its own stories in its own particular way, even if that means that large international audiences remain unfamiliar with the form. Building on folk tales and modern urban myths, the narratives in Nollywood can feel otherworldly, with a tendency to explore social ills through melodrama and extravagance. But as Jonathan Haynes (2016) states, with the current development of "New Nollywood," showing the modern urban elites fascinated by fashion and wealth, films are again becoming more expensive to make as filmmakers look to make better quality films that are screened at the growing number of multiplex cinemas in Nigeria and at global film festivals.

While women have always had a space in the industry as actresses, Nollywood has been dominated by negatively stereotyped images of women. Given its immense popularity globally, this negative portrayal impacts on a huge population: "these images promote continuous domination by men and subordination and subjugation of women" (Usaini 2016, 127). Nollywood has been criticised for its portrayal of women as cold-hearted, materialistic, vengeful sex objects. Moreover, women's roles are usually depicted in domestic spaces, showing them as mothers, housewives, or in other domestic roles. Esan nuances this somewhat by pointing out the enormous diversity of roles available to women, but she does admit that very often these roles still function as antagonistic to the success of a man, and the relationship between man and woman continues to be combative. While she asserts that Nollywood is starting to become more self-reflexive and critical of its stereotypical tropes, the harmful images of women remain substantial. We could presume that these stereotypical portrayals of women would be more nuanced if women take a place behind the camera.

Historically, it has been rare for women to be in charge in Nollywood, either as directors or producers. Esan notes that in television women have been active for quite some time, and are increasingly calling the shots in Nollywood. One example of a pioneering female filmmaker and an inspiration for young New Nollywood filmmakers was Amaka Igwe, who died in 2014. For years, Igwe was the only female Nollywood director. Director Tope Oshin Ogun says "Igwe is that one person, who took me out of this mindset that women are worth less: [she said] if you have the talent, go ahead and be what you want to be!" (Campion and Denton 2017). Likewise, Genevieve Nnaji, arguably Nollywood's most famous actress, dedicated her feature directorial debut *Lionheart* (2018) to Amaka Igwe. There is now a small corpus of work emerging from female Nollywood directors that may be able to rectify the negative image of women in Nollywood.

British-Nigerian Michelle Bello studied filmmaking in the US, and her two films so far, *Small Boy* (2008) and *Flower Girl* (2013) are both easily digestible boy-meets-girl stories. Stephanie Okereke Linus, a very prolific actress in Nollywood (she has starred in over 100 films), also studied filmmaking in the US, and served as director, scriptwriter, producer and actress for her debut *Through the Glass* (2008). For her second film *Dry* (2014) she again fulfilled all these roles herself. *Dry* is a particularly important film as one of the first to take on controversial issues like fistula and underage marriage. It is the story of Halima, a 13-year-old girl who is married off to a 60-year-old man who rapes her. When she falls pregnant, she suffers from fistula (VVF) and is abandoned by her husband and the community. Zara, a doctor played by Linus herself, decides to help Halima and dedicate her career to other girls in the same situation. A heroine story with a feel-good ending, it is far removed from any critical arthouse treatment, but it was an important widely-viewed work in a slate of issue-based films that touched on gender politics in Nigeria.

Another is Tope Oshin Ogun's *Journey to Self* (2012). It "has no male protagonists, but four women telling their own stories, stories that many Nigerian women struggle with in silence, about child marriage, domestic abuse, divorce and the pressure to conform to other people's expectations" (Utor 2017). While the film was not popular, it was one of the first Nollywood stories with only female protagonists. The film was made in response to the contemporary inaction on the part of the government on the Gender Equality Bill which was stuck in Parliament between 2010 and 2018. The filmmaker explains that "the Bill basically said women should have equal opportunities at work, salaries, and the way they are treated" but it was rejected in 2018 due to "religious sensibilities" (Payton 2016). Despite this setback, Ogun expresses hope that New Nollywood remains strong on the women directors front.

Like *Journey to Self* and *Dry*, Remi Vaughan-Richards' *Unspoken* (2016) casts a critical spotlight on the issue of child brides. It is quite a didactic story but when it was taken on a tour of remote parts of the country, Richards said in an interview that the response was encouraging. Very young mothers came to the screenings and understood the importance of letting young girls finish education before getting married (Utor 2017).

In the same year, Kemi Adetiba's *The Wedding Party* (2016) became the top box office winner by a woman and the highest grossing Nollywood film ever. Also breaking box-office records was Bunmi Ajakaiye's *My Wife and I* (2017), a body swap comedy in which a husband and wife are forced to learn to understand one another's lives (including the man struggling to understand a woman's period). Ajakaiye was assistant director on *The Wedding Party*. Model and actress Blessing Effiom Egbe also turned to directing, and *The Women* (2017) created some controversy because of its negative portrayal of women as disloyal gold-diggers. The director emphasises that in her view women are complex and competitive beings, often antagonistic towards each other.

Thus, while we see an increase in the number of women making films in Nollywood that are increasingly successful, we also see a move away from the emancipatory power in the films' thematic strengths. Where the earlier issue-based films by women like Linus, Oshin Ogun and Richards tackled serious topics pertaining to women's rights and emancipation, with moderate success, the younger filmmakers like Adetiba, Ajakaiye and Egbe seem to be putting the emphasis on ensemble casts and New Nollywood standards, breaking box office records with global audiences, but these later films once again portray women subject to patriarchal societies and conservative norms. So we can wonder whether, and why, we have gone past an emancipatory representation and returned to more patriarchal portrayals. Perhaps this is due to a widespread disappointment with the failure of the Gender Equality Bill or because of increased sensitivities regarding religion. But Genevieve Nnaji's new film, *Lionheart*, about a young business woman fighting the patriarchy with her intelligence and business acumen is a successful combination of an emancipatory story and a New Nollywood aesthetic. She says:

> *Lionheart* stemmed from my desire and hunger to shed light on, and to speak the truth of what it's like to be a young [woman] trying to make it in a world that is dominated by men. That being said, it was equally important to me that the movie was light-hearted and warm, so the environment in which it was told was crucial as well.
>
> *(Rogo 2019)*

Lionheart portrays a carefully supportive patriarchy slowly but surely putting its trust in the future of young women. The film is itself an illustration of this pragmatic feminist ethic. For decades this actress was the darling of Nollywood, and she recently made history by screening the film in Toronto where Netflix bought the worldwide rights for millions of dollars, making Nnaji the first Nollywood naira billionaire.

Central Africa: Democratic Republic of Congo

In stark contrast to the many studies of Nollywood, there is a real dearth of scholarly work on cinema from the DRC, especially in English. Most of the historical resources we used have come from francophone authors, and most of that research focuses on the male missionaries who initiated filmmaking before the 1960s and the male pioneers of Mobutu's Zaire and of DRC since 1997. Gansa Ndombasi (2008) regrets the lack of interest in, and information available about, Congolese cinema, taking it upon himself in his short study to describe the history of Congolese cinema since the missionaries of the early twentieth century. He divides Congolese cinema history into three distinctive parts: from the early twentieth century until Mobutu's time in the 1960s was a period of didactic, Catholic filmmaking with the sole purpose of evangelising local communities. Mobile cinemas were used to spread messages of a religious, moral and educational nature. This period of filmmaking is also extensively researched by Belgian anthropologist Guido Convents (2006). The second period Ndombasi identifies stretches from the early 1960s until 1997, a period of monopartism under President Mobutu, where cinema still served a moral purpose but now in the service of the head of state and a return to traditional values and nationalism. During this time even imported films, very popular with the wider population, were vetted in the service of Mobutu's rule. The third period Ndombasi identifies, "Cinéma Congolais," follows from the Mobutu era, when Zaire became the Democratic Republic of Congo once again. Cinema flourished both due to so-called Revivalists' investments in religious cinema but also through independent efforts mostly from the strong and emancipated diasporas, usually (co-)produced with cinematically strong countries such as France and Belgium.

What the first two periods have in common is a complete lack of women's contributions to cinema. In fact, as Ndombasi, Convents and other scholars point out, the female characters in the films conformed to stereotypes of domesticity and wifedom on the one hand and promiscuity on the other hand as the only possible traits attributed to women in cinema. Indeed, women featured in films only in so far as they were relevant to the male protagonist's story. Similarly, "Cinema Congolais" since 1997 has been dominated by male filmmakers, but in recent years a number of, often very young and cosmopolitan, women have taken up filmmaking. Three women with hyphenated identities, Monique Mbeka Phoba, Ibéa Atondi-De Cointet and Claude Haffner, have specialised mostly, and with some success, in documentary filmmaking. As far as fiction filmmaking goes, they have stuck to short films. One very recent exception is Machérie Ekwa Bahango, whose debut feature fiction film *Maki'La* screened at Berlinale in 2018. While she defied the odds to make this film, she recognises as well "that women artists in the Congo need help [...] especially to discover themselves and know that they are capable of doing great things" (Vourlias 2018a). We discuss this film in more detail in Chapter 6.

African feminisms

As we argue in the introduction, we want to position this study within an African feminist framework because we regard feminist ways of doing and thinking as inseparable from a study interested in women's creative practices. Of course, this framework has to be rooted in, and based on, the lived experiences of African women, and as such, Western understandings of the development and applications of feminist thought have to be decolonised. Whether feminist theories are suitable and appropriate when writing about African women's films is a valid question, not least because some filmmakers do not self-identity as feminists, and not all films by African women can be described as feminist, although we maintain that a politically female sensibility is visible in all the work we cover in this book. It is important to create a space where diverse opinions and approaches can coexist. Moreover, the reality of divergent perspectives on African feminism is not necessarily a generational issue: Safi Faye (born in 1943) has been outspoken about her resistance to the term, and clear about her commitment to supporting the African notion of gender complementarity, whereas Egyptian author and activist Nawal El Saadawi (b. 1931) has devoted her entire career to women in Islam, with resolutely feminist opinions. For her, feminism is not a Western invention, but is embedded in the culture and struggle of all women all over the world (Krishnan 2018). We argue that a feminist framework of study should allow for a multiplicity of positionings, and should also be a space for contestation, disagreement and debate. While feminism is central to our study of African women's cinema, we also acknowledge that embracing it is a strategic, ideological, political and pragmatic choice, intended to enhance the relevance of our research globally. Many African women, especially the younger generations, are outspokenly feminist, and we stand with the over two hundred African feminists who, at the first African Feminist Forum held in Ghana 2006 developed a Charter of Feminist Principles for African Feminists, "seeking to re-energise and reaffirm African feminism in its multiple dimensions":

> Choosing to name ourselves feminists places us in a clear ideological position. By naming ourselves as feminists we politicise the struggle for women's rights, we question the legitimacy of the structures that keep women subjugated, and we develop tools for transformatory analysis and action. We have multiple and varied identities as African feminists. [...] Our feminist identity is not qualified with "ifs," "buts" or "howevers". We are Feminists. Full stop.
>
> *(Ahikire 2014, 7)*

Of major significance to our approach of underlining the multiplicity and plurality of African feminisms is a transnational understanding of feminism, linked to the transnational subject positionings of individual filmmakers, transnational film economies, and the inherent and indeed originary transnationalism of African cinema. It is an approach that respects the nation as a basis for specific cultural and political starting points, but prioritises regional, continental, international and global connections above national positionings. We do this with a political and ideological agenda, but also in a practical and industrial sense when considering issues such as training, funding, production, exhibition and distribution. While transnationalism, when used in relation to film and also more broadly, is a contested term, we wish to emphasise its optimistic, constructive nature as opposed to its association with the negative and unequal consequences of neoliberalism, capitalism and globalisation. Our focus is on collaboration, solidarity and friendship across borders, races, and ethnicities, while retaining specificity and particularity where necessary.

The two most important feminist theorists of transnationalism, in our view, are Chandra Talpade Mohanty and Ella Shohat, who have written together and commented on each other's work. In her seminal essay "Under Western Eyes," Mohanty maintains that "Third World women" are not a homogenous mass and that the politics of difference need to be emphasised. She also advocates a transnational solidarity between women of colour, White women and women from regions known as the "Third World". She acknowledges the need for a shared frame of reference and a "search for a common feminist political project, within a framework of solidarity and shared values" (Mohanty 2003, 502). She further argues that this feminist solidarity must be based on the realisation that women across the globe live with "common differences," which means that diversity and specificity must not be eroded away through generalisations, but should encourage women everywhere to find a common agenda. Ella Shohat likewise "emphasizes the particularities and diversity of local struggles for gender equality, and recuperates gender and sexuality from universalising narratives of national history" (Murphy and Williams 2007, 14). Shohat (2003) focuses on films in which women reclaim their bodies from the nation state. While Shohat accepts the particularities of nationalist struggles and the consequences for the nation's women, she refuses to subscribe to any notion of a globalised sisterhood. She argues for a general acceptance of the national's hybridity while recognising its particularities.

Setting up a suitable framework for African feminist analyses requires us to carefully consider the origins and development of African feminism, unpack its oppositional and complementary stance towards Western feminisms, and to unravel and critique longstanding assumptions. The inherent intersectionality of African and postcolonial feminism is central to this work: as Susan Andrade argued, while European/Western feminist critics tend to gloss over race, postcolonial critics often ignore the category of gender (1990, 93). Andrade argues that for Eurocentric feminists, race is merely a trope for gender, another way to understand the larger oppression of women. For masculinist cultural critics, the privileged category of race subsumes all others; gender serves as a lens through which the greater oppression of Non-Europeans can be understood. Neither of these theoretical positions offers a space from which an African feminist criticism can be articulated, because neither is able to address the heterogeneity that analysis of African women's texts must foreground. As women have been written out of history, women writers and filmmakers (re-)inscribe themselves into it now, and an intersectional approach to these efforts is necessary in order to achieve solidarity across global feminist idealisms.

The development of African feminism has a layered history. The establishment of a feminist movement on the continent was delayed by the predominance of nationalist concerns during liberation struggles – men and women united in this struggle, and their common enemy was colonial oppression. The historiography of the liberation struggle has not allowed enough scope for feminist concerns, with nationalism typically privileged over feminist concerns. In contrast, films by female directors show how African women actively participated in nationalist movements as resistance fighters and party activists. After independence(s), women's interests were betrayed by nation states with the realisation that military activity and other central contributions to the liberation struggle do not necessarily translate into progressive national gender politics. This led to contradictory constructions of women in nationalist ideologies, for example in the call for "new women" versus "women as upholders of traditions and customs, reservoirs of culture" (Mama 2001, 259). Amina Mama further argues that nationalists who inherited power from colonial bureaucrats were overly conservative in their sexual politics. The authoritarian control of women that existed during the colonial period therefore often went unchallenged in postcolonial regimes. After independence it became clear that the norms in pre-colonial and in postcolonial Africa both rest on patriarchal pillars, and that there is an urgent need for these structures to be examined and critiqued. Postcolonial times also crushed the hopes that had infused the struggle for independence. Nigerian feminist Obioma Nnaemeka describes African women's lives as a balancing act "subject to internally imposed patriarchal structures and externally engineered imperialistic contexts" (2005, 31). It is within the complex context of the persistence of traditional patriarchal gender structures, gender patterns introduced by Christianity, Islamisation and colonial oppression, as well as the modification of gender roles under neo-colonialism and continuing Western cultural imperialism, that contemporary African women are shaping their identities and subjectivities.

Mama describes the collective African experience of imperialism and colonial penetration as a violent and gendered process (2001, 253). This process of White penetration into Africa shows the gendered violent nature of colonialism, which led to the re-evaluation of both feminine and masculine roles in African societies. While colonial oppression brought about the emasculation, as well as the questioning and re-definition of African masculinity, it is African women's social and individual positions during and after colonisation that are really in need of critical examination. Mama shows how the history of colonisation reveals a patriarchal process with its origins in the witch hunts and inquisitions of the Middle Ages and the Industrial Revolution's treatment of the working classes and of women. With the advent of imperialism, Europe's racist ideologies and practices established Black people as the exotic other, who became a metaphor for Africa: "the dark and unknown continent, waiting to be penetrated, conquered and despoiled" (ibid., 255). The racist gender values enforced under colonialism commodified African women in a process that speedily degraded the legal status of women.

A significant obstacle in the development of African feminism is the fact that the term "feminism" is seen as a Western concept, and Western feminist principles do not necessarily offer solutions relevant to the concerns and needs of African women. Desiree Lewis (1992) emphasised that the resultant binarism between Western feminism and African/Black feminism needs to be addressed: "the blindness of Western feminists to the realities of Third-World women's lives is still an issue," she stated (ibid., 36). Sweeping terminology like "global sisterhood" presumes that feminism is a universally accepted term, but as feminists we need to dig much deeper into our own privilege and biased points of view, influenced by institutionalised and systemic hierarchies. The basics of White privilege are certainly gaining attention. As many African intellectuals and cultural practitioners have shown, decolonisation and women's liberation should be seen as inextricably intertwined issues, an interconnectedness of gender, race and class oppression that forms the complex context within which African women formulate socio-political agendas and negotiate social and economic identities.

Criticism of attempts to universalise Western feminist principles and to translate these ideologies into the realities of African women's lives has contributed to the development of a specifically African feminist discourse. It has to be understood that African women are often empowered *differently* from those in the West. For instance, multiple historical examples exist of matrilineal structures that gave women prominent societal roles and political status. Andrea Cornwall, for example, argues that these could be seen as "proto-feminist underpinnings of women's collective action" (2005, 10), which gave rise to collective militancy, riots and rebellion of women in the struggle against colonialism. Women's active participation in anti-colonial struggles as well as their representation in contemporary African governments, point at the convenient categorisation of and the assumptions that African women are less emancipated than Western women. This assumption is the result of a Western gaze onto Africa and underlines the urgency with which the world needs to recognise that modes of emancipation are culturally specific rather than universal.

Gwendolyn Mikell stated that African feminism is "distinctly heterosexual, pro-natal and concerned with 'bread, butter and power' issues" (1997, 4). She argued that Western women emphasise individual emancipation and self-determination, while African women concentrate on emancipated public participation within their communal and broader societal spheres. Some African feminists indeed emphasise the politics of complementarity and co-operation between women and men. However, Mikell's position has been critiqued by African scholars such as Josephine Ahikire who argues against "the conservative dynamics that work to undermine the critical edge of African feminism, creating a sense of urgency about the need for the feminist movement to re-assert and re-energise itself" (2014, 7). For Ahikire, African feminism is far from being constructed in a simple opposition to Western feminism, as African feminism constitutes a multitude of diverse experiences and positions. Mikell's "bread, butter and power" feminism is, Ahikire says, not only conservative but it also undermines the progressive work of women's movements and generations of women dedicated to pursuing bolder and more radical agendas, particularly in the contentious areas of sexuality, culture and spirituality, often trapped in the stranglehold of "tradition" (ibid., 8). The younger generation of African feminists criticise

> the 'hypocritical' and 'sexist' defence of African culture and tradition to justify discrimination against women; the practice of giving women token positions of power; sexist attitudes when it comes to sexual and reproductive health and rights; the use of notions of motherhood and state policies to minimise women's contributions; and the feminisation of HIV/AIDS and poverty.
>
> *(Badri and Trip 2017, 5).*

African feminism(s) should be seen as a plural endeavour, a body of scholarship and activism that

> speaks to and for the multiplicity of experiences on the continent. Feminism encapsulates myriad theoretical perspectives emanating from the complexities and specifics of the different material conditions, and identities of women, informed by the diverse creative ways in which we contest power in our private and public lives.
>
> *(Ahikire 2014, 8)*

Akin-Aina argues for an epistemology of African feminism that goes beyond "bread, butter, culture and power," arguing that

> the African feminist movement is characterized by: an ongoing process of self-definition and re-definition; a broad-based membership; a resistance to the distortions and misrepresentations by Western global feminism; a 'feminism of negotiation'; as well as efforts to reconcile power dynamics on the continent, nationally and within the movement.
>
> *(2011, 67)*

The first Feminist Forum held in 2006 in Ghana reflected a shift in thinking about African feminism, which has become clear in feminist discourse and discussion on websites, blogs, journals and social media over the past decade (Badri and Tripp 2017, 6). For example, Nigerian writer Chimamanda Ngozi Adichie's feminist pamphlet *We Should All Be Feminists* (2014) outlines a direction for African feminism for the twenty-first century.

We believe, then, that our first task as feminist observers and scholars is to recognise and indeed celebrate the historical presence of women in the African film industries, and that the continuing creativity of contemporary female directors and the telling of women's stories has to be admired in light of these pioneers' efforts. Second, female filmmakers not only provide alternatives to representations of African women in the Western media and to patriarchal African discourses, but they are also developing innovative forms of homegrown feminist aesthetics. Returning to Shohat, in the early 2000s she called for a style of feminist filmmaking which should challenge the masculinist contours of the "nation" in order to continue a feminist decolonisation of African historiography through a "multi-cultural feminist aesthetics of resistance" (2003, 54). *Women in African Cinema: Beyond the Body Politic* charts the extent to which this call has been answered, showcasing how African women film-makers have long contributed to revising stereotypical images of African women, moving towards a multivocal feminist lens.

Notes

1   For more in-depth studies of colonial cinema in Africa, we recommend Glenn Reynolds (2015) *Colonial Cinema in Africa: Origins, Images, Audiences.* Jefferson, NC: McFarland & Co.; Lee Grieveson and Colin MacCabe (eds) (2011) *Empire and Film.* London: Palgrave Macmillan; and Tom Rice (2019) *Films for the Colonies: Cinema and the Preservation of the British Empire.* Berkeley, CA: University of California Press.
2   See, for example, Armes (2006); Bakari and Cham (1996); Barlet (2000; 2016); Diawara (1992; 2010); Dovey (2009); Givanni (2001); Gugler (2003); Harrow (1999; 2007; 2013; 2017); Murphy (2000); Murphy and Williams (2013); Pfaff (2004; 2010); Saul and Austen (2010); Tcheuyap (2011); Thackway (2003); Ukadike (1994).

Bibliography

Adichie, Chimamanda Ngozi (2014) *We Should All Be Feminists.* London: Fourth Estate.

Ahikire, Josephine (2014) "African feminism in context: Reflections on the legitimation battles, victories and reversals," *Feminist Africa*, 19, pp. 7–23.

Akin-Aina, Sinmi (2011) "Beyond an epistemology of bread, butter, culture and power: Mapping the African feminist movement," *Nokoko*, 2, Institute of African Studies, Carleton University, pp. 65–89.

Andrade, Susan Z. (1990) "Rewriting history, motherhood, and rebellion: Naming an African women's literary tradition," *Research in African Literatures*, 21(1), pp. 91–110.

Andrade-Watkins, Claire (1999) "Portuguese African cinema: Historical and contemporary perspectives, 1969–1993." In Kenneth W. Harrow (ed.) *African Cinema: Postcolonial and Feminist Readings.* Trenton, NJ: Africa World Press, pp. 177–200.

Armes, R. (2006) *African Filmmaking: North and South of the Sahara.* Bloomington, IN: Indiana University Press.

Austin, Guy. (2012) *Algerian National Cinema.* Manchester: Manchester University Press.

Badri, Balghis and Aili Mari Tripp (2017) *Women's Activism in Africa.* London: Zed Books.

Bakari, I. and M. Cham (1996) *African Experiences of Cinema.* London: BFI Publishing.

Baldé, Assanatou (2016) "Cannes Film Festival, Rahmatou Keïta: 'The future of cinema in Africa'," *Afrik.com* (24 May). Available online: www.afrik.com/festival-de-cannes-rahma tou-keita-l-avenir-du-cinema-est-en-afrique [Accessed January 2019].

Balseiro, Isabel. and Ntongela Masilela (eds) (2003) *To Change Reels: Film and Film Culture in South Africa.* Detroit: Wayne State University Press.

Barlet, O. (2000) *African Cinemas: Decolonizing the Gaze.* London: Zed Books.

Barlet, O. (2016) *Contemporary African Cinema.* East Lansing, MI: Michigan State University Press.

Bisschoff, Lizelle (2012) "Reconciling the African nation: Fanta Régina Nacro's *La Nuit de la Vérité.*" In Lizelle Bisschoff and Stefanie Van De Peer (eds) *Art and Trauma in Africa: Representations of Reconciliation in Music, Visual Arts, Literature and Film.* London: I.B. Tauris, pp. 213–230.

Bisschoff, Lizelle (2015) "Cinema in East Africa," *Journal of African Cinemas*, 7(2). Intellect.

Blignaut, J. and M.P. Botha (eds) (1992) *Movies Moguls Mavericks: South African Cinema 1979–1991*. Cape Town: Showdata.

Botha, Martin P. (2004) "The song remains the same: The struggle for a South African audience 1960–2003," *Kinema*, 21 (Spring), pp. 67–89.

Botha, Martin P. and Adri Van Aswegen (1992) *Images of South Africa: The Rise of Alternative Film*. Pretoria: Human Sciences Research Council.

Campion, Mukti Jain and Nadia Denton (2017) *Nigeria: Shooting it Like a Woman*, produced for BBC World Service.

Convents, Guido (2006) *Images et démocratie. Les Congolais face au cinéma et à l'audiovisuel. Une histoire politico-culturelle du Congo des Belges jusqu'à la république démocratique du Congo (1896–2006)*. Kessel-Lo, Afrika Filmfestival: Aden Diffusion.

Cornwall, Andrea (ed.) (2005) *Readings in Gender in Africa*. Oxford: James Currey.

Dangaremgba, Tsitsi (2019) "Double bind: Women filmmakers in Africa are edited too soon," *Daily Maverick* (29 April). Available online: www.dailymaverick.co.za/opinionista/2019-04-29-double-bind-women-film-makers-in-africa-are-edited-too-soon/ [Accessed May 2019].

Davis, P. (1996) *In Darkest Hollywood: Exploring the Jungles of Cinema's South Africa*. Athens, OH: Ohio University Press.

Diawara, Manthia (1992) *African Cinema: Politics and Culture*. Bloomington, IN: Indiana University Press.

Diawara, M. (2010) *African Film: New Forms of Aesthetics and Politics*. New York: Prestel Publishing.

Dovey, L. (2009) *African Film and Literature: Adapting Violence to the Screen*. New York: Columbia University Press.

Dovey, Lindiwe (2012) "New looks: The rise of African women filmmakers," *Feminist Africa*, 16. Available online: http://www.agi.ac.za/agi/feminist-africa/16/ [Accessed April 2018].

Ellerson, B. (2000) *Sisters of the Screen: Women of Africa on Film, Video and Television*. Trenton, NJ: Africa World Press.

Ellerson, Beti (2018a) "Kenyan women in cinema, visual media and screen culture." Available online: http://africanwomenincinema.blogspot.com/2009/08/glance-at-kenyan-women-in-cinema.html [Accessed January 2019].

Ellerson, Beti (2018b) "Lucy Gebre-Egziabher: A woman on a mission." Available online: http://africanwomenincinema.blogspot.com/2018/02/lucy-gebre-egziabher-woman-on-mission.html [Accessed January 2019].

Esan, Oluyinka (2018) "Women in Nigerian films: Roles and tropes." Keynote Lecture, Doing Women's Film and Television History IV: Calling the Shots – Then, Now, Next, University of Southampton.

Gavshon, Harriet (1992) "Women in the South African Film Industry." In J. Blignaut and M.P. Botha (eds) *Movies, Moguls, Mavericks: South African Cinema, 1979–1991*. Johannesburg: Showdata.

Grieveson, Lee and Colin MacCabe (eds) (2011) *Empire and Film*. London: Palgrave Macmillan

Gugler, J. (2003) *African Film: Re-imagining a Continent*. Bloomington, IN: Indiana University Press.

Guru-Murthy, Krishnan (2018) "Egyptian feminist Nawal El Saadawi," in *Ways to Change the World Series*, Series 1, Episode 13. Broadcast 13 June 2018. Available online: www.channel4.com/news/ways-to-change-the-world-a-new-channel-4-news-podcast-nawal-el-saadawi [Accessed January 2019].

Gutsche, T. (1972) *The History and Social Significance of Motion Pictures in South Africa, 1895-1940*. Cape Town: H. Timmins.

Harrow, K. (1999) *African Cinema: Postcolonial and Feminist Readings*. Trenton, NJ: Africa World Press.

Harrow, K. (2007) *Postcolonial African Cinema: From Political Engagement to Postmodernism*. Bloomington, IN: Indiana University Press.

Harrow, K. (2013) *Trash: African Cinema from Below*. Bloomington, IN: Indiana University Press.

Harrow, K. (2017) *African Filmmaking: Five Formations*. East Lansing, MI: Michigan State University Press.

Haynes, Jonathan (2016) *Nollywood: The Creation of Nigerian Film Genres*. Chicago: University of Chicago Press.

Hees, E. (1991) *The National Film Board of South Africa: A Short History*. University of Stellenbosch.

Hillauer, Rebecca (2005) *Encyclopedia of Arab Women Filmmakers*. Cairo: American University of Cairo Press.

Kassahun, Eyerusaleam (2018) "Women's participation in Ethiopian cinema." In Michael W. Thomas, Alessandro Jedlowski and Aboneh Ashagrie (eds) *Cine-Ethiopia: The History and Politics of Film in the Horn of Africa*. East Lansing: Michigan State University Press, pp. 119–140.

Lewis, Desiree (1992) "Myths of motherhood and power: The construction of 'black woman' in literature," *English in Africa*, 19(1) (Spring), pp. 35–51.

Mahoso, Tafataona (2001) "Unwinding the African dream on African ground." In June Givanni (ed.) *Symbolic Narratives/African Cinema: Audiences, Theory and the Moving Image*. London: BFI Publishing, pp. 197–226.

Maingard, J. (2007) *South African National Cinema*. London: Routledge.

Mama, Amina (2001) "Sheroes and villains: Conceptualizing colonial and contemporary violence against women in Africa." In Gregory Castle (ed.) *Postcolonial Discourses: An Anthology*. Oxford: Blackwell Publishers.

Marx, Lesley (1992) "Where Angels fear to tread: Three white women and a camera." In J. Blignaut and M.P. Botha (eds.) *Movies, Moguls, Mavericks: South African Cinema, 1979–1991*. Johannesburg: Showdata.

Mboti, Nyasha (2014) "The Zimbabwean film industry," *African Communication Research*, 7(2), pp. 145–172.

Mikell, Gwendolyn (ed.) (1997) *African Feminism: The Politics of Survival in Sub-Saharan Africa*. Philadelphia: University of Pennsylvania Press.

Modisane, L. (2013) *South Africa's Renegade Reels: The Making and Public Lives of Black-Centered Films*. London: Palgrave Macmillan.

Mohanty, Chandra Talpade (2003) "'Under Western Eyes' revisited: Feminist solidarity through anticapitalist struggles," *Signs*, 28(2), pp. 499–535.

Murphy, D. (2000) *Sembene: Imagining Alternatives in Film & Fiction*. Melton: James Currey Publishers.

Murphy, David and Patrick Williams (2007) *Postcolonial African Cinema. Ten Directors*. Manchester: Manchester University Press.

Ndombasi, Gansa (2008) *Le Cinema du Congo Democratique*. Paris: L'Harmattan.

Obioma, Nnaemeka (2005) "Mapping African feminisms." In Andrea Cornwall (ed.) *Readings in Gender in Africa*. Oxford: James Currey, pp. 31–40.

Payton, Matt (2016) "Nigerian Senate votes down gender equality bill due to 'religious beliefs'," *The Independent* (17 March). Available online: https://www.independent.co.uk/news/world/africa/nigerian-senate-votes-down-gender-equality-bill-due-to-religious-beliefs-a6936021.html [Accessed January 2019].

Pfaff, F. (2004) *Focus on African Films*. Bloomington, IN: Indiana University Press.

Pfaff, F. (2010) *A l'écoute du cinéma sénégalais*. Paris: Editions L'Harmattan.

Reynolds, Glenn (2015) *Colonial Cinema in Africa: Origins, Images, Audiences*. Jefferson, NC: McFarland Publishing

Rice, Tom (2019) *Films for the Colonies: Cinema and the Preservation of the British Empire*. Berkeley, CA: University of California Press.

Rogo, Paula (2019) "Genevieve Nnaji makes history with Netflix's first Nigerian original film Lionheart," *Essence* (4 January). Available online: www.essence.com/celebrity/p retty-dope/nigeria-genevieve-nnaji-history-lionheart-netflix/ [Accessed January 2019].

Saks, L. (2010) *Cinema in a Democratic South Africa: The Race for Representation*. Bloomington, IN: Indiana University Press.

Saul, M. and R.A. Austen (2010) *Viewing African Cinema in the Twenty-First Century: Art Films and the Nollywood Video Revolution*. Columbus, OH: Ohio University Press.

Shohat, Ella (2003) "Post-Third-Worldist culture: Gender, nation, and the cinema." In Anthony R. Guneratne and Wimal Dissanayake. *Rethinking Third Cinema*. London: Routledge. pp. 51–78.

Tcheuyap, A. (2011) *Postnationalist African Cinemas*. Manchester: Manchester University Press.

Thackway, Melissa (2003) *Africa Shoots Back: Alternative Perspectives in Sub-Saharan Francophone African Film*. Oxford: James Currey.

Tomaselli, K. (1989) *The Cinema of Apartheid: Race and Class in South African Film*. London: Routledge.

Tomaselli, K. (2006) *Encountering Modernity: Twentieth Century South African Cinemas*. Amsterdam: Rozenberg Publishers.

Ukadike, N. Frank (1994) *Black African Cinema*. Berkeley: University of California Press.

Ukadike, N. Frank (2002) *Questioning African Cinema: Conversations with Filmmakers*. Minneapolis: University of Minnesota Press.

Usaini, Suleimanu, Ngozi, M. Chilaka and Nelson Okorie (2016) "Chapter 8: Portrayal of Women in Nollywood Films and the Role of Women in National Development." In *Impacts of the Media on African Socio-Economic Development*, Hershey, PA: IGI Publishing, pp. 126–140.

Utor, Florence (2017) "Shooting it like a woman: The evolution of Nigerian females behind the screen," *The Guardian Nigeria* (5 November). Available online: https://guardian.ng/a rt/shooting-it-like-a-woman-the-evolution-of-nigerian-females-behind-the-screen/ [Accessed January 2019].

Verschueren, Bernard (2002) "Fanta Nacro: Hope in female form," *The Courier* (January-February), pp. 2–5.

Vourlias, Christopher (2018a) "Berlin director Bahango hopes to inspire Congolese women to pick up cameras," *Variety* (16 February). Available online: https://variety.com/2018/ film/spotlight/berlin-film-festival-2018-bahango-makila-berlinale-1202696635/ [Accessed January 2019].

Vourlias, Christopher (2018b) "For black women in South African film biz, equality still a struggle," *Variety* (21 July). Available online: https://variety.com/2018/film/news/black-wom en-in-south-african-film-biz-equality-a-struggle-1202880315/?fbclid=IwAR07OI5WbA7Cn x09Ecq-AN7iz0QyH4Cm7P2jNGJHYqobOG95idXR3YmEYlw [Accessed January 2019].

Filmography

34 South, Dir. Maganthrie Pillay, South Africa, 2005

A Close-up on Bintou, Dir. Fanta Régina Nacro, Burkina Faso/France, 2001

A Costa dos Murmúrios / The Murmuring Coast, Dir. Margarida Cardoso, Portugal, 2004

A Dry White Season, Dir. Euzhan Palcy, USA, 1989

À mon âge je me cache encore pour fumer/I Still Hide to Smoke, Dir. Rayhana Obermeyer, France/Greece/Algeria, 2016

A peine j'ouvre les yeux / As I Open My Eyes, Dir. Leyla Bouzid, Tunisia/France/Belgium/ United Arab Emirates/Switzerland, 2015

Atlantique, Dir. Mati Diop, France/Senegal/Belgium, 2019

A World Apart, Dir. Chris Menges, UK/Zimbabwe, 1988

Aala Kaf Ifrit/Beauty and the Dogs, Dir. Kaouther Ben Hania, Tunisia/France/Sweden/ Norway/Lebanon/Qatar/Switzerland, 2017

Alda and Maria, Dir. Pocas Pascoal, Portugal, 2012

Anonymes / Buried Secrets, Dir. Raja Amari, Tunisia/Switzerland/France, 2009

Apatride / Stateless, Dir. Narjiss Nejjar, Morocco/France/Qatar, 2018

Asfour Stah / Halfaouine: Boy of the Terraces, Dir. Férid Boughedir, Tunisia/France/Italy, 1990

Atlantique, Dir. Mati Diop, Senegal/France/Belgium, 2019

Aya de Yopougon / Aya of Yop City, Dir. Marguerite Abouet & Clément Oubrerie, France, 2013

Bab Al-Sama Maftuh / A Door to the Sky, Dir. Farida Benlyazid, Morocco, 1989

Baby Mamas, Dir. Stephina Zwane, South Africa, 2018

Bakar, Dir. Mona Abu El-Nasr, Egypt, 2001

Balageru, Dir. Hermon Hailay, Ethiopia, 2012

Barakat!, Dir. Djamila Sahraoui, France/Algeria, 2006

Bedwin Hacker, Dir. Nadia El Fani, France/Morocco/Tunisia, 2003

Bezness, Dir. Nouri Bouzid, France/Tunisia/Germany, 1992

Born Free, Dir. James Hill & Tom McGowan, UK/USA, 1966

Casa Nayda, Dir. Farida Benlyazid & Abderrahim Mettour, Morocco, 2007

Come Back, Africa, Dir. Lionel Rogosin, USA, 1959

Corps étranger / Foreign Body, Dir. Raja Amari, France/Tunisia, 2016

Cry Freedom, Dir. Richard Attenborough, UK, 1987

Deux femmes sur la route / Two Women on the Road, Dir. Farida Bourquia, Morocco, 2007

Dry, Dir. Stephanie Okereke Linus, Nigeria, 2014

Everyone's Child, Dir. Tsitsi Dangarembga, Zimbabwe, 1996

Fad'jal, Dir. Safi Faye, Senegal, 1979

Farewell Ella Bella, Dir. Lwazi Mvusi, South Africa, 2018

Fatma 75, Dir. Selma Baccar, Tunisia, 1975

Femmes aux yeux ouverts / Women with Open Eyes, Dir. Anne-Laure Folly, Togo, 1994

Femmes de Niger / Women of Niger, Dir. Anne-Laure Folly, Togo, 1993

Fiela se Kind, Dir. Katinka Heyns, South Africa, 1988

Flame, Dir. Ingrid Sinclair, Zimbabwe, 1996

Flower Girl, Dir. Michelle Bello, Nigeria, 2013

Freedom Fields, Dir. Naziha Arebi, UK/Libya, 2012

From a Whisper, Dir. Wanuri Kahiu, Kenya, 2008

Frontieras / Borders, Dir. Farida Benlyazid, Morocco, 2013

Frontières / Borders, Dir. Apolline Traoré, Burkina Faso/France, 2017

Granny's Flags, Dir. Naziha Arebi, Libya, 2012

Hang Time, Dir. Ngozi Onwurah, UK/Nigeria, 2001

Hotel Rwanda, Dir. Terry George, UK/South Africa/Italy, 2004

Imani, Dir. Caroline Kamya, Sweden/Uganda, 2010

Inch'Allah Dimanche, Dir. Yamina Benguigui, France/Algeria, 2001

Indivision / Joint Possession, Dir. Leila Kilani, Morocco/France/United Arab Emirates/Qatar, 2018

Jemima and Johnny, Dir. Lionel Ngakane, South Africa/UK, 1966
Jit, Dir. Michael Raeburn, Zimbabwe, 1990
Journey to Self, Dir. Tope Oshin Ogun, Nigeria, 2012
Kaddu Beykat, Dir. Safi Faye, Senegal, 1976
Kare kare zvako: Mother's Day, Dir. Tsitsi Dangarembga, Zimbabwe, 2005
Keïd Ensa / Women's Wiles, Dir. Farida Benlyazid, Morocco/France/Switzerland/Tunisia, 1998
Keletat, Dir. Kidist Yilma, Ethiopia, 2015
King Solomon's Mines, Dir. Compton Bennett & Andrew Marton, USA, 1950
King Solomon's Mines, Dir. J. Lee Thompson, USA, 1985
L'amante du rif / Rif Lover, Dir. Narjiss Nejjar, Morocco, 2011
L'arbre aux esprits / The Tree Spirit, Dir. Cilia Sawadogo, Burkina Faso, 2005
L'Éveil / The Awakening, Dir. Selma Baccar, Tunisia, 1966
La femme mariée à trois hommes / The Woman with Three Husbands, Dir. Cilia Sawadogo & Danièle Roy, Burkina Faso/Canada, 1993
La Noire de… / Black Girl, Dir. Ousmane Sembène, Senegal/France, 1966
La Nouba des femmes du Mont Chenoua, Dir. Assia Djebar, Algeria, 1979
La nuit de la vérité / The Night of Truth, Dir. Fanta Régina Nacro, Burkina Faso/France, 2004
La saison des hommes / The Season of Men, Dir. Moufida Tlatli, Tunisia/France, 2000
La trace / The Trace, Dir. Néjia Ben Mabrouk, Tunisia, 1988.
La vida perra de Juanita Narboni/Juanita from Tangier, Dir. Farida Benlyazid, Morocco/Spain, 2005
La Zerda, ou les chants de l'oubli, Dir. Assia Djebar, Algeria, 1983
Laïcité, Inch'Allah!, Dir. Nadia El Fani, Tunisia/France, 2011
Laila, Dir. Stephan Rosti, Egypt, 1927
Land Apart, Dir. Sven Persson, South Africa, 1974
Le challat de Tunis / Challat of Tunis, Dir. Kaouther Ben Hania, Tunisia/France, 2013
Le gardien des forces / The Guardian of the Forces, Dir. Anne-Laure Folly, Togo, 1992
Les oubliées / The Forgotten Women, Dir. Anne-Laure Folly, Angola, 1997
Les Silences du palais / The Silences of the Palace, Dir. Moufida Tlatli, Tunisia/France, 1994
Les yeux secs / Cry No More, Dir. Narjiss Nejjar, Morocco/France, 2003
Lionheart, Dir. Genevieve Nnaji, Nigeria, 2018
Maki'la, Dir. Machérie Ekwa Bahango, Democratic Republic of the Congo, 2018
Mamlambo, Dir. Palesa Letlaka-Nkosi, South Africa, 1997
Marock, Dir. Laila Marrakchi, Morocco/France, 2005
Meba, Dir. Kidist Yilma, Ethiopia, 2015
Même pas mal, Dir. Nadia El Fani, France, 2012
Monangambé, Dir. Sarah Maldoror, Angola, 1968
Moolaadé, Dir. Ousmane Sembène, Senegal/Burkina Faso/Morocco/Tunisia/Cameroon/France, 2004
Mossane, Dir Safi Faye, Germany/Senegal, 1996
My Wife and I, Dir. Bunmi Ajakaiye, Nigeria, 2017
Nos lieux interdits / Our Forbidden Places, Dir. Leila Kilani, Morocco/France, 2008
Nos Seins, Nos Armes, Dir. Nadia El Fani, Tunisia/France, 2013
Number 37, Dir. Nosipho Dumisa, South Africa, 2018
One Evening in July, Dir. Raja Amari, Tunisia, 2001
Ouled Lenine / The Children of Lenin, Dir. Nadia El Fani, Tunisia/France, 2007
Out of Africa, Dir. Sydney Pollack, USA/UK, 1985
Pumzi, Dir. Wanuri Kahiu, South Africa/Kenya, 2009
Queen of Katwe, Dir. Mira Nair, USA, 2016
Quest for Love, Dir. Helena Nogueira, South Africa, 1988
Rachida, Dir. Yamina Bachir-Chouikh, Algeria/France, 2002

Rafiki, Dir. Wanuri Kahiu, Kenya/South Africa/Germany/Netherlands/France/Norway/ Lebanon, 2018

Raya, Dir. Zulfah Otto-Sallies, South Africa, 2001

Rear Window, Dir. Alfred Hitchcock, USA, 1954

Rebuni, Dir. Kidist Yilma, Ethiopia, 2015

Riches, Dir. Ingrid Sinclair, Zimbabwe, 2001

Rock the Casbah, Dir. Laila Marrakchi, France/Morocco, 2013

Saikati, Dir. Anne Mungai, Kenyan, 1992

Sambizanga, Dir. Sarah Maldoror, Angola/France, 1972

Satin rouge / Red Satin, Dir. Raja Amari, France/Tunisia, 2002

Selbé et tant d'autres / Selbe: One Among Many, Dir Safi Faye, Senegal, 1983

Shooting Dogs, Dir. Michael Caton-Jones, United Kingdom/Germany, 2005

Simba, Dir. Brian Desmond Hurst, UK, 1955

Small Boy, Dir. Michelle Bello, Nigeria, 2008

Something Necessary, Dir. Judy Kibinge, Germany/Kenya, 2013

Sometimes in April, Dir. Raoul Peck, France/Rwanda/USA, 2005

Sorry, Mr. Law, Dir. Inas El-Degheidy, Egypt, 1985

Sur la planche / On the Edge, Dir. Leila Kilani, Germany/Morocco/France, 2011

Tanger, le rêve des brûleurs / Tangier, the Dream of the Burners, Dir. Leila Kilani, France, 2003

Taza, Dir. Kidist Yilma, Ethiopia, 2017

Terra Sonâmbula / Sleepwalking Land, Dir. Teresa Prata, Mozambique/Portugal, 2007

The Girl from Carthage, Dir. Albert Samama Chikly, Tunisia, 1924

The Wedding Party, Dir. Kemi Adetiba, Nigeria, 2016

The Women, Dir. Blessing Effiom Egbe, Nigeria, 2017

Through the Glass, Dir. Stephanie Okereke Linus, Nigeria, 2008

Trader Horn, Dir. W.S. Van Dyke, USA, 1931

Un certain matin, Dir. Fanta Régina Nacro, Burkina Faso, 1991

Uno's World, Dir. Bridget Pickering, South Africa/Nigeria/Namibia, 2001

Unspoken, Dir. Remi Vaughan-Richards, Nigeria, 2016

Yaltasebew, Dir. Hermon Hailay, Ethiopia, 2013

Yefikir Wagaw, Dir. Hermon Hailay, Ethiopia, 2015

Yema, Dir. Djamila Sahraoui, Algeria/France/United Arab Emirates, 2012

Zaineb takrahou ethelj / Zaineb Hates the Snow, Dir. Kaouther Ben Hania, Tunisia/France, 2016

Zin'naariya! / The Wedding Ring, Dir. Rahmatou Keïta, Burkina Faso/Niger/France, 2016

Zohra, Dir. Albert Samama Chikly, Tunisia, 1922

2

THE MULTIPLICITY OF FEMALE IDENTITIES

Embracing plurality

In the Senegalese documentary *Selbé et tant d'autres/Selbe: One Among Many* (1983), Safi Faye's intimate but unobtrusive camera observes the life of a 39-year-old Serer peasant woman, Selbé, and her precarious existence in a Senegalese village. While the film focuses mainly on a single remarkable individual, the title is indicative of the representative nature of her life, a life shared by many other Serer/Senegalese/African rural women. Faye was one of only a handful of Black sub-Saharan African women active in the film industry at the time, and her film represents the multiplicity of female identities inhabited by rural African women. The eighties was a time of economic hardship in many African regions, as a result of the Structural Adjustment Programmes imposed by the World Bank and International Monetary Fund, and Selbé's life is marked by a struggle to provide for her family, in the absence of a husband who has left for a neighbouring town in search of work, only to return empty-handed. Selbé works on the fields, with a baby tied to her back, and takes on all domestic tasks in the quest to feed and raise her nine children. In times of particular hardship, she collects mussels in order to buy millet, rice and fish to sell. In voice-over, she tells the viewer how she once had to leave the village for eight months to find work in Dakar in an attempt to pay off her debts. The economic climate has relegated the men to unemployment and has disrupted traditionally complementary gender roles in the domestic sphere, unsettling marriage and family life. "The strength of my own arms is all I can rely on," she says, "I can pull down a tree, but I'm only a woman." Nonetheless, her life is not entirely one of adversity, as she teaches a song to her children that she learnt from her own mother, and she finds solidarity and friendship among her fellow village women. Selbé is a Senegalese Serer woman, a daughter, mother, wife, friend, homemaker, entrepreneur, agricultural worker, labour migrant and transmitter of culture. Her individual, cultural, gender, national, ethnic and economic identities are all intertwined, converging to present a complex picture of a particular African woman.

This chapter lays the groundwork for the following chapters, which are all concerned to some degree with identity politics. We start with an overview of the concept of identity and its complexities and then move on to theoretical descriptions and cinematic examples of gendered identities, traditional versus modern identities, racial identities, national identities and, finally, transnational identities, followed by our two selected case studies. African filmmaking has, since its inception, been used as a tool in the process of negotiating African identities. African cultural practitioners, including filmmakers, take part in discursive processes analysing and critiquing the suitability of an identity built around assumed "natural" categories. The violent and oppressive systems of colonisation and apartheid have made the process of negotiating and defining identity imperative for postcolonial Africa. This process has become even more complex and critical under the conditions of continuing cultural and economic imperialism imposed on Africa by the West and the East, unequal globalisation, and questions of the place and positioning of modern Africa in the contemporary, global world as well as the importance of the African diaspora to a greater plurality of African identities. It is important to view identity as an ongoing process rather than a fixed position. Cultural theorist Stuart Hall described identity as "never unified, increasingly fragmented and fractured; never singular but multiply constructed across different, often intersecting and antagonistic discourses, practices, and positions. They are subject to a radical historicisation, and are constantly in the process of change and transformation" (Hall and du Gay 1996, 4). Hall's conception of identity encourages us, therefore, to think of identity as a process of negotiation between continuity and difference, an approach that seems pertinent to understanding African identities. Negotiating identity and delineating subjectivity is a collective as well as an individual or personal experience, since identity subsumes various elements like nationality, culture, race and ethnicity, class, religion, gender and sexuality. The intersection of these elements in forging an individual, social and cultural identity in modern Africa means that identity is always complexly layered, hybrid, de-essentialised and even contradictory. However, the conflicts ensuing from the internal or external contradictions and confrontations when shaping and interrogating one's identity are often a productive force that can lead to growth and maturation, of an individual and a society.

Female identities

Female African filmmakers very often use film as a way of negotiating identity, as a creative process of self-definition and of expressing individual, collective, social and cultural identities. In African women's films, gender, racial and cultural identity (either self-determined or imposed) tend to intersect with the politics of representation (Mistry and Schuhmann 2015, xi). It is precisely because film can be used as a form of cultural self-determination that it is such a powerful tool in postcolonial Africa. Film historian Roy Armes states that the question of African cultural identity has been and remains a major concern in African filmmaking (2006, 67–68). Armes uses Hall's article "Cultural Identity and Cinematic Representation" (1989) as an analytical framework for examining the construction of identity in African film. Within this framework, identity should not be seen as an already accomplished historical fact represented through film, but should instead be viewed as a "production," which is never complete, always in process and always constituted within, and not outside of representation. "Identities are the names we give to the different ways we are positioned by, and position ourselves within, the narratives of the past," wrote Hall (Armes 2006, 111). Viewed as an instrument in mediating identity, filmmaking then becomes a means of self-definition and self-determination. Indeed, this book is intended as a counter and a response to foreign (mis)presentations of Africa, illuminating how female African filmmakers talk and "shoot" back at stereotypical and misguided representations of their identities, histories and cultures.

Selbe: One Among Many might be seen as a depiction of the two stereotyped polar opposites by which African women have been defined: the image of the strong, resourceful woman as backbone of her society and "mother of the nation" on the one hand, and the African woman as silent, helpless and impoverished victim, on the other hand. However, such a reading ignores the nuances of the multiple subject positionings depicted in the film. Most films by African women depict the diversity of identities that form part of African womanhood. As we show in this chapter and in the book as a whole, the multiple roles that African women fulfil in their societies, and the different but often overlapping spheres of gender, race, class, nationality, ethnicity and sexuality that inform their subjectivity, mean that female identity in Africa, as elsewhere, is fluid and plural. The positioning of identity is further informed by the effects of tradition and modernity, of rural versus urban spaces, often depicted in conflict with one another but often actually interacting in a complementary way. While discourse – political or academic – can be tempted by dichotomies and oppositions, art and cultural production often serve as a challenge to facile treatments of life and people in order to convey a more sensitive approach to the reality of the lived experience. As such, filmmaking can be used as part of the process of negotiating the tradition versus modernity and rural versus urban dyads, to recover and celebrate suppressed pasts and traditions, but also as part of the process of forging a modern identity in the world. The women's films that we are concerned with in this chapter show how individual and personal identities exist alongside social, cultural and communal ones, including urban, rural, diasporic and mixed-race female identities. The case studies in particular are indicative of the transnational identities that so many African women occupy in the contemporary world.

Gendered identities

Gender identity, specifically the self-identification as female, is central to our interest in identity as a broad social construct. But being female means different things to different women, and means different things in a Western/non-Western, European/African, or colonial/postcolonial context. It includes a variety of individualities such as mother, wife, daughter, sister, partner, business woman and homemaker, among others. Gender identity is central to identity politics, as it prescribes to a large degree how we view ourselves as individuals and in relation to other people. Identity is always individual *and* social, constructed by personal characteristics as well as group identifications. Collective female identity in an African context is sustained by the communal nature of many traditional societies, but at times African women might also prefer a focus on an individual identity. There is a danger in over-emphasising the communal nature of African cultures, as it could lead to a stifling of attempts to gain female emancipation. The emphasis placed on the role of the African woman in relation to her various community ties could in some cases even reinforce the oppression of women. It could, for example, restrict or inhibit women who want to pursue ambitions outside of the home, or who choose not to have children. As such, it becomes necessary for women to explore alternatives, which can entail an emphasis on individual emancipation and expression. Identity is not a natural given, characterised by fixed, objective criteria. Political and historical contexts determine the formation of identities, rendering the processes of human self-expression dynamic, fluid and diverse. If we view identity as ever-changing, this problematises Armes's claim that there has been a dominant continuous strand of sub-Saharan African filmmaking since its inception in the early 1960s that accepts identity as a given, based on a sense of a common historical experiences and shared cultural codes (Armes 2006, 111). Even within the social realist genre, African identity has never been treated as unproblematic by filmmakers like Sembène and Faye, who both pay close attention to postcolonial Africa's conflicting and intersecting dualities.

Certain strands of African filmmaking increasingly deal thematically with diasporic relations, with an emphasis on individual experiences and desires, which could lead to multiple and even conflicting subject positionings. In contemporary African cinema, female identity is inevitably depicted as hybrid, as women in African societies fulfil a diverse range of roles with aspects of race, class, generation and gender being complexly intertwined. French film historian Olivier Barlet claims:

> It is by opening up the cracks in their identity, the fissures they sense within, the contradictions between the essential values of their origins and the possible perversion of those values which tradition forces upon them, that women themselves advance, and also bring about social progress.
>
> *(1996, 106)*

Indeed, the films under discussion in this chapter engage in multiple ways with identity formation and social progress, with the fluidity of identity and with the cracks and fissures in identities that lead to challenging, affective and in many cases transnational narratives.

With Faye's ethnographic documentaries providing an antecedent, the beautifully stylised documentaries about rural traditions of female wall-painting by Senegalese/French director Katy Léna N'diaye offer examples of how women perform and recreate their gendered identities, in an individual and collective way.

N'diaye has made two films on the subject, *Traces, empreintes de femmes/Traces, Women's Imprints* (2003) on the tradition of wall paintings by the Kassena women in southern Burkina Faso, followed by *En attendant les hommes/Waiting for Men* (2007) about the traditional wall decoration by women in the Mauritanian town of Oualata (we discuss these further in Chapter 3). The performative elements of these documentaries are emphasised, as the women are encouraged, within the safe and intimate space in which they are being filmed, and through the trust that exists between the filmmaker and her female subjects, to reveal a lot about themselves. Thus, the making of the documentaries allows them a space in which to "perform" their gender subjectivity differently than they might in other situations. Some of the women, for instance, speak quite frankly about their relationships, including sharing intimate details about their sexual lives.

Likewise, in the documentaries by Izza Génini from Morocco, the filmmaker achieves a safe space for female musicians and travelling bands to speak openly about their gendered and religious roles on the festival circuit in Morocco. Made in 1988, *Aïta* is a short film that challenges the patriarchal nature of the *moussems* (or festivals) and the traditionally dominant male presence in performances at these *moussems*. Génini films the female singers, or *cheikhat*, during their performances but also at intimate moments in their hotel room. The contrast between these two contexts decreases as the film develops: first, the filmmaker sets up a relationship with, and a space for, the singers and dancers to talk about their limitations and freedoms; then, the film arrives at a performance that showcases individual characters, the spirit of solidarity among the women and an insight into the performance they bring to the stage. Their observations of the men in their audiences at the *moussems* adds a level of performativity to gender and religion that reveals a complicit relationship with various audiences, beyond the screen. In both *Waiting for Men* and *Aïta*, the traditional roles of womanhood are performed, knowingly and on multiple levels, revealing a subtle irony and solidarity between African women.

Racial identities

Racial identity is perhaps nowhere more pertinent on the African continent than in South Africa, a country whose brutal history of White minority rule has been shaped by processes of racialisation during the apartheid era. South African society was systemically and determinedly "racialised," in the sense that the term is used by cultural theorist Kwame Anthony Appiah (1992), creating a society characterised by racism and racial discrimination – one of the many destructive legacies of South Africa's past which has to be dealt with in the post-apartheid era. During the transitional period from apartheid to democracy post-1994, the concept of a "rainbow nation" was coined by Archbishop Desmond Tutu to designate the multiracial and multicultural realities of contemporary South Africa, and the term has been widely applied since then. However, the usefulness of "rainbowism," as the ideological application of this notion became known, has also been criticised for not dealing with the complex legacy and consequences of racism in the new South Africa. The continuing rise of violent xenophobic attacks in the country, mostly against labour migrants from other African countries, is one example of the failure of rainbowism. South African writer, author and poet Jeremy Cronin has warned:

> Identity formation as well as the myth of the "rainbow nation" and its performative intention have served to discursively create a national identity that has been top-down in its constitution and implementation. As a result, true reconciliation has been foregone in place of a simplified and somewhat candy-coated myth of peace that has served to reconcile those on the inside whilst pitting them against those on the outside.
>
> *(Cronin 1999)*

Being mixed-race, or "coloured," in the South African context is a particularly complex racial identity, and its intersection with gender is explored by a number of female filmmakers, among others in Kali van der Merwe's documentary *Brown* (2004). The film traces the personal journey of a female singer, Ernestine (Ernie) Deane, who calls herself "brown," as she attempts to recover her family's history in order to claim a space for herself and her unborn child. Ernie's heritage is mixed: she is part Zulu, Khoi and Dutch, and her partner is part Irish and German. In an attempt to explore this diverse ethnic and racial heritage, Ernie embarks on an enquiry into her own background. Similarly, multidisciplinary artist and filmmaker Zara Julius draws on her personal experience of being mixed-race in South Africa in her short film *Mixed Space* (2017), consisting of interviews with mixed-race adults that explore their experiences against the paradoxical background of a multiracial, post-apartheid South Africa. Annalet Steenkamp's documentary *I, Afrikaner* (2013) probes white Afrikaner identity exploring her family background over four generations of South African farmers, for whom a connection to the land is central to their ethnic and national identity.

The exploration of mixed-race identity also informs French/Ivorian filmmaker Isabelle Boni-Claverie, who lives and works in Paris and is of mixed-race heritage. She explores individual female identity in her short *Pour la nuit/For the Night* (2004), a film which, through its intimate portrayal of female sexuality and personal choice, is quite atypical as an African film. Her own positioning as part of the African diaspora is certainly embedded in the style and subject matter of the film. The focus on individual female longing and desire, and the intimate camerawork and framing contribute to the film's experience of a personal journey that explores how racial and female identities are performed by a mixed-race woman from the African diaspora. Boni-Claverie's documentary *Trop noire pour être française?/Too Black to be French?* (2015) explores the persistence of racism in France, in particular against its colonial past. Burkinabe director Apolline Traoré similarly explores mixed-race identity in her feature film *Sous la clarté de la lune/Under the Moonlight* (2004), in which a young mixed-race girl returns to Burkina Faso to reunite with her African mother. *Valley of the Innocent* (2003) by Welsh/Nigerian filmmaker

Branwen Okpako is set in Germany, and tells the story of Eva, a woman of mixed race, looking for her origins. Having grown up in an orphanage, the adult Eva longs to find her real father, who is Black, and starts a journey of discovery by searching for information in the archives of East Germany. This uncovers a convoluted plot to hide her birth and protect the family name – secrets that metaphorically mirror Germany's troubled past. It is a story that was undoubtedly inspired by Okpako's own mixed-race identity. We see in these films a recurring theme of narratives woven around hybrid female identities, often reflected in the filmmakers' own hybrid positionalities. Our case studies explore these themes further.

Nationalism and identity

National identity is extremely complex in the African context and should be regarded as an incomplete and insufficient marker of African identity. Nationalism and notions of national identity and belonging are fraught because of the enormous diversity existing within most African nations and the idiosyncrasies of national borders. Because of the devastating consequences of colonialism and the way in which European nations divided Africa up in countries and areas, the formation of nation-states after independence often involved a process of joining diverse ethnicities and regions on the one hand, and partitioning regions in a way that forced regional redefinition on the other hand (Guneratne and Dissanayake 2003, 62). The postcolonial era has shown that nationalism has failed in many African countries, something that is particularly pertinent for African women, who felt betrayed by the nationalist project. African feminists often critique the ideals of nationalism that did not allow scope for feminist concerns to emerge, even though women took on various roles in African countries' struggles for independence. In fact, some would even argue that the nationalist movements concealed crucial female concerns which resulted in postcolonial societies that continue the patriarchal oppression of women as it became clear that independence did not result in gender equality.

The idea of nationalism and the nation-state is thus a problematic and unstable concept in postcolonial Africa, with a shifting significance within African political discourse. Nationalist ideologies, often inadequately and insufficiently conceptualised, were rapidly developed and disseminated during independence struggles. This is problematised further by the fact that, as Pines and Willemen argue, the West invented nationalism, initially in the form of imperialism and colonialism, as nation-states extended their domination over others. This created the paradox of the hegemonic sense of "national culture" and the "problem" of national identity for the colonised territories (1990, 18). A unified national-cultural identity within colonised territories arose primarily in response to the oppressor, giving rise to a sometimes oppositional and contradictory nationalist discourse. Consequently, contemporary African nation-states emerged as artificial entities, by nature multi-ethnic, multilingual and very diverse (Shohat 2003, 57). The resulting African nationalisms that occurred after independence tend to be ill-defined and often contradictory ideological constructs. This emerging nationalism has been variously described as a return to the traditional values of precolonial Africa (as proposed by Léopold Senghor's concept of Negritude for instance); as the progress of Africa from the dark ages of traditionalism into the era of modernity; as the hegemony and control of one ethnic group over others; or as the overcoming of ethnic differences as a way of countering imperialism (Cobham 1992, 46). In many cases, the optimism of the anti-colonial struggles gave way to uncertainties and a sense of disillusionment, also surrounding issues of gender in relation to national ideals. A simplistic invocation of women-as-nation, of women's bodies as nationalist trope, has become, as the title of our book indicates, obsolete.

Critiquing patriarchy and negotiating gender relations in the postcolonial African nation-state is a process in which male and female African novelists and filmmakers are actively taking part. The notion of "national identity" will always be a contested terrain, challenged in particular by those on the margins of society, including women. When Shohat (2003, 54) states that "[a]ny serious discussion of feminist cinema must engage the complex question of the 'national'," she calls for a style of feminist film- and video-making that challenges the masculinist contours of the "nation." Shohat argues that any definition of nationalism must take class, gender and sexuality into account and must allow for racial difference and cultural heterogeneity to emerge. Within this dynamic movement, any simplistic or static idea of the nation must be abandoned in favour of viewing the nation as an evolving, imaginary construct rather than an "originary essence." The negotiation of national identity becomes a complex process that has to take into account the multiplicity and intersectionality of various subject and identity positionings. Shohat further argues that in film such a perspective would result in cinematic forms that expose the fissures in essentialist views of gender, class, ethnicity and race (55). Similarly, Nnaemeka writes that the "motherland" trope in nationalist mythologies hides the traumas, disruptions and ambiguities of personal and collective stories. Filmmaking by African women can fill in the gaps in these "official" and dominant nationalist ideologies, with women becoming agents of change, actively participating in alternative forms of nation building and historiography (1997, 2).

Female African filmmakers are taking part in (re)constructing the nation and redefining nationalism, and they have done so since the beginnings of filmmaking on the continent. The role of women in the African liberation struggles has been well documented by female filmmakers. Sarah Maldoror's *Sambizanga* (Angola, 1972), set during the Angolan war for independence, prioritises female experiences of the liberation struggle as a woman, Maria, goes on a journey in search of her imprisoned husband. This physical journey also leads to the awakening of her own political consciousness. In Algerian director Assia Djebar's *La Nouba des femmes du Mont Chenoua* (Algeria, 1979), a young woman, Lila, returns to her homeland 15 years after the end of the Algerian war to interview communities of women and listen to their stories of resilience, strength and anti-colonial resistance. Deborah May's documentary *You Have Struck a Rock!* (South Africa, 1981) describes the history of nonviolent resistance by Black South African women to the use of the notorious and much-hated passbook imposed by the apartheid government. Ingrid Sinclair's *Flame* (Zimbabwe, 1996) is the first fiction feature film from Zimbabwe to deal with the role of women in the Zimbabwean liberation struggle – a protracted war that lasted from 1964 to 1979 – as two young girls decide to join the struggle as guerilla fighters. We reflect further on these representations of revolutionary women in Chapter 4.

More recently, Ateyyat El Abnoudy's *Days of Democracy* (Egypt, 1996) traces the role of women in the 1995 Egyptian parliamentary elections. Fanta Régina Nacro's *La nuit de la vérité/The Night of Truth* (Burkina Faso, 2004) is a fiction feature film that deals with national reconstruction after years of interethnic conflict between two fictional West African tribes, centralising the diverse roles that women play in nation-building. In Taghreed Elsanhouri's documentary *Our Beloved Sudan* (2012), a nation's troubled history is told through the story of mixed-race family. Mixed-race and hybrid identities problematise any simplistic or homogenous understanding of the nation, as the next section shows.

From nationalism to transnationalism

In the quest to define the (largely postcolonial) history of African cinema on its own terms, the transnational nature of cinema has been neglected by scholars and historians of African film in favour of a cultural and historical relativism that focuses on individual auteurs and national(ist) freedoms and limitations. However, when studying all aspects of film – from the training and approaches of its filmmakers, through funding, production and dissemination, to themes, genres and styles – we need to look beyond the national cinemas of the continent, not only in a pan-African but also in a manifestly transnational way. In fact, African cinema has been transnational in nature since the very beginning, even in colonial times, and increasing globalisation, travel and migration, digital de-territorialisation and post-national identity formation, necessitate a thinking beyond the limitations of the nation. Transnational cinema focuses on the interactions and encounters, some-times conflicting, between two or more cultures, ethnicities, or nationalities. When it comes to women's concerns, transnational feminism likewise presents a theore-tical lens that utilises the shifts within monolithic notions of national identity, in order to forge transnational connections between female identities, relations and experiences. Such an approach goes against the notion that one type of feminism can be seen as global or universal – something earlier waves of Western feminism have been accused of – and instead proposes that feminist philosophies and activism from different parts of the world could productively inform each other.

Through an emphasis on the effects of globalisation on people across nations, ethnicities, races, genders, classes, generations and sexualities, transnational femin-ism is inherently intersectional. Drawing on postcolonial feminist theories, trans-national feminists such as Inderpal Grewal, Caren Kaplan and Chandra Talpade Mohanty argue that legacies of racism, White privilege, colonialism and oppression continue to shape the social, economic and political oppression of people across the world, while emphasising that gender inequality manifests itself differently in varying contexts and locations. Where and when necessary, transnational feminism speaks against White feminism and its collusion with racism and imperialism, highlighting the specificity of gendered and racialised experiences while simultaneously striving for feminist solidarity, exchange and collaboration. Transnational feminism recognises the importance of feminist networks that reach across the borders of nation-states, as promoted, for instance, by the UN women's conferences from the 1970s onwards. Indeed, the UN women's conference held in Mexico City in 1975, at which 1976–1985 was designated as the UN Decade for Women, brought together for the first time, feminist activists and scholars from across the globe (more about this in Chapter 3). It is essential that African feminism should be part of this transnational feminist dialogue, even if it was crucial for African feminist scholars to firstly define African feminism on their own terms (as we showed in Chapter 1).

On the level of individual identity, a transnational positioning is often embedded in the experiences of African filmmakers and in the stories they tell. Many have studied and worked temporarily or settled permanently in locations different from the original home countries, or have always had multiple origins, as in the case of mixed-race filmmakers with origins from both inside and outside of Africa. These multiple and complex layers of experiences, influences, identities and backgrounds inevitably influence filmmaking practices and approaches. Ellerson (2015, 5) shows how the increased migration of Africans to North America for study and work, coupled with the coming-of-age of Africans born and/or raised within African diasporas in the West, have resulted in changing dynamics in the construction of identities. The exploration of dual identity in African women's films has a long history, since Safi Faye's *La passante* (1972), in which a young Senegalese woman deals with cultural alienation on her arrival in France. Despite our privileging of transnational identities and cinematic practices, we also need to acknowledge that the national does not simply disappear as we move towards the transnational. Indeed, for some filmmakers the national remains the more familiar framework for the production and consumption of their films. While some women filmmakers inhabit striking transnational characteristics in their personal backgrounds, their chosen themes and narratives, and their approaches to film production, others work within a firmly national context.

Experiences of complex identity positions that span nations and cultures are reflected upon in the lives and work of filmmakers such as French/Burkinabe Sarah Bouyain (whose feature film, *Notre étrangère/The Place in Between*, is analysed below) and French/Moroccan Souad El-Bouhati (whose film *Française/French Girl* is discussed below as well), French/Algerian Assia Djebar, German/Egyptian Viola Shafik, French/Tunisian Nadia El Fani, French/Congolese Pauline Mulombe, Paris-based Rwandan Jacqueline Kalimunda, French/Ivorian Isabelle Boni-Claverie, Welsh/Nigerian Branwen Okpako, French/Congolese Claude Haffner, French/Senegalese Mati Diop, world traveller Jihan El-Tahri, Ghanaian/American Frances Bodomo and Akosua Adoma Owusu, and many others. The hybridity of these identities is manifest in their films as well, with themes of identity fragmentation, the pains and gains of a positioning marked by liminality and interstitiality, and the complex quest for belonging and home. Ellerson (2017) points out that these transnational positionalities and their influence on filmmaking styles and practices relate to Hamid Naficy's concept of "accented cinema" (2001). Naficy's accented cinema describes exilic, diasporic and postcolonial filmmaking, and the tension between homeland and host land is central to his understanding of the exilic, transnational filmmaker. According to him, political idealism, nostalgia and economic motivations lie at the basis of the filmmakers' lived experience and their concerns in their films. Living, working and dreaming in the interstices between host land and homeland prompts them to navigate a "third space," as proposed by Homi K. Bhabha (2004, 55). For Naficy, establishing this third space "goes beyond the sum of its binary antecedents of homeland and host society," as it creates an alternative that bears resemblances to the homeland and the host society, while also being utterly different and new (2001, 220). Our selected case studies exemplify these in-between positionalities and identities, as they both deal with exile, diaspora, return, belonging, bi- or multilingualism, the interracial family, and mixed-race identity. These are, indeed, some of the most prominent themes that occur in the accented films of transnational female African filmmakers.

Case study: *Notre étrangère/The Place in Between* (Sarah Bouyain, France/Burkina Faso, 2010)

Sarah Bouyain's feature film *Notre étrangère/The Place in Between* (2010) was presented in competition at the 2011 FESPACO film festival, where it won two awards. The film's narrative draws on the director's own transnational positionality, providing clear autobiographical references. Bouyain was born in France and is a mixed-race writer and director with a Burkinabe father and a French mother (a parental heritage she reverses in the film). Bouyain has explained in interviews that she is the granddaughter of a mixed-raced woman and her first film, the documentary *Les enfants du blanc/Children of the White Man* (2000), explores the story of her grandmother, the daughter of a French soldier and a kidnapped African woman. Bouyain has described her heritage as dual mixed-race, which is where her affinity for Burkina Faso derives from. While she grew up in France, her father, who intended to return to Burkina Faso, spoke about his home country continuously. This significantly shaped the social location of her work. She acknowledges that she might project in her films a certain non-specific fantasy of "Africa" that grew out of her father's eternal wish for return (Ellerson 2011). Thus, the oscillation between the country of origin and the adopted host country leads to an interstitiality, an in-betweenness of being suspended between two cultures, as the title of the film indicates.

The Place in Between is a gentle, quiet and intimately female-focused film, with very few male characters, as it depicts the physical and emotional proximity between its female protagonists. It centres around Amy (Dorylia Calmel), a young mixed-race woman living in Paris with her French family – her White stepmother and half-brother – who plans to return to Bobo-Dioulasso in Burkina Faso after the death of her White French father, in order to reunite with her Burkinabe mother from whom she was separated when she was eight years old. On her return to Burkina Faso she encounters a culture she feels alienated from, exacerbated by the fact that she finds her mother's compound deserted and dilapidated, with only her aunt there, who does not recognise her at first and with whom she cannot communicate. Amy's story is juxtaposed, through parallel editing, with that of her mother Mariam (Assita Ouédraogo), a middle-aged Burkinabe woman who works as a cleaner in France and develops a friendship with Esther, a White French woman whom she teaches Dyula, Mariam's native language. The complex cultural connections between Burkina Faso and France, between Africa, Europe and its diasporas, form the broader historical backdrop to a deeply personal and intimate story of alienation, estrangement and the search for belonging. The continuous parallel editing, shifting between Amy's point of view – firstly in France and then in Burkina Faso – and that of her mother working and living in France, follows the physical, emotional and psychological journeys of both women and establishes the connection between them, even though they are physically separated.

The film opens with a silent shot of a woman, whom we later surmise is Amy's mother, Mariam, arriving at work at dusk. Her presence in the early morning deserted office block where she works as a cleaner emphasises her solitude and isolation, as she works alone and changes from jeans back into an African dress once her shift is finished. This scene then cuts to our introduction to Amy, as we learn that Amy has a desire to travel to Burkina Faso to reunite with her African mother. Very little is known about Amy's mother: her half-brother Elliot says he thought she was not spoken about because she was dead. In addition to Amy's impending physical journey, a map of Africa on her bedroom wall gives another hint at her inner identity search. Amy's desire to reconnect with her African heritage causes concern in her French family, especially her stepmother, as her half-brother tells their mother: "She's afraid of hurting us, especially you."

While Amy clearly enjoys the embrace of a loving family in France, as a mixed-race woman separated from her biological African mother as a child, she does not find full belonging with them, prompting her search. Mariam, on the other hand, is clearly an outsider in France, living almost invisibly on the margins of a society that does not accept her. We observe a disturbing racist incident when a White man pushes her on a station platform, and the camera often lingers on her face that carries an expression of sadness. Mariam lives in a women's hostel and shares a room with another African immigrant. Their bedroom walls are covered with photos, pictures and letters from loved ones they left behind: nostalgic visual markers of the life of an outsider in a hostile and culturally alienating environment. The hostel is a prototypical Third Space, an in-between, temporary and indeterminate place marked by the pain of exile, and inhabitants clutching onto memories of home. Mariam's solitude is alleviated by her developing friendship with Esther, a manager in the office block where she works. She starts teaching Esther Dyula and beyond the language lessons they also start sharing more about their lives, and their similar life journeys of both being unmarried and childless. In a particularly poignant exchange, Mariam explains to Esther that a greeting in Dyula always has to be accompanied by an extended enquiry into the wellbeing of one's mother, daughter, husband and so on, but only if one has these familial connections. Mariam longingly looks at photos on Esther's walls – black and white snapshots of her as a child. Indeed, photographs as repositories of memories play a crucial role in how we construct our individual and social identities.

Mariam's cultural and social alienation in France is echoed by Amy's experiences when she arrives in Bobo-Dioulasso. Her first stop is at a tailor where she changes into an African dress and loosens her hair, clearly wishing to reconnect with the outward African part of her identity. On the back of a moped we are introduced to the new environment through her eyes: the camera follows her eyeline as she observes the everyday scenes of people, animals and life on the street. Upon her arrival at her mother's old compound she encounters two women – one is her aunt, Acita, who does not recognise her at first, and the other a young girl, Kadiatou, who was taken in by Acita when she was rejected by her father's new wife after her mother's death. Amy's first reaction is to run away from the compound, going back to her hotel, distraught. When she returns to the compound, she greets her aunt who welcomes her warmly in an emotional reunion, and calls her Aminata, a return to her African name highlighting Amy's dual identity. Amy does not speak Dyula and cannot understand her aunt, but the young Kadiatou acts as their interpreter and Amy learns that her mother left for France a long time ago. As Amy attempts to learn more about her mother's departure, the language barrier causes frustration and emotional distance as it becomes clear that her aunt is hiding some facts and that Kadiatou is not translating everything fully. Nonetheless, they grow closer when Amy suffers a bout of diarrhoea (as travellers in new environments often do) and is cared for by her aunt and Kadiatou.

Amy's estrangement from the Burkinabe environment and the conflict between her African and European identities is played out, at times humorously, in her changing back and forth between traditional African and casual European dress. Dressed in a t-shirt, slacks and trainers in one scene, a shoe seller calls out "White girl!" (*fille blanche*) to her on the street. Amy's inner conflict is externalised when she trips over her voluminous African dress in a café and is accosted by an older man. Clothing is of course a highly visible and at times significant marker of cultural and group identity, and Amy eventually reaches a compromise by wearing an African-style top combined with tan-coloured slacks, a fusion of fashion symbolic of her dual cultural identity. Clothing is also connected to Mariam's past and identity, as she tells Esther she used to travel a lot, taking the bus to Bamako to buy fabric to bring back to Bobo to sell. Living in France, she has only left Paris once, her world shrunken and lonely. Mariam's solitary life has parallels with her sister Acita's loneliness, who only has the young Kadiatou as company in the abandoned compound, her childlessness and solitude having driven her to alcoholism.

As the familiarity between Amy, her aunt and Kadiatou grows, Amy gradually learns some Dyula, communicates better with Acita and becomes more comfortable in the Burkinabe environment. The film's dual narrative reaches a parallel climax when Esther finally reveals to Mariam that the reason she is learning Dyula is because she is in the process of adopting a child from an orphanage in Banfora (a smaller city about 50 miles from Bobo-Dioulasso). Despite Esther's protests that the child's mother is unable to look after him, Mariam is outraged, the revelation clearly opening the emotional wound of her own lost daughter. "I wish I could take back every word I taught you" she tells Esther. In Burkina Faso, Amy finally confronts her aunt about the truth of her mother's departure, leading to a tense confrontation between them, visualised through rapid shot reverse shot close-ups. Acita tells Amy that her mother was not well shortly after Amy's birth, longing for news of her husband in France. When Amy's father sent for her from France, Mariam let her go with the blessing of her family, but she fell apart and eventually disappeared, bringing shame onto the family and tearing them apart. This emotional revelation leads to a reconciliation between Amy and her aunt, and, with the introduction to a friend of Amy's father who can help her locate her mother in France, the scene is set for a potential mother-daughter reunion and the start of a journey of healing. While the film does not offer an explicit happy ending, there is visual closure through the film ending exactly as it began – Amy's mother, Mariam, arriving at work in the early morning and changing into her work clothes. She observes herself fleetingly in the mirror, with a changed expression, as if she is seeing herself differently, for the first time. Both women's journeys are continuing – Amy had to leave France and travel to Burkina Faso to reconnect with the African part of her identity, and, paradoxically, to get closer to her African mother who now lives in Paris.

The mother-daughter relationship, marked by presence and absence, is central to the film. The alternating narrative structure through which Amy and Mariam's stories unfold, visualises the biological and psychological connection between them while also emphasising their separation. The importance of motherhood is underscored in Amy's close relationship with her stepmother, in Esther's desire to adopt a baby, and in Amy's childless aunt who raised her as a young girl and later welcomed the abandoned Kadiatou as a surrogate daughter. The importance of motherhood, so often valorised in an African cultural context, is also emphasised when Acita attends a ceremony for a new-born baby but sits to the side, physically marginalised and removed from the young mothers. "Children are a woman's wealth," declares a male visitor, while Acita looks on wistfully. In the emotional climax of the film, Acita reveals to Amy that her childlessness drove her to desperate measures, even visiting a witch doctor in search for solutions. The fractured relationships between and the absence of mothers and daughters, are therefore the key themes of the film, but ultimately the narrative points towards female relationships forged not only by biological, but also by social, cultural and emotional ties, through – as we argue in Chapter 5 – a transformed ability to communicate effectively across generations.

Language and communication are central tropes in the film, represented through Amy's inability to communicate with her aunt in Dyula, forcing them to understand each other through body language and facial expressions. Mariam seems more at ease with bilingualism, although when she teaches Esther Dyula, at some point she needs to search for the correct translation of a French word into Dyula, indicating a loss of language, a common experience for the bilingual expat or migrant. Presumably Amy spoke Dyula as a child but having left Burkina Faso for France at eight years old, she has entirely forgotten her mother tongue. Language and identity are closely connected, language serving not only to express but also to construct identity. The close connection between language, culture and identity is evident in that culture and language shape one's social and individual identity. Indeed, language can be seen as a verbal expression of culture, conveying cultural ties and social belonging. As Amy and Acita gradually overcome the communication barriers between them, as their emotional bond grows, she also starts to learn some Dyula, making tentative steps towards reconnecting with a forgotten language and a lost past.

The two main protagonists in the film, Amy and Mariam, carry multiple identities that inform their subjectivity and positionality, ranging from their intimate relationships (as daughter, mother, sister, niece, friend and so on), to their social and cultural positioning, both being migrants, and Amy being mixed-race. Both of their identities are suspended between two cultures, offering them multiple places of belonging or being an outsider. This in-betweenness could be a source of productive cultural hybridity but also of great inner conflict and fragmentation, described by African American writer W.E.B. Du Bois as a "double consciousness" (1994). As this analysis shows, this double consciousness impacts considerably on the way one constructs one's identity, how one views oneself and how one builds relationships with others. Reconciling and reconstructing several aspects of one's identity in the face of immense heterogeneity is a recurring theme in African women's cinema. Living in-between two cultures often leads to being simultaneously insider and outsider, of remaining a stranger in both spaces, and of constructing a Third Space. In *The Place in Between* both director Sarah Bouyain and the character Amy, as mixed-race women, also pose questions about what it means to be African or to claim Africanness as part of one's identity. An authentic African identity, the film says, is elusive. The multiplicity of Bouyain's identity is emphasised in an autobiographical detail she inserted in the film's French title – *notre étrangère* translates as the paradoxical phrase "our foreigner," which, Bouyain reveals, is what her mixed-race grandmother called her as a child (Ellerson 2011).

Case study: *Française/French Girl* (Souad El-Bouhati, France/ Morocco, 2008)

Franco-Moroccan filmmaker Souad El-Bouhati (b. 1962) started her career as a social worker and became a script assistant. She graduated in film directing from the Sorbonne in Paris and worked for the production company Movimento. *Française* (2008) is her debut feature film. As in *The Place in Between*, the filmmaker has borrowed autobiographical elements as inspiration for the film. Like her protagonist in *Française*, El-Bouhati was born in France and she based the inspiration for the story of her feature film on an experience from her childhood: the sudden disappearance of a friend with Algerian origins and the responses she received when she asked where the friend had gone. People told her "she has returned home," but as far as El-Bouhati was concerned, France was her home. This puzzle regarding her identity and her belonging stuck with her. Hafsia Herzi, the main actress in the film, has gone through similar experiences. She says: "A journalist recently asked me if I was 'integrated'. Into what? I am French" (Moutaatarif 2008). Herzi is very proud of her Tunisian-Algerian background, as evidenced by the Tunisian, Iraqi, Moroccan and Algerian identities she has taken on in film, but she is, like Sofia in the film, a *Française* first and foremost.

The physical and emotional journey that people of Maghrebi backgrounds go through in France is the subject of a prolific type of filmmaking, Beur cinema. The opposite journey, the one from France back to the so-called "Bled" or home country is likewise a popular narrative in Beur cinema. But *Française*, being a rare example of Beur cinema by a woman, challenges stereotypes that are usually subscribed to in Beur cinema. Beur narratives usually show the extremely complex process of integration, whereas Sofia feels entirely French from the start. The "Bled" is usually a space for a rite of passage, leading to the conclusion that France is the absolute home. *Française*, however, offers a spectrum of attitudes towards France and Morocco and a plurality of meanings for concepts like "home" and "abroad". It explores Sofia's identity as a transnational rather than a national one.

The plot shows us the early life of Sofia (Hafsia Herzi), with Moroccan parents, who spends a happy childhood in a small provincial French city, until she is suddenly torn away from her school and friends one day, when her parents force her into the car and drive off into the night. Barely thirteen minutes in, the film shows the cruelty of subjecting an unsuspecting child to the traumatic process of displacement. Before this though, numerous references have already been made to Sofia's multiple identity: during a lesson on Africa, the teacher tells the class that one of them, Sofia, is from Africa. Questioning faces look at her and Sofia is clearly displeased with this assertion, as her friend Elodie asks "That's where you're from? So what are you then, African, French, Moroccan or Arab?" Tellingly, Sofia refuses to answer the question. Increasingly she notices her mother and father are unhappy and depressed. Her father hardly speaks. Recently unemployed, he feels useless. Meanwhile, Sofia's mother reprimands her when she innocently talks about her grandparents' country as "their" place: "It's your country too. You come from the land of your ancestors." The parents suffer from increasing homesickness while Sofia takes refuge in her studies and friends, trying to ignore her family's bitter reality. The reality of her parents' depression and nostalgia hits hard when she is forcefully taken from her home to Morocco. Ten years on, as the films jumps ahead, Sofia is nearing adulthood and divides her time between working alongside her father on the farm and her studies. She takes both very seriously: working the fields and olive groves allows her to keep busy and escape domestic work, while studying lends focus on the future: taking her baccalaureate, to be able to return to France, where she is from.

Sofia has a very close bond with her father, Rachid, he is a confidant and a role model. She spends all her time at home with him, making sure he is around as she avoids being alone with her mother. This is, again, a complex relationship where Sofia projects onto her father what she herself longs for: freedom of movement and acceptance of the self. However, Rachid is the person concealing her French passport. He is the one who passively keeps her in Morocco and attempts in plain sight to attach her to his country, by encouraging her bond with the land he works. Sofia's adoration of her father is mocked by her mother, who tells a friend that "Sofia is his favourite child." In Rachid we see the struggle between responsibility and understanding, between forceful parenting and a secret admiration of Sofia's inner strength and determination. He appreciates her stubbornness and her hopeful outlook on her imagined future in France. But he also has the responsibility to explain why he is keeping her passport from her until she comes of age: "Don't you understand, for them we will never be French," showing her his vision of the schism between race and ethnicity, Morocco and France, home and abroad.

While it is her father who hides her passport, it is Sofia's mother, Fouzia, who more strictly wants Sofia to fit in with traditional gender roles. She may be the tomboy on the farm, but Fouzia wants her to take on traditionally gendered domestic tasks. She wants Sofia to marry a Moroccan, like her eldest daughter who conforms more easily to the roles of housewife and fiancée. Surprisingly, it is Fouzia who finally manages to understand Sofia's fervent wish to return "home," and starts to accept it. One evening she overhears Sofia quietly read to herself a poem by Baudelaire: "L'invitation au voyage" from *Les Fleurs du mal*, and it makes her understand her daughter's deep melancholia.

> Mon enfant, ma soeur,
> Songe à la douceur
> D'aller là-bas vivre ensemble!
> Aimer à loisir,
> Aimer et mourir
> Au pays qui te ressemble!

> Think, would it not be
> Sweet to live with me
> All alone, my child, my love?
> Sleep together, share
> All things, in that fair
> Country you remind me of?[1]

The camera turns to her hand, writing in close-up the Arabic translation of this poem. As in *The Place in Between*, language and identity are intertwined, as the Arabic and French language, which she both masters entirely, help to express and construct her multiple identity. Translating this first poem, she marks out her future career. Also, upon hearing Sofia read out the poem so melancholically,

Fouzia is finally able to recognise in her daughter's longing for France the longing she felt to return "home" to Morocco. She recognises Sofia's double consciousness and is finally able to also give her an explanation for her behaviour as she gives Sofia her passport: "I did not think it would be so hard for you. Here we are at home. I did not want to see my kids done wrong."

Sofia gets along well with her brother, who sympathises with her naively but does not understand her plight as a young woman with responsibilities and expectations weighing her down. But both Sofia's siblings have a negative attitude to her intellect: her brother expects her to do his homework, while her sister resents her for "bragging about your classical Arabic" and for being a good student. Echoing her sister, Sofia's friend Touria blames her for "bragging about your lessons, bragging about Amar, and bragging about France." These accusations of bragging trigger a violent reaction in Sofia, and she runs away from the boarding house to enact a foiled escape that reminds of the North African "*harragas*," or illegal migrants.[2] Because she does not have a passport when she sets out for the harbour, her captors assume she is an illegal migrant. Her parents intensify their mission to keep her in Morocco by pushing the arranged marriage. This triggers another crisis: Sofia cuts off her hair and refuses to speak. She mirrors the facial expressions and physical postures of her parents when they were increasingly depressed in France. Communication between all family members breaks down. Sofia only uses her voice when she reads to herself. It is at this point that her mother and father break their silence and return her passport, as they finally see their own desperation for home reflected in her. It is also at this point, when Sofia receives her French passport, that she is able to take her first adult decision.

Just like in *The Place in Between*, the title of the film encloses an internal paradox. The film juxtaposes Sofia's connection to the land with her intellectual nature. As someone with her gaze firmly fixed on the future, she occupies one space in her head (France) but another in her physical reality (Morocco). In France, this is obvious to everyone except herself. As a Maghrebi child, Sofia is marked out by her physical appearance. Yet she performs her Frenchness naturally. As a maturing young adult, she increasingly performs the Frenchness as something that sets her apart. The juxtaposition is that, while performing her Frenchness, she studies classical Arabic, has a Moroccan boyfriend and is intensely connected to the Moroccan landscape. Her double consciousness becomes increasingly visible in her choice of clothes and the way she behaves. Her work on the farm, her loving gaze over the countryside and her care for the land, trees and crops, link her physically with Morocco, but her Frenchness is externalised through the colours she wears, red, white and blue: blue dungarees and white or red t-shirts. Her bandana is equally an expression of a French, even a feminist, position.

It is not only her outward appearance that express her double consciousness. Sofia's mannerisms and habits set her apart from other women as well. The femininity expressed in the title refers to an emancipated identity as a young woman used to knowing what she wants and getting her way. Sofia believes that emancipation comes through education, as shown in the scene where Sofia wants to teach a young

Moroccan worker to read and write so that she can emancipate herself and get a better job. Likewise, instead of walking, Sofia strides and runs. These large strides show her confidence, energy, purpose. She runs towards her future, cannot wait to come of age and return to France, she looks up jobs in France, and moulds her education so that she is certain of jobs in her future. Having found job vacancies in France for translators, she is pragmatic about her double identity: as a translator she can use her Moroccan-ness and her knowledge of the Arabic language to return to France confidently and put her acquired skills to good use.

She also runs away from people and obstructions (indeed, often people are the obstruction): her various attempts to escape are represented in her running away from her mother and jumping into her father's car, in getting out of Amar's car when he asks her to marry him, in jumping from the tractor to escape her duties. The camera is in constant motion, enacting her restlessness. Montages of short and jerky shots accentuate her impatience. But the motif of running stands in opposition to that of the closed gates, doors and windows that trap Sofia in a fixed frame. Whether it is the close-up of her face behind the bars reflected in the windshield of the family car bound for Morocco, or that of the young woman behind the bars of the bathroom window after her botched escape from the boarding house: several suggestive aesthetic frames and lines mimic the bars of the triple prison that encloses Sofia: her Moroccan roots, her status as a woman, and her status as a teenager dependent on her parents' choices.

Slowly but surely the strides she takes and the suggestions of having to escape prisons fade, once she has gained her independence, and she has again visibly chan-ged both her looks and her attitude when she walks out of the city office at the end of the film. Her strides have become steps, her face is smiling, and her whereabouts are ambiguous. She is translating classical Arabic into French in a French-speaking office with an international workforce of White, Black and Arab employees. As Sophia leaves the office, we are left to figure out whether she is in France or in Morocco. We hear the muezzin's call to prayer, see a multitude of styles and fash-ions, and shops with French signs. It could easily be a multicultural city in the south of France. But it is Morocco – the car licence plates finally give it away. Once her freedom, that is to say her independence (from school, parents, the farm, from being stuck without a passport) is won, Sofia fully assumes her life choices and consolidates her complex personality. She has escaped the interstitial space that is the "prison" of dependence and youth, and now that she can make her own decisions, she accepts her double consciousness. It is this Sofia, calmly strolling through the streets smiling, who achieves her hopes and dreams independently, because she has finally come to accept and embrace her complex and multiple identity. Being suspended between two cultures is Sofia's plight, but this burden becomes lighter to carry as she matures and when she emancipates herself as someone who actively decides that she does not have to choose one identity over the other. Throughout the film she uses her cul-tural hybridity to her advantage in a pragmatic and impassioned view of the future, even if this is sometimes unconscious and almost accidental. It becomes increasingly purposeful when she settles down in a self-acceptance that enables her to produc-tively move beyond the uneasy double consciousness.

Souad El-Bouhati transmits through this film a desire to escape the stereotypes of the Arab-African woman. The independence of Moroccan women often passes for an impossible ideal. Sofia studies, has a boyfriend, dreams of escape and freedom. She experiences a deep-seated wish for independence, both as a girl, as a woman and as someone who accepts her multiple identity. Rather than opting for one country or one identity to the detriment of another, she embraces both. The film is above all about finding the freedom to choose; she develops into a young adult able to make a wise and unbiased choice. France is no longer the haven she imagined, nor is being Moroccan a limitation. The ambiguity of the ending is exciting and Sofia's wholehearted acceptance of her multiple identity, her transnational strengths, are optimistic in nature.

★★★★

This consideration of female African identities in film has demonstrated that identity is always complex and plural, constructed from within and from without, and through a multitude of markers such as ethnicity, race, language, class, generation, culture, religion, gender, sexuality and nationality. As shown in these films, for a very diverse range of people with African roots identity has become hybrid and globalised, as many did not grow up in the culture and language of their African ancestral homeland. This multitude of identity markers and positionalities could lead to a conflicting and at times painful process of constructing a unified view of oneself, through a desire to integrate and find belonging. African women of the diaspora often occupy a liminal and marginal position, a transnational existential space, but, in the words of Naficy, "liminality becomes a passionate source of creativity and dynamism" (2001, 208). These women are navigating and negotiated their identities within a Third Space, marked by the interstitiality of simultaneously being an insider and an outsider. As we have seen through the two case studies, embracing this Third Space leads to filmmaking that explores what it means to live in a transnational age, with increased mobility and travel, voluntary or involuntary exile, the formation of diasporas, and a continuous fluctuation of positionality between multiple home and host countries and cultures.

Notes

1 Trans. Edna St. Vincent Millay
2 "*Harragas*" or "burners" is a word describing people from North Africa who burn their identity papers before crossing the Mediterranean towards Europe. Without papers, they cannot be identified officially as Maghrebi or African, and cannot be sent back.

Bibliography

Appiah, Kwame Anthony (1992) *In My Father's House: Africa in the Philosophy of Culture.* Oxford: Oxford University Press.
Armes, Roy (2006) *African Filmmaking North and South of the Sahara.* Edinburgh: Edinburgh University Press.
Barlet, Olivier (1996) *African Cinema: Decolonizing the Gaze.* London: Zed Books Ltd.

Baudelaire, Charles (1936) "Invitation to the voyage." In *Flowers of Evil*. Trans. Edna St. Vincent Millay. New York: Harper and Brothers.

Bhabha, Homi K. (2004) *The Location of Culture*. London and New York: Routledge.

Cobham, Rhonda (1992) "Misgendering the nation: African nationalist fictions and Nuruddin Farah's maps." In Andrew Parker et al. (eds), *Nationalisms and Sexualities*. New York: Routledge.

Cronin, J. (1999) "A Luta dis-continua? The TRC Final Report and the Nation Building Project." *TRC: Commissioning the Past*. Johannesburg: Centre for the Study of Violence and Reconciliation.

Du Bois, W.E.B. (1994) *The Souls of Black Folk*. New York: Gramercy Books.

Ellerson, Beti (2011) "Sarah Bouyain: Notre étrangère/The Place in Between," Interview with Cineuropa, *African Women in Cinema* blog. Available online: http://africanwomenincinema. blogspot.com/2011/02/sarah-bouyain-notre-etrangerethe-place.html [Accessed January 2019].

Ellerson, Beti (2015) "African women in cinema: An overview." In J. Mistry and A. Schuhmann (eds) *Gaze Regimes: Film and Feminisms in Africa*. Johannesburg: Wits University Press, pp. 1–9.

Ellerson, Beti (2017) "Traveling gazes: Glocal imaginaries in the transcontinental, transnational, exilic, migration, and diasporic cinematic experiences of African women," *Black Camera*, 8(2), pp. 272–289.

Guneratne, Anthony R. and Wimal Dissanayake (2003) *Rethinking Third Cinema*. London: Routledge.

Hall, Stuart (1989) "Cultural identity and cinematic representation," *Framework*, 36: 68–81.

Hall, Stuart and Paul du Gay (1996) *Questions of Cultural Identity*. London: Sage.

Mistry, J. and A. Schuhmann (eds) (2015) *Gaze Regimes: Film and Feminisms in Africa*. Johannesburg: Wits University Press.

Moutaatarif, Yasrine (2008) "Une étoile nommée Hafsia," *Le Courrier de l'Atlas*, 16 (June), pp. 76–77.

Naficy, H. (2001) *An Accented Cinema: Exilic and Diasporic Filmmaking*. Princeton: Princeton University Press.

Nnaemeka, Obioma (ed.) (1997a) *The Politics of (M)Othering: Womanhood, Identity, and Resistance in African Literature*. London and New York: Routledge.

Pines, Jim and Paul Willemen (1990) *Questions of Third Cinema*. London: British Film Institute.

Shohat, Ella (1991) "Gender and culture of empire: Toward a feminist ethnography of the cinema," *Quarterly Review of Film and Video*, 13(1–3), pp. 45–84.

Shohat, Ella (2003) "Post-Third-Worldist culture. Gender, Nation and the Cinema." In A. Guneratne and W. Dissanayake (eds) *Rethinking Third Cinema*. London: Routledge, pp. 51–78.

Filmography

Aïta, Dir. Izza Génini, Morocco, 1988

Brown, Dir. Kali van der Merwe, South Africa, 2004

Days of Democracy, Dir. Ateyyat El Abnoudy, Egypt, 1996

En attendant les hommes / Waiting for Men, Dir. Katy Léna N'diaye, Belgium/Senegal, 2007

Flame, Dir. Ingrid Sinclair, Zimbabwe, 1996

Française / French Girl, Dir. Souad El-Bouhati, France/Morocco, 2008

I, Afrikaner, Dir. Annalet Steenkamp, South Africa, 2013

La Nouba des femmes du Mont Chenoua, Dir. Assia Djebar, Algeria, 1979

La nuit de la vérité / The Night of Truth, Dir. Fanta Régina Nacro, Burkina Faso/France, 2004

La passante, Dir. Safi Faye, Senegal, 1972

Mixed Space, Dir. Zara Julius, South Africa, 2017

Notre étrangère / The Place in Between, Dir. Sarah Bouyain, France/Burkina Faso, 2010

Our Beloved Sudan, Dir. Taghreed Elsanhouri, Sudan/UK, 2012

Pour la nuit / For the Night, Dir. Isabelle Boni-Claverie, France, 2004

Sambizanga, Dir. Sarah Maldoror, Angola/France, 1972

Selbé et tant d'autres / Selbe: One Among Many, Dir Safi Faye, Senegal, 1983

Sous la clarté de la lune / Under the Moonlight, Dir. Apolline Traoré, Burkina Faso, 2004

Traces, empreintes de femmes / Traces, Women's Imprints, Dir. Katy Léna N'diaye, Belgium, 2003

Trop noire pour être française? / Too Black to be French?, Dir. Isabelle Boni-Claverie, France, 2015

Valley of the Innocent, Dir. Branwen Okpako, Germany, 2003

You Have Struck a Rock!, Dir. Deborah May, South Africa, 1981

3

FEMALE FRIENDSHIPS IN FILM

Affinities, affiliations and activism

The 2018 blockbuster *Black Panther,* directed by Ryan Coogler and based on a Marvel comic, was hailed as a breakthrough superhero film because of its representation of Black and African characters. The film centralises Black characters and experiences, so often marginalised in comics and superhero films, and it also, importantly, features a strong army of female warriors, the fictional Dora Milaje, or "adored ones." There is in fact a historical antecedent to this army of female warriors in the women fighters of the African Kingdom of Dahomey. Located in present-day Benin, the Kingdom existed from the 1600s until 1894 when the region was colonised by France (Maggs 2018, 108). The Dahomey Amazons, so named by French explorers who compared them to the warriors of Greek mythology, represent the idea of a political system in which men and women control political and military institutions jointly, and African historians have argued that this system can be found in the true history of precolonial African reality, only later distorted by colonial intervention (Coleman 2018). We know from historical accounts that the Dahomey warriors trained through intense physical exercise, learnt survival skills and indifference to pain and death, and were extremely disciplined (Dash 2011). In a predominantly patriarchal world, these fierce women warriors have continued to capture imaginations and, despite the brutality of a military regime that focused on violent expansion and practiced slavery, the Dahomey Amazons stand as a symbol of female solidarity, bravery and strength.

Such historical, fictional and mythological examples of the power, independence and influence of groups of women draw attention to the fact that women's identities are not only dependent on the formation of the self, or in relation to a male partner. We are interested in representations that challenge and problematise heteronormativity, that reject the notion that female identity is predominantly forged through a relation to men. In this chapter, we explore female affinities and affiliations in their many manifestations: female friendships, communities, activism, movements, alliances and transnational connections, in incidental, formal and informal settings. The chapter also investigates the communities of women on-screen and asks whether these are defined by a matrilineal past or tradition, by a coincidental absence of men or by a deliberate prioritising of female relationships. Female friendships and affiliations exist across all cultures and religions, in the form of sororities, sisterhoods, covens, assemblies, networks and, as we saw in the examples above, even armies. Thus, we want to explore the multiple communal and societal ties of African women as represented on-screen, and while we are mostly interested in the positive and affirmative manifestations of these relations, we acknowledge that female affiliations are complex and can at times also be destructive and harmful. We also argue that negative depictions or views of female relationships are often informed by patriarchal and misogynist agendas. African women have formed affinities of friendship, intimacy and care that often play out in the private and domestic sphere, but they have also formed powerful alliances in the public sphere to promote women's rights, fight oppression, colonisation and apartheid, influence politics, challenge patriarchal cultural norms, and enhance women's social and economic emancipation and independence.

Critical and theoretical work on fictional and factual narratives of female friendships is abundant, especially in Euro-American spheres. There is, however, less academic work on friendships between women of colour, with Renée Larrier's work on the representations of female friendship in francophone Africa and the Caribbean (1993) being one of the first studies of female friendship in African and Caribbean women's fiction. Larrier's work draws attention to the "best friend" character (for which there is a special word, *kawaye*, in Hausa) that is often found in African women's literature (1993, 181). She shows that depictions of relationships between co-wives and intergenerational mentoring are common in oral and written African narratives, emphasising the mutuality and reciprocity evident in women's friendships (ibid, 182). Werewere Liking and Marie-José Hourantier's *Contes d'initiation féminine du pays bassa* (1981), which translates as "female initiation tales," is a seminal text of female friendship, consisting of two stories told by Bassa women exclusively for female audiences. Representations of female friendship have also been discussed in relation to film, even if to a lesser extent than in literature, but again, there is a dearth of critical work on female friendship in African film.

In what follows we outline some of the existing theorisation of female friendships, followed by a section on female filmic affiliations and finally, an overview of female political activism and women's movements, informed by filmic examples. The chapter then continues with two case studies of films with affinities and friendships at the heart of their narratives.

Theorising female friendship

Female solidarity has been at the heart of many feminist movements, with an emphasis on women's friendships based in principles of equality rather than the inequalities evident in patriarchal heteronormative – heteropatriarchal – structures

(Okech 2013, 19). Sasha Roseneil (2006, 322) describes how friendships have been fundamental to feminist politics, identities and communities, and argues that this focus on female friendship within feminist theory could be seen as a "radical challenge" to the heteronormativity of most social science theory. Roseneil goes as far as to say that "[w]ithout powerful, chosen bonds of affection and care between women, feminism would be unthinkable, women's movements impossible, everyday life in inhospitable environments lonely" (ibid). Women's same-sex friendships and ties of affection, solidarity and support are thus a crucial part of rethinking and transforming gender roles and relations. As evident in feminist movements, we argue that female friendship is also embedded in political solidarity between women, and powerful feminist movements have formed through the belief in a shared collective goal.

Feminism has evolved from the notion of a global "sisterhood" to a privileging of solidarity as main uniting principle (Okech 2013, 2). This development reveals a critique of Western feminist movements that ignore or underplay the racial and class differences that often sharply shape the experiences and livelihoods of women of colour. The concept of solidarity is argued by feminists of colour like bell hooks and Chandra Talpade Mohanty to be strategically more useful and powerful than the idea of a sisterhood based on likeness and similarity merely because of one's female gender. The roots and basis of oppression are not the same for all women, as intersectional and transnational feminism have shown us. Patricia Hill Collins identifies three safe spaces for Black women; "social spaces where Black women speak freely" (2000, 100). One of these safe spaces is within Black women's relationships with one another, in informal settings as well as more formal and public spaces. While these feminists make us aware of the importance of recognising and acknowledging the differences between and nuances of lived experience, networks based on solidarity also enable us to seek affinities across socio-cultural conditions and various intersections of identities. Black feminists in particular argue against the idea of a shared global sisterhood and point out that there are many different ways of finding solidarity. The work of these feminists, Okech argues, shows us that "[t]he inner bond that would naturally lead to solidary was not a pregiven, stable phenomenon, [...] but should be constructed in practical political struggles" (Okech 2013, 2). These political struggles are transformative, context-specific and adaptable, just as the ideal of solidarity is not an essentialist perspective that sees all women as connected through an "inner bond." Just as hooks argued that solidarity needs to be a sustained, ongoing commitment, Mohanty's transnational feminist approach requires solidarity to be established through practice and lived experience. Feminist politics become a politics of coalition building, affinity and partnership.

Despite these positive attributes, representations of female friendships and relationships have often focused on jealousy and competition between women, in Africa for instance within the social context of polygamous marriages. This is evident in the patriarchal misogynist myth that women are each other's worst enemies. A well-known example of an African film on this theme would be Sembène's *Xala* (Senegal, 1975), in which the main male character is shown to marry a third, very young wife, to the chagrin of his older, traditional first wife and modern, materialistic second wife. These three wives represent archetypal characters, lacking nuance and dimension. Similarly, Nigerian director Blessing Egbe's *The Women* (2017) follows the events that occur when a group of four women and their male partners go on a weekend getaway for a birthday party. The film's tagline, "where two or three women are gathered, there is war," regenerates a stereotypical narrative of female competition, jealousy and strife. We would like to move beyond the notion of female conflict, however, in order to focus on the positive and productive aspects of female friendship, and a focus away from the dominant tendency in mainstream cinema worldwide to show women primarily in relation to men, amongst the legion of films that reach their narrative conclusions by heteronormativity, and heterosexual coupling, being restored.

Critics have shown that lifelike and true representations of women's relationships, friendship and female bonding in film are rare, whereas male "buddy" movies are an established well-loved genre (Donahue 2016; McGill 2018). Given the general underrepresentation of female characters and filmmakers, it is not surprising that cinema has also underrepresented interaction between female characters. Prioritising female characterisation, representation and relationships is central to the Bechdel Test, popularised by Alison Bechdel's comic *Dykes to Watch Out For* (1983) (www.bechdeltest.com). This test requires a film to have at least two women in it, who talk to each other about something other than a man. Despite the simplicity of the rules of the test, it remains astonishing how many films fail the test. It is also revelatory to note that films that do pass the test are overwhelmingly written and directed by women, as shown in most of the case studies contained in this book.

The Bechdel Test challenges a heteronormative worldview that regards women only in relation to men. Representations of bonds of friendship and intimacy between women take the focus away from the nuclear family and the heterosexual couple as the foundation of social organisation. It draws attention to the fact that networks of care and support exist outside of the family, and thus female friendships can challenge, transgress and indeed threaten heteronormativity. Meg Rickards's feature film *Tess* (South Africa, 2016), is an example of a narrative that focuses on the affirmative aspects of female friendship and solidarity. Based on the novel *Whiplash* by South African author Tracey Farren, it tells the story of Tess, a feisty twenty-year-old woman who makes a living as a prostitute in Cape Town. Destitute and desperate, she suffers horrendous abuse and violence at the hands of multiple men, but it is the supportive community of women that offers salvation from her oppressive circumstances, lifts her out of poverty and abuse when she unexpectedly falls pregnant, and aids her in her spiritual and physical healing. Crucially, her redemption is shown not to lie in heterosexual coupling or in family ties but in female friendship. Our case studies at the end of this chapter, Apolline Traoré's *Frontières/Borders* (Burkina Faso, 2017) and Rayhana's *À mon âge je me cache encore pour fumer/I Still Hide to Smoke* (Algeria, 2017) offer further examples of films that prioritise and centralise strong female friendships and solidarity.

Anthropologists and historians have found that many African societies have been inherently matrilineal in structure and kinship organisation, offering historical examples of powerful females such as Queen Nefertiti of Egypt, Queen Makeda of Ethiopia, Queen Candace Amanirenas of Nubia, and the Rain Queen Modjadji of South Africa, arguing that it is the introduction of Islam and Christianity and the advent of colonialism that imposed patriarchal rule (Moloi 2012). There are historical examples of both matrilineal and matriarchal social organisations in various African contexts, and contemporary women's movements in Africa often find their roots in these indigenous women's strategies, as well as in women's collective action in anti-colonial and liberation struggles, as we discuss in Chapter 4. As our outline of African feminisms in Chapter 1 reveals, a significant new development from the mid-2000s onwards was that women's rights activists in Africa increasingly began to refer to themselves as feminists, even if, as Badri and Tripp explain (2017, 4), many female activists still do not self-identify as feminists, because of a prevailing prejudice against what is perceived as a Western import and an anti-men stance. This reluctance to self-identify as feminist is, however, rapidly changing as younger generations of African women are redefining and reclaiming feminism on African terms, as evident from the Charter of Feminist Principles for African Feminists formulated during a 2006 gathering of African women in Accra, Ghana. Women have been organising themselves politically, socially and culturally for centuries, igniting and sustaining worldwide women's liberation movements with a multitude of local manifestations in specific socio-political and cultural contexts. At the heart of these women's liberation movements lie political affinities, shared solidarities and, indeed, female friendships and networks of support and care, as the following two sections will show.

Filmic affiliations

On 11 November 2018 300 women gathered at Constitution Hill in Johannesburg (a former prison complex now converted into a museum memorialising South Africa's troubled past), as part of the Joburg Film Festival. Their aim was to talk about gender disparities in the South African film industry, and to create a space for women to engage with issues of gender inequality in the film, television and cultural landscape of South Africa. A spokesperson for Sisters Working in Film and Television (SWIFT), Zoe Ramushu, said of the gathering:

> The conversation around diversity is not a new one but because of the joint effort women across Africa and around the world have put in, it has become "the conversation". Because we work in such a visible industry it's important that they lead the conversation and keep it in the spotlight. Every movement has its time and our time is now.
>
> (Joburg Film Festival 2018)

We believe that affiliations and networking between women is a crucial part of addressing gender inequalities, in both private and public domains, in order to strengthen capacity, share skills, information and expertise, and mobilise change. The development of women's organisations, structures and networks to support and expand funding, training, production, distribution and exhibition opportunities is essential for building more gender equal film industries. There are many examples of female affiliations in the African film industries, as we showed in the introduction, from the historic FESPACO women's gathering of 1991 which led to the founding of the National Union of Women Working in Film in Burkina (UNAFIB), to the African Women in Film Forum (AWIFF) and Women Filmmakers of Zimbabwe (WFoZ), both established in the 2000s, African branches of the international organisation Women in Film and Television (WIFT), and the more recent SWIFT in South Africa, the Ladima Foundation and the African Women Filmmakers Hub. All these organisations address the underrepresentation of women in the African film industries in a variety of ways and by prioritising specific approaches, such as capacity building through training and mentorship schemes, nurturing and shaping creative ideas and script development through dedicated support structures, mobilising or leveraging funding, or offering production and distribution support and advice. Often these affiliations aim to establish infrastructures for national, regional, continental and international networking and support, bolstered by a public agenda or manifesto. In patriarchal societies where women are often neglected or silenced by men in the workplace, it is crucial that safe and supportive female-dominated spaces are created and maintained.

As with many grassroots, self-regulated and self-directed cultural or political movements worldwide, the sustainability of these female networks is often precarious, leading to many of these initiatives having limited lifespans, periodically appearing, disappearing and sometimes reappearing. This is a major challenge to small, often non-hierarchical and democratically organised women's movements with limited funding and support from official channels or substantial donors or funders. Women founding and spearheading these initiatives regularly do so voluntarily, juggling a number of different personal and career roles and responsibilities. Public funders or donors and potential corporate sponsors demand professionalism and a convincing track record, which can be difficult for organisations to achieve, especially ones that emerge out of voluntary and passionate efforts. Representatives of these organisations and networks could make recommendations for addressing gender inequality in the African film industries, and regularly do so at public panel discussions and events. However, real political will and financial commitment are necessary for economic, regulatory, legal and cultural frameworks to transform in favour of film industries that practise equality of opportunity across gender, class, race, sexuality and ability. All the while it is crucial that these issues remain high on public agendas and that women's coalitions, networks and affiliations in the African film industries continue to push these issues to the foreground. An example of a positive initiative to promote women in film is the South African National Film and Video Foundation's Female Only Filmmaker Project in 2017–2018, aimed at providing ten women, particularly those from historically disadvantaged backgrounds, with an opportunity to make a film in collaboration with other (more experienced) women.

When it comes to collaboration between women in creating art, Laura Marks – whose work on touch and the senses in film has been revolutionary – has looked at friendships between artists in her book *Hanan al-Cinema* (2015). She describes how audio-visual artists take on so many roles in their creative process that they often end up working for and with one another. Marks explores how "friendships perturb our systems" and "catalyze potentials," as such always "channelling a flow of change that produces and continually shapes individuals" as being part of a larger community (24). By increasing one's consciousness of being part of a bigger whole of affiliative networks, friendships can highlight the larger potential of individuals in an expanding, increasingly communal system. Women working together in the film industries can bring out the best in one another and stimulate each other in their cinematic endeavours. This is the nature of affinity and affiliations, leading to trusting relationships and friendships, resulting in increasingly successful films. This power of female friendships is increasingly revealing its power in the African film industries.

Female political activism and women's movements

Women activists in Africa have been engaged in a variety of movements and forms of collective action before colonisation, during the struggles for liberation, and after independence, engaging in issues ranging from land rights and inheritance, to increasing female political representation, ending cultural and traditional practices that are harmful or discriminatory to women, and addressing domestic abuse and violence (Badri and Tripp 2017, 1). While some of these movements have been inspired and informed by international feminist movements and supported by external agencies and international donors, African women have also contributed significantly to global understandings and realisations of women's rights (ibid.). African women have certainly not passively absorbed or adopted external agendas and definitions of feminism. In fact, Badri and Tripp (2017, 9) reveal how African women's movements have influenced global trends at least since the seventies. The Association of African Women for Research and Development (AAWORD) is a pan-African non-governmental organisation based in Dakar, Senegal, formed in 1977 as one of the first regionally based organisations of women in Africa. The organisation undertakes and supports research, networking, training and advocacy with the intention of promoting the economic, political and social rights of African women. Its founding was partly inspired by a desire to offset the domination of research on women in Africa by Western scholars and to tackle the dearth of research on women in Africa at the time. Ellerson details the impact of a seminar organised by AAWORD in 1984, entitled "Women, Communication, Development," which underscored AAWORD's understanding of the importance of women working at the intersection between media and African development, including filmmaking (Mistry and Schuhmann 2015, 3).

Tripp et al. (2005, 235–236) identified general patterns and trends in women's mobilisation in the context of political liberalisation, from women's organisations during the earlier post-independence period focused on religious, welfare and domestic concerns, to the organisations that have emerged since the nineties prioritising women's socio-economic emancipation and promoting the use of information and communication technologies. The expansion of media coverage of women's issues, greatly enhanced in the digital age, provided mainstream media outlets with alternative coverage of women to counter the often-patronising portrayal of African women in the media. Digital technology could also be utilised by women in other productive ways, such as the South African female friendship app Girl Crew, developed in 2018, which enables women to share their interests, hobbies and activities and connect with similar women wishing to forge new friendships (Kamau 2018). Such female specific technologies provide a much safer space for women than relationship apps such as Tinder, building female communities and networks and taking female friendship into the digital age.

Positive and more diverse media representations of African issues include depictions of African women who are increasingly taking up leadership positions in areas where they have historically been excluded from power. Women's campaigns, not only at governmental but also at grassroots levels, continue to promote the socio-political and economic emancipation of women and fight against traditional customs that are perpetuating women's oppression. Some of these movements have gained international visibility and recognition, such as the Green Belt Movement led by Kenyan environmental activist Wangari Maathai. Kenyan director Wanuri Kahiu (who also directed *Rafiki*, discussed in Chapter 7) directed the documentary *For Our Land* (2009), which charts Nobel Peace Prize laureate Wangari Maathai's environmental and political activism and reveals how European colonial policy is implicated in environmental destruction in Africa. The documentary *Pray the Devil Back to Hell* (2008) documents the activism of another remarkable African woman, Liberian social worker Leymah Gbowee, also a Nobel Peace Prize laureate. Gbowee founded the movement Women of Liberia Mass Action for Peace, which grew into a large peace movement that mobilised and united thousands of Christian and Muslim women in Liberia into a political force against violence and an oppressive government, and led to the election of Ellen Johnson Sirleaf in 2006, the first female African head of state. As we outline in Chapter 4, women have also been at the forefront of movements for political reform in Morocco, Tunisia and Egypt during the Arab Spring, as well as in liberation and revolutionary movements across the continent, and in post-conflict and reconciliation initiatives.

Africa has produced women who are worldwide leaders in the political representation of women, spearheaded recently by Rwanda, which became the first country in the world in 2016 where women parliamentarians exceeded 50% (Badri and Tripp 2017, 10–11). Women's groups have played a hugely important role in advancing debates on women's political leadership and the use of gender quotas, forcing changes on governmental, legal and judiciary levels (ibid., 13). These achievements have been documented in various films directed by women. *Sisters in Law: Stories from a Cameroon Court*, directed by Cameroonian Florence Ayisi and British Kim Longinotto (2005), portrays the work of female lawyers in the judicial system in Cameroon, centring around four cases involving violence against women. South African Jane Thandi Lipman's film *Courting Justice* (South Africa, 2011), features the lives, personal journeys and public work of seven women judges serving in various South African courts, revealing the challenges they face working in predominantly male institutions. *Whispering Truth to Power* (South Africa/Netherlands, 2018) is another South African documentary in which filmmaker and human rights lawyer Shameela Seedat follows the courageous work of Thuli Madonsela, South Africa's first female Public Protector, as she builds a case against the country's then-president, Jacob Zuma, in the face of false allegations, public humiliation and death threats against her. All these films document the remarkable work of African women fighting injustice and promoting democracy, women's and human rights. However, female leadership should not only be measured by highly visible positions of leadership such as these examples of political and legal representation, as it also includes many other forms of spiritual leadership (see Chapter 8), rural women's localised collectives, economic emancipation through small-scale entrepreneurship, and individual emancipation within the domestic sphere.

These grassroots women's collectives have been documented by female African filmmakers, originating perhaps from Senegalese director Safi Faye's ethnographic docu-fictions in which she centralised the role of women in the Serer societal structures and traditions. Her 1975 film *Kaddu Beykat* depicts how twentieth century colonial export crop and labour policies have brought about shifts in the gendered division of labour, in some cases reinforcing a feminised subsistence in the food economy. Writing from a feminist anthropological view, Jane Guyer argues that

> [f]or the 1970s feminists, Africa's female farmers seemed living proof – analogous to woman-the-gatherer – of women's original and massive contribution to the productive economy, of the possibility of integrating childcare with independent work, and of the historically late and derivative nature of women's regulation to the "domestic domain."
>
> *(Guyer 2005, 103)*

As such, female farming threw light on a range of feminist concerns such as the historical bases of patriarchy, the social status of women, and the effects of state policies. An African ethnographic perspective, as depicted in Faye's films, views African farming not as an example of a primitive period but as a system of knowledge and practice with its own history, innovations and prospects. Farming is a role that women have adopted due to labour migration and changes in the traditional gendered division of labour, but this role is always combined with other roles such as wifehood and motherhood.

Microfinancing and localised female entrepreneurship have also played a significant role in improving women's economic status, especially when we consider that most African women work in agricultural or informal sectors. Burkinabe director Fanta Régina Nacro's humorous short film *A Close-up on Bintou* (2001) is a playful take on female emancipation within the domestic sphere. It focuses, similarly to Faye's work in the Senegalese context, on the experiences of women in rural Burkina Faso. It tells the story of Bintou, an oppressed housewife, who fights tirelessly against the domestic abuse she suffers, by starting a business sprouting millet for beer-making in order to earn money to send her daughter to school. Bintou's husband, Abel, feels threatened by her entrepreneurial endeavour and attempts to ruin her chances of success by smashing her sprouting pots. He succeeds once but fails the second time, when Bintou casts a spell that traps him as he bends over her pots with a hammer, keeping him immobile throughout the night. Abel believes that Bintou's real reason for wanting to become financially independent is that she is having an affair, but he soon finds out that her absences are due to her attending the gatherings of a women's support group. Through sheer determination and the support of other women, Bintou ultimately succeeds in starting up a successful business and sending her daughter to school. Female entrepreneurship is also celebrated in South African director Sara Blecher's *Ayanda* (2015), in which the titular character, a young modern South African woman, is a successful mechanic taking over her father's business. On a similar theme, the Burkinabe documentary *Ouaga Girls* (2017) by Theresa Traoré Dahlberg, charts the journeys of a group of young women from Ouagadougou who are studying to become car mechanics. Both films depict the struggles of young women in a personal coming-of-age journey to establish themselves in a traditionally male career.

Women's movements lobby for cultural rights, and particularly for changes in cultural traditions, such as customary law and the authority of traditionally and religiously patriarchal institutions that conflict with or undermine women's rights and freedoms. As such, these groups advocate new cultural norms that promote equality, non-discrimination and healthy, fulfilling lives for both men and women (Badri and Tripp 2017, 18). Anne-Laure Folly, an international lawyer and filmmaker from Togo, has addressed cultural and women's rights in a range of documentaries. One of her best-known films, *Femmes aux yeux ouverts/Women with Open Eyes* (1994) consists of interviews with women at grassroots level in West Africa, tackling sensitive issues such as female circumcision, forced marriage and HIV/AIDS. Given the importance of grassroots activism by African women that we want to emphasise in this chapter, *Women with Open Eyes* is a particularly significant example of a documentary made by an African woman that engages with the issue of female genital mutilation in a much more complex way than the plethora of foreign-produced documentaries on this topic. Folly's film surveys, in a transnational manner, the social conditions faced by women in Burkina Faso, Mali, Senegal and Benin in the 1990s, providing a platform where women speak for themselves and address the camera directly. This activist feminist film was intended for African audiences and has been screened to enthusiastic female audiences across West Africa, highlighting the importance of female spectatorship mentioned above (Brière 2005, 166). Moreover, Folly's film does not only focus on issues of FGM, but on a range of topics affecting women in West Africa, thus giving a deep sense of balance and recognising that the emancipation of African women is tied to a range of intersecting issues. In *Women with Open Eyes* women are given the opportunity to assert themselves, as they occupy the entire audio-visual space and speak for themselves in the absence of an authoritative voice-over. It depicts women organising at a grassroots level positioning themselves as "natural feminists" (Brière 2005, 172).

More recently, female solidarity, maternal lineages and the cultural and societal affinities of women have been celebrated on screen by Senegalese-French film-maker Katy Léna N'diaye, who made two documentaries about traditions of female wall-painting and decoration. *Traces, empreintes de femmes/Traces, Women's Imprints* (2003) observes the tradition of wall painting by the Kassena women in southern Burkina Faso, and *En attendant les hommes/Waiting for Men* (2007) deals with traditional wall painting by women in the Mauritanian town of Oualata on the edge of the Sahara Desert. Given the importance of N'diaye's documentaries in discussions on female communities and networks of friendship and support, we pause briefly on these two films.

The skill of wall painting in *Traces* is shown to be a legacy handed down in the female lineage, from mother to daughter, generation after generation. Whereas wall art is the domain of the women, the men make bricks and construct the walls of the mud buildings, in a clear traditional stratification of gender roles. Four female characters introduce the viewer to their art: a young girl Anetina and her three grandmothers – Anmea, Akoune and Anouyere. The film opens with no dialogue or narration, with only a quiet focus on the women's work and close-ups on their faces and hands. Anetina's three grandmothers are introduced through static, frontal close-ups. The way in which women are framed by the camera is significant as they occupy the entire frame-space, resulting in a dominant female subjectivity. The interplay between tradition and modernity is detailed in the tra-dition of wall painting, through individual portraits of women from different gen-erations. As such, the main themes of the film are female communal support, solidarity and collective action. These women now collectively guard the tradition of decorating the walls of Kassena households. Particularly evocative and beautiful is the ending of the film, where the camera focuses on the meticulous preparation of the paint and the walls, and on the ways in which the decorative paintings take shape under the women's hands in a collaborative and organic female process. The film has a sensual richness focusing on texture, colour and touch: the camera's close-up on the women's hands decorating the walls imbues the film with an entirely tactile quality. *Traces* ends as it begins: with the identical point of view shot that now reveals exactly how the compound is decorated, and as such its circular movement encapsulates the completion of an entirely female task.

Waiting for Men is very similar in style to *Traces*: formally framed shots of three women being interviewed, relating intimate details about their lives and sharing views on economic emancipation, relationships, sexuality and desire. One of the women paints *tharkas* for an income (decorative patterns on the walls of the buildings), the second is a nurse, and the third one runs a small shop, dreaming of becoming a wealthy business woman. The title of the documentary refers to those women whose husbands have left due to labour migration, but this passive position is subverted by the subjects, as they do much more than wait for their men: they form networks, create art and generate an income. While the film certainly deals with aspects of female economic emancipation through the tradition of painting *tharkas*, it is actually an exploration of the intimate lives of the women. Once again, as in *Traces*, we observe women creating wall decorations, in silent close-ups of their hands and of the intricate *tharka* designs, while listening to, and learning about, how they have all created their own livelihoods while their husbands are away. Scenes of groups of women drinking tea together and playing *wari* in the sand (a popular African game played with beads or seeds), emphasise the importance of female friendships and companionship to develop the women's creative and independent community. In what follows, filmic solidarity, friendship and affinity are further explored in our two selected case studies. *Borders* and *I Still Hide to Smoke* are both exemplary in their depictions of these themes, as it is the interactions and developing friendships and solidarity between multiple female protagonists that drive forward the narratives in both films.

Case study: *Frontières/Borders* (Apolline Traoré, Burkina Faso/France, 2017)

Apolline Traoré is part of a younger generation of Burkinabe filmmakers, following in the footsteps of the pioneering directors from Burkina Faso such as Fanta Régina Nacro, Gaston Kaboré and Idrissa Ouédraogo, who was her mentor. She spent part of her childhood and studied filmmaking in the US and returned to Burkina Faso to commence her career in film and television. It should be noted that, with several shorts and television productions and four feature fiction films in her oeuvre, Traoré is one of the most prolific female directors in sub-Saharan Africa. Her four feature films have all been in competition at FESPACO, and all contain primary female protagonists and female-centred narratives. Traoré has described in interviews how she returned to a male-dominated film industry in Burkina Faso, in a society where her male elders demanded a level of deference that often hampered her ability to direct on set (Bavier 2017). Her focus on female storytelling is inspired by her frustration with persisting two-dimensional portrayals of African women on screen, and she has stated: "Having women in the industry is very important. We have a different vision. We see things differently" (ibid.)

Frontières/Borders focuses on the developing friendship between four women as they travel on public transport across West Africa: from Dakar in Senegal via Mali, Burkina Faso and Benin, to Lagos in Nigeria. Their friendship is forged through the hardships they encounter, predominantly the ever-present threat of male harassment and violence manifested in corrupt policemen and custom officials, highway robbers, thieves, rapists and traffickers. Border areas are often volatile and dangerous zones, partly because of the idiosyncratic and arbitrary way in which Africa was carved up by European colonisers who did not respect pre-colonial borders or ethnic geopolitics, but also because border areas in many places are exploited for human trafficking and corruption. Despite this seemingly ominous setting of the film, its transnational framing is its major strength – Traoré is herself a director with a transnational background, and *Borders* is an African feminist road movie that carries its transnational positioning not only in its narrative setting, but also in its casting, languages, production and funding. The road movie as genre is more readily associated with male heroes and protagonists, sometimes with a female adjunct character, exactly because the genre is associated with the myth and luxury of unlimited freedom and mobility that women do not have access to, confined by domestic duties, childcare, monthly menstrual cycles and other restrictions. Road movies often focus more on the journey than the destination, with the main protagonist(s) undergoing a moral, spiritual or psychological change or transformation over the course of the narrative. Although this character progression is certainly also present in *Borders*, in this film the characters are not willingly undertaking journeys of self-discovery but are travelling out of economic necessity and other needs.

The film introduces us to Adjara (Amélie Mbaye), a Senegalese trader who is travelling to Lagos to buy merchandise for the women's association she is a member of, and Emma (played by the famous Ivorian actor Naky Sy Savane), a trader from Ivory Coast, who is travelling to Lagos to sell bazin fabrics from Mali. During their journey they meet Vishaa (Unwana Udobang), a Nigerian woman living in Burkina Faso, who is on her way to her sister's wedding, and Sali (Adizétou Sidi), a Burkinabe student who is getting married soon and is travelling to Lagos to make a delivery for her fiancé. The lone female itinerant trader is prevalent in many parts of Africa, as entrepreneurial African businesswomen cross borders to buy and sell goods. Despite or perhaps precisely because of the vulnerability of these female travellers, solidarity and camaraderie develops between them on these long, slow bus journeys on potholed African roads, as depicted in *Borders*. All five countries featured in the film are part of the ECOWAS economic union (the organisation also part-funded the film). Regional affinity and transnational friendships and solidarity are forged despite the multitude of differences that exist between the characters; the diversity of their languages, cultures, customs, traditions, religions and ages. They speak French, as well as Wolof, More, Bambara, English, Portuguese, Yoruba and other languages. This linguistic variety cements the film's transnational character but regardless of the differences between the women, they find solidarity through a shared African-ness and positionality as women travelling together.

When Emma boards the bus in Bamako, the older Ivorian traveller is at first surly and aloof. "Company is another word for trouble," is her snappy retort to Adjara's friendly approach. Emma is travelling with a bulk of fabrics that she hides under her clothes in order to avoid excessive export and import charges. Adjara spots her covertly layering the fabrics under her clothes behind a tree and then waddling back to the bus. It is a humorous scene with well-timed comic rhythm; the film is interspersed with moments of light cathartic relief in an otherwise dramatic narrative. When Emma's neighbour complains about the space she and her load take up on the seat, Adjara offers to sit next to her, and they conspire at the next border crossing, misleading the official to pay only a small custom charge.

Incidences of bribery and corruption, always by male policemen and custom officials, abound in the film and Adjara repeatedly mentions the ECOWAS regulations that should enable the free movement of goods and people across these borders. It is clear that, despite the political ideology of regional support and solidarity, economic need and greed take precedence. When Adjara questions Emma about why she did not confront the official, she responds, "a lion does not show his claws to the elephant," indicating the gendered power imbalance that exists between female travellers and male agents of state authority. A hostile and aggressive patriarchal public space presents serious challenges and restrictions to the women who dare to enter it.

As Sali, a Burkinabe student, and Vishaa, a Nigerian running a restaurant in Bobo-Dioulasso in Burkina Faso join the journey, the four women gradually open up and get to know each other. Emma reveals that she has been travelling as a trader for 15 years, initially to pay for her two children's European educations, but now that they are independent, she has continued her travelling because of an inner disquiet caused by loneliness and the anger at her husband's untimely death. Adjara is undertaking her first journey, selected by the women's group she belongs to, to purchase merchandise in Lagos for their start-up business. Her need for independence and female companionship and support is partly motivated by an abusive husband. Sali is travelling to deliver a suitcase in Benin for her fiancé, an errand that could pay for their wedding, and Vishaa is on her way to her sister's wedding in Lagos. Emma's hardened stance finally softens when the bus passes an accident scene and she demands they stop to help the injured. Her action is prompted by the fact that she lost her own mother in a road accident. This revelation serves as a catalyst for Sali to share with her new-found friends that she was orphaned at 12 years, when the hostel her parents owned burnt down. The sharing of personal histories, dreams and aspirations lends the four women's budding friendship some depth. They may be sharing circumstances over which they have little control, but the companionship that develops between them is voluntary, and essential for their survival. They are from different nationalities, backgrounds and ages, they speak different languages, and each has her own reason for travelling, but their solidarity is formed through a connection with the road.

The women's precarious situation escalates when, on entering Cotonou in Benin, Sali is arrested. The revelation that the suitcase she is carrying for her fiancé contains illegal drugs emphasises her naivety as she has unwittingly been used as a drug mule. Adjara notices that Sali is being taken away by a police officer, and when she and Emma follow, they find her being raped by the policeman in a shed. Survival instincts kick in and they kill him with a huge rock. As the three women flee from the shed, Sali surreptitiously steals the policeman's gun.

They are now fugitives but manage to get away when Vishaa distracts the police. They are later picked up by a car enabling them to cross the border into Nigeria, hiding Sali in the trunk and disguising her in a long robe and hijab in order to get onto the next bus to Lagos. The characters' dialogue references stereotypes of Nigerian corruption, materialising in a highway robbery with aggressive men ordering all passengers off the bus, demanding they hand over their phones, jewellery and money. Adjara, who is carrying all the money entrusted to her by the women's organisation, refuses to hand over her money bag, agitating one of the robbers who threatens to shoot her. In a moment of heightened female solidarity and self-sacrifice Vishaa pushes the robber away, only to get shot and killed. Their journey comes to a devastating end when they reach the coast in Lagos, a literal and spiritual ending to the journey, with the three remaining women contemplating the events sitting on the beach, resigned and defeated. They visit Vishaa's family to share the tragic news of her death, and a female family member leads the group in a song of mourning. In a final conversation before they part ways, Emma encourages Sali to report her fiancé and work on her dream to rebuild her parents' hostel. She implores Adjara to never allow another man to beat her, especially with the financial independence she will gain from the women's business. Adjara advises Emma to make peace and be less angry. "It's already done, and thanks to you, my friends," are her final words to them.

The real purpose of the physical and psychological journeys that the women have undertaken, bolstered by their growing friendship, is to free themselves from the authority and abuse of patriarchy and to assert their female agency. In the final scenes of the film we see Emma taking a taxi home, looking serene, her endless journeying having come to an end. Adjara crosses the road with her young daughter, both have smiles on their faces. And Sali visits her fiancé. A powerful voice-over recaps the film's message:

> They say a woman can handle anything, must be able to handle anything.
>
> They say God created woman with a back strong enough and shoulders wide enough to carry the world.
>
> [...]
>
> The aim of our journey, of our quest: to feed our family, to grow, to survive, to become independent, or to be an example to our children.
>
> [...]
>
> We set off on this journey with promises.
>
> [...]
>
> But, for lack of anything better, we rise when we must, and get onto the bus.
>
> [...]
>
> That's what we learn on the road. We don't really know each other until others stand up before us like mirrors. And then we see our own fear, our own strength, our own generosity too.
>
> [...]
>
> And when it's all over, we go back home, back to our daily routine, wondering if we are condemned.
>
> We tell ourselves that in any case, we must put on a brave face in coping with our misfortune.
>
> But from putting on a brave face, under the weight of too much misfortune, one day, we will explode.

The voiceover is a feminist manifesto of female strength, solidarity and friendship, and its final line a grave warning to patriarchy. In the very final scene of the film, Sali enters her fiancé's room and points the gun, which she has kept since her rape, at him. A shot is heard as she simultaneously calls the police. The film's narrative has shown us that Sali is unlikely to receive justice or protection from any authority, but she is taking her destiny into her own hands nonetheless. It is a drastic act, but it is tempered and balanced by Adjara and Emma's positive and empowering choices. All three women have found support and courage through their friendship and solidarity, enabling them to reject heteropatriarchy and renounce their oppression. No longer will they be putting on a brave face; in seeing the reflections of themselves in each other, they have found their true inner strength.

Case study: *À mon âge je me cache encore pour fumer/I Still Hide to Smoke* (Rayhana Obermeyer, France/Greece/Algeria, 2017)

I Still Hide to Smoke (2017) is a recent triumph of Algerian feminist cinema. In a long tradition of rare but powerful feminist stories since *La Nouba* by Assia Djebar, Rayhana Obermeyer has created a film based on a theatre piece that she wrote herself. The film focuses on Fatima (played by the versatile Palestinian actress Hiam Abbass) and a number of very different female characters engaged in opinionated conversation, far removed from the limiting and strictly policed discourse inside Algeria. As such, the film was largely shot in Greece and only a few of the shots – those on rooftops looking out over the Mediterranean Sea – were filmed in Algiers. The enclosed setting of the film gives it a claustrophobic feel, contrasting with the freedom of speech enacted within the safe space of a women-only bathhouse, where the majority of the action takes place. The film offers a representative, diverse image of women in Algiers. It also represents a variety of experiences, depending on the women's class, religion and generation. Rich in dialogue and loyal to the unities of classical theatre, the film's condensed development, space and time offer a concentrated plotline, contrasted with a variety of female voices and faces in the action of the film and drawing attention to the solidarity found among the women in the bathhouse.

While Algeria is historically best known for its preoccupation with revolutionary cinema, the War for Independence and its heroes (see Chapter 4), recent films have shown a confident surge of young women telling women's stories. Yamina Bachir-Chouikh was a precursor of this movement, and her debut film, *Rachida*, focuses on the communities of and friendships developed between women of different generations, living in an oppressive patriarchal society. *Rachida* evokes memories of the worst atrocities of the Islamist terror campaign in Algeria in the nineties, on a personal and a political scale. However, the film foregrounds the power of solidarity between and among young and older women in the face of increasing Islamisation and violence perpetrated by men. In the film, young teacher Rachida refuses to plant a bomb in her school and is cold-bloodedly shot in the belly and left for dead. Women clad in haïks (long, enveloping white gowns specific to Algeria) rush to cover her body lovingly with their veils. The veil becomes a symbol of protection and female solidarity. Miraculously, she survives, but the trauma leaves its marks on her body and psyche. To recover, she goes into internal exile with her mother, to a rural village in the north of Algeria. However, Islamist terrorist groups operate in the wilderness in and around the village too, kidnapping and raping women and killing indiscriminately.

A feminist solidarity is central to the historical context in which *Rachida* was produced, and it remains highly relevant in our discussion of *I Still Hide to Smoke*. Both films examine how female solidarity challenges violent and chaotic male environments. Different communities of women come together to protect young women. In *I Still Hide to Smoke* (2017) we witness a powerful female solidarity that enables women of different backgrounds, generations and religious conviction to stand together for survival. The film paints a portrait of Fatima, who runs a women's hammam, and subtly orchestrates a safe feminine space not only for physical cleansing but also for emotional friendships and battles. The women in the all-female cast in the warm, humid space of the hammam have strong political opinions and polemical discussions that offer insight in the broad scope of identities and relationships in an unnamed city in Algeria. It is so safe that even at the climax of the story, men cannot enter the hammam when one of the elderly women shouts "get lost, no men in here, this is the women's time." As such, the schism between inside and outside spaces, and the division of genders within those spaces is emphasised.

In this film, outside, between safe spaces, women cover entirely with veils and focus their gazes on the ground. In the voice-over that frames the film, Samia – a young spinster who works in the hammam with Fatima – explains that women are not allowed outside, and that the only space where she is free is on the terrace of her roof. But even then, there are certain rules she has to abide by: her mother tells her she can go up there and look at the sea only if she is also usefully busy. So, she goes there to wash and hang up the clothes to dry. She says that aside from water, electricity, oil and sugar, the thing women lack most in Algeria is love. Indeed, even inside the houses women are persecuted, as Fatima is seen being raped by her husband and fleeing to the hammam to clean herself. Samia, meanwhile, day-dreams naively of finding a husband, and of the sea and the boats leaving across the Mediterranean. She testifies that Algeria is a prison and thinks how even her brother is "in the belly of a boat, searching for a new horizon." She longs for a new horizon in Algeria, beset by the sounds of bombs and muezzin, the city increasingly besieged by fundamentalist problems.

The intergenerational dialogues offer different perspectives on women's freedoms and limitations, but all agree on the importance of being "sisters" and supporting one another in an increasingly complex and tumultuous reality outside. The hammam serves as a women-centric refuge, depicted as steamy, dominated by amber and pinkish colours, and warm naked female bodies. Filming her subjects in various natural states of undress is, given the context, a political act in and of itself, but

Rayhana's plural identity allows her to use the trope of the hammam as a tool in her film's overall feminist message of solidarity among women. This is highlighted with comforting talk, communal baths and mutual massages between young children, teenagers, young women about to be married, mature and aging women. All shed their hijabs and any other outer layer to reveal their similarities underneath and to escape the oppressive politics of the outside world. Inside, the bathers discuss intercourse, orgasms (one particularly humorous conversation shows how there is no Arabic word for "orgasm") and related topics, a rarity in Algerian cinema.

It is a young woman, Meriem, who heightens tensions within the hammam when she enters the story, by bringing outside influences inside. The 16-year-old has been secretly pregnant but is now being chased around town by her vengeful brother Mohamed. She finds shelter in the arms of Fatima upstairs in the hammam, while the other women are unaware of her presence. However, the upheaval of her brother's threats and the imam's interruptions initiate her labour and she gives birth in the hammam. A recent widow, who lost her fundamentalist husband and is herself becoming increasingly extremist in her ideals, helps with the delivery of the baby as she was previously a student of medicine. Even those women who do not see eye to eye due to their diametrically opposed positions on and experiences of religion, band together and assist with the safe delivery of the baby, vowing that they will take care of Meriem and her child. As such, the dynamics of this diverse and fascinating group of women benefit from a gendered affinity, within which friendships resolve acute tensions.

The diversity of the group of women warrants some attention, especially as Fatima declares in a very domineering way that "no politics are allowed in the hammam." There are some devastating stories, for example from an elderly woman who reminisces about getting married and about her first night with her husband. She reveals that she was only 11 years old and that she was "so afraid I peed myself." Her husband was much older and very heavy lying on top of her. He hurt her, and they never had kids, but she bore six children by another man, whom she loved dearly but secretly. Nadia, a young divorcée, celebrates getting her "certificate of independence" and is harshly criticised by Zahia, the widow of a fundamentalist. They fight verbally and physically, until Nadia shows the scars left by an acid attack perpetrated by one of Zahia's fundamentalist relatives for wearing a dress instead of a veil. A teacher testifies she wears a hijab only because "they threatened me." This teacher is particularly fond of Leila, a young teenage girl who does not speak. Later it becomes apparent why: she screams loudly when she sees a young woman menstruating onto her white chemise and the teacher explains that Leila is traumatised as she witnessed fundamentalists raping her sisters and disembowelling her mother while chanting verses from the Quran.

Religion is very harshly criticised in the film, in particular when Zahia, after delivering the baby, turns against the group of women and betrays them to her fundamentalist brethren. But in a moment of inspiration, Samia suggests that they follow the Greek legend of Ulysses, where they escape the island of the Cyclops by disguising as sheep. When they leave the hammam, the women all wear haïks and pretend to be pregnant so that the men cannot identify Meriem. Visually this becomes a very powerful contrast between white female veils and black male garments, positing the women as one group of blameless victims and the men as an evil perpetrating power. The women's veiled solidarity is a controversial move, because the haïk – a symbol of maturity and purity in elderly women – demands respect in Algerian culture, and the men indeed back off slightly. However, a tragedy does unfold in spite of the ruse, as Samia, wearing Meriem's red shoes, is wrongly identified as Meriem: Mohamed lunges forward with a knife and kills her. In an act similar to Sali's final act of revenge in *Borders*, Fatima, who loves Samia as her protégé running the hammam, takes the knife and kills Mohamed. She frees her friends from the Islamists' patriarchal power through sacrifice and accepts her punishment.

The film ends with Samia's voice-over, again emphasising the power of solidarity as expressed beyond different generations and through the symbol of the veil. Similar to *Borders*, the voice-over here sounds defiant and strong, with a clear message of love for the future of Algeria's women. As we witness Leila, Meriem and the baby being looked after by the teacher, on the roof of her house and hanging up washed clothes to dry, Samia says that she is taking all the headscarves of Algeria with her on her journey to death, "because I love you, Leila." This final expression of affinity between a tragic heroine and her beloved younger friend, beyond death, is emotionally and visually striking, as we see countless black scarves flying away in the wind over the sea, like a murmuration of birds taking off towards the horizon. As it does in so many films, the sea symbolises a sense of freedom and escape. We see this in *Borders* too, when the women's journeys, paradoxically restrictive because of the threats and violence they are subjected to on the road, come to an end when they reach the ocean, and they are finally free.

★★★★

The parallels between *Borders* and *I Still Hide to Smoke* are almost uncanny, which might be exactly because they are both films that focus so intimately on female community and solidarity, set within hostile male environments. In both films the groups of women form friendships and allegiances in spite of and across religious, ethnic, class, generational, national and linguistics differences, forced together by circumstances often stained by tragedy. Rape, revenge and sacrifice are powerful narrative tropes, as female characters are subjected to male sexual violence and deal with it in different ways. Female alliances across generations are paralleled in the films too, as older women take on a caring role in educating younger women, whereas the younger women search for a balance between accepting their status as victim and rallying together in their urge to achieve emancipation. Above all, both are female-directed films that centralise female friendship and depict the powerful female force that can emerge when women come together.

Bibliography

Badri, Balghis and Aili Mari Tripp (2017) *Women's Activism in Africa: Struggles for Rights and Representation*. London: Zed Books.

Bavier, Joe (2017) "Burkina Faso director gives African women authentic voice," *Reuters* (5 March). Available online: www.uk.reuters.com/article/us-burkina-filmfestival-direc

tor/burkina-faso-director-gives-african-women-authentic-voice-idUKKBN16C0WP [Accessed January 2019].

Brière, Eloise A. (2005) "Confronting the Western Gaze." In Obioma Nnaemeka (ed.) *Female Circumcision and the Politics of Knowledge: African Women in Imperialist Discourses.* Westport, CT and London: Praeger, pp. 165–183.

Coleman, Arica L. (2018) "There's a true story behind black panther's strong women. Here's why that matters," *Time* (22 February 2018). Available online: http://time.com/5171219/black-panther-women-true-history/ [Accessed January 2019].

Collins, Patricia Hill (2000) *Black Feminist Thought: Knowledge, Consciousness and the Politics of Empowerment.* London and New York: Routledge.

Dash, Mike (2011) "Dahomey's women warriors," *Smithsonian Magazine* (23 September). Available online: www.smithsonianmag.com/history/dahomeys-women-warriors-88286072/ [Accessed January 2019].

Davis, Evans and J. Lorber (2006) (eds) *Handbook of Gender and Women's Studies.* London: SAGE Publications.

Donahue, Anne T. (2016) "Female friendship in the movies, for better and for worse." Available online: www.tiff.net/the-review/female-friendship-on-film/ [Accessed January 2019].

Ekine, Sokari and Hakima Abbas (eds.) (2013) *Queer African Reader.* Cape Town: Pambazuka Press.

Ellerson, Beti (2015) "African women in cinema: An overview." In Jyoti Mistry and Antje Schuhmann (eds.) *Gaze Regimes: Film and Feminisms in Africa.* Johannesburg: Wits University Press, pp. 1–9.

Elgrably, Jordan (2017) "Algerian new wave: When words are lacking – that's where cinema comes in," *Middle East Eye* (24 November). Available online: www.middleeasteye.net/in-depth/features/new-wave-filmmakers-brings-algeria-light-1869705340 [Accessed January 2019].

Guyer, Jane I. (2005) "Female Farming in Anthropology and African History." In Andrea Cornwall (ed.) *Readings in Gender in Africa.* Oxford: James Currey, pp. 103–110.

Joburg Film Festival (2018) "Over 300 women gather to talk gender disparity at the Joburg Film Festival," *Screen Africa* (2 November). Available online: www.screenafrica.com/2018/11/02/film/business/over-300-women-gather-to-talk-gender-disparity-at-the-joburg-film-festival/ [Accessed January 2019].

Kamau, Vanessa (2018) "Meet the South African women that built a female only friendship app," *TechMoran* (5 September). Available online: www.techmoran.com/2018/09/05/meet-the-south-african-women-that-built-a-female-only-friendship-app/ [Accessed January 2019].

Larrier, Renée (1993) "Inscriptions of orality and silence: Representations of female friendship in francophone Africa and the Caribbean." In Janet Doubler Ward and Joanna Stephens Mink (eds) *Communication and Women's Friendships: Parallels and Intersections in Literature and Life.* Bowling Green State University Popular Press, pp. 181–194.

Liking, W. and M. Hourantier (1981) *Contes d'initiation féminine du pays bassa.* Issy les Moulineaux: Les classiques africains.

Maggs, Sam (2018) *Girl Squads: 20 Female Friendships That Changed History.* Philadelphia: Quirk Books.

Marks, Laura (2015) *Hanan Al-Cinema: Affections for the Moving Image.* Cambridge, MA: MIT Press.

McGill, Hannah (2018) "Girl friends on film: the rare case of lifelike female friendships on the big screen," *Sight and Sound* (March). Available online: www.bfi.org.uk/news-opinion/sight-sound-magazine/features/girl-friends-film-lifelike-female-friendships-big-screen [Accessed January 2019].

Mistry, J. and A. Schuhmann (eds) (2015) *Gaze Regimes: Film and Feminisms in Africa*. Johannesburg: Wits University Press.

Moloi, Vusi (2012) "The organic roots of the African matrilineal society," *New Afrikan*, 77. Available online: www.newafrikan77.wordpress.com/2016/01/05/the-organic-rootsor igin-of-afrikan-matrilineal-societies/ [Accessed January 2019].

Mulvey, Laura (1975) "Visual pleasure and narrative cinema," *Screen*, 16(3), pp. 6–18.

Okech, Awino (2013) "'In sisterhood and solidarity': Queering African feminist spaces." In Sokari Ekine and Hakima Abbas (eds) *Queer African Reader*. Cape Town: Pambazuka Press, pp. 9–31.

Roseneil, S. (2006) "Foregrounding friendship: Feminist pasts, feminist futures." In K. Davis, M. Evans, and J. Lorber (eds) *Handbook of Gender and Women's Studies*. London: Sage Publications, pp. 322–341.

Tripp, Aili Mari et al. (2005) *African Women's Movements: Changing Political Landscapes*. Cambridge: Cambridge University Press.

Filmography

A Close-up on Bintou, Dir. Fanta Régina Nacro, Burkina Faso/France, 2001

À mon âge je me cache encore pour fumer / I Still Hide to Smoke, Dir. Rayhana Obermeyer, France/Greece/Algeria, 2016

Ayanda, Dir. Sara Blecher, South Africa, 2015

Black Panther, Dir. Ryan Coogler, USA, 2018

Courting Justice, Dir. Jane Thandi Lipman, South Africa, 2011

En attendant les hommes / Waiting for Men, Dir. Katy Léna N'diaye, Belgium/Senegal, 2007

Femmes aux yeux ouverts / Women with Open Eyes, Dir. Anne-Laure Folly, Togo, 1994

For Our Land, Dir. Wanuri Kahiu, Kenya, 2009

Frontières / Borders, Dir. Apolline Traoré, Burkina Faso/France, 2017

Kaddu Beykat, Dir. Safi Faye, Senegal, 1976

La Nouba des femmes du Mont Chenoua, Dir. Assia Djebar, Algeria, 1979

Ouaga Girls, Dir. Theresa Traoré Dahlberg, Sweden/France/Burkina Faso/Qatar/Netherlands/Finland/South Africa, 2017

Pray the Devil Back to Hell, Dir. Gini Reticker, US, 2008

Rachida, Dir. Yamina Bachir-Chouikh, Algeria/France, 2002

Rafiki, Dir. Wanuri Kahiu, Kenya/South Africa/Germany/Netherlands/France/Norway/Lebanon, 2018

Sisters in Law: Stories from a Cameroon Court, Dir. Florence Ayisi & Kim Longinotto, Cameroon/UK, 2005

Tess, Dir. Meg Rickards, South Africa, 2016

The Women, Dir. Blessing Effiom Egbe, Nigeria, 2017

Traces, empreintes de femmes / Traces, Women's Imprints, Dir. Katy Léna N'diaye, Belgium, 2003

Whispering Truth to Power, Dir. Shameela Seedat, South Africa/Netherlands, 2018

Xala, Dir. Ousmane Sembène, Senegal, 2017

4

WOMEN IN REVOLUTION AND REVOLUTIONARY CINEMA

Al-Khoroug Lel-Nahar/Coming Forth by Day (Hala Lotfy, Egypt/United Arab Emirates, 2012) shows how revolutions on film do not always translate into fast-paced, energetic images or outspoken opinions. Recent Egyptian film production cannot avoid the revolution of 2011, but it can visually challenge the expectations of the revolution, both celebrating and lamenting the initial optimism and contemplating the impasse of post-revolutionary governance. Focusing on the relationship between a daughter and her largely absent parents, in a slow, modest and condensed fragment of a story, the emphasis is on loneliness, disappointment and suppressed feelings. More of a pressure cooker of feelings than a trajectory of development, the film refuses to engage outspokenly with the revolution. There is a sense of fear of engaging with the outside world, which is encapsulated in the elimination of space and time. A stagnating and entrapped life is portrayed in a film that refuses the classic or historical tropes of revolutionary cinema. Instead these films change film language and form to engage with the shortcomings of cinema and of life, in their inability to cope with and represent the deflated nature of a failed revolution. Its defiance of expectations stands out and heralds a new approach to revolutionary cinema in Egypt.

All revolutions, big or small, personal or political, are intended to bring about change. Films about conflict, war, liberation struggles and revolutions are the subject of countless studies regarded as seminal in the field, in particular those films that depict the heroic soldier and the strategising political leader (see Eberwein 2004; Chapman 2008; Cunningham and Nelson 2016). It is also these films that often win the major prizes at international film festivals or awards ceremonies. If we take a cursory glance at some of the most popular or most highly rated films in film history like *Battleship Potemkin* (Eisenstein, 1925), *Seven Samurai* (Kurosawa, 1954), *Good Morning, Vietnam* (Levinson, 1987) and *Indigènes/Days of Glory* (Bouchareb, 2006), it is clear that conflict and war narratives are central to global film history.

Revolutionary cinema movements inspired the most impactful changes in the course of film history. With the term "revolutionary cinema" we particularly refer to those films that revolutionise the medium: films that inspire changes in form, style and approach to filmmaking on a practical and intellectual level. For this reason, these movements are often called "waves" or "new" cinema. Conflicts and revolutions are eventful and offer a clear narrative arc beneficial to storytelling, and revolutionary stances on changing the form of storytelling for ideological reasons respond to a stalemate in the representational approach to these events.

This chapter will show how revolutionary filmmaking has defined African filmmaking in many ways, but also how expectations regarding revolutions and conflicts on screen are constantly challenged by younger generations of female filmmakers. Starting with an in-depth look at the history of Third Cinema and its African directions, specifically in Algeria and Angola, we then focus on the most recent and mediatised revolutions in North and South Africa: respectively the Arab Revolutions in Tunisia and Egypt and the anti-apartheid struggle in South Africa. Of course, the continent as a whole has seen its fair share of revolutions and revolutionary cinema. Indeed, we highlight that Nigerian films are increasingly tackling complex historical issues such as the Biafran War; that Congolese cinema is a space in which to address the consequences of violent conflict and conflict resolution; and that Rwandan cinema has been used as a powerful tool to address reconciliation in the post-genocide era. But our focus moves from an exploration of the history of revolutionary filmmaking in the spirit of Third Cinema, to "new waves" of political cinema in North and South Africa, stemming from the revolutionary spirit of the anti-apartheid struggle and the 2011 wave of Arab revolutions. All the while we look at how, in the hands of female filmmakers, films about revolution become revolutionary films.

Women in war and revolution

Miriam Cooke charted the emerging tradition of women's contributions to the "War Story" (1996). The master narrative – as the term implies, completely reserved for the male experience – requires alternatives that challenge the authority of the singularly male experience. Cooke shows how women who write (or film) themselves and their experiences into the war story undo a male contract with violence, sexuality and glory. Terms like "grand narrative" or "master narrative" (perceived to be the standard) obscure the diversity of experiences and have for too long defined the way we think about conflict and revolution. Even where conflicts and revolutions took place in perceived "masculine" spaces such as battlefields and frontlines, women have been present in a variety of roles. Furthermore, when warfare moved away from specifically designated battlefields into civilian spaces, the line between combat zones and safe zones was blurred. As such, women's and other "different" stories contest and break down the acceptance of a dichotomous world (home vs. front, civilian vs. combatant, war vs. peace, victory vs. defeat) that have framed, and ultimately promoted, conflict.

When it comes to gender roles in films about war, conflict and revolution, the grand narratives of history have by and large focused on the "male" theatre of war, seeing conflictual situations as an exclusively male environment. In these stories, revolutionary leaders, soldiers, generals and politicians are presumed to be male. However, women have historically always been part of wars and revolutions, they have just not been represented, not been given the time or space to develop women's narratives of war and revolutions, at least not in canonical films. Moreover, the stereotype of the woman as the long-suffering victim of war rather than as an active agent needs to be dispelled. Women in war and in the war film act as nurses, doctors and other carers; they can be soldiers or generals and part of the more violent theatre of war; they can certainly be victims, just as men can, although gendered violence can be used as a particularly dreadful weapon of war; and women can act as strong reconciliatory forces in post-conflict situations.

As Thomas Sankara, leader of the Burkinabé liberation movement, said: "The revolution cannot triumph without the genuine emancipation of women" (2007, 51). Though in some respect his words were patronising, he was also pragmatic, and called for women to assert themselves. Indeed, women are a basic necessity for the revolution to succeed and be victorious, in a process of liberating all women from reactionary policies and hypocrisies, in order to "build a free and prosperous society in which women will be equal to men in all spheres" (ibid., 43). The Marxist fervour clearly inherent to the spirit of Sankara's speech remains relevant. Turshen and Twagiramariya argue that the enduring war-time picture of the active male and the passive female "has depended on the invisibility of women's participation in the war effort, their unacknowledged, behind-the-lines contributions to the prosecution of war, and their hidden complicity in the construction of fighting forces. [...] Once these activities are revealed," they state, "it is no longer possible to maintain the innocence of all women" (1998, 1). In modern forms of war, especially civil wars and liberation struggles, women are also combatants and resistance fighters and even when they are not actively involved, they support war efforts in multiple ways.

It is important to point out that when filmmakers create agency-driven narratives of women's experiences of revolution and conflict, they are not rewriting history, rather they are addressing gaps in, and challenging the singular focus of, accepted male-dominated historiography. Just as the canon of (African) cinema needs to be addressed and women need to be inscribed into it, so too should women's previously neglected or ignored contributions be continually reintegrated into historiography.

In her research on African women in war and conflict, Uwakweh describes how the aftermath of conflicts not only brings political change (for better or worse), it can also initiate new forms of violence and related gender challenges (2017). Articulating the consequences of war for women and children remains a major challenge as we need a deeper understanding of the new sources of violence and aggression perpetrated against women, the gendered challenges of reintegration in the aftermath of violence, and of the consequences of gendered violence for the African continent. While it is certainly important to acknowledge gendered victimisation and violence, we would also warn against blanket victimisation of women and their experiences of conflict and revolution. As we have seen in other films in this book, African women are strong, independent, have the power to speak, and the revolution or conflict they survive often gives them an opportunity to be heard and seen as well. We would opt for an emphasis on the power of the postcolonial, transnational African woman who is not stuck (nor has she ever been stuck) in a gendered victimhood but emancipates herself from the role she has been assigned in the cultural canon. Since women started making films in Africa, the woman on screen is a much more powerful, inspiring force of agency and inspiration.

Historical revolutions on the screen

Some of the pioneering films by women from the African continent are those that "insert" women into the grand narratives of history: for example Sarah Maldoror's *Monangambé* (1968) and *Sambizanga* (1972); Safi Faye's *La Passante* (1972) and *Kaddu Beykat* (1976); Selma Baccar's *L'Éveil/The Awakening* (1966) and *Fatma 75* (1975); and Assia Djebar's *La Nouba* (1979). While not all these films deal directly with violent conflict, they are all concerned with women's roles in recently independent societies struggling with an oppressive colonial past and "grand narratives" of official historiography. The films are directly or indirectly concerned with the aftermath of independence or with revolutionary movements that led up to it. In fact, a lot of the earliest women's films from the continent can be seen as inherently revolutionary, where movements like Third Cinema in the late sixties inspired a revolutionary fervour, addressing the atrocities of the colonial past inflicted on women.

Algerian cinema in particular is often seen as a cinema entirely defined by revolutionary sentiments. For instance, Salmane states that "Algerian cinema was born out of the war of independence and served that war" (Salmane 1976, 5), illustrated by films such as *L'Algérie en flammes/Algeria in Flames* (Vautier, 1958) and *La battaglia di Algeri/The Battle of Algiers* (Pontecorvo, 1966). The latter film achieved iconic status as the ultimate militant Third Cinema film. In hindsight, this cinema has also served as a memory of the war – mythologising the liberation struggle and dealing with trauma. This revolutionary cinema is popularly called *cinéma moujahid* or freedom fighter cinema. Officially sanctioning the memorialisation of resistance, it is a "filmic reflection of glowing official martyrdom" (Austin 2012, 22). But the role of female freedom fighters has been conspicuously absent from *cinéma moujahid*, as the official history of the liberation struggle focused on heroic men fighting for the country. Initially, *cinéma moujahid* was an expression of the Third Cinema movement, but in Algeria it developed into a stale replication of itself. In what follows we briefly outline the inspiration behind, and shortcomings of, Third Cinema, the lack of women in the movement being our foremost concern.

As the ideas of Third Cinema were taken up around the world, on the African continent the Third Cinema Manifesto influenced militant cinema in previously colonised areas at the same time as the New Arab Cinema Collective announced its aesthetic and thematic plans for cinema in the Arab world after 1967 (Van de Peer 2017, 4–6). Reacting against the dominance of specific film styles and forms that were rooted in Hollywood (First) and European (Second) cinemas, the Manifesto and its followers sought to use the camera to "shoot back" and revolutionise film-making. These revolutionary cinema movements, emphasising a political message of rebellion against oppression of any kind, reveal a preoccupation with everyday reality and the aim to mobilise the audience. The cinema this global anti-colonial movement envisaged had a politicised content that aims to turn passive consumers into active contributors and ignites involvement in the struggle against the "System." The Manifesto publicised an aesthetic of anger and militancy, whereby the revolution can only be successful if it is highly political and violent. The Manifesto's Latin American authors, Solanas and Getino (as well as others such as Glauber Rocha and Jorge Sanjinés), were more concerned with the masses, themes, information, truth and aggression than with the artistic and visual quality of the film.

The consensus today is that Third Cinema was the product of a very specific moment in history and its continuing relevance was contested by Teshome Gabriel in the eighties and Ella Shohat in the early 2000s. Most interestingly for us, Shohat shows that Third Cinema doubly marginalised women, "both as filmmakers and as political actants" (Guneratne and Dissanayake 2003, 17). Many women in the "Third World" have nevertheless made extensive use of film to express their own participation in the struggle for national independence. They have just not received the attention they warrant. These women claim their agency and their power in images. Shohat's main point is that the Third Cinema Manifestoes were homogeneous and overgeneralising, male and heroic in their terminology. In this context, Third Cinema was "produced mainly by men [...] and often favored the generic and gendered space of heroic confrontations" (Shohat 2003, 59). As an alternative, she suggests a post-Third Cinema women's aesthetic that rewrites cinema history and reinstates women into that history gradually but confidently. In women's hands, revolutionary content engenders a revolutionary form.

Sarah Maldoror's career as a filmmaker illustrates the impact of Third Cinema on women's revolutionary cinema. She was assistant director on *The Battle of Algiers* and soon thereafter made a strong political documentary examining torture techniques used by the French in the Algerian war, *Monangambé* (1968). Her feature film *Sambizanga* (1972) is still exemplary today as an early feminist expression of the Third Cinema ideology. Born in France and of Guadeloupean heritage, she is regarded as a pioneering female African filmmaker because of her long and deep involvement with filmmaking on the continent. She was a co-founder of the theatre group Compagnie d'Art Dramatique des Griots in Paris in 1956, which trained and supported Black actors. She left the company in the early sixties to study cinema at VGIK in Moscow on a scholarship (Bassori 2016). Maldoror had a particular affinity with Angola, as she married the leader of the Liberation movement, poet and philosopher Mário Pinto de Andrade. With her interest in the emancipation of the Black artist, as well as her activism in liberation struggles, all her films look at the liberation of African countries.

Maldoror focuses in great detail on women's experiences of the liberation struggle. *Sambizanga* has attained cult status in its own right, as one of the first feature films made by a Black woman in Africa, but also because the only surviving copy of the film on 16mm with English subtitles is preserved in the New York Public Library. The film is based on a novella by Angolan author José Luandino Vieira and was shot in Congo-Brazzaville. Maldoror used guerrilla filmmaking practices with the aim of mobilising its viewers, in particular Western viewers unaware of the brutality of the Portuguese colonial regime. The film was subsequently banned in Portugal and thus also in its "province" of Angola. It won prestigious prizes in Berlin and in Carthage but was only screened in Angola after independence.

Sambizanga is the name of the working-class neighbourhood in Luanda that housed a Portuguese prison where Angolan militants were taken to be tortured and killed. The film begins with the arrest of revolutionary Domingos Xavier by Portuguese officials. Xavier is taken to Sambizanga prison where he is at risk of being tortured to death for not giving up the names of his fellow dissidents. The rest of the narrative focuses on Xavier's wife, Maria, who searches from jail to jail to find out what has become of her husband, experiencing excruciating emotional and physical pain during the journey while persisting in her struggle and showing immense perseverance. Her experience of solidarity among women is empowering both for her and for those around her. Emphasising the central presence of women in historiography Maldoror has said that "African women must be everywhere. They must be in the images, behind the camera, in the editing room and involved in every stage of the making of a film. They must be the ones to talk about their problems" (Sezirahiga 1995). She thus combines her activism behind the camera with a fight to get women on screen in African cinema.

Other revolutionary cinema movements and manifestoes that came into existence around the same time have not received the same scholarly attention as Third Cinema. A year before the Third Cinema Manifesto, in 1967, a "defeat-conscious" Arab attitude instigated by the defeat by Israel found its filmic culmination in the New Arab Cinema Collective, or Alternative Cinema (Bouzid 1995). A new generation of young filmmakers reenergised a collective new outlook on realist cinema. The search for new forms at this time was based in "a series of refusals" – a rejection of three main tendencies: gratuitous aestheticism, mediocrity of form and prostitution of great themes (Hennebelle 1976, 6). "[They] want to reawaken the public and bring it to share the fight" (ibid.). Férid Boughédir shows in *Caméra arabe* that New Arab Cinema thrived on a multiplicity of themes and genres, approaches and innovations, such as taking the camera outside into the real world, and making space for women interested in making films, a vision of reality that corresponded much more with the audience's lived experience. It is worth quoting the Manifesto at some length here, to lay bare the overlaps with Third Cinema:

> The Alternative Cinema Manifesto [...] held that the authenticity of film and its closeness to the social and political reality of a society is a measure of its value nationally and internationally. [...] The manifesto said: what we need is a cinema that records and studies the movement of society and analyzes its new social and political relations, a cinema that would discover and reveal the meaning of life for the individual in the midst of these relations.
>
> *(Samak 1977, 14)*

In parallel with the Third Cinema Manifesto, these filmmakers were working towards what was real and urgent for the people. Cinema was more than ever concerned with contemporary reality, which was – since 1967 – a less complacent and more self-conscious reality. Realism became the dominant strength of film, reflected in a content intrinsically linked to the form.

While Third Cinema had overlooked the role women played in filmmaking and in revolutions, New Arab Cinema became an opportunity for women in Egypt in particular to reclaim their position behind the cameras, which had been lost in the fifties (see Chapter 1). In the early seventies – with the advent of new realism, waves of revolutionary filmmaking and second wave feminism finding its feet worldwide – women reclaimed the camera. Both feminism and realism need a material platform for expression. Both are politically inspired forms of opposition to mainstream assumptions. Politically and socially engaged films thus became preoccupied with the specificity of representation and serving as a platform for oppressed voices.

Egyptian Ateyyat El Abnoudy (1939–2018) admitted to being heavily influenced by both Third Cinema and New Arab Cinema. Her first films in the early seventies referred to revolutionary and anti-colonial filmmaking practices in the global "Third World." Her films are concerned with social inequalities in Cairo, and the audience is given the responsibility of watching and listening differently than they would with other Egyptian films. She experimented in particular with the voice of a film. In the shorts *Horse of Mud* (1971), *Sad Song of Touha* (1972) and *The Sandwich* (1975), El Abnoudy's revolutionary impulses are encapsulated in her approach to the gaze and the voice. The juxtaposition of observational social realism and a lyrical, aesthetic contemplation on reality shapes an engagement with the lower classes rooted in admiration and respect. Her later work continued a preoccupation with the lower social classes, women and children, and became increasingly political, culminating in her most successful film, *Days of Democracy* (1996). Juxtaposing recorded speeches by female politicians with the exchange of concerned gazes, engenders a revolutionary spirit in its audiences and highlights the lack of women in parliament.

South African revolutionary film: women during and after apartheid

As in other revolutions, women in South Africa played a dominant role in the anti-apartheid struggle, while building a culture of resistance that kept Black communities going by sustaining their political identity through an emphasis on awareness and education (McQuiston 1997, 193). Forms of resistance did not only come from Black South African women in positions of political or social power (like Winnie Mandela and the ANC) but also from Black women who were not necessarily politically affiliated. From the seventies onwards, the horrors of apartheid were increasingly exposed to the international community, often in documentary and fiction films. Anti-apartheid films, produced by Europeans and Americans (and a handful by South Africans living in exile), reveal a gaze into South Africa from the outside. Only a small number of alternative films were produced clandestinely by liberal, White and male South Africans living in the country.

Documentary filmmaking in particular contributed substantially to critiquing the racist nationalist doctrine of the apartheid state, making efforts to redefine national identity in the post-apartheid nation. After the arrival of television in South Africa in 1976, documentary was carefully controlled by the state apparatus, and depictions of political reality were censored altogether (Verster 2007, 109). Even though strong political movements saw the light of day in anti-apartheid documentary making from as early as the fifties, these were not accessible to the public until well into the nineties. Often these films were made under very dangerous conditions: after two States of Emergency in the eighties, freedom of speech was heavily curtailed. The extremely oppressive policies of apartheid prevented film from being used as a tool in the liberation struggle to the extent that it was done in countries like Algeria, Angola or Mozambique. However, a number of anti-apartheid films did emerge during the eighties. Made clandestinely, these documentaries played an important role in alerting the rest of world to the horrors of the apartheid system.

Of particular interest are a number of female-directed anti-apartheid documentaries focusing on the participation of women in the liberation struggle. Two examples of South African documentaries of this nature are *You Have Struck a Rock!* (1981) by Deborah May and *Liberation Women* (1985) by Beata Lipman. May's film mainly deals with the remarkable women's campaigns against the pass system in the fifties. This system was designed by the government as a method of influx control that confined the majority of Black South Africans to the rural, undeveloped and largely infertile "homelands" (described by Winnie Mandela as "concentration camps" in *Liberation Women*). In 1955 and 1956 women organised nationwide protests against the hated pass laws; the first involved 2,000 women in Durban and Cape Town, and the second 20,000 women who marched to the government buildings in Pretoria. On their arrival at the government buildings they handed over petitions and stood resolutely in protest for 30 minutes. They sang an anthem of defiance: "Now you have touched the women you have struck a rock, you have dislodged a boulder, you will be crushed." This march took place on 9 August 1956 and marked what is now celebrated as Women's Day in South Africa. May's documentary of this non-violent civil disobedience movement, crushed at the 1960 Sharpeville massacre, and the banning of anti-apartheid organisations, is assembled through a montage of archive material, photographs, newspaper articles and interviews. *Liberation Women* focuses on a number of prominent women in the anti-apartheid struggle: Winnie Mandela, Helen Joseph and Amina Cachalia. Lipman returned to South Africa from exile to make the film clandestinely. Consisting mostly of interviews, the film addresses the hopes and dreams of South African women from different backgrounds, united in their fight for the abolition of apartheid.

A number of South African documentaries from the eighties emphasise the smaller, often forgotten, narratives of women who suffered severely under the system, in contrast to the above examples celebrating heroic women's collective and individual actions. *South Africa Belongs to Us* (1980) is a German production that tells the stories of five Black women from different areas and diverse socioeconomic backgrounds, revealing how Black South African women, no matter which social class they belonged to, were most affected by apartheid. Each of the five narratives is bookended by interviews with female leaders like Winnie Mandela and Fatima Meer (ex-president of the Black Women's Federation), but it is the individual narratives of marginalised Black women, and the film's meticulous and unhurried focus on the lives of women who survive on the periphery of society, that create the greatest impact. The contrasts between the heroic vision of the African woman which is commonly encountered in official history and filmic representation – especially in liberation struggle narratives – on the one hand, and the day-to-day struggles of women's everyday lives on the other hand, suggest that grand narratives have to make way for the micro-narratives of "other" women to be heard as well. These films have become part of the collective memory and of the discourse recounted and remembered in the post-apartheid era.

More recently, *Standing on their Shoulders* (2018) by South African filmmaker Xoliswa Sithole, is a historical journey through time that connects various female resistance movements. The starting point is the 1956 women's march documented in *You Have Struck a Rock!* This mantra functions as a testimony to the resilience of some remarkable female activists, including Albertina Sisulu, Lilian Ngoyi and Helen Joseph. The documentary continues to the end of apartheid, reminding us of the unwavering strength and courage of Winnie Madikizela-Mandela and other ANC women, and into the contemporary era with the continued struggles against patriarchy fought through the "fallist" movements of Rhodes Must Fall and Fees Must Fall. While women's voices in political movements are still silenced and marginalised, the film gives a powerful platform to feminist activists, scholars, students and political leaders to highlight the work that women continue to do in fighting patriarchy, race and class oppression.

Women's post-conflict and reconciliation efforts

As elsewhere on the continent, in South Africa the optimism that existed during the liberation struggles – which for women included the hope that life after independence would result in fuller gender equality and increased opportunities for female emancipation – did not fully deliver in the postcolonial era. Nnaemeka shows that nationalist discourses disguise women's issues in a way that requires women to frame their concerns firstly within a national ideology, as a prerequisite for being considered "political." She says "the truth of the matter is that most of the time […] nationalist politics depoliticizes women's politics, forcing the repoliticization of women's politics back on the national agenda only as an aftermath of nationalist struggles" (Nnaemeka 1997, 2). Laray Denzer sums it up: "When it came time for the distribution of rewards for loyalty, sacrifice and hard work, however, women found their male colleagues surprisingly obdurate and chauvinistic" (Denzer 2005, 217). Gender equality for Black women has been delayed by the historical fact that Black nationalism was privileged over feminist concerns. African women actively participated in nationalist movements as resistance fighters and party activists, but after independence women's interests were betrayed by nation states. Even military contributions did not translate into progressive gender politics, and women remained marginalised from active participation in the political and economic life of the newly liberated nations.

A filmic representation of this marginalisation can be found in Zimbabwean feature *Flame* (Ingrid Sinclair, 1996). Telling the story of Flame and Liberty, two young women who decide to join the Zimbabwean liberation struggle as soldiers, the film shows the harshness of their training – exacerbated by some male comrades using food to get sexual favours from female fighters – and their involvement in the struggle, eventually leading to complete disillusionment. At Flame and Liberty's reunion in present-day Zimbabwe at the end of the film, the two women realise that no comprehensive public memory exists of the liberation of the indigenous Zimbabweans from colonial rule, and that what is remembered has been told from a male perspective. But as we argue in Chapter 2, African women have always been at the forefront of progress and change, and increasingly occupy positions of leadership. Correspondingly, historiographies need to take into account the central roles that women have played in liberation struggles. Badri and Tripp (2017, 17) also remind us of the remarkable contributions of women to peacemaking and peacebuilding, as African women activists are involved in ending the African conflicts of the nineties and noughties, both at local and national level, by demonstrating against war, negotiating the release of kidnapped people, and organising ceremonies and amnesties to turn in arms. These reconciliation initiatives have served as peacebuilding templates in other post-conflict regions.

Fractures in the optimism that existed during the struggles for liberation and the ideals of national unity are heightened in the civil wars, inter-ethnic strife and brutal conflicts that have plagued many African countries in the post-independence era. Film can be seen as a tool that helps to safeguard memories while it can also be a preventative force, often through documentaries enabling previously marginalised voices to be heard. An example of this is the *Landscape of Memory* series (1999), a series of films addressing issues of truth and reconciliation in Southern Africa, three of which were directed and produced by female filmmakers. As the title of the series suggests, the premise of the project is that remembering can work to prevent atrocities from happening again. *Soul in Torment* by Zimbabwean director Prudence Uriri for example deals with the civil war that broke out in Matabeleland shortly after independence from Britain in 1980. Renowned South African poet Antjie Krog directed *The Unfolding of Sky*, which reported on the proceedings of the Truth and Reconciliation commission.[1] This film portrays a dialogue between Krog, an Afrikaner, and Deborah Matshoba, an African woman who suffered solitary confinement, torture and detention during apartheid. The two women explore the notion of reconciliation. For Matshoba it means forgiveness, creating a culture of *ubuntu*. For Krog it means that as an Afrikaner she has to be forgiven. Mozambican filmmaker Karen Boswall directed *From the Ashes*, the third film by a female filmmaker in the *Landscape of Memory* series, which deals with the civil war that wrecked Mozambique a few years after independence was gained.

Johannesburg-based Aliki Saragas's 2017 documentary *Strike a Rock* (invoking the 1956 women's march, but in a different context), tells the story of two mothers and best friends, Primrose Sonti and Thumeka Magwangqana, who live in Marikana, a settlement that developed around a platinum mine. Marikana was the site of a horrific tragedy in which 34 miners were killed and dozens injured when the police opened fire on a crowd of miners striking for higher pay and improved living conditions in 2012. Public commemorations of the Marikana massacre have typically focused on the slain and surviving male miners, while the stories of the widowed wives were neglected. *Strike a Rock* documents the struggles of two remarkable women fighting for improved living conditions. Primrose and Thumeka founded women's organisation Sikhala Sonke/We Cry Together. The film shows how these two inspiring women develop into leaders in their struggle for social and economic justice. Similarly, Reabetswe Moeti's award-winning short film *Mma Moeketsi* (2018) depicts a female story of the Marikana massacre, as domestic worker Mma Moeketsi from rural Lesotho hears news of the strike. As she watches the unfolding events on television, she waits for news from her son with intensifying dread. The Kenyan film *Something Necessary* (2013), which we discuss later in the chapter as a case study, further illuminates the effects of conflict and violence on women, as well as women's roles in post-conflict reconciliation efforts.

Contemporary revolutions: narrating revolutionary moments

Since the early 2010s, revolutions have once more sent a "new wave" through North African filmmaking. The so-called Arab revolutions that began in North Africa and spread to the rest of the Arab world have completely dominated cinema made in the MENA region ever since. As the wave of revolutions was sparked by the self-immolation of Mohamed Bouazizi in Sidi Bouzid, Tunisia, and as the "Jasmine Revolution" remains the only one that could (at least partly) be called successful, the earliest films about the Arab Revolutions came from Tunisia. However, some of these films were commissioned by European organisations or festivals, and the impulse behind these commissions needs to be taken into consideration. Lebow revealed the danger of revolutionary filmmakers being subjected to this type of profit-inspired interest by Western programmers (2014, 63). But the wave of political change in Tunisia also made way for young women filmmakers like Kaouther Ben Hania, whose *Le challat de Tunis/Challat of Tunis* (2013), *Zaineb takrahou ethelj/Zaineb Hates the Snow* (2016) and *Aala Kaf Ifrit/Beauty and the Dogs* (2017) directly reference the revolution along with Leyla Bouzid's *A peine j'ouvre les yeux/As I Open my Eyes* (2015). Both filmmakers respond to a new freedom of expression, using cinema as a valve that guides their future-thinking for women, through a reckoning of the past on screen.

However, even in those North African countries – like Morocco and Algeria – where the Arab Revolutions have not (yet) taken hold as intensively as they did in Tunisia and Egypt, there is also a veritable "new wave" of young, daring filmmakers emerging. In Morocco the increase in productivity has been largely due to the change in politics since the late nineties. Directors like Laïla Marrakchi, Leïla Kilani, Narjiss Nejjar and others continue to address the oppressive history of colonial and neo-colonial (and neoliberal) tendencies in Moroccan cinema. In Algerian cinema, the very recent wave of new cinema and the dramatic increase in the number of Algerian films on the international scene is interestingly led by a number of young women. Women used to be seen as exceptions within a small, male-dominated cinematic output from a country plagued by cultural and political oppression of women, but recently young female filmmakers like Rayhana (with *I Still Hide to Smoke*, 2016 – Chapter 3) and Sofia Djama (with *Les bienheureux/The Blessed*, 2017) have really taken centre stage. These directors have claimed that they became filmmakers out of a desperate need to break with the singularly male stories coming from Algeria. Amel Blidi, for example, made two short documentaries, *Demain est un autre jour/Tomorrow is Another Day* in 2013, and *In the Shadow of Words* in 2016. She says:

> I don't think there's anything haphazard about this new wave. We survived a long and difficult time. Now we need to speak to each other, to come out of our silence and that ambience of suppression. When words are lacking – when it's hard to talk about what you've just lived through in Algeria – that's where cinema comes in.
>
> *(Elgrably 2017)*

She confirms the power of cinema to deal with past and present revolutions, and acknowledges the need for women to use their voices to give shape to the stories of conflict and revolution. This is a cinematic revolution in its own right.

Case study: *Al-Khoroug Lel-Nahar/Coming Forth by Day* (Hala Lotfy, Egypt/United Arab Emirates, 2012)

Coming Forth by Day (2012) is Hala Lotfy's debut feature. She made a number of shorts and a series of documentaries for Al Jazeera, which cemented her interest in urban politics. Born in 1973, she studied economics and politics before her degree in filmmaking. She set up Hassala Productions in Cairo, a filmmakers' cooperative dedicated to supporting independent filmmakers with mentorships and technical workshops. As such, Hassala Productions enables the production of non-commercial films, and provides concrete support throughout the complex (administrative) process of filmmaking. Lotfy says she was inspired to do this because she believes in the power of independent cinema to deal with issues that are relevant to local communities and because of her conviction that film plays an important role in spreading knowledge and raising awareness (Synergos).

She started writing *Coming Forth by Day* in 2008 and filming in 2010 but the revolution interrupted the production process, delaying the film by six months. The disappointment with the revolution became an inherent part of the production process. Indeed, the revolution in Egypt changed nothing, in Lotfy's view, and cinema needed to do more in order to continue the struggle. She says: "We were on the streets and really in danger," adding that crew members were arrested during production. "We realized that we needed to deliver a sense of revolution into our work" (Allen 2013). With that mentality, Lotfy resumed work on the film, and for her, it became the act of making the film that was revolutionary in itself:

> It was an act of resistance, because the film scene in Egypt is so established that it makes it hard for individuals to make a name for themselves. It's a very good example of how the country lacks democracy.
>
> *(Allen 2013)*

Amir Taha argues that cinema is the artistic field that benefited most from the 2011 revolution in Egypt (Taha 2017). But as Lotfy says, this film came about in spite of the revolution, and in spite of Egyptian cinema being a male-centred industry. Edited by Heba Othman and production designed by Chahira Mouchir, *Coming Forth by Day* is an entirely female effort in a male-dominated film industry. Hala Lotfy is one of the frontrunners of a new, feminist cinema movement. *Coming Forth by Day* is about those left behind by a corrupt system, the nameless faces continuing to live unnoticed lives. The film works with a new type of Egyptian realism – one where the art of the image becomes more important than that of the voice, because the voice is drowned out by other post-revolutionary noise. The protagonist, Soad (Donia Maher), is a thirty-something woman who lives in a small Cairo flat with her parents. She is her elderly father's carer. He is bed-bound, immobile and silent; an emasculated man. Soad's mother is an exhausted nurse who barely communicates with her daughter. The unity of space, time and purpose in the first half of the film cannot prevent the outside coming in through the open windows: traffic, voices, calls to prayer and general street noise enter the flat without offering an idea of the outside world, but Soad does escape into Cairo. However, instead of the outside affording respite from the claustrophobic flat, Cairo actually increases the oppressive atmosphere. The slowness of the day, the overpowering brightness and the focus on unfamiliar bodies and faces emphasise the physical effects of the Egyptian stasis on the poor, on women and on those disenfranchised by a failed revolution. This heralds the new treatment of a revolutionary reality that has come to a standstill. The revolution and the change a revolution is intended to bring, as a long and slow process with interruptions and disappointments on the way, is condensed into a hopeless moment.

In this new Egyptian cinema, films are revolutionary in understated ways: their pace is slow and they are aesthetically challenging rather than revolutionary in the way we would expect from the legacies of Third Cinema or Alternative Arab Cinema. In *Filming Revolution*, a project on revolutionary cinema in Egypt, Alisa Lebow describes a blunt resistance to narrating the revolution, which has led to radical changes in form and aesthetic approach to art. It includes a filmic focus on the slowness of the moment, reflecting the lack of change, and a focus on what is (versus what was or will be) resulting in a cinema with little narrative causality or character development. In interviews with filmmakers she noticed how some spoke strenuously against the very idea of making a film about the revolution, and others simply felt that the revolution was too overwhelming a topic – but *any* films being made in Egypt since the revolution are "about" the revolution.

(Lebow, 2018)

Films made about, or since, the Egyptian revolution are concerned with depicting the atmosphere, or the stillness of life *in spite of* the revolution. Indeed, time – and especially the slowness of time – is one of the main aspects that have come to define Egyptian filmmaking since 2010. *Coming Forth by Day* is an outstanding example of this preference for slowness and the stretching of time. It is a stylistic strength that indicates a deep awareness of slow change, a meditation on the relevance of past and future, and translating these reflections into a string of moments rather than a narrative causality. Characters in the film spend a lot of time in bed, under the covers, unwilling or unable to wake up, and prolonged moments of staring out the window without engaging with what they see. Instead, the camera lingers on their faces and on the back of their heads, contemplating in close-up the self-reflections of characters in a depressed state of stasis.

The city of Cairo itself turns out to be a city of the dead. After a night of aimless wandering in the dysfunctional city, Soad visits the actual City of the Dead, the necropolis in Cairo. The title of the film refers directly to the ancient Egyptian *Book of the Dead*, or, in its literal translation, the *Book of Coming Forth by Day*. It consists of a number of texts that can be described as spells used to assist the dead person's passage into the underworld and the afterlife, in the company of Osiris. When Soad wanders into the City of the Dead, an area of graves and mausoleums now used as the living quarters of the poorest inhabitants of Cairo, the atmosphere shifts. For some, living among ancestors is a blessing, for others the City of the Dead is the slum into which they have been driven. In the film, the City of the Dead is depicted as a space of peaceful, lonely meditation for Soad: she sits down, and calmly watches dawn arrive. This moment, although dark, does offer some relief as the oppressive silence turns into a cool sense of quiet. So far, the three protagonists have been non-living, and have been suffocating one another in the flat, but the dead in the City of the Dead stand peacefully side by side, and Soad finds new purpose in going home as she witnesses the sunrise. She transitions into the light of a new day and this offers some solace as she walks home and accepts that her father will soon pass into the afterlife. The last (and first) conversation between Soad and her mother reveals an acceptance of death. They pose a final – unanswered – question: "Where are we going to bury him? Where is our cemetery located?"

Beyond the characters' suffocation developing into acceptance, Lotfy shows how the revolution itself has become a fiction, a fabrication that bears little resemblance to any kind of reality. By implication, she throws into question the entire project of narrating such a history. Focusing on Soad's one-day journey into Cairo, seeing people from all religious convictions being dealt the same uncertainty in a city that has lost its lustre, *Coming Forth by Day* implicitly negotiates the status of women in

Egypt, as it breaks the religious and social taboo of death. In the first half of the film Soad remains inside the flat, and the film emphasises the immobility of Soad's father, the family's failure to communicate meaningfully, and their exhaustion and depression. But it does this in a sensitive and haptic manner. The second half of the film sees Soad escaping the oppressive atmosphere inside, to go walking aimlessly through the city doing impulsive, meaningless tasks. The city is an unfamiliar space, no one really communicates – rather people shout at one another and talk to themselves – and everyone presents a potential threat. Moreover, the brightness of the light presses down onto the dusty Cairo streets, and it is not until darkness falls and Soad feels unseen that she is able to look up at the sky. The film focuses on the image and keeps quiet: representations, implications and interpretations are entirely dependent on the visual power of the film. Where Egyptian cinema is stereo-typically very dialogue-driven, this revolutionary film is quiet and self-reflexive. Lotfy says: "We don't enjoy anything and are just rolling over day by day – because of the economic crisis, because of a lack of understanding. This feeling, the lack of hope and total despair, is something I cannot express, but it hangs in the air" (Allen 2013). Similarly, another young women director, Jasmina Metwaly, acknowledges that the revolution is "not a subject so much as a state of being, [and] so to make a film 'about' the revolution is in essence to miss the point" (Lebow 2018). Instead, she talks of making films from "within" the revolution, stretching time and accepting life rather than explaining political stasis.

The film's revolutionary nature is thus entirely post-revolutionary: narrative is replaced by impressions and sensations. In fact, human tragedies, everyday injustices, political oppression and social suffering are of no importance to the plot; they are not the topic, they are just there. And that is precisely where the revolutionary spirit of the film lies: in its power to reveal the everyday banality of injustice in the Egyptian capital, with no beginning and no end. The film aims to activate one's instinctual senses rather than any intellectual or revolutionary speech. This idea of a feeling, a scent, a sensuous experience of the city might be what makes the film part of a feminist look at the revolution and its aftermath (the way stream of con-sciousness-writing and *écriture féminine* did in French literature). Quite a few female Egyptian filmmakers have come to the conclusion that rationalising this feeling *and* the revolution is difficult. Films such as *Arij, Scent of Revolution* (2014) by Viola Shafik, show a very fragmented and subjective, intensely personal and self-reflexive thought-process on the far-reaching consequences of the events throughout Egypt. In *Arij* Shafik allows the overwhelming incoherence of the revolution to lead the halting, disconnected film – a form expressed in the film's title through the immaterial nature of the "scent." As such, the films are dominated by long takes, minimal camera movement, and simple and direct cuts, lighting and sound designs that encourage a cinema of the senses, of instinct and of feelings rather than explanations. The film thrives on a quiet and non-judgmental observational quality.

When it comes specifically to women's experiences of the revolution, Lebow explains that the beginning of the revolution seemed to be clear: "the demands were very general, calling of course for the fall of the Mubarak regime but also for 'bread, freedom, and social justice'" (2018). However, increasingly there was a need to make specific demands for women's rights,

> when women protesters were being targeted in a particularly gendered form of violence at the hands of the state but also by unorganized bands of men who felt entitled to police women's bodies in public spaces (this included everything from grabbing breasts and genitals to stripping women of their clothes and digitally penetrating them, and even gang rape).
>
> *(Lebow 2018)*

By the end of 2011, gender shaming had grown to such proportions that it was forced into prominence (Lebow 2018). Videos on this topic are extremely hard to watch, especially as a woman, and filmmakers have wondered about strategies to deal with and/or represent such traumatic and traumatising events. Indeed, one of the main questions of the Egyptian revolution is whether women's rights can be inferior to human rights or social and political equality.

Case study: *Something Necessary* (Judy Kibinge, Germany/Kenya, 2013)

In January and February of 2008, inter-ethnic and political tensions that had been brewing for decades in Kenya culminated in a period of severe post-election violence that resulted in over 1,000 deaths, 350,000 displaced persons, 2,000 refugees, numerous victims of sexual violence, and the destruction of huge numbers of properties (CSIS 2009). While the violence erupted initially because citizens perceived the elections as rigged by the government, it turned into an inter-ethnic and geopolitical conflict with members of the Kikuyu and Kisii communities, believed to be associated with the president's Party of National Unity (PNU), being targeted in the Rift Valley and on the coast. In Western Kenya the violence and destruction were directed towards government facilities. It was widely believed that politicians, influential businessmen and village leaders colluded in perpetrating the violence through recruiting criminal gangs of unemployed and dispossessed youths. In Nairobi, Kikuyu gangs were mobilised to carry out violence against the Luo, Luhya and Kalenjin peoples, and drive them from their properties. Ethnically driven sexual violence was committed against women and girls in the form of individual and gang rapes (ibid.). This paints the traumatic and horrific socio-political context of Judy Kibinge's 2013 film, *Something Necessary*.

Kibinge is one of Kenya's most high-profile filmmakers. She entered filmmaking after a very successful career in advertising. Her debut feature film, *Dangerous Affair* (2002) is credited with ushering in a new wave of Kenyan filmmaking, a sharp departure from the previous predominance of NGO-funded, awareness-raising documentaries that have burdened the anglophone sub-Saharan African film industries in particular (see Chapter 1). With its romantic love story that centres on female characters, depicts the everyday lives of the young Kenyan middle class, and is set in an urban surrounding in vibrant and modern Nairobi, *Dangerous Affair* contains a homegrown narrative and aesthetic that appealed to local audiences. In line with our argument concerning revolutions in content and in style, Kibinge's work can be seen as an important artistic intervention that subverted the status quo in Kenyan filmmaking in the early noughties. In her other documentary and fiction films, she regularly addresses social and cultural issues relevant to modern Kenyans. Kibinge is multi-talented: among many other achievements, she is a founding member of the leading African literary magazine *Kwani?* and the founder of Docubox, an East African documentary film fund. Her films have been recognised internationally, she has been a jury member for the International Documentary Festival Amsterdam (IDFA) and in 2017 she was invited to act as a voting member for the Academy Awards.

Something Necessary focuses on Anne (Susan Wanjiru) who begins her path to recovery after her husband Steve is murdered and her son Kitu lies in a coma as a result of the post-election violence. Parallel to her story runs that of Joseph, a young man who was part of the gang that burnt down Anne's farm, murdered her husband, attacked her son and raped her. Joseph is desperate to leave behind his life of violence, to escape the clutches of the gang and to repent for his part in the brutalities committed against Anne and her family. *Something Necessary* is a slow and contemplative film which, similar to *Coming Forth by Day*, shows the aftermath of violence in which survivors are at times paralysed by their trauma and incapable of moving on. Fear and apprehension permeate the decisions and actions of the characters, as in the Egyptian film, and the outside world in particular is perceived as a hostile space, keeping Anne in physical and psychological entrapment. Through Anne's slow and uneven journey to recovery, the film focuses in particular on the effects of violence and conflict on women, as well as women's roles in post-conflict reconciliation efforts.

The film opens with archival footage of the post-election violence, as gangs attack people and their properties, wielding machetes and other weapons. Kibinge has explained in interviews that the decision to open the film with clips of real footage was a strategy to present the type of audio-visual news material that international audiences would be familiar with in representations of conflicts on the African continent. Watching this kind of footage in the safety of the home has a desensitising effect; the violence is committed by anonymous, non-individualised mobs that reinforce stereotypical views of Africa held by foreign viewers. It is the kind of fast-paced and frenzied footage that we might more readily associate with visual documentation of revolutions and societal conflicts. However, when the film cuts to Anne, who is recovering in hospital, the pace changes completely: we are intimately drawn into the emotional torpor of an individual struggling to cope with the psychological and physical scars left by violent trauma. Long takes follow her wordless contemplation, her expression dazed and bewildered as she stares out of the window. Viewers are compelled to empathise with Anne, to try and comprehend something of her pain and suffering – an impossible quest, but one of the aims of creative expression that artists have never stopped pursuing.

A similarly ambiguous opposition between inside and outside spaces as in *Coming Forth by Day* is also present in *Something Necessary*. The inside of a hospital room or a bedroom in her damaged farmhouse are spaces where Anne could sleep for endless hours and be safe from the dangerous outside world or the memories of violence. But it is also a claustrophobic space that keeps her trapped and immobilised. The outside is depicted with wide shots of the vast, beautiful Kenyan countryside, but it is an exposed space that represents threat and emphasises Anne's vulnerability. When she leaves the hospital, she decides to slowly rebuild her farm (ironically called The Haven) piece by piece, as a way of reconstructing her fractured life. Her husband's brother, Lesit, and her sister, Gathoni, regard this as an irrational decision and repeatedly advise against it. Gathoni accuses her of being self-obsessed and Lesit dismisses her request for help with a misogynistic sneer: "Steve was the farmer. But you.... You are a woman. And a widowed woman. It's not right for you to live there."

At the same time, Joseph is also attempting to forge a new life for himself, initially finding a job at a factory. Both characters are haunted by the past, Joseph by his own violent deeds and Anne by flashbacks to the night of violence and by visions of her dead husband, representative of the post-traumatic terror that she is experiencing. Members of the gang Joseph is trying to escape from continuously harass and threaten him, and when he misses work after being beaten up, he loses his job but is offered another as a loader for a delivery company. Coincidentally this job takes him back to Anne's farm to deliver materials for the rebuild, intensifying his need for penance. He overhears a conversation between his co-workers about Anne's defencelessness alone on the unprotected farm, which prompts him to build a barbed wire fence around her farm at night. This becomes his atonement for his part in the violence that devastated Anne's life.

In a feminist act of self-determination, Anne gradually starts taking back control of her life through the stone-by-stone rebuilding of her farm and returning to her work as a hospital nurse. When she discovers that she is a pregnant as a result of the gang rape, she steals medicine from the hospital, checks herself into a cheap hotel and takes abortion pills to terminate the pregnancy. High angle shots frame her crouched in the corner of the hotel room writhing in pain, until she eventually washes away the blood from the aborted foetus in the shower. Anne's physical and emotional suffering is translated into scenes that are extremely difficult to watch. Temporary reprieve comes when her son wakes up from his coma and Anne is allowed to take him home. But their relationship is damaged. Kitu is angry and fearful about being back on the farm. When her depression and apathy set in again, leading Anne to neglect his welfare, her sister unceremoniously announces that she is taking Kitu away.

Joseph is depicted as both a perpetrator and a victim, roles that are often conflated at times of conflict and chaotic violence. The origins and perpetration of political violence can be inscrutable, especially where previously non-violent people, living peacefully side-by-side suddenly turn on each other, committing violent acts, as a result of historic tensions and prejudices. In lived experience there is no simple resolution or easily identifiable and clear-cut victim/perpetrator, good/ evil binary. Early on in *Something Necessary* Joseph and other gang members are shown in a crowded room watching the news of a power-sharing agreement between President Mwai Kibaki and his opponent. They are outraged by this betrayal as they have been fighting for the land they believed was stolen from them in the elections. "We fight for what is ours, even till death," they vouch. Trapped within these continuing cycles of violence, Joseph is unable to escape the wrath of the gang for deserting them, and they eventually beat him to death, dumping his limp body on his mother's doorstep. His fate is a sobering reminder of the consequences of violence.

A Commission of Inquiry into Post-Election Violence (CIPEV) was implemented by the government in the wake of the conflict, and in *Something Necessary* Anne hears about the Commission and is prompted by her friend to attend the hearings. It had a mandate to investigate the facts and the conduct of the state security agencies, by giving people a platform to deliver testimonies and eyewitness accounts. As in other historical examples of truth and reconciliation commissions, the film depicts people's distrust of a government that has betrayed them, and scepticism about the effectiveness of the Commission to achieve any real benefits or restitution for ordinary citizens. It is seen by some as a ploy by politicians to avoid prosecution by the International Criminal Court, but Anne decides to attend a hearing and listens to various testimonies of people having lost their livelihoods and their loved ones. Anne's own testimony is represented to the viewer not in words, but through flashbacks to the night of the attack, commencing with the gang approaching the farmhouse with flaming torches. The sound is muffled as we witness fragmented snippets of the attack, ending with close-ups of family photographs disappearing in flames. These flashbacks are a physical manifestation of the violent rupture in her life. Anne's journey to peace and healing is not over, and the film remains open-ended. She never identifies Joseph as the anonymous do-gooder rebuilding her fence, and reads the new fence as a positive sign. The film ends with her picking up her son in a tearful reunion, leaving open the possibility of life after trauma.

Like *Coming Forth by Day, Something Necessary* depicts a nation in pain, at an impasse after political conflict, devastating violence or disillusionment. Kibinge has explained that the film was completed at a tense time, in early 2013 just before the next elections. Kenyans were apprehensive and fearful that the violence could be repeated, and local audiences found it a difficult, and potentially re-traumatising film. She sees the film as a repository for collective memories, and an attempt to find answers. Her first film after the post-election conflict was a documentary entitled *Peace Wanted Alive* (2009), the title borrowed from a phrase a graffiti artist sprayed on the walls of buildings in Kibera, a slum outside of Nairobi. That film documented the ways in which various artists and cultural workers attempted to create something positive out of the violence, to offer a different depiction of the events from what popular media could. It was Kibinge's way of ending the paralysing effect of the violence on her own psyche. She said:

I think violence of this kind happening, forces you to ask yourself whether, as a writer or as an artist or as a filmmaker, you have any kind of responsibility – and I always used to say "no," "no, of course not – I just make film." But then suddenly here this thing is and you do have at your hands something that you can use to do something a little bit wider. So it was a coming of age time, for me at least.

(Wallis, 2013)

★★★★

Our two case studies, both made in the aftermath of political conflict, show the difficult recovery process after violence. This shared theme results in many other similarities. Stylistically the incapacitating effect of trauma on individuals is depicted through long takes and minimal camera movement. Both films attempt to individualise those nameless faces who have to continue their lives after a violent disruption. Death looms large over both narratives. In *Something Necessary*, Anne is not even offered the ceremonial closure of attending her husband's funeral, as Lesit informs her they buried him while she was in hospital. Both films show women looking after loved ones and coming to terms with violence perpetrated by men. As the films attempt to capture the stasis of the current moment, they do not present conclusive narratives, but they do offer some hope for their central female protagonists. Narrating and representing trauma in a truthful way is highly complex; some would say impossible. But in both the Egyptian and Kenyan contexts, these post-revolution and post-conflict periods presented a fertile time for artists to explore what happened and why it happened, even if these questions remain unanswered. Art presents the opportunity to reach at least the possibility of catharsis. While we need to be realistic about art's capacities and limits to contribute to peacebuilding and conflict resolution, revolutionary films like *Coming Forth by Day* and *Something Necessary* are significant female testimonies that attempt to enable audiences to sympathise with those experiencing violence.

Note

1 Krog wrote *Country of My Skull* (2002) about her experiences in the TRC, made into the film *In My Country* in 2004.

Bibliography

Allen, Kristen (2013) "Act of resistance – making an independent film in Egypt," *Spiegel*. Available online: www.spiegel.de/international/world/director-hala-lotfy-on-making-independent-films-in-egypt-a-883254.html [Accessed January 2019].

Austin, Guy (2012) *Algerian National Cinema*. Manchester: Manchester University Press.

Badri, Balghis and Aili Mari Tripp (2017) *Women's Activism in Africa: Struggles for Rights and Representation*. London: Zed Books.

Bassori, Timité (2016) "Un théâtre nègre à Paris: La compagnie Les Griots," *Africultures* (21 November). Available online: http://africultures.com/un-theatre-negre-a-paris-la-compagnie-les-griots-13855/ [Accessed January 2019].

Bouzid, Nouri and Shereen El Ezabi, (1995) "New realism in Arab cinema: The defeat-conscious cinema," *Alif: Journal of Comparative Poetics*, 15, pp. 242–250.

Chapman, James (2008) *War and Film*. London: Reaktion Books.

Cooke, Miriam (1996) *Women and the War Story*. Oakland, CA: University of California Press.

CSIS (2009) "Post-election violence in Kenya and its aftermath," *Centre for Strategic and International Studies* Blog (August 11). Available online: https://csis.org/blogs/smart-global-health/post-election-violence-kenya-and-its-aftermath [Accessed January 2019].

Cunningham, Douglas A. and John C. Nelson (2016) *A Companion to the War Film*. London: Wiley-Blackwell.

Denzer, LaRay (2005) "Gender and decolonization: A study of three women in West African public life." In A. Cornwall (ed.) *Readings in Gender in Africa*. Oxford: James Currey, pp. 217–233.

Eberwein, Robert T. (2004) *The War Film*. New Brunswick, NJ: Rutgers University Press.

Elgrably, J. (2017) "Algerian new wave: 'When words are lacking – that's where cinema comes in'." *Middle East Monitor*. Available online: www.middleeasteye.net/features/algerian-new-wave-when-words-are-lacking-thats-where-cinema-comes [Accessed 20 September 2019].

Fanon, Frantz (1967) *The Wretched of the Earth*. Harmondsworth: Penguin.

Gabriel, Teshome (1982) *Third Cinema in the Third World. The Aesthetics of Liberation*. Ann Arbor, MI: UMI Research Press.

Guneratne, A. and W. Dissanayake (eds) *Rethinking Third Cinema*. London: Routledge, pp. 1–28.

Hennebelle, Guy (1976) "Arab cinema," *MERIP Reports*, 52, pp. 4–12.

Krog, A. (1999) *Country of My Skull*. London: Vintage Books.

Lebow, Alisa (2014) "Filming revolution: Approaches to programming the 'Arab Spring'." In Dina Iordanova and Stefanie Van de Peer (eds) *Film Festival Yearbook 6: Film Festivals and the Middle East*. St Andrews: Film Studies, pp. 61–74.

Lebow, Alisa (2018) "Narrating the revolution," *Filming Revolution*. Available online: https://filmingrevolution.supdigital.org/article/316/narrating_the_revolution [Accessed November 2018].

Lebow, Alisa (2018) "Women," *Filming Revolution*. Available online: www.filmingrevolution.supdigital.org/article/323/women [Accessed November 2018].

McQuiston, Liz (1997) *Suffragettes to She-Devils: Women's Liberation and Beyond*. London: Phaidon.

Nnaemeka, Obioma (ed.) (1997a) *The Politics of (M)Othering: Womanhood, identity, and resistance in African literature*. London: Routledge.

Salmane, Hala (1976) "Historical background." In H. Salmane, S. Hartog and D. Wilson (eds) *Algerian Cinema*. London: British Film Institute, pp. 5–7.

Samak, Qussaï (1977) "The politics of Egyptian cinema," *MERIP Reports*, 56, pp. 14.

Sankara, Thomas (2007 [1990]) *Women's Liberation and the African Freedom Struggle*. Second, revised edition. Atlanta: Pathfinder Press.

Sezirahiga, Jadot (1995) "Sarah Maldoror: 'Il faut prendre d'assaut la télévision,'" *Ecrans d'Afrique*, 12.

Shohat, Ella (2003) "Post-Third-Worldist culture. Gender, nation and the cinema." In A. Guneratne and W. Dissanayake (eds) *Rethinking Third Cinema*. London: Routledge, pp. 51–78.

Solanas, Fernando and Octavio Getino (1969) "Towards a third cinema." In B. Nichols (1976) *Movies and Methods: An Anthology*, Volume 1. Oakland, CA: University of California Press, pp. 44–64.

Synergos (no date) "Hala Lotfy: Synergos social entrepreneur and founder, Hassala," *Synergos*. Available online: www.synergos.org/network/bio/hala-lutfy [Accessed January 2019].

Taha, Amir (2017) "Hala Lofty's coming forth by day: Towards a new Egyptian cinema," *Mise-en-Scène – The Journal of Film and Visual Narration*, 2(2), pp. 19–34.

Turshen, Meredeth and Clotilde Twagiramariya (eds) (1998) *What Women Do in Wartime: Gender and Conflict in Africa*. London: Zed Books.

Uwakweh, Pauline Ada (2017) *African Women Under Fire: Literary Discourses in War and Conflict*. Lanham, MD: Rowman and Littlefield.

Van de Peer, Stefanie (2017) *Negotiating Dissidence: The Pioneering Women of Arab Documentary*. Edinburgh: Edinburgh University Press.

Verster, François (2007) "Redefining the political: A short overview and some thoughts on personal documentary films from the new South Africa." In M. Botha (ed.) *Marginal Lives and Painful Pasts: South African Cinema After Apartheid*. Parklands: Genugtig Uitgewers.

Wallis, Kate (2013) "QandA: Judy Kibinge – Writer, director and filmmaker," *Africa in Words*. Available online: https://africainwords.com/2013/11/08/qa-judy-kibinge-writer-director-and-film-maker/ [Accessed January 2019].

Filmography

À mon âge je me cache encore pour fumer / I Still Hide to Smoke, Dir. Rayhana Obermeyer, France/Greece/Algeria, 2016

A peine j'ouvre les yeux / As I Open My Eyes, Dir. Leyla Bouzid, Tunisia/France/Belgium/United Arab Emirates/Switzerland, 2015

Aala Kaf Ifrit / Beauty and the Dogs, Dir. Kaouther Ben Hania, Tunisia/France/Sweden/Norway/Lebanon/Qatar/Switzerland, 2017

Al-Khoroug Lel-Nahar / Coming Forth by Day, Dir. Hala Lotfy, Egypt/United Arab Emirates, 2012

Arij, Scent of Revolution, Dir. Viola Shafik, Egypt/Germany, 2014

Battleship Potemkin, Dir. Sergei M. Eisenstein, Soviet Union, 1925

Caméra arabe, Dir. Férid Boughedir, Tunisia, 1987

Dangerous Affair, Dir. Judy Kibinge, South Africa/Kenya, 2002

Days of Democracy, Dir. Ateyyat El Abnoudy, Egypt, 1996

Demain est un autre jour / Tomorrow is Another Day, Dir. Amel Blidi, Algeria, 2013

Fatma 75, Dir. Selma Baccar, Tunisia, 1975

Flame, Dir. Ingrid Sinclair, Zimbabwe, 1996

From the Ashes, Dir. Karen Boswall, Mozambique, 1999

Good Morning, Vietnam, Dir. Barry Levinson, USA, 1987

Horse of Mud, Dir. Ateyyat El Abnoudy, Egypt, 1971

In My Country, Dir. John Boorman, South Africa, 2004

In the Shadow of Words, Dir. Amel Blidi, Algeria, 2016

Indigènes / Days of Glory, Dir. Rachid Bouchareb, Algeria/France/Morocco/Belgium, 2006

Kaddu Beykat, Dir. Safi Faye, Senegal, 1976

L'Algérie en flammes / Algeria in Flames, Dir. René Vautier, Algeria, 1958

L'Éveil / The Awakening, Dir. Selma Baccar, Tunisia, 1966

La battaglia di Algeri / The Battle of Algiers, Dir. Gillo Pontecorvo, Italy/Algeria, 1966

La Nouba des femmes du Mont Chenoua, Dir. Assia Djebar, Algeria, 1979

La passante, Dir. Safi Faye, Senegal, 1972

Le challat de Tunis / Challat of Tunis, Dir. Kaouther Ben Hania, Tunisia/France, 2013

Les bienheureux / The Blessed, Dir. Sofia Djama, Algeria/Belgium/France, 2017

Liberation Women, Dir. Beata Lipman, South Africa, 1985

Mma Moeketsi, Dir. Reabetswe Moeti, South Africa, 2018

Monangambé, Dir. Sarah Maldoror, Angola, 1968

Peace Wanted Alive, Dir. Judy Kibinge, Kenya, 2009

Sad Song of Touha, Dir. Ateyyat El Abnoudy, Egypt, 1972

Sambizanga, Dir. Sarah Maldoror, Angola/France, 1972
Seven Samurai, Dir. Akira Kurosawa, Japan, 1954
Something Necessary, Dir. Judy Kibinge, Germany/Kenya, 2013
Soul in Torment, Dir. Prudence Uriri, Zimbabwe, 1999
South Africa Belongs to Us, Dir. Chris Austin, West Germany, 1980
Standing on their Shoulders, Dir. Xoliswa Sithole, South Africa, 2018
Strike a Rock, Dir. Aliki Saragas, South Africa, 2017
The Sandwich, Dir. Ateyyat El Abnoudy, Egypt, 1975
The Unfolding of Sky, Dir. Antjie Krog, South Africa, 1999
You Have Struck a Rock!, Dir. Deborah May, South Africa, 1981
Zaineb takrahou ethelj / Zaineb Hates the Snow, Dir. Kaouther Ben Hania, Tunisia/France, 2016

5

DAUGHTERS AND THEIR MOTHERS

Between conflict and acceptance

In Tunisian classic *The Silences of the Palace* by Moufida Tlatli (1994), Alia, a 25-year-old wedding singer, returns to her place of birth and reminisces about her mother's life as a servant and mistress in the palace of the Beys. The lower grounds of the palace not only function as the servants' quarters but also as a safe space, metaphorically warm and humid, almost womb-like, for a community of women and young girls who talk a lot but do not speak about certain hidden truths. It is this contrast between disclosure and concealment that marks out mother–daughter relationships in the films under discussion in this chapter. As the women/mothers in *The Silences of the Palace* are domestic workers but also servants at the beck and call of the Beys' sexual whims, the oppressive outside patriarchy invades the women's quarters too often and retains control over what is said and what is known. A lack of good communication skills and (occasionally misplaced) protective attitudes from the mothers towards their daughters, all exacerbated by the constant presence of the spectre of the colonial past and pending independence, complicate communication across generations. As Alia considers the past and struggles to accept her own fate as a mother and mistress to an unfaithful man, a new understanding of her mother's sexuality and servitude enables her to decide to raise her child as a single mother in an independent Tunisia.

In *Buried Secrets* (Tunisia, 2009), a film inspired by *The Silences of the Palace*, fellow Tunisian filmmaker Raja Amari similarly explores her three characters' complex inter-generational relationships. A lower-class mother and her two daughters take refuge in the downstairs quarters of an abandoned villa and spy on a young wealthy couple secretly consummating their love before marriage. The youngest of the daughters, Aicha, is drawn to the couple and obsessed with their sexual relationship. The relationship with her mother and sister suffers because of her interest in these outsiders, and also because of secrets that her mother has kept from her: it is her sister who is actually her mother, being the victim of an entirely suppressed sexual relationship with her own father. Aicha, practically mute and the carrier and embodiment of this secret, is a very oblique character, enacted by the sensuous Hafsia Herzi. After breaking out of her oppressive situation, where her mother(s) have not been able to establish the subterranean safe space Alia's mother did in *The Silences of the Palace*, Aicha takes revenge on those who have not listened to her silence or noticed her internal struggles with the secrets surrounding her. Due to the complete failure of communication across class and generations, she is the only one to escape the confines of the past and of the lower, womb-like quarters of the house, in this case in spite of her mother.

These narratives showcase the rich and intense complexity of mother-daughter relationships in cinema. Motherhood remains a fundamental part of many African women's lives, and has historically been depicted extensively in African women's films, including the joys, fears and complexities of childbirth and the mother-child relationship. Motherhood is a highly contentious social issue in all feminist contexts, whereas being a daughter is seen as the less problematic or interesting position. However, we want to question this position, and consider the immense responsibility put on daughters to grow up in a patriarchal world. As such, we choose to focus here on the neglected positionality of the daughter. As we show, mother and daughter form a complex alliance that develops along the lines of a scale between solidarity and support, and opposition and rejection. It seems to us that the generational differences between older and younger women are the hardest to overcome. And we argue here that they are usually only overcome if intergenerational communication fails and is then restored.

Cinematic mother-daughter relationships

The relationship between women of different generations but the same kin is one of the most dynamic relationships there is, precisely because it is both constant and constantly in flux. Women make films about women in order to address inequalities and imbalances in the representation of women's identities and subjectivities on screen. We emphasise that motherhood is not always an inherently traditional or old-fashioned cinematic identity for women: in many cases the films narrate the intergenerational struggles that drive the narrative forward. At the same time, motherhood is often included in African delineations of feminism, sometimes in opposition to Western feminism. However complex conceptualisations of motherhood are in feminism, or perhaps precisely because of its polemical nature, it is imperative to discuss the history and agency of motherhood and the range of approaches to these women's identities in African cinema. However, we want to enrich our reflections on the sociological and anthropological understandings of motherhood with discussions of daughterhood: the female child often being the character left out either in the range of protagonists in the narrative or in scholarly work on relationships on the screen. Additionally, we prefer not to limit our understanding of the child to children: adults are someone's children as well. The daughters we discuss in this chapter are young adults who, in the coming-of-age stories, make decisions and assert their ideologies independently from their mothers.

In an African context, while there have been plenty of mother-daughter relationships on screen, these have not received the critical attention they merit. Moreover, in the rare cases where these relationships are part of the narrative, they often emphasise either an antagonistic relationship, or a co-dependency: one of two extremes possible on a whole spectrum of developing feelings. In what follows, we present a non-exhaustive overview of some of the most memorable mother-daughter relationships in African cinema, after which we focus on feminist and other approaches to mothers and daughters. We want to show how constructive these relationships can be, with a specific interest in the success or failure of intergenerational communication. In its discussions of mothers and daughters, this chapter engages with the concepts of socialisation and education; with the tension between closeness, similarity and solidarity and the struggle for difference, independence and change; and with the generational struggles between kin. The two case studies focus on *Mossane* (Safi Faye, Senegal, 1996) and *À peine j'ouvre les yeux/As I Open my Eyes* (Leyla Bouzid, Tunisia, 2015). We look at issues of gender, genre and generation, and how these three concepts relate to each other, in order to explore how mothers and daughters structure their dynamic relationships and navigate their identities on screen.

When films focus on female children, female filmmakers mostly focus on the affirmative aspects of motherhood, with motherhood seen as a choice and an experience, with its own struggles and rewards. In the same way, the choice not to have children can be an act of self-determination. Daughterhood, likewise, is depicted as a complex but enabling position that allows young women to discover their own agency. While daughters are often ignored, the concept of motherhood features dominantly in discourse on African womanhood and African feminism. There is the assumption that all African women are mothers even if they do not have their own biological children. The communal nature of some African societies leads to women (and men) taking on parental roles which can be non-biological. African feminism generally rejects radical feminism's critique of motherhood, focusing rather on the notion that motherhood is both a biological *and* social role. Criticism is aimed at attempts to universalise Western feminist principles, seeking instead opportunities to translate these ideologies into the realities of African women's lives. This has contributed to the development of a specifically African feminist discourse.

In this context it is important not to read African women's experiences exclusively in terms of (maternal) sacrifice or victimisation, a remnant of colonialism where the continent was essentially gendered as "Mother Africa." The role of women is regularly defined in terms of traditional structures, and in nationalist rhetoric anywhere women are often upheld as mothers of the nation. But these grand narratives obscure debates around issues exclusively affecting women, like polygamy, the lack of access to education and the underrepresentation of women in public spheres. African womanhood and motherhood are typically invoked as a symbolic and allegorical representation of the nation, where women become a trope in idealising national identity rather than as characters with their own personalities, struggles and successes, and their own agency. Going beyond this discourse, as the title of our book asks, requires us to go into it first.

Geographical or emotional distance between mothers and their daughters is one of the main tropes in mother-daughter films. In Pauline Mulombe's short film *Tout le monde a des raisons d'en vouloir à sa mère/Everyone has Reasons to be Angry with their Mother* (DRC/Belgium, 2010), the mother/daughter relationship, through issues of multiculturalism, tradition and modernity, are explored from the perspective of African daughters growing up in Europe. This is also explored in Sarah Bouyain's debut feature *Notre étrangère/The Place in Between* (France/Burkina Faso, 2011) (see Chapter 2). Apolline Traoré's *Sous la clarté de la lune/Under the Moonlight* (Burkina Faso, 2004) has a similar theme, as an African mother reunites with her mixed-race daughter snatched away at birth by the girl's French father. French-Ivorian director Isabelle Boni-Claverie's short film *Pour la nuit* (*For the Night*, 2004) depicts a single night on the streets of Marseille as a young mixed-race woman experiences psychological turmoil on the eve of her African mother's funeral. A lost mother is also one of the themes of Kenyan director Wanuri Kahiu's *From a Whisper* (2008), in which a young, rebellious daughter is in search of her mother who has been missing since a terrorist attack in Nairobi. Sara Blecher looks at girlhood experiences in *Ayanda* (South Africa, 2015), the coming-of-age story of a tenacious young woman struggling to build a productive relationship with her mother while coming to terms with her father's death, and *Dis ek, Anna/It's me, Anna* (2015) again deals with the dark side of the parent/daughter relationship in a story centred around child sexual abuse and failed parenthood, in particular the failure of the mother as protector.

The theme of mothers sacrificing everything in order to provide a better life for their daughters is equally prominent. In another Traoré film, *Moi Zaphira* (Burkina Faso, 2012), Zaphira is a mother unsatisfied with her life, wishing a better future for her daughter, which leads to a painful separation and estrangement between the two. South African Stephina Zwane's *Baby Mamas* (2018) follows the lives and friendship of four single mums. Zimbabwean director Tsitsi Dangarembga's short film *Kare kare zvako: Mother's Day* (2005), shows, in a highly symbolic style, the lengths a mother will go to in order to provide for her children during a time of drought. The film is based on a Shona folk tale, with the narrative structure replicating the repetitive structure of oral African storytelling traditions. It is a fable about motherhood and hunger set in rural, pre-colonial Zimbabwe, in which the role of provider has fallen on the mother.

In North Africa, the best-known films by women that explore mother-daughter relationships include early pioneering feminist films as well as some of the most recent work. We mentioned Tlatli's *The Silences of the Palace*, one of the foundational feminist film narratives in Maghreb, Arab and African cinema, dealing with several mother-daughter relationships. The legacy of this film is huge, as several Tunisian, Moroccan and Algerian films have shown. A number of Moroccan films have explored how life changes for daughters who become mothers. *L'enfant endormi/The Sleeping Child* by Yasmine Kassari (Belgium/Morocco, 2004) is set in a women's village, as most men have migrated to Europe. When Zaineb and her sister Halima both fall pregnant, their mother reacts very differently to her two daughters, and as they grow in their motherhood, the two sisters take a distance from their elders in order to turn their attention to one another and to their own daughters' realities. This film followed Narjiss Nejjar's initial explorations of mother and daughterhood in her debut feature *Les yeux secs/Dry Eyes* (Morocco/France, 2003) also set in a women-only village, where daughters change as they become mothers. Nejjar has built up a body of work that continues to centre its themes and treatment on the complexity of the mother-daughter bond: in *Apatride/Stateless* (Morocco, 2018) Henia lives alone in north east Morocco, on the border with Algeria. She and her father were, alongside 45,000 other Moroccan families, deported from Algeria in 1975. Her mother remained behind. Since then, Henia has been longingly gazing across the border in search of her mother, but she is unable to cross over. Because of her own impending motherhood, in an appropriately silent and defiant manner she plunges herself into the sea, crossing the water in order to pursue the search for her mother. In Algerian films, daughters often search for a mother figure who is absent because of the legacy of war. Finding female solidarity across generations, in *Barakat!* by Djamila Sahraoui (2006), Amel, a young doctor, and Khadidja, a veteran of the war for independence, search for Amel's disappeared husband. Amel and Khadidja are not biological mother and daughter, but their respective roles start to reflect the care inherent to a daughter and mother relationship.

As becomes clear from the above, themes like geographical and emotional distance between mothers and daughters, the deep-seated urge in mothers to make better lives for their daughters, and the life-changing rite of passage in which daughters become mothers are some of the powerful life-altering experiences mothers and their daughters go through, together or separately. These quintessential female developments relate to the reality of women on the African continent, where the diaspora, migration and having to contend with socially and politically challenging limitations define the female condition. In what follows we look in more detail at some historical and theoretical discussions of motherhood and daughterhood respectively, in order to set us up for the case studies.

Motherhoods

From a socio-political recognition of the importance of cultural heterogeneity, over the acknowledgement of tradition and communal responsibility, to the psychology of a transformative experience of motherhood, female theorists and historians confirm the wide variety of mothering personalities and the collective yet personal experience of motherhood. The central idea we want to highlight is the complexity and plurality of the motherhood experience and its representations. A lot of the theory on African motherhood and the way in which it fits into ideas of feminism comes from anthropology and literature rather than film studies, arguably because women making films on the African continent is not yet a widespread enough phenomenon. In the largely male canon of African cinema, motherhood is often either a position of deference or a matter of antagonism (Ukadike 1994). The mythic mother, explored in patriarchal mythology or psychoanalysis, can be an intimidating and overbearing creature, causing a painful power struggle or an uncaring relationship with female offspring. Feminist anthropologists and historians challenge this one-dimensional vision of motherhood in order to foreground mother figures positioned between confinement in a male world and a powerful independence as life-giver. A feminist motherhood can simultaneously be shelter and prison. Desiree Lewis shows that in African feminisms, "mothering is represented as a pivotal and extensively supportive activity which coordinates acquisitions of selfhood" (1992, 36). We would add that feminist cultural products challenge static identities, and examine women's representations as a constituent part in the hierarchical network. Lewis criticises a male vision of motherhood, where "the canonized mother demonstrates physical fortitude and self-sufficiency, while simultaneously registering extreme psychic repression" (ibid., 45). We need to rupture the canon by consciously revealing how thinking in binaries works counterproductively: African films show how the diverse positions of a mother and her daughters are complex and plural.

Rather than delegate venerating visions of a mythical motherhood to traditional matriarchy, Nigerian anthropologist Ifi Amadiume looks at the fundamental differences between matriarchy and matriliny. While both kinship theories certainly indicate the importance of motherhood, both also (problematically) emphasise the "construction of woman as an object to be moved or owned" (1997, 75). The difference lies in power structures dependent on the women in a community versus belonging and kinship descent. Furthermore, she shows that definitions of womanhood and motherhood in African societies usually rely on a woman's capacity to run an independent economy that contributes to the building of the household – not necessarily a nuclear family household but the sustainability of a community in which she functions as an economic and psychological agent. Likewise, Obioma Nnaemeka emphasises the centrality of mothering roles in a community rather than as an individual, and the responsibilities this requires (1998). In Africa, she claims, motherhood is a central component of the heterogeneous conceptualisation of womanhood. As such, focusing on women as mothers permits an emphasis on relations between women, thus allowing for the interesting but neglected relationship between mothers and daughters to take centre stage. Nnaemeka stresses that motherism has contributed significantly to social change and indeed has heavily influenced non-Western versions of feminism.[1]

Building on Amadiume and Nnaemeka's ideas of communal motherhood, Femi Nzegwu gears her discussion of motherhood towards spiritualism. She shows how "in ancient religious traditions of Africa we find again and again the predominance of the mother goddess; the valorisation of the female principle; the earth symbol" (2001, 14). At the same time, this spiritual motherhood is not just mystical: it is also dominated by a sense of economic independence and dominance, industriousness, and control over economic activity and its proceeds (ibid., 16). In other words, motherhood is not *either* a mystical *or* a pragmatic position, but *both* simultaneously. The collective responsibility of women towards youth – namely to steer society's growth in a particular direction according to prescribed norms and values – indicates the role of women as mothers to a community and specifically to young women. Female elders therefore act as powerful instruments of social change and progress, both individually and collectively. As Nzegwu shows, motherhood is a supreme position that remains inclusive and refuses to exclude women on the basis of biological shortcomings. Instead, it is a position from which to enact affection, solidarity and prosperity for the future of the younger generation. Child rearing (not only bearing) is equal to ensuring the best character development, which is a communal responsibility.

Motherhood is never only biological. Motherhood assumes heterogeneous meanings in different cultures and religions. It is not an "automatic set of feelings and behaviours that is switched on by pregnancy and the birth of a baby. It is an experience that is profoundly shaped by social context and culture" (Akujobi 2011, 2). The difference between choice and expectation lies in the perception of motherhood as an institution versus it being treated as an experience (Nnaemeka 1998, 5), and the socialisation of daughters is central to their development. Motherhood is a transformative moral experience that needs to be demystified. We now turn our focus to daughters, young women who are socialised and educated in pragmatic, balanced relationships. On the one hand, this relationship embraces loyalty and solidarity through gendered affiliation and, on the other hand, it foregrounds a transformation due to generational differences. Daughters inspire us to readdress the role of women in their journey towards shaping individual personalities, defining their own lives and developing their growth as protagonists in their life's journeys. In our case studies we illustrate how maturing daughters are not simply individuals that function within a hegemonic binary, but complex human beings with their own psychology and spirituality, who function in a socio-historical, cultural and spatial context.

Daughterhoods

Motherhood is a political act: through procreation women define posterity. Having a daughter ensures continuation of the gender and changing the future for women. Daughterhood is a political act as well: in maturing, a female child learns to make choices and joins a history of womanhood. But daughterhood is often neglected, as children are seen as passive, innocent and naïve – especially young female children. But this perception of innocence and naivety is a European construct. We do not subscribe to a sentimentalised and diminutive representation of children as victims worthy of compassion, and in need of protection. We need to see daughters as having their own particular brand of agency, from girlhood to adulthood.

Suzanna Danuta Walters reacts against the psychology of mothers and daughterhood represented in popular culture, often by male filmmakers (1992). Mother/

daughter relationships rarely take centre stage where the Oedipal mother/son epic is very often the narrative arc. In contrast, Walters shows how the mother/daughter relationship is characterised by a mix of love, responsibility and blame. This formative relationship is interesting precisely because of its pull and push factors. The pull between generations is established through nurture and the socialisation process, framed by solidarity. The push describes the context of separation, the cutting of the apron strings through conflict, resulting in widely diverse and recognisable narrative developments. It is in a shared womanhood – as the daughter imitates and rejects, fears and loves, searches for role models and creates her own identity – that the fluidity of the roles appears. Overlaps between generations are where the wealth of experience lies, but because women have been relegated to the margins, or to the private sphere, storytellers do not always have access to these narratives. Walters asks us to consider the relationship's fluidity in a cultural and social context where we see living relationships changing, connecting and critically influencing one another's positions. Now is the time to use intergenerational relationships as the central thread through a female-led narrative structure. We are no longer looking at a relationship constructed in conflict but at the fluidity of closeness and sympathy, of independence and experience.

There is hardly any critical material on the mother-daughter relationship in African popular culture, and no sources that have studied this relationship on African screens. We need to have a closer look at the voices of young women as daughters, because "contemporary girls are actively involved in constructing and producing what needs to be seen. They are making themselves heard, [...] through narratives of their relationships with family members, and through participation in civic and other social movements" (Mitchell and Reid-Walsh 2010, 1–2).[2] From childhood to adolescence, female children intensively contribute to society. We call for an increased examination of the ways in which girls and young women negotiate family settings and personal relationships to have an impact on their communities. Digging deeper into the cinematic construction of daughterhood, we take in the agency and self-determination of a daughter who is an active part of the community, and whose voice is central to this role.

One of the main international theorists of childhood in film, Karen Lury (2005), explains that children often embody the symptoms of society's failures. While they certainly bear the brunt of it, we'd like to highlight that they can also represent ways out of these failures. When children show up at the centre of cultural and political debates, adults usually see them as inactive, passive bearers of meaning rather than agents. A child is also an emblematic figure that shoulders society's fantasies of the past and the future. However, this same child can serve as the active catalyst for change and narrative development. In that context, children are storytellers. Essentially, new generations see the world differently and live in a different world: precisely what intrigues the adult filmmaker whose memory is troubled and whose traumatised state of mind is perhaps envious of the child's lack of a memory. Lury deconstructs the idea that the child remains a passive object that has emotional baggage loaded onto it. Instead, she shows that the child, when observed or engaged with in its own right, is an agent. She asks how the child's agency – as disruptive, impossible, unintelligible – is imagined and portrayed. But it may be more rewarding to look at how children and childhood are performed: the daughters in the films discussed here are aware of what they are doing, both within the narrative as well as in the production of the film.

In heteronormative societies, children (usually the sons) continue the human race, by ensuring and protecting the continued existence of the nation. If children represent the memory of the adult, reproduction replays the memory of the self, and guarantees the continuity of the family name, the race, and the nation. In films, the significance of children plays on this everyday understanding of the child's role in society. If, however, we see children as independent agents, then we can ask whether – if sons are seen as the agents of the future – female children represent the past and the present. Do daughters serve as memory, as storytellers? Certainly, this is what we see confirmed in the fact that female filmmakers and their protagonists both assume the role of storytellers. Safi Faye and Leyla Bouzid are storytellers who ensure a (re-)telling of history that pays attention to and includes girls in their narratives.

Case study: *Mossane* (Safi Faye, Germany/Senegal, 1996)

Safi Faye's *Mossane* (1996) is one of the most important films in the history and development of women's filmmaking in sub-Saharan Africa. It is Faye's last film, and unusual as a feature fiction film in her oeuvre of ethnographic documentaries and docufictions. It was included in the Un Certain Regard section at the 1996 Cannes Film Festival, screened at FESPACO in 1997 and released in France in 1998 but due to a protracted and troubled production history it has not been widely seen, particularly in the anglophone world. Because of its historical and critical importance, however, it has been widely referenced in African film scholarship; its significance in Faye's career, in histories of African women's filmmaking and in African filmmaking as a whole, secures its prominent place in African film history. Through our reading of daughterhood in *Mossane*, we aim to add to critical and analytical perspectives of the film, underscoring its importance in a study of the work of women filmmakers.

The film tells the story of Mossane (Magou Seck), a beautiful 14-year-old girl coming of age in a Serer village in Senegal. Her name is derived from the Serer word "moss" which means beauty, purity, innocence or virtue. Indeed, Mossane's beauty is so extraordinary and ethereal that humans, nature and the ancestral spirits of the metaphysical plane are all infatuated with her. Even Mossane's own brother, Ngor, is enthralled by her beauty. Mossane, however, loves Fara, a poor student who has temporarily returned to the village because of university strikes. At birth she was promised to Diogoye, a well-to-do young man working in France. Mossane's mother insists on the marriage taking place because of the financial benefits it would give the family, and Mossane's rebellion against the impending wedding results in a tragic fate: she drowns in the river by the village, seemingly preferring death to an unwanted marriage. The film centres on the intergenerational conflict, the complexities of the mother-daughter relationship and the coming-of-age of a young woman who is claiming her own agency and independence from parental control. If read in this way, Mossane is representative of young teenage girls anywhere in the world. But while these are clearly universal themes, the film is set in a specifically African ontology, with depictions of traditional rituals, highly metaphorical and proverbial dialogue and metaphysical, spiritual narrative interlocutions that render it mythical and poetic.

The production of the film started in 1990, but it took six years from shooting to post-production due to a legal battle with the producer. Faye entrusted the financial aspects of the film to a French accountant who, without her knowledge, took over the rights to the film. It took a six-year court battle for Faye to regain the rights, a struggle that left her emotionally exhausted. In an interview with Ukadike she said: "I had to fight a lot to save my last film, Mossane, and now I have no more ideas. I am afraid to make films again," and: "I am no longer ready to make a film like Mossane. It is my last big film, because I do not want to be destroyed anymore. If something bad should happen to me, my child will lose everything" (Ukadike 2002, 31–35), statements that explain her regretted absence from filmmaking since.

Being the mother of a daughter she adores was her main inspiration, as Faye's own daughter was the same age as the title character when she started working on the film:

> I wanted to place the accent on the ephemeral beauty of adolescence, to sing this confusing time when the body changes and the teenager is unsure of him/ herself [...] I wanted the most beautiful girl in the world to be African, and I sung her praises because I am a mother.
>
> *(Thackway 2003, 155)*

Faye also said that the transformations she observed in her own daughter at the age of 13½ is what she wanted to recreate in the film (Pfaff 2004, 195). For Faye, her daughter was at a magical age, a specific moment in her life where her transformation was distinctive (ibid., 187). The starting point of the narrative is a Serer legend foretelling the tragic fate of a young girl born every two centuries whose beauty is so extraordinary that she can only know a fatal destiny. Daughterhood, and specifically the transition between childhood and womanhood – a slippery interstice – is mystified and mythologised. We would argue that it is important to read the film as a myth and its ending as a symbolic act of defiance rather than as a literal punishment for her rebellion. If we view the adolescence of a young girl on the verge of womanhood as the transient moment that the film attempts to capture, it makes it possible to see why Mossane cannot stay in this world. Mossane does not commit suicide but fulfils her destiny by returning to the ancestors: she never belonged to this world and was always only passing through. Motherhood and daughterhood are depicted as pragmatic, spiritual and metaphorical: they denote a kinship relationship marked by solidarity and closeness, conflict and defiance but also a transcendental moment.

Despite *Mossane*'s seemingly clear generic positioning as a fiction film, Safi Faye has problematised this categorisation by saying that she is not persuaded that she has made a fiction film, because her imagination comes from what she has lived, the values instilled in her, and the education she has received (Ellerson blog). She has said that the boundaries between fiction and documentary are not clear-cut, a position that echoes through her ethnographic films, which contain elements of both fiction and documentary. It is crucial though, not to read the representations of ritual and tradition in the film as anthropological "truths": Faye has clarified that many of these depictions were of her own invention. Even though arranged and forced marriage does of course have a real-world referent in certain cultures, it does not occur in Faye's Serer culture and as such, the film is not intended as a moral tale attempting to raise awareness of this issue. It is a product of her imagination, shaped by her lived experiences as a Senegalese woman, with the many esoteric and ritualistic depictions and descriptions in the film left to the viewer's imagination to interpret and understand. At the press conference after the screening of the film at FESPACO in 1997, a rather volatile discussion ensued when several European audience members insisted on an anthropological explanation for some parts of the film, which Faye refused to give. For Faye this suggests that, in European eyes, Africa remains a continent that can be explained in anthropological studies that have been the foundation for Eurocentric research in Africa for eons (Ellerson in Pfaff, 2004, 190). It is, she has said, "as if an African filmmaker were prohibited from exercising the artistic authority to create from her own imaginary" (ibid.). Whereas intergenerational conflict can often be mapped onto a tradition/modernity dichotomy, as indeed many African films do, Faye rejects this binary as playing into the hands of simplistic Western understandings of African customs and traditions. The film challenges our understanding of gender, genre and generation in its provenance, its motivation, and in its resulting style, story and meaning.

In terms of a gendered reading, *Mossane* foregrounds the female experience, as all Faye's films do. Thackway pointed out how the film poses a subtle but radical challenge to the way Black femininity and Black beauty have historically been feared and exoticised (2003, 155). A simultaneously corporeal and spiritual female presence is central from the opening of the film, in which we hear a female griot singing about Mossane's beauty, while we see Mossane, from a distance and in silhouette, as she is bathing in the river. The voices of a female griot choir punctuate the entire narrative, in itself a significant choice as West African griots are usually male. The opening sequence establishes Mossane's association with water, a familiar spiritual link between the female force and water, and a connection that is echoed throughout the film. There are several moments that reinforce the significance of water: shots of the river; libations offered under a baobab tree on the riverbank as the villagers implore the ancestors for rain and a good harvest; scenes of Mossane, her mother and her friend Dibor washing with buckets of water and soap; and Mossane fetching water in the well, a place she later briefly contemplates throwing herself into to escape the unwanted marriage. The narrative concludes with Mossane's disappearance in the river at night as she is finally reclaimed by the ancestral spirits of the river. In a highly symbolic and prophetic image, the blood of a sacrificial bull flows into the river and mixes with the water. Mossane's destiny is also foreshadowed in the opening praise song, which laments that the pangools – the ancestral spirits depicted in otherworldly but recognisably human form – "have come, since the dawn of time, to contemplate their chosen one, to admire their favourite." She must return to the river, the song tells us, "where the spirits dwell amid the churning waters."

As expected from virtuous daughters, Mossane fulfils a number of domestic tasks: she cares for her ill brother Ngor, struck down by a mysterious illness later revealed by a diviner to be caused by the curse of Ngor's inappropriate and incestuous infatuation with Mossane. We see her sewing in the yard of the compound and preparing food and drink for her parents and their guests. The interactions between mother and daughter are typical of the push-and-pull dynamic of this complex relationship. There are moments of intimacy and closeness as Mossane rests her head on her mother's lap, soothed by her gentle words, and when her mother asks her to scrub her back while she is bathing. But there are also increasing moments of conflict due to Mossane's growing rebellion against the unwanted marriage. Significantly, Mossane's father is all but absent from the narrative, occasionally referred to and only a couple of times seen on screen. On the verge of womanhood, Mossane is in the interstice between child and adult, wanting to acquiesce to her mother's authority but simultaneously feeling the pull of her own awakening agency, personality and desires. This is also a time of sexual curiosity and education, provided not by her mother Mingué, but by Mossane's older friend Dibor, a more benevolent mother-figure. Together they peer at a racy magazine, idealising the freedom of the women in the pictures. Dibor is the antidote to Mingué, offering a maternal guidance and encouraging Mossane's agency. An intimate lovemaking scene between Dibor and her husband Daouda is remarkable in its own right, as it depicts female sexual assertiveness and choice – and is a reflection on Dibor's freedom and her role as an example to Mossane. In the act of love, Dibor is on top and she is the one to call an end to it when they hear Mossane approaching, despite her husband's protestations that he is on the verge of climaxing. Mossane is curious and eager to learn, anticipating the next step in her physical relationship with Fara. She asks Dibor: "How do I go about it with Fara, without the worst happening?" Dibor responds: "Fara can rub you with the tip of his sex softly, and from your clitoris, pleasure will spread through your body." She emphasises the important thing is to be careful in order to avoid an unwanted pregnancy. There are intimate, stolen moments between Mossane and Fara, but their relationship is still one of innocence. Emphasising the pleasure of the sexual act over becoming a mother indicates how Dibor thinks beyond biology and procreation, focusing rather on the young woman's agency. As such, the film foregrounds and celebrates female beauty, sensuality and sexuality, but Faye's camera does not depict these scenes in a voyeuristic or exoticised way. Rather, by keeping the camera at eye level with Mossane, it is the young woman's agency that is prioritised once more.

Mossane's beauty is not only a cause for celebration and adoration, but also of rivalry and conflict. An uncle, the diviner examining Ngor, declares that a ritual is necessary to cure the unwanted infatuation, and that, in addition, Mossane must be married off as soon as possible. The ritual takes place outside of the village at a crossroads, where the siblings are tied together, back-to-back, and left in a hole in the ground for the night. When Mossane expresses fear to her brother during the night, he tries to calm her by asking her to look at him. "I'd like to look into your eyes until you go blind," she declares, a forceful statement rejecting his gaze, and by extension the admiring and sometimes leering gazes of others in the village. Through this statement Mossane claims ownership of the gaze, as the one looking and deciding.

In addition, not all villagers agree with Mossane's parents that she should be married off to Diogoye. Dibor in particular is outraged that no one is taking Mossane's feelings into account and that they are allowing vague promises and financial gain to destroy her happiness. Dibor enlists the help of her grandmother, who unsuccessfully attempts to make Mossane's mother see the folly of her decision. Young village boys describe Mossane's parents as vultures, declaring that they hope Fara gives her a child. Mossane is such a powerful and central female presence in the village that everyone is discussing her fate and future. Their attempts are meaningless, of course, as Mossane, in a social realist and literal interpretation, resists an unwanted decision about her future. In a spiritual and metaphorical way Mossane has never belonged to the real world with its conflict, problems and pains.

While the wedding shows the villagers arriving with gifts, singing and celebrating, Mossane is sitting alone in a room separate from the celebrations, covered in a white shroud-like veil. She passes down her wedding gifts to her friends, and storms out of the room to angrily declare her refusal to marry Diogoye in front of all the villagers:

> If marriage were merely a question of bank notes, I'd give in to your wishes. But I refuse to be cornered by the mob. No one asked for my opinion. My heart does not love Diogoye. Send back his dowry. This wedding will never take place.

She thus highlights the complete lack of communication and understanding between herself and her mother, who arranged the marriage. Her mother's single-minded focus on the money Diogoye will bring to the family has destroyed the bond between mother and daughter as Mossane defies her mother's wishes. That night she looks for Fara at his house, only to find out that he has gone back to university, with the strike being over and Fara being painfully aware of his inability to provide to Mossane materially what Diogoye can offer. She runs away in anguish, first to the well where she stares down into the black water, and then to the river, rowing away in a pirogue. We hear the ominous voices of the pangools, as the boat drifts off and disappears out of frame. When morning breaks the wailing of women confirms Mossane's disappearance. The soundtrack of the female griot choir starts up again as Mossane's lifeless body is carried ashore. "Mossane is gone!" the singers declare. Her death had been prophesied: she would only see 14 rainy seasons. She is now at peace, and her struggle has ended. "Who chose our village? And left Mossane on our shore?" is the repeated refrain over the end credits. These words support a symbolic and mythical interpretation of the narrative: Mossane was only temporarily lent to the earth and never really belonged there.

When Ukadike interviewed Faye about *Mossane* in 1997 at FESPACO, he asked whether the film received a cinematic release. We know that, after its festival screenings at Cannes and FESPACO, Trigon in Switzerland organised a commercial run in 1996–1997, it was released in France in 1998, and Sembene's company distributed the film in Africa. Ukadike pushed her further on the issue of distribution but she was evasive and philosophical:

> Perhaps it is better for me to wait. People can inquire about the film or offer proposals for distribution, but I will exercise some degree of restraint. Remember that I created the story and invented the spirits; nobody can see spirits or represent spirits, so when you show them in a film, maybe the spirit will find a way to bring something good for the future. For me, spirits do not belong to this world, and if they come, heads must bow.
>
> *(Ukadike, 2002: 37)*

When we attempted to screen *Mossane* in the early years of the Africa in Motion Film Festival around 2006, Faye told us that she entrusted the single surviving English-subtitled 35mm print of the film to the Museum of Modern Art in New York and that she does not allow this print to travel. At the time, the only way to view the film (apart from this inaccessible print), was through a French-subtitled DVD held at the Médiathèque des Trois Mondes in Paris. Finally, in 2017, through a grant from the Arts and Humanities Research Council (AHRC) in the UK, we worked closely with Faye and her preferred company Titra Film in France to create a high-quality digital version of the film with English subtitles. At the time of writing, this version had been screened or was due to screen at Africa in Motion in Scotland, BFI Southbank in London, Zanzibar International Film Festival, and several other film festivals and cinemas internationally. As such, we contributed in a small way to making this hugely significant film more widely seen. We agree with what Faye said back in 1997: "I am sure *Mossane* will be universal and eternal. For that, I can wait" (ibid.). Twenty years after this interview, *Mossane* was still as relevant and magical as the daughter in the film.

Case study: *A peine j'ouvre les yeux/As I Open My Eyes* (Leyla Bouzid, Tunisia/France/Belgium/United Arab Emirates/Switzerland, 2015)

Leyla Bouzid's debut feature film, *As I Open My Eyes* weaves the coming-of-age experience of a young woman into the events leading up to the Jasmine Revolution in 2011. In an interview she said:

> When the [Jasmine] Revolution happened, the desire to film and document that period was very strong. Many documentaries were shot then — all full of hope, all focused on the future. I, too, really wanted to film. Not the revolution, but what everyone had lived through and been subjected to: the suffocating everyday life, the total power of the police, the surveillance, the fear and paranoia of the Tunisian people over the past 23 years.
>
> *(Bouzid, 2018)*

Both the film and this statement of intent show the previously widespread state repression in people's daily lives in Tunisia, and offers a rich and fertile ground for storytelling once that pressure of silence has been lifted.

The protagonist, 18-year-old Farah (Baya Medhaffer), sings in a band and has a loving sexual relationship with her musician boyfriend Borhène. In pre-revolution Tunis, she is the charismatic, attractive, and outgoing lead singer of an underground rock band who are discovering their voice and struggling with the oppressive nature of censorship and taboo subjects. At the same time as the general stifling and silencing atmosphere towards the end of Ben Ali's reign, Farah specifically experiences issues of gender inequality and the continuing exclusion of women in Tunisia despite their active struggle for equal rights and the country's relatively progressive laws. Tunisia has a rich history of women fighting for independence and gaining rights in the independence era, as has been documented by Tunisia's first political filmmaker Selma Baccar in her feminist essay film *Fatma 75* (1975). In *As I Open my Eyes*, music plays a central role: it transcends cultures and languages, and the lengthy musical interludes demonstrate a kind of escapism as well as a deep awareness of politics. At the dawn of the Arab Spring, the music of Farah's band addresses complex issues in her home country. The music was purpose-written for the film by Iraqi-British lute-master Khyam Allami to fit lyrics by Bouzid's poet friend Ghassan Amami: Bouzid said that

> Khyam Allami made the rock music I dreamed of with the lute, inspired by traditional Tunisian music with Arabic lyrics. He composed the music for the main actress. I had to find a young girl able to sing and act.

The fact that it is a young girl performing the lyrics emphasises how she struggles with that extra layer of oppression of being a young woman.

The film really is about the energy of youth and music, and the struggle between different generations to communicate effectively across the age-gap. It shows a mother-daughter relationship influenced by the tensions in a pre-revolution Tunis, and the divergent ways in which mother and daughter deal with their inner revolutions. The film is set at the time immediately before the revolution and the atmosphere in the country leading up to the revolution – which did not come out of nowhere even if it surprised many. The fiery, stubborn, revolutionary voice is Farah's, a young woman at a crossroads where she needs to make important decisions about her future: is she going to study musicology or medicine? She is living at a time when the tensions inside Tunisia are coming to a boiling point, and these tensions are mirrored in the relationship between mother and daughter. Farah's father Mahmoud is mostly absent, like Mossane's, as he works far away in the phosphate mines of Gafza. He is a liberal who refuses to join "The Party." If he did join, that would enable him to live in Tunis with his family, but it would also compromise his political integrity. This is another hint of political repression, because the mines of Gafza are a significant location: it was one of the first areas where workers rose up in 2011. His principles suggest a liberal upbringing for Farah, but his absence also highlights the relationship between mother and daughter.

But this does not mean her mother does not have a voice: at several occasions the film suggests that Hayet used to be like her daughter but was ground down by the system and disappointments (both in love and in life). Farah seems unaware of this, and insists on finding out on her own how she can negotiate her passions within the culture she lives in, which wants her to temper these passions. Hayet does not have consistent authority over her daughter. It can be presumed that they previously had a fairly close, liberal relationship, but as Farah gains agency and starts to dominate her mother, their relationship disintegrates. The fact that the mother figure is performed by superstar and singer Ghalia Benali adds another layer of complexity to the female voices in the film. Her acting history and reputation as a singer influence the reception of the film, especially since the film is about women in music. We know relatively little about Hayet (played by famous actress and singer Ghalia Benali) and her reputation in the film rests mostly on suggestions and suspicions, but the impression is given that she is a strong, independent and modern woman, who supports her daughter up until the moment where life becomes dependent on the revolution and she feels she needs to protect Farah from herself. They stop communicating and Farah ends up in trouble with the police. This trouble is caused by a secret policeman who has a role in Hayet's past, which is left ambiguous. So, it is not until both mother and daughter learn to talk *with* each other through effective communication that is honest and straightforward rather than *at/towards* each other – enacting what is expected of them – that the relationship finds an equilibrium.

Farah is the singer in the film, performing the role that Ghalia Benali may feel she has served in the past. Living through the exceptionally complex circumstances of the Jasmine Revolution in Tunis, the actresses switch roles to perform their mother-daughter relationship. They blend into and out of each other, they are one and the same person while they both struggle to gain independence from one another and from their oppressors. At the same time, through this struggle between being alike and wanting to be different from one another, they also realise they need one another. Farah is learning to find her freedom as she realises her responsibilities, and Hayet needs to trust and have patience with her daughter. Most of all, they need to learn to communicate with one another on a balanced and equal level, and they need to acknowledge one another's agency. Mother and daughter must develop the understanding that they need to accept one another, even if they do not understand each other.

It is interesting to discover that Bouzid's favourite Tunisian films (Bouzid, 2018) are historical examples of mother-daughter films: the first is Moufida Tlatli's *The Silences of the Palace* (1994), which examines the women working and living in the household of a powerful local governor on the eve of independence in the 1950s. Bouzid especially admires how the film highlights the silences between the women and the powerful mother-daughter relationship, which is sensitive and sensual but highlights a double oppression: an economic and a gender oppression. Bouzid's other favourite film is Raja Amari's *Satin rouge/Red Satin* (2002), which looks at the life of a middle-aged widow who breaks out of the monotony of her everyday life by taking up belly-dancing and taking on a younger lover (for an extended reference to this film, see Chapter 7). This film also highlights the generational differences and difficulties between a mother and her daughter, as the younger lover of the mother turns out to be the daughter's boyfriend. In both films it is a (re-)discovery of the balance between what is unsaid and what is brought out into the open that enables mother and daughter to find peace with their own role and with the other, as well as with their agency in a context of oppression. As such, the act of breaking the gendered silence between generations is liberating and empowering.

The mother-daughter relationship in *As I Open my Eyes* is very dynamic and multi-layered: Hayet is a liberal if somewhat suppressed independent woman, the actress who plays her is a rebellious singer like Farah. Initially Hayet trusts her daughter and sets her free. But as Farah becomes more and more politicised in Tunis' nightlife, Hayet is bothered by Moncef, someone from her past who threatens her that her daughter will be in trouble. He is a secret policeman and he texts Hayet: "It's about your daughter: Farah hangs out with people known to the police. If she carries on like them, she'll be in trouble." Hayet answers confidently that she knows her daughter, but the secret policeman says "So you know she was drunk in a man's bar last night? She sang as well, a song about our country. She reminds me of you at her age." Hayet becomes increasingly worried as the communication with her daughter is short-circuited: they seem to understand each other but cannot accept one other, and they stop talking altogether when Hayet forbids Farah to perform and Farah exasperatedly shouts "everything is forbidden and dangerous with you, you drive me crazy!" She later locks her mother's bedroom door and escapes to go singing with the band.

The combination of fear and pride Hayet feels for her daughter are reflected in the lyrics of Farah's songs:

> Oh country, my country of dust, your gates are closed and bring misfortune, turn up the volume. The starving are eating insults, your dog's teeth are made of gold but the gums of the poor are toothless, the thirsty are drinking blood, tomorrow they'll be exiled.

The title song also denounces Tunisia's unfair treatment of its people:

> As I open my eyes
> I see those deprived of work or food
> and a life outside their neighborhoods.

Despised, aggrieved,
up to their eyes in problems,
they breathe through the soles of their feet.

As I open my eyes
I see those retreating into exile,
crossing the ocean's immensity
on a pilgrimage to death.
With the country's troubles,
people lose their minds,
looking for new troubles,
different from those they know.

As I open my eyes
I see people who are extinguished,
trapped in their sweat, their tears are salty,
their blood has been stolen
and their dreams have faded.
On their heads, castles are being built.

Once back home after this incendiary gig, Farah feels guilty about locking in her mother, and says "Don't be angry mum, nothing happened to me." But Hayet is at the end of her tether and whispers "Do what you want, don't speak to me, if you need anything, ask your dad." Later Hayet announces at a family celebration that Farah got into medical school. At this gathering it becomes clear that there is tension between Hayet and her mother as well: grandmother has repeatedly said she wants Farah to go to medical school, but Hayet has stood up for her daughter's dream of doing musicology. But here Hayet does what her mother wants, and adds "What is musicology anyway?" and this turnaround raises suspicion with grandmother – another breakdown of communication between a mother and her daughter. Farah runs away and asks her boyfriend whether she can come live with him because "I can't stand my mother anymore, we'll end up killing each other."

The second half of the film sees Farah's dramatic rebellion reach its climax as she is taken by the secret police after the band is informed on by their manager, who has been filming them. After the violent police intervention, there is a moment of continued traumatic silence between mother and daughter until Hayet opens up about being like Farah, and they sing together. Their communication has been revived and Hayet explains that "when I was young I was like you: passionate. I thought I had wings. I loved and lost my youth." Farah asks: "What did you do?" and Hayet answers, with a proud smile: "I had you. You, who stops at nothing." When they sing together, they sing: "When I see this world of closed doors, I'm inebriated. I close my eyes and every time a girl appears to me. Sometimes I think it is her. The same one. In the end, is it her? It's another!" The lyrics draw attention once again to the difficult position of young women in the Tunisian dictatorship. When Farah hears herself, she turns to her mother and stops singing, Hayet encourages her: "Sing! Sing!" and they whisper the rest of the song together.

The focus of the film and the song lyrics then is on the consequences of living in a repressive state and the fear it generates in diverse layers of the population who differ through gender, race and class. Hayet's past courage was deformed by fear and coercion. One example is when she enters a bar frequented by the band while Farah is in prison. She is the only woman there, and the whole bar falls silent. She is reduced to the status of a gendered object. Her past remains obscure even though it informs her present decisions: she is a sympathetic character, but tries to stifle Farah's ambition and is motivated by maternal protectiveness. She clearly identifies with her daughter's rebelliousness. She also uses her past connections with the secret policeman to free Farah from prison. Hayet oscillates between being a practical, pragmatic mother and one dominated by feelings, passion and her own nature. It is clear however that the lack of acceptance between mother and daughter is fed by the state's irrationality and the daily threat of incarceration. Like her mother before her, Farah is a free spirit struggling with authority, including her mother's, boyfriend's, the state's and the manager of her band. Farah's arrest and interrogation are very harsh, depicted in an intense single take, and intended to break her strong spirit. Despite the demise of the band and the destruction of Farah's vibrancy and naivety, viewers are made aware of the role played by youth in the Jasmine Revolution. The film captures the far-reaching influence of the police state and the growing restlessness of youth and workers, which eventually led to the end of Ben Ali's corrupt regime.

★★★★

Every woman is a also someone's daughter. We have shown that while motherhood is a very fertile narrative, so is daughterhood. Seen from the perspective of two very forceful women filmmakers, the daughters in the films we have discussed here are strong and wilful. They drive the narrative forward through their spiritual, social, political and cultural awakening. Their lives and decisions impact on those around them, and in some ways liberate their mothers from the constraints of gendered and generational presumptions. The two daughters we have chosen to focus on in this chapter, Mossane and Farah, are inspirational young women who find their agency and deal with obstructions in the way in which their era and situation force them to. Leyla Bouzid made her film about but well after the Jasmine Revolution. The spirit of increased freedom and the importance of young women's voices in the future of Tunisia is of vital importance to the changes the country is undergoing. Mossane, in another era and another political context entirely, likewise makes her own decisions and refuses to compromise. Both young women are knocked back by tradition, patriarchy and a breakdown of communication across generations, but neither of them gives in to that constriction: Farah sings again, even if it is quietly, and Mossane decides to enact her fate. Both forcefully voice their opinions and struggles through their bodies, and even if they are in some respects let down, they refuse to become victims and they do not lose their agency. They reclaim their voices and follow their instincts.

Paying attention to the dynamic between mother and daughter is in itself a substantial and important way to start to tell stories about women in relation to one another. Daughters and their mothers provide a multi-layered narrative of idealism and experience, that do not always correspond but can productively inspire each other. It is the breakdown of the symbiotic or co-dependent relationship between older and younger women that provides the clean slate from which to start to build a relationship of equals with individual thoughts and agencies. Mossane and Farah have shown that a youthful stubbornness develops into a maturity of thought and communication, and could lead to successful new relationship dynamics.

Notes

1 While we are less interested in motherism, we do want to acknowledge it as an aspect of African feminism's interest in motherhood. These ideas on motherism have been developed by Catherine Obianuju Acholonu, who sees motherism as an inherent form of African feminism, going beyond biological motherhood (1995). For more info, see: Acholonu, Catherine Obianuju (1995) *Motherism: The Afrocentric Alternative to Feminism*, Afa Publications.
2 The timing of the journal in 2010 is significant in the sense that it the year of the Dakar Declaration on Accelerating Girls' Education and Gender Equality, where a commitment was made towards girl-children's education.

Bibliography

Acholonu, Catherine Obianuju (1995) *Motherism: The Afrocentric Alternative to Feminism*. Abuja: Afa Publications.

Akujobi, Remi (2011) "Motherhood in African literature and culture," *Comparative Literature and Culture, CLCWeb: Comparative Literature and Culture*, 13(1). Available online: https://docs.lib.purdue.edu/cgi/viewcontent.cgi?article=1706andcontext=clcweb [Accessed October 2018].

Amadiume, Ifi (1997) *Reinventing Africa: Matriarchy, Religion and Culture*. London: Zed Books

Bouzid, Leyla (2018) Interview published in DVD booklet for As I Open my Eyes.

Ellerson, Beti (2010) "Safi Faye: Role model," *African Women in Cinema*. Available online: http://africanwomenincinema.blogspot.co.uk/2010/05/safi-faye-role-model.html [Accessed November 2018].

Lewis, Desiree (1992) "Myths of motherhood and power: The construction of 'black woman' in literature," *English in Africa*, 19(1), pp. 35–51.

Lury, Karen (2005) "The child in film and television: Introduction," *Screen*, 46(3), pp. 307–314.

Mitchell, Claudia and Jacqueline Reid-Walsh (2010) "Girls seen and heard," *Girlhood Studies*, 3(2), pp. 1–10.

Nnaemeka, Obioma (1998) *Sisterhood, Feminisms and Power: From Africa to the Diaspora*. Trenton, NJ: Africa World Press.

Nzegwu, Femi (2001) *Love, Motherhood and the African Heritage: The Legacy of Flora Nwapa*. Senegal: African Renaissance.

Pfaff, Françoise (2004) *Focus on African Films*. Bloomington: Indiana University Press.

Thackway, Melissa (2003) *Africa Shoots Back: Alternative Perspectives in Sub-Saharan Francophone African Film*. Oxford: James Currey.

Ukadike, N. Frank (1994) "Reclaiming images of women in films from Africa and the black diaspora," *Frontiers: A Journal of Women Studies*, 1(1), pp. 102–122.

Ukadike, N. Frank (2002) *Questioning African Cinema: Conversations with Filmmakers*. Minneapolis: University of Minnesota Press.

Walters, Suzanna Danuta (1992) *Lives Together, Worlds Apart: Mothers and Daughters in Popular Culture*. Berkeley, CA: University of California Press.

Filmography

A peine j'ouvre les yeux / As I Open My Eyes, Dir. Leyla Bouzid, Tunisia/France/Belgium/ United Arab Emirates/Switzerland, 2015

Anonymes / Buried Secrets, Dir. Raja Amari, Tunisia/Switzerland/France, 2009

Apatride / Stateless, Dir. Narjiss Nejjar, Morocco/France/Qatar, 2018

Ayanda, Dir. Sara Blecher, South Africa, 2015

Baby Mamas, Dir. Stephina Zwane, South Africa, 2018

Barakat!, Dir. Djamila Sahraoui, France/Algeria, 2006

Dis ek, Anna / It's me, Anna, Dir. Sara Blecher, South Africa, 2015

Fatma 75, Dir. Selma Baccar, Tunisia, 1975

From a Whisper, Dir. Wanuri Kahiu, Kenya, 2008

Kare kare zvako: Mother's Day, Dir. Tsitsi Dangarembga, Zimbabwe, 2005

L'enfant endormi / The Sleeping Child, Dir. Yasmine Kassari, Belgium/Morocco, 2004

Les Silences du palais / The Silences of the Palace, Dir. Moufida Tlatli, Tunisia/France, 1994

Les yeux secs / Cry No More, Dir. Narjiss Nejjar, Morocco/France, 2003

Moi Zaphira, Dir. Apolline Traoré, Burkina Faso, 2013

Mossane, Dir Safi Faye, Germany/Senegal, 1996

Notre étrangère / The Place in Between, Dir. Sarah Bouyain, France/Burkina Faso, 2010

Pour la nuit / For the Night, Dir. Isabelle Boni-Claverie, France, 2004

Satin rouge/Red Satin, Dir. Raja Amari, Tunisia, 2002

Sous la clarté de la lune / Under the Moonlight, Dir. Apolline Traoré, Burkina Faso, 2004

Tout le monde a des raisons d'en vouloir à sa mère / Everyone has Reasons to be Angry with their Mother, Dir. Pauline Mulombe, DRC/Belgium, 2010

6

AFRICAN WOMEN'S BODIES

Journeys into womanhood

Actress, editor and writer Ghalya Lacroix has been central to some of the most significant films made in Tunisia, like *Bezness* (Bouzid, 1992), *The Silences of the Palace* (Tlatli, 1993) and *Hedi* (Ben Attia, 2016). She also regularly contributes to her husband Abdellatif Kechiche's films as a script writer and editor. Among others, she adapted the life-story of Sara Baartman into a film script for *Vénus noire/Black Venus* (2010) and contributed to the writing of the dialogues in that film. This film is one of a number of fiction films and documentaries dedicated to Baartman, a subject of European racism and the objectification of the Black female body. In the early nineteenth century, Sara Baartman, a Khoikhoi woman, was taken from the Cape in South Africa to Europe where she was toured around so-called freak-shows and her body exhibited at large zoo exhibitions in the UK and France. Because of her large posterior and bust, she was the subject of pseudo-scientific research, but her body was mostly displayed for large audiences, for whom she was obliged to perform exotic dances.

Baartman's body has continued to be the subject of much interest across the world in media stunts. The miss-telling of her story remains controversial, and her body continues to be claimed by Black celebrities. For example, in Kim Kardashian's photoshoot by which she hoped to "break the internet" in 2014, Kardashian's posterior received comparisons to Baartman's. Beyonce was rumoured in 2016 to be working on a script based on Baartman's experiences, although, if true, this has not yet materialised. It is clear then, that Baartman represents the "enduring image of an African woman, reduced to a body" (Abrahams 1997, 18), but as Gordon-Chipembere shows, this only evidences the European perspectives from which her legacy has been created historically (2011). Her story remains obscure. During her lifetime and after her death she was compared to an animal and subjected to colonial exploitation, sexism and racism. She was ridiculed and commodified, seen as dumb and submissive, presumed to be the "missing link between animal and human" (Parkinson 2016). After her death in 1815 her brain, skull and genitals were displayed at the Musée de l'Homme in Paris until 1974. Her body is the testimony of an enduring victim of European racism and sexism. In fact, Sara Baartman's body, both during her lifetime and after her death, speaks volumes about the lasting sexualisation of the body of Black women. In 1994, President Nelson Mandela formally requested that France return her remains and, after much legal wrangling, France finally acceded to the request in 2002. Her belated burial on South Africa's National Women's Day in 2002 finally enabled the crucial recognition of her body as the physical manifestation of a person who deserves to be treated as a human being rather than as an object of curiosity and ridicule. In this chapter we look in some detail at Black women's bodies and how they are represented on screen by women filmmakers, acknowledging the diverse experiences and agencies, and most importantly, the stories these women tell embody.

When discussing the female body in African women's films, we want to draw attention to the many different ways in which the body has been approached in film studies internationally, in order to see how African scholars and filmmakers have responded to these approaches, and how they have constructed different visions of the female African body on the screen. Our ideas stand in strong opposition to the simplistic division of body and mind, but also to the stereotype of women's bodies representing the political status of their nation, as in the concept of mothers of the nation, or – in an African context – the colonialist idea of "Mother Africa." We conceptualise the body in film as a space where divergent complex approaches collide: the material and the symbolic, the individual body as it functions in relation to others' bodies, or as it is assigned labels by others. The female body is a rich source of inspiration, both for filmmakers and for film scholars. It is also a vast topic, and we place our discussion firmly within a transnational context while focusing our analyses on specific aspects of the body: physicality, race and power. In this chapter we look at the corporeality, physicality and power of the female body, which offer avenues to explore the African female body's fullest potential.

Any experience of the body is first and foremost individual: it is the subjective and personal, physical manifestation of a person. This leads to a second consideration of the body as a social construct, where the body is a reflection of the society in which it functions. This societal thinking on the body considers power positions and performance within specific cultural contexts. Third, the body is always both an individual and a communal entity, as it moves and changes within space and time, and constructs human agency and different subject positions depending on the space it occupies. These three discourses on the body can be summed up in an imagined development from physical and psychological "object," to a philosophical "subject." We follow Sara Ahmed's theorisation in *Strange Encounters* (2000), where she deconstructs the fetishisation of "strangers," which bolsters Western agency and identity construction at the expense of strangers, who are rendered as static, lacking in agency, and as pre-existing objects (rather than subjects) of knowledge. Like bell hooks, she asks that we "see black females as subjects, and not objects." She dares us to "look and see differently" (hooks 2014). In this chapter we enable readings that acknowledge the female African body as a physical, psychological and philosophical manifestation of the body – where all three approaches intersect to enable the body to come to its fullest fruition through its beauty and its power.

The female body in cinema

Approaches to studying the female body in relation to cinema include, in Western scholarship, an established critical framework of psychoanalytic feminist film theory that critiques the phallocentric male gaze onto the female body, in the work of theorists such as Laura Mulvey (in particular her seminal essay "Visual Pleasure and Narrative Cinema" first published in 1975) and E. Ann Kaplan (for example *Women and Film: Both Sides of the Camera*, 1983 and the edited volume *Psychoanalysis and Cinema*, 1989). This approach is not the most suitable for analyses in African contexts, as it focuses, as Kaplan admits, on "female representation within capitalist states" (1983, 189). The analyses that these scholars offer are focused on White female bodies, and the very practice of psychoanalysis is rooted in Western theory.

We find it more interesting to look at the philosophical turn in film studies which has explored the body as a "phenomenon," where spatial awareness of the other leads to the possibilities for affect and tactility, in a phenomenological approach. Phenomenology accepts that "an other" can experience the same receptivity to an event or an object as "the self." An other body is understood as a subject *and* an object, and an intersubjective understanding of an other body allows for empathic thinking and feeling. Sara Ahmed carefully unfolds the meanings of subject positions and the presuppositions of the phenomenologists when they talk about perceiving the "other." She describes how Whiteness is usually the position of scholars discussing the body. In her analysis of the non-White body, she shows that race and history are always present, though usually below the surface of the phenomenological body (Ahmed 2007, 153). And so, whatever our subject position, when considering "other" bodies it is crucial to consider the object-ness *and* the subject-ness of bodies of different colour. In film phenomenology, the visual powers of the camera – distance to the subject/object, the camera angle, mise-en-scene – can reveal the position of the filmmaker towards the body, while the orality of the medium constructs its own contribution to film-language. As such, the film aesthetics define the perception of the body on screen and determine the degree of perception and embodiment. Bearing in mind the necessity for intersectional approaches to audio-visual representation, seeing the limitations of a single-colour-worldview is an important first step towards recognising that other individuals everywhere share experiences, which enables affiliation, if not identification. For every separate individual the body is lived-in, a site of life, corporeality, inhabited, and is not only a site of vulnerability but also of pleasure and possibilities. In other words, we have to *decide* to accept life and the experience of life as a shared one.

There is, of course, also a danger of minimising differences. Our experiences and perceptions are not universally shared, while solidarity and intersubjectivity relate to a shared experience. A focus on shared experience could be perceived as simplistic, utopian and perhaps even homogenising. Moreover, we are concerned here with film, an art form that in and of itself carries ideological stances, also in the representation of bodies. It is important therefore to always also engage with the social and political history of bodies beyond their objectness and move into subjectness: "configuring the black girl as object [...] makes her susceptible to racial violence" (Ohito and Khoja-Moolji 2018, 278). The body, and specifically its outer layer, the skin – the first point of contact or recognition – determines one's political experience of the world. As Carla Peterson says:

> as we observe bodies (ours or others'), we need to acknowledge that we are never just looking at individual bodies; by comparison, we connect these to other bodies, placing them within groups – most especially those of gender, family, race and nation – and endowing them with a group identity. These differing perspectives on the body [...] may overlap, but, just as significantly, they may also diverge and conflict with one another.
>
> *(Peterson 2001, ix)*

As Ohito and Khoja-Moolji phrase it: "instead of seeing black feminised bodies as already distinct and determined by defined and static boundaries, we [have to] show how they are always becoming – how their surfaces are repeatedly re-constituted upon contact with other bodies" (Ohito and Khoja-Moolji 2018, 279). This ambiguity needs to be recognised in films by African women as well.

Shohat warns against universalising Western parameters and using ahistorical psychoanalytical categories such as "desire," "fetishism," and "castration" which might lead to a discussion of the "female body" and "female spectator" that is ungrounded in many different women's experiences, agendas and political visions. "Whereas a white 'female body' might undergo surveillance by the reproductive machine, the dark 'female body' is subjected to a dis-reproductive apparatus within a hidden, racially coded demographic agenda," she writes (Shohat 2003, 53). African systems of relation have a different ontology to which psychoanalytical approaches are not necessarily applicable. We suggest that a film-philosophical approach through inter-subjectivity, and one that takes into account the embodied film experience and a human respect for the other's body as a fellow human being, does stand a chance at understanding global cinema, and thus also African cinema. The emancipated intersubjective gaze in film recognises its positionality and implicitly *and* explicitly subverts the objectifying orientation Ahmed critiques. Retaining ownership of their bodies also entails for African women the affirmation of the Black body as a material and a conceptual manifestation of the Self. This Self entails ideals of both female beauty and female power, leading to a struggle for female agency to overturn within a patriarchal context the view of the anomalous Black female body as created in the colonialist imaginary. Postcolonial theorist

Robert Young (1995) describes this view of the African female body as a reaction against a "desiring machine" which created a simultaneous desire and repulsion in the colonial mind. Rather, we are interested in how self-assigned and confident African female physicality and power interact in physical, social and spatial environments through film.

Objectification of the Black female body is a perennial issue for African women and female African filmmakers, who critique colonialist ideologies that eroticised and exoticised the female African body. The "desiring machine" and its view of the Black female body is still perpetuated in film, advertising and visual media worldwide. As we will show here, African women filmmakers act against this view, and as such one might find some parallels, in a transnational sense, between the critical strategies employed by Western feminist philosophy and theory, and the attempts of African feminists to transform the African woman from object to subject within African visual culture. The issue at stake is the awareness that the African woman has not always owned her own body – the female body has and continues to be a battlefield of (White) male concerns. In terms of representation, it becomes a question of how a woman becomes an active subject, as opposed to a passive object being observed. It is, then, important to consider who makes images for whom, and how they represent women in that equation. In what follows, we look into the physicality of the body and its impact on women's complex psychology, in order to move on to describing the power of the bodily subject in film.

Beauty and (physical and psychological) health

A lot of the scholarship, activism and much of the filmmaking about African women's bodies is the result of a reaction against Western(ised) or Eurocentric conceptions of, and insistence on, beauty and health. Indeed, beauty is usually seen as a reflection of the condition the body is in, and its overall health. Specifically, when it comes to standards of beauty, Black women are often under pressure to meet Western ideals in terms of body type, skin colour and hair texture. The more they approach White standards of beauty, the more they are perceived as beautiful. According to Sekayi (2003) and De Casanova (2004) the tall, slim, light-skinned and blue-eyed, muscular body is a Western ideal of health and power. The "body beautiful" is regarded as synonymous with success and a concern with health and self control. Ronald E. Hall's edited collection on skin colourism in the twenty-first century (2012) shows the complex psychology and the actual suffering young people of colour experience in their socialisation into these Eurocentric standards. The incremental but enormous changes in these standards first necessitated and then moved away from attitudes such as "Negritude" and "Black is Beautiful" (Hall 2012). But these attitudes and the studies on colourism are focused primarily on African American realities, whereas our concern here is bodies on the African continent. The African American context in relation to bodies and race is very specific, as Chimamanda Ngozi Adichie wrote in *Americanah*: "I did not think of myself as black and I only became black when I came to America" (2013, 359).

This complex idea of Blackness as being outside of the norm is subtly dealt with in *Aji-Bi: Under the Clock Tower*, a documentary by Raja Saddiki from Morocco (2016). This film looks at how a small group of Senegalese women living in Morocco, and stuck there illegally on their migratory journey north to Europe, work as informal beauticians on the streets. Set in Casablanca in a community of enterprising women that hustle for business at the iconic clock tower, twenty-year-old Mereme considers her journey and flits between settling in Morocco or continuing to Europe. She is part of a group of women of all ages who are organising themselves to survive in a Moroccan society that can be both generous and hostile to outsiders. Of course, the fact that the film is made by a young Moroccan woman is significant in the representation of the Senegalese women, and the awareness that the artist as an observer is, strictly speaking, an outsider looking in and balancing the xenophobia and hospitality of Morocco. The title-word Aji refers to a common woman's name in Senegal, to a particularly enterprising and successful personality, as well as the Arabic word Hadja or Hadji, a title of respect awarded to a pilgrim who has undertaken the pilgrimage to Mecca. The Aji-Bi in the film work hard and organise themselves as they contemplate their own pilgrimage to Europe, and work to earn enough money to support their families in Senegal. The multi-layered nature of their experience as Black trans-migrants, entrepreneurs and community-centred groups stuck in Morocco, where racial and sexist discrimination persist (Aidi 2016), is foregrounded, while their community spirit and female solidarity provides the documentary with an optimistic note towards the end.

The changing perceptions of, and engagement with, beauty standards in art and in the media show that there is no such thing as a universal or timeless beauty. Indeed, Black women critique the generalisations of Western, White beauty standards: "Western beauty standards are based on idealized depictions of White women's physical features (e.g., fair skin, long straight hair, thin lips, small nose) which can be difficult and impossible to attain for many Black women" (Walker 2014, 1). Scholars have highlighted the need for attention to those aspects of beauty that "extend beyond body type and shape in research pertaining to Black women's body image" (ibid.). In fact, the degree to which European standards in beauty and physicality are internalised globally needs to be continuously critiqued. What perhaps started with movements such as Black is Beautiful, Black Power and Black Consciousness in the 1960s is still a painfully urgent and relevant agenda. "Even though history has been terribly unkind to the African body," Bakare-Yusuf writes, "the body was and still is capable of being something quite beautiful, quite sensuous, quite joyous. There is always a memory of the 'flesh', of the flesh that was once liberated" (1999, 312). As our retelling of Sara Baartman's tragic life story at the start of this chapter indicates, the fascination with the Black female body during slavery and colonialism turned the African female body into a spectacle and an object of erotic desire and repulsion, which denied African women subjectivity. It has been argued that historical remnants of these processes have been internalised by African women, and are exacerbated by the infiltration of contemporary models of Western standards of beauty in a globalising world, as is clear from the number of hair straightening and skin whitening products which can be found in shops in African cities all over the continent. African female filmmakers explore and critique these issues and notions of female beauty through the depiction of women's relationships with their bodies.

Kenyan filmmaker Ng'endo Mukii's animated short film *Yellow Fever* (2012) explores skin colourism and self-image among young African women. Through an innovative stylistic mix of animation, collage, live action, spoken word and dance, the film focuses on the effects of media-created and perpetuated ideals on African women and their perceptions of beauty. Mukii has stated that African media is saturated with beauty ideals that are hard to obtain, often unhealthy and harmful to African women as they strive to conform to a globalised and homogenised Western concept of beauty (Mukii 2018). These ideals include chemical hair straightening, the use of hair weaves, and skin bleaching. The title of the film references a Fela Kuti song, *Yellow Fever*, that reproaches women who use skin-bleaching products, and whose skins, with the reduction of melanin, turns yellow. Mukii sees this phenomenon as a media-induced psychological condition not dissimilar to eating disorders and other body-dysmorphic medical conditions. As we stated above, skin and skin colour is not only a physical identity marker, but is also always political and psychological, and it is the deeper roots of practices that compel African women to attempt to change their bodies, that Mukii explores in *Yellow Fever*. There are a number of other films by African women that explore similar themes, including Ghanaian-born Akosua Adoma Owusu's *Me broni ba* (2009), which translates as "my White baby," an experimental documentary featuring hair salons in Kumasi in Ghana, in which women practice hair braiding on discarded white dolls from the West. South African director Omelga Mthiyane's *Body Beautiful* (2004) explores the body image of Black South African women through following the lives of four women from different demographic backgrounds and with different body shapes. *Fantacoca* (Agnes Ndibi, Cameroon, 2001) and *A Gentle Magic* (Lerato Mbangeni and Tseliso Monaheng, South Africa, 2017) are both documentaries that examine and question the practice of skin bleaching by African women, and the short film *Black Barbie* (Comfort Arthur, Ghana, 2016), similarly to *Yellow Fever,* addresses the issue through the use of animation.

The same juxtaposition/opposition between White and Black skins appears when tackling feminist issues such as the struggles of the women's movements over reproductive rights, sexual choice and bodily integrity. These struggles reveal different perspectives on abortion, fertility control, women's health, sex education, female circumcision, child spacing and demographic growth (Campbell 2003, 170). Female African filmmakers consistently address these themes and explore notions of the Black female body in relation to issues such as sexuality, motherhood, health, initiation and rites of passage ceremonies, including FGM. Rather than rejecting corporeality and embodiment altogether, they aim through their work to reclaim ownership of the Black female body, and to reinsert female subjectivity and agency through representation of these extremely challenging topics, rather than avoiding them. In what follows we go into more detail on issues related to subjectivity, beauty and power, followed by analyses of *Maki'la* (2018) by Congolese director Machérie Ekwa Bahango and *High Fantasy* (2017) by South African filmmaker Jenna Bass.

Beauty and power: philosophical embodiments

The body as a tool in the development of a subject and that subject's agency is a less concrete and more socio-philosophical concept. Here we want to engage with how the look and feel of a woman's body impacts on her daily life, on the power she has or lacks, and on the status she manages to achieve in the society in which she functions. Price and Shildrick point out that "the body, then, has become a site of intense enquiry, not in the hope of recovering an authentic female body unburdened of patriarchal assumptions, but in the full acknowledgement of the multiple and fluid possibilities of differential embodiment" (1999, 12). We explore the possibility of the existence of different capabilities and powers, unlimited possibilities, as well as limitations in the manner that Black African women characters' bodies are constructed. We specifically follow Canning in her history of the body in feminist studies, when she says that "if discursive and social bodies have frequently figured as abstractions, studies of individual or collective 'material' or bodily experiences often have the reverse problem: they can be overly concrete, undertheorised or cast too simply in terms of resistance/subjection." Instead, she argues that "historical specificity in analysing bodies, inscriptions, and embodiment might help us contemplate the very different methods required for reading the body as symbol versus reading the processes of embodiment, inscription and reinscription." Indeed, it is the "merits of charting the connections and convergences of the material and the discursive that make bodies such difficult objects of historical analysis and such intriguing sites of memory, agency and subjectivity" (Canning 1999, 513).

Sociologist Felly Nkweto Simmonds (1999) describes the racialisation and objectification of the Black body as a double complication for Black women by being female and being Black.

> As an African woman my 'certain private information' is not only inscribed in disciplines such as anthropology, but also in colonial narratives, literatures, photographs, paintings and so on. Here the 'facts' created by social theory and the 'fictions' created by literature can be difficult to separate. At times social theory itself becomes a fiction. [...] In this white world, the Black body, my body, is always on display.
>
> *(Simmonds 1999, 52–53)*

These words remind us of the opening to this chapter, and the representation of Sara Baartman. Indeed, with reference particularly to slavery, Bibi Bakare-Yusuf (1999, 311) maintains that physical brutality and force transformed the African body to an always captive one. Under the slave economy and colonisation two kinds of bodies were produced: the body of knowledge (the oppressor) and the body of labour (the oppressed). The body has become the most celebrated site for addressing a wide range of cultural configurations, in particular from a feminist perspective, and many studies on the body address numerous ways of deconstructing the body-mind dualism in Western metaphysics.

As described above, the feminist philosophical turn moves away from psychoanalysis in order to conceptualise the body in a framework of self-awareness as well as solidarity with an other's body, as a physical manifestation of the other. An awareness of the subjectivity of the other, and her similar experience of objects in the world, is called inter-subjectivity: a realisation that the other is not an other but rather a subject who experiences the self as similar to the other. This development from psychoanalysis towards philosophy and the increasing interest in the body as a material, self-identifying subject rather than a manifestation of the complex human object and its visual pleasure came through the theorisation by Laura U. Marks of embodied or haptic filmic experiences in intercultural cinema. An embodied experience is one where all the senses – beyond the audiovisual ones – are called upon to make and experience cinema. She writes: "Haptic images invite the viewer to respond to the image in an intimate, embodied way, and thus facilitate the experience of other sensory impressions as well" (Marks 2000, 2). While we acknowledge that Marks' intercultural cinema does not engage with African films, we do see African cinema as an inherent part of intercultural cinema, as African film so often engages with the meetings of cultures, "tracing the effects of racist, colonial, and imperial mis- (or non-)representation on the lives on now-diasporic peoples," or transnational peoples.

Beti Ellerson, when discussing the female African body in film as a symbol or as a metaphor for change, looks only at male filmmakers' work, e.g. Ousmane Sembène, Djibril Diop Mambéty, Souleymane Cissé, Kwaw Ansah and Désiré Ecaré. She points out that in their films, the female body is a medium of culture, inherent to and highly visible in society as the result of a performance of femininity, and that it occupies a space: it is carried, moved, adorned, and reveals corporeal practices (Ellerson 1997). As such, it is a reflection of culture, society and environment. While we agree with these points on the body functioning within and being an expression of culture, society and environment, we do not want to do so by expressing a multitude of dichotomies in film the way Ellerson does, as she analyses the men's films on women's bodies through the discourses of tradition vs. modernity, higher vs. lower class, rural vs. urban or power vs. powerless. We want to show that in women's films, these dichotomies are abandoned as simplistic, unproductive tropes within which to analyse African film, and we want to illustrate how women's films and their treatment of female African bodies are rather more complex, constructive and realistic. While we acknowledge the historical and the continuing contemporary struggle for emancipation on many levels, in our view women's films deal with bodies in a much more pragmatic way: the body is first and foremost a physical manifestation of the self, of the subject, and a subject has power over their individual appearances, so we want to link beauty and power, the outward appearance of the body to the inward development and the outward expression of that power. Beauty in this sense is not merely an appreciative stance of aesthetically pleasing features and characteristics, but rather beauty in these films is engaged with charisma, pride, independence, and development. As such, embodied experiences can de-westernise beauty. It has become a socio-political and emancipatory tool that enables expressions of female empowerment and emancipation. Beauty and power, as such, are intertwined and dependent on one another.

Case study: *Maki'la* (Machérie Ekwa Bahango, DRC, 2018)

Since 1997, women filmmakers such as Monique Mbeka Phoba and Ibea Atondi have played an important role in cinema in DRC, but in recent years, a couple of often very young and cosmopolitan women have taken up filmmaking. One example is Machérie Ekwa Bahango, whose debut feature *Maki'la* (2017) screened at Berlinale in 2018. Although there is a dearth of English language scholarly or critical work on cinema from the DRC that barely ever mentions women, and very few films by women are made, what there is, is very strong cinematic material. When *Maki'la* screened at the Berlinale, there was a sense of excitement surrounding the film, as Bahango is a self-taught filmmaker in her early twenties. She worked on various film sets for a couple of years before she became the translator on Alain Gomis's prize-winning Kinshasa-set *Félicité* (2017), assisting with transforming the script into Lingala, the local language. Gomis himself is French-Senegalese, and admits he very much felt like an outsider in Kinshasa, not knowing the language or the culture (Grey 2017). Nevertheless, his film is a confident depiction of a very strong woman, the eponymous singer Félicité (actress Véro Tshanda Beya), whose son needs urgent hospital treatment, for which she does not have the money. Bahango says about her experience working with Gomis, whose film focuses on a very strong central performance by a Congolese woman, that this inspired her to make her own dream of making a feature film a reality. When Gomis realised that his translator had filmmaking aspirations, he invited her onto the set more often so that she could gain insight into how a professional set works, and he introduced her to his own network of cinema professionals (Sambou 2018). This experience inspired her to take up the camera herself, as she had been researching and penning the script for *Maki'la* for a couple of years. The film was produced by Tosala Films, a production company based in the DRC, significant as an indication of the development of home-grown cinema in the country.

In a 2003 article on the DRC, women and war by Nadine Puechguirbal, the author illustrates how prior to the ongoing conflict, there was "a gap between the law relating to women's rights and realities" (Puechguirbal 2013, 114): the law states equality, reality however shows that there is no such thing. Like in other patriarchal societies, family law has it that the husband is the head of the household and must provide for the family. Even though women therefore do not hold positions of power on the markets, 90% of market traders are women. Puechguirbal expands that women have been seen as victims of war and conflicts in DRC and not as valuable contributors to the post-conflict efforts to changing the DRC's situation. And yet, there is an increased general awareness of women's indepen-dence and self-confidence, their pragmatic stance towards providing for the family, and a refusal to give in to the pressures to conform to norms that prevailed before the war (ibid., 117). Even though the conflict in DRC is ongoing, read in this context of post-conflict self-awareness, *Maki'la* perhaps embodies the potential of the powerful, determined and self-sufficient post-conflict DRC woman. The film offers a correction of the vision of DRC women as victims, vulnerable and pow-erless, and rather shows women as inhabitants of a revised reality shown on screen by an equally defiant young filmmaker.

Maki'la (Amour Lombi) is the eponymous heroine of the story. She is married to Mbingazor, a local gangster, but they have an entirely non-domestic set-up, living in group and fending for themselves, male and female spheres separated from one another. Maki'la is pragmatic: she manages to get by with friends and a gang of younger street children stealing for her. When one of these kids, a young boy, defies her and decides to go to football school instead in order to pursue his own future, she loses a little bit of her authority and simultaneously takes on a new, young orphaned girl, Acha, to teach her to survive in the chaotic urban sprawl of Kinshasa. Through this experience of "training" Acha and learning to listen to her stories, the children that work for her seem to change from useful objects whose bodies serve to make Maki'la money, to subjects with individual needs and dreams. Acha makes Maki'la more aware of the connections that can be set up between people, which can be productive beyond the exploitation of their skills. This is also important for the filmmaker: to name the ambitions and dreams of the children and listen to their stories, even if they are unpleasant. Though they'd been stigmatized by society, Bahango recognised "that they also have dreams, that they are living life like everyone else" (Vourlias 2018a). This is perhaps most beautifully shown in the blossoming sisterly relationship between Maki and Acha. Initially Maki treats Acha as her minion, but gradually they grow fond of one another, as Acha starts to call Maki her "big sister." They sleep, eat and work together, and they tell one another their life stories. Their mutual respect grows as they bond and recognise themselves in one another.

In *Maki'la*, power is overtly linked to the body: taller, stronger women rule a roost of young chubby kids. At the same time, Mbingazor is the leader of his gang because as an albino he is believed to be a White sorcerer. The physicality of the body, and specifically skin, are foregrounded in an ambiguous and com-plex way. The albinism of Mbingazor is never mentioned, except in the group when they call him "white." These references to skin colour do not at first sight have anything to do with race but rather with mystical powers, and his status at the head of the gang of boys. He stands out as different, tough, violent and loud: he is consistently filmed from a low angle perspective, he looks down (literally) on his gang and on Maki'la as he sits much higher up on the wooden structure they inhabit, and this downward look is emphasised by droopy eyelids that are the effect of constant drug use.

Nevertheless, the women in the film are much stronger emotionally and physi-cally than the men. Their pragmatic struggle to survive on the mean streets of

Kinshasa ensures that they stick together and though they fend mostly for them-selves, they also form loosely structured "gangs" to ensure loyalty and power in numbers. Indeed, the intro of the film illustrates this point excellently. Maki and two of her friends are sitting by the side of the road, doing one another's hair. Suddenly Mbingazor's gang appears in front of them, posing like "*sapeurs*" – well dressed and with a proud cosmopolitan attitude to boot – introducing themselves to the girls and to the audience. They freeze in their stances like proud cockerels, with a view to being admired by the girls, who instead laugh at them and gaze at the performance mockingly. It is a game, but it illustrates the film's emphasis on physicality, as well as the dynamics between the boys and girls as separately allied and perhaps even in competition.

In addition, the relationship between the two protagonists is presented immediately as troubled: Mbingazor comes to Maki to touch her and hold her in a vice-like grip, and tells her she should not be out on the streets on her own, while she says it is of no business of his whether she is alone or not as she can take care of herself. She calls him by his real name, Jonathan. She shouts "let go of me!" and complains that "all you do is get drunk and do drugs." He is, in her and wider society's eyes, a bad husband because he does not provide for her. She pushes him over, literally, as he falls on the ground drunkenly and he shouts, "Don't call me Jonathan, whore!" She is unim-pressed, and her pragmatic, entrepreneurial stance is affirmed in the way in which she moves on with life, hustling and fighting for her survival in Kinshasa.

Maki's emotional strength is also emphasised by her physical appearance. She lives on the streets and wears filthy clothes but carries herself proudly, straight and tall, lean and muscular. Her chin is always held up high and even though she is described by the filmmaker as a "scrappy heroine," she retains an element of ele-gance and self-assured pride. Having been orphaned at the age of 13, Maki suc-ceeds in ruling a posse of street kids who steal money, food and drink for her. She has friends and enemies, she commands fear from some and gets disdain from others, and she works within the limits that are imposed upon her life. But she also bears the consequences of a lack of education, the plight of poverty and the uncomfortable life of a street child. Bahango has said in interviews that she did not want to "shy away from the darker plot twists" of life on Kinshasa's streets. Pov-erty, hunger, and loneliness feed Maki's anger. In spite of her pragmatism and day-to-day struggle for survival she is also naive in many ways. Although he is an albino, Maki believes that Mbingazor is white and as such ascribes his powers to his whiteness. This perception adds a layer of complexity to Maki's internalised acceptance of white power. Her belief that he is not only white but also a wizard extends this complexity into the spiritual realm. Her attitude towards him is, on the one hand, determined by her disappointment in him as a husband: he is just like the others, a useless drugged up drunkard. But at the same time he is a powerful gang leader and a sorcerer, a white man often seen in an upward angle, looking down on his gang members and on his wife. When she starts to suspect the link between Mbingazor and Acha, Maki'la's protegee, she asks a fellow prostitute: "can a white and black be brothers?" Her colleague laughs at Maki's naivety and says

"Mbingazor is albino, not white," which seems to come as a surprise to Maki. She had not even considered this possibility. Psychosocial issues such as the belief that albinism is unnatural and that the body parts of affected people make powerful medicine, persist in Central and East Africa, particularly in DRC (Kromberg 2018). In *Maki'la*, it emphasises the importance of the body and its skin. In the film there is a lack of solidarity between the protagonists and the body is a site of power and suffering. Even if the film shows the pragmatism of street children, it highlights the vulnerability of the young female body, how easily young women are harmed, and rejects the body as a site of pleasure as a privilege of those with wealth and power.

Maki earns money with her body but also pays the price for doing this. She is compelled by hunger and poverty to start working for a madam outside her zone. Her madam talks of Maki as "a new little whore from the red zone," someone they don't get along with, and someone who is not educated. But as long as they bring in money, young prostitutes are useful and can work. This is the prelude to a sequence towards the end of the film, when Maki is with a male client who hires her services as a prostitute but needs her only to assist him with his sorcery. The man, who drives a big car and is corpulent and very tall, uses magic on her so that she cannot move and is in a lot of pain. Again, Bahango claims, this is "a reality that I cannot hide," indicating the connection between the spiritual or metaphysical and the material body that exists in many cultures. Prostitution, HIV and human trafficking go hand in hand in DRC, where rich business men still sacrifice poor girls for money as if their vulnerable bodies are commodities. But Maki escapes in spite of the physical pain. Her naivety and the fact that she is uneducated do not mean that she is passive: she uses the physical power in her own tall and muscular body to escape and return to Acha.

Enfolded within these tragic storylines and the darker aspects of the film, are a few moments in which Maki opens up. The manner in which Bahango approached her plot was through meetings with orphans on the streets of Kinshasa and by encouraging them to share their stories. Even within the storytelling, the body features dominantly: when a protagonist steals food and has to run away from those pursuing her, the diegetic sound fades out and the intense breathing and the heartbeat of the runaway dominates the soundtrack. Likewise, Maki's storytelling goes together with physical nourishment: as she takes Acha under her wings, they bond over dinner and the act of eating enables them to speak and listen to one another. Even though Acha speaks only French and Maki does not speak any French, insisting on Lingala, they do communicate. They speak with their mouths full: Maki tells Acha that her parents were killed, that she had no one, that no one helped her and that she was so angry that she wanted to kill everyone until she met Mbingazor. He was "a real sorcerer, no one goes against him, he taught me everything I know: to kill and to steal, everything that is forbidden." In a flashback to their makeshift wedding the gang explains that they don't steal, they just take. Maki wonders whether being a street child is a sin. She says it is just a shame that it means nothing but bad things. But she is assured that Mbingazor is going to change that when he becomes a minister. In their own ways then the gang want to fight for their dreams, just as Bahango says. The gang is an alternative for a family, and giving someone like Mbingazor power gives sense to a hopeless situation: their belief in the magical powers of the albino provides hope for the future.

After Maki's story, we also witness Acha's story. She is from Lubumbashi, her mother died at birth, and she has since then lived with an aunt and uncle. The uncle regularly raped her but in spite of this she kept on dreaming about one day having enough money to buy a beautiful white Barbie doll and a car, and live like a princess. She also wants to find her long lost brother, Jonathan. The time spent storytelling between the two girls, is also the time in the film when close-ups dominate the screen. This emphasises the importance of the moment of storytelling and the sharing of food, and the growing bond between Maki and Acha. This moment of telling and listening also becomes a moment in which the viewer is invited to really see the girls up close. Acha explicitly states that Maki is her big sister: "You're my only family, don't leave me" and she does not even know how true that is – as Maki slowly realises that Mbingazor is Jonathan and Acha's big brother, which would make Maki and Acha sisters-in-law. Maki realises that she knows more than Acha and Mbingazor but delaying to share this knowledge turns out to be her biggest mistake, as she effectively leads Mbingazor to Acha. Mbingazor rapes Acha, not knowing she is his little sister, and later, as Maki takes too long with her struggle to figure out what to do and where her loyalties lie, Mbingazor and Maki kill one another as Acha survives.

This tragic ending of their lives and of the film shows how the abuse of power, in any form, has devastating consequences. Maki'la lives in a world where rape and violence against women are commonplace, where sex is a weapon and where the body is a commodity, especially women's bodies, which are seen as objects and not as subjects. As soon as Maki and Acha tell one another their stories, and we would expect or hope that their subject positions become increasingly certain and emphasised, they remain defined by their environment and their circumstances. The lack of education, of guidance, of solidarity between street children in a world where power is inherently unbalanced and unfair, the weak, poor and young are unprotected and incapable of really emancipating themselves. Apart from Acha, who represents the only sparkle of hope in the film, this tragic tale shows how DRC's poor populations suffer from the consequences of colonialism and neo-colonialism, of the ongoing conflict in the country and the enormous power imbalances. The fact that Bahango inserts, in the middle of the film, a moment of reprieve where two female friends eat together and tell one another their stories, only serves to emphasise the hopeless situation for women in DRC. In spite of her body being used and abused, Acha's survival finally shows the power in Maki's sense of responsibility towards the younger girl. She protects Acha with her body, sacrifices her life and her body for Acha, also explaining who Mbingazor really is. Even though there is devastation in realising that her own brother raped her, the lack of solidarity throughout the film is lifted in that one tragic moment of ultimate dedication: Acha beats Mbingazor to protect Maki and Maki gives up her own life and her body so that Acha can survive. The fact that Acha then puts on Maki's clothes shows her emancipation and independence. Perhaps the ending of the film, with the survival against all the odds of Acha, is a visual metaphor for the hope Bahango represents in Congolese film culture: a few bright young women are telling stories and sharing knowledge against the odds to pass on to new generations of women filmmakers establishing themselves.

Case study: *High Fantasy* (Jenna Bass, South Africa, 2017)

Jenna Bass's *High Fantasy* is a body swap political satire set in the new South Africa, and, given its appropriation of this well-known genre with its central supernatural deceit, it provides a fertile opportunity for analysing matters of race, gender, psychology, politics and power as it pertains to the female body. Bass is a prolific director and writer whose work is regarded as part of the "new wave" of South African cinema. She is one of the creators of *Jungle Jim*, an illustrated pulp-literary magazine for African fiction, indicative of the aesthetic and artistic sensibilities prevalent in her work. Her films have premiered around the world, including at Toronto, Sundance, Berlinale, Göteborg, Busan and Durban. Her most recent feature, *Flatland*, a contemporary female Western, was selected to open the Berlinale Panorama section in 2019. As a young, White female director working in the contemporary South African context, all her work is infused with the complexities of post-apartheid South Africa, particularly in relation to young South Africans of different genders, races, socio-economic and -cultural backgrounds attempting to negotiate their place in a hugely diverse and intricate society.

The premise of the film is a camping trip that a group of four young South Africans embark on: Xoli (Qondiswa James) is a politically conscious Black woman with a radical activist leaning; Lexi (Francesca Varrie Michel) is a White woman who struggles to come to terms with her guilt about the atrocities of apartheid perpetuated by her people; and Tatiana (Liza Scholtz) is a mild-mannered and polite mixed-race woman who feels less comfortable with politically charged conversations. The fourth member of the crew is Thami, a Black male, who is friends only with Lexi and brought along because her uncle insisted the three women had a man with them to protect them. As such, the characters present a very broad range of South African demographics and identities, and their differences and squabbles, present from the start of the film, set the scene for an explosive adventure. To add to this promising premise, Bass gave the actors iPhones to film themselves, and left most of the conversations unscripted. This gives the film a low-budget DIY aesthetic. The "found footage" material is intercut with post-trip documentary style interviews in which the characters describe and reflect on the curious happenings at the camping trip.

Bass is somewhat of an artistic agitator, rebelling against cinematic conformism and convention as she grew increasingly frustrated with the slow and difficult process of making fiction feature films in South Africa. Her debut feature, *Love the One You Love* (2014), is a similar improvisational film shot entirely on iPhones, also exploring issues of youth identity in contemporary South Africa. In 2018 she announced that she was establishing an "alternative film school" that would challenge the way film has been taught traditionally in South Africa (Vourlias 2018b). The weekly classes would be a step toward "decolonising education" and acknowledging the influence of race, gender, class and sexuality in determining opportunity and power in the South African film industry. Bass is deeply aware of the complexity of intersectional identities and has stated that changes in the South African film industry are privileging White women rather than women of all colours. She says:

> As a white woman in the South African film industry, despite the challenges I have experienced due to gender, I have nonetheless managed to pursue my own work. However, I see that the glass ceiling remains a stark reality for many of my black colleagues – which should be unacceptable in our country.
> *(Lyra 2017)*

Bass's acute awareness of the complex entanglement of gender, race and class in the so-called "rainbow nation" of the "new" South Africa informs the narrative of *High Fantasy*. From the start of the film, tensions run high as Xoli and Tatiana are annoyed with Lexi for inviting a man, the aggressive and sexist Thami, without asking them. As they drive towards their camping spot through the vast flat planes of Lexi's family farm, Thami expresses his anger at the fact that one White man owns all this land. Tatiana states that land ownership in South Africa is tainted because the farm was stolen by Lexi's family generations ago, and property law meant that they could keep the farm. With its body swap plot twist complicating their political views on race in South Africa, *High Fantasy* is a political makeover of a well-utilised storytelling device, and generic conventions are further referenced in conversation about horror films – the desolate setting of course providing an obvious link – as they banter about the stereotypical horror narrative in which the Black guy has to die first and the White girl survives to the end. While their road trip conversations are filled with small talk and mockery, the underlying tensions and the vast differences between them continuously threaten to bubble to the surface. As they set up camp on arrival, Thami upsets the women with his sexist language, and Xoli admonishes him for his ignorance of the oppressive legacy of "the system" and the "systematic mind rape" to which Black people have been subjected. Thami ridicules Lexi for connecting with Black guys on Tinder, and she scoffs at him that the only reason he is there is because her uncle wanted her to bring a guy along. We witness physical performances of real and imagined identities as the friends entertain each other: Xoli tells them that she is of Khoi and Xhosa ancestry and performs a traditional song and dance for them; Lexi clumsily attempts to recite a Xhosa poem, struggling with the consonant clicks to the amusement of her friends. As night falls and Thami wants to join the women in their tent to escape the cold, the gender boundaries are drawn as he is warned: "You are in female territory now."

As morning breaks the four friends wake up in consternation as they discover they have inexplicably swapped bodies during the night. The Black male Thami is now inhabiting Xoli's Black female body, Xoli is in Lexi's White body, mixed-race Tatiana is in Thami's body, and Lexi's consciousness has been transferred to Tatiana's body. Xoli's reaction is the most violent and hysterical as she shouts, "Get your white shit off me!," disturbed and upset as she is by the fact that she is in Lexi's White body. She wonders whether it happened because the White ancestors returned for revenge. It cannot be her Black ancestors, she reasons, as they would never put her in this situation. She is literally inhabiting the body that oppresses her. In the post-trip interview Xoli explains that she was freaking out because she did not want a White girl's hair or skin, and Lexi acknowledges honestly that "It must be fucking awful to have a white person's body if you're black." When Xoli storms off trying to rip out her light-brown Caucasian hair, Lexi runs after her demanding that she leaves her hair alone. Tatiana confesses in her interview that she was glad that Lexi had her body because she knew that she wouldn't do any harm to it. If Thami got into her body he might have sexually abused it, perhaps finger himself, "You never fucking know," she says, "it's a guy." Thami discloses that the hardest part for him was to understand why he was so upset that he turned into a woman. He realised that is was because he was terrified that all the things he was doing to girls would start happening to him. For Tatiana, being in a male body is a deeply alienating experience, as we observe her in close-up examining her new body, its Black skin, flat nipples, muscular knees and scars. Their reactions reveal the complex ways in which our identities are carried within our bodies, marked by our gender, race and sexuality, our physicality and psychology, and the political, ideological and cultural meanings of the body formed by memories of our individual and collective pasts and experiences of the present inscribed in our flesh.

In the context of our preoccupation with the Black African female body in this chapter, Xoli's positionality and identity is of most interest here. She is an archetypal "strong Black woman," as she informs the others that Black women "have to be stronger than our pain, stronger than our struggle." In a symbolic reading of the Black female body as a site for the inscription of multiple cultural and political configurations, Xoli's reaction to the body swap, and her reflection on what it means to inhabit a Black female body, gain significance. Under apartheid, the Black female body was abused, exploited and devalued, but Black women used the physical force and literal presence of their bodies to resist this oppressive system, through protests, strikes and marches, as we describe in Chapter 4. Naked protests in particular have been used by Black women, historically and in the contemporary era, to denounce sexual abuse and other forms of oppression. This is significant in an African context, in particular when enacted by older women, as their naked bodies on public display brings shame to the patriarchy that oppresses them. Women protests in South Africa not only have historical significance, as the more recent "fallist" movements of Rhodes Must Fall and Fees Must Fall have shown (student protests against colonial legacy and continuing inequality in South Africa). When the group swap back into their own bodies after swimming in a dam, Lexi is visibly upset and walks off, disappearing for hours. Xoli in particular is very angry at her, as her inconsiderate behaviour delays their departure. She is upset about the emotional and physical toll that Lexi's disappearance is inflicting on the others, which we could read as justified anger at a system that privileges White bodies at the expense of Black bodies. Xoli reminds the others of the Fees Must Fall protests of which she was part of in 2015, when she "put her body on the line." Xoli is thus part of a lineage of Black South African women who have placed their physical bodies in the face of threat and danger as a literal manifestation of activism and protest. When Tatiana tries to appease her by stating that it is not about the fact that Lexi is White, her plea falls on deaf ears, as for Xoli this is exactly the issue. She declares that she doesn't care about Lexi, as "my body is for Black lives." Xoli's character therefore not only invokes the South African fallist movements, but also the broader international context of the Black Lives Matter movement. Her outrage at Lexi's selfish and inconsiderate behaviour reminds us of the vulnerability of Black bodies and the constant struggle for agency and emancipation.

Lexi's distress at swapping back into her own White body could be understood as her revolt against this reminder of her guilt and complicity in a system where White privilege prevails and Black bodies continue to be systematically oppressed. As Lexi eventually reappears at the camp, Thami is there to meet her and she rebukes his concerned questions with: "Do I feel relieved? Why would anybody be relieved to be like this?" pointing at her White body. Lexi and Thami start kissing and eventually have sex, with Tatiana and Xoli later discovering them asleep and naked. A cut to Xoli's post-trip interview shows her exasperation at the interviewer's questions, as she has nothing left to add because this story was about Lexi, she was the main character: "I am supporting cast," she scorns. Lexi is embarrassed and apologetic as she wakes up to find her female friends filming then, which outrages Thami: "I'm a black man and I'm a fucking problem." The group's reactions bring into sharp focus the complex gendered and racial tensions that serve as a microcosm of the broader South African society. They pack up in the dark and as they are leaving the camera lingers on a South African flag draped over a camping chair, an ironic reminder of the disillusionment with the rainbow nation. Xoli has the last word as she says it is perhaps a good thing for a White woman to be inside a Black women's body, as she can learn something from walking on someone else's shoes.

However, it is exactly this probability of "walking in someone else's shoes," of intersubjective understanding and real empathy, that is questioned in *High Fantasy*. The body swap trope employed here, in which the characters learn what it is like to literally inhabit someone else's skin, configures the body as both material and symbolic, and draws attention to the physical, psychological and political meanings and manifestations of the body. We are reminded of the firstly subjective, individual and personal experience of the body, which is precisely why the body swap is so painful and uncomfortable. Earlier in this chapter we showed the phenomenological possibility that a spatial awareness of the other could lead to affect and tactility, through which we may understand someone else's body as both subject and object. But as the film shows, this experience is also open to confusion and misunderstandings, signalling perhaps the impossibility to be truly empathetic. It is not identification that is the goal here, but affiliation, as the characters grapple with understanding the experience of being female from a male perspective, of being Black from a White perspective. In the South African context, with its brutal history of racial segregation that rendered Black bodies into objects denied subjectivity and humanity, the quest for intersubjective understanding seems utopian. As such, *High Fantasy* has an inconclusive and open ending, intending to be a catalyst for conversation rather than offering any solutions. Bass has stated her disappointment in the body swap genre in general, because it usually concludes with everyone having learnt lessons and gained mutual understanding. Instead, she wanted to subvert any neat narrative conclusion. In the South African context, the process of recognising an other as a subject is extremely hard given South Africa's history. The notion of the South African rainbow nation has failed, and there is a continuing struggle against injustice between oppressed bodies and privileged bodies. In her awareness of her own White privilege, Bass relinquished power to the cast by putting them in control of capturing their experiences and interactions. In this way, she aligned the filmmaking process with the content of the film – she did not want to enforce her White experience of identity politics. The DIY aesthetic of the film also creates an immediacy through the removal of a cinematic interface, a technique that brings us closer to Marks' notion of haptic cinema. As a spectator, we are under an illusion of direct access to the events, because of the point of view shots and the documentary aesthetic of the mobile camera lens. There is the possibility then that as spectators of this film we might develop a hint of empathy with specific characters, and a mutual understanding with them, more successfully than the characters in the film.

****

Both *Maki'la* and *High Fantasy* prompt us to consider the physical, psychological, philosophical and ideological construction of the Black female body in particular. Neither films have restorative conclusions, and such endings deliberately disclose, in the case of the DRC, that society is still a patriarchal construct that perpetuates violence on women's bodies, and, in the case of South Africa, that the post-apartheid utopia has been replaced with a more sober, and sombre, consideration of the possibilities and limits of reconciliation and political change, particularly for women. African women's bodies have long been battlegrounds of physical and metaphorical violence, but the time has come to imagine women's bodies beyond symbols of the nation. As long as women stay trapped in those patriarchal nationalist configurations, gender equality on all levels – material, political, economic, social and cultural – will not be achieved in post-independence nations such as DRC and South Africa. Freedom and liberation mean that the female body must also be freed from the constraints of the past and the present: it is a crucial part of the journey into womanhood.

Bibliography

Abrahams, Yvette (1997) "The great long national insult: 'Science', sexuality and the Khoi-san in the 18th and early nineteenth century," *Agenda*, 13(32), pp. 34–48.

Adichie, Chimamanda Ngozi (2013) *Americanah*. New York: Anchor Books.

Ahmed, Sara (2000) *Strange Encounters: Embodied Others in Post-coloniality*. New York: Routledge.

Ahmed, Sara (2007) "A phenomenology of whiteness," *Feminist Theory*, 8(2), pp. 149–168.

Aidi, Hisham (2016) "Morocco: 'Neither slave, nor negro'," *Al Jazeera Online* (10 April). Available online: www.aljazeera.com/indepth/opinion/2016/03/morocco-slave-ne gro-160330082904386.html [Accessed October 2018].

Bakare-Yusuf, B. (1999) "The economy of violence: Black bodies and the unspeakable terror." In Janet Price and Margrit Shildrick (eds) *Feminist Theory and the Body: A Reader*. New York: Routledge, pp. 310–323.

Campbell, H. (2003) *Reclaiming Zimbabwe: The Exhaustion of the Patriarchal Model of Liberation*. Claremont: David Philip Publishers.

Canning, Kathleen (1999) "The body as method? Reflections on the place of the body in gender history," *Gender and History*, 11(3), pp. 499–513.

De Casanova, Erynn Masi (2004) "'No ugly women,' concepts of race and beauty among adolescent women in Ecuador," *Gender and Society*, 18(3), pp. 287–308.

Ellerson, Beti (1997) "The female body as symbol of change and dichotomy: Conflicting paradigms in the representation of women in African cinema," *African Women in Cinemablog*. Available online: www.africanwomenincinema.org/AFWC/FemaleBody.html [Accessed November 2018].

Grey, Tobias (2017) "Alain Gomis on Felicite and feeling like an immigrant everywhere," *Financial Times* (24 October). Available online: www.ft.com/content/24293056-b7db-11e7-bff8-f9946607a6ba [Accessed October 2018].

Gordon-Chipembere, Natasha (2011) *Representation and Black Womanhood. The Legacy of Sarah Baartman*. London: Palgrave Macmillan.

Hall, Ronald E. (2012) *The Melanin Millennium: Skin Color as 21st Century International Discourse*. Berlin: Springer Science and Business Media.

hooks, bell (2014) *Black Looks: Race and Representation*. New York: Routledge.

Kaplan, E. Ann (1983) *Women and Film: Both Sides of the Camera*. New York: Routledge.

Kaplan, E. Ann (1989) *Psychoanalysis and Cinema*. New York: Routledge.

Kromberg, Jennifer G. (2018), "Chapter 9: Psychosocial and cultural aspects of albinism." In *Albinism in Africa: Historical, Geographic, Medical, Genetic, and Psychosocial Aspects*. Amsterdam: Elsevier, pp. 171–201.

Lyra H. (2017) "TIFF 2017 women directors: Meet Jenna Bass – 'High Fantasy'," *Women and Hollywood* (5 September). Available from: https://womenandhollywood.com/tiff-2017-wom en-directors-meet-jenna-bass-high-fantasy-5dd5135f9826/ [Accessed January 2019].

Marks, Laura (2000) *The Skin of the Film: Intercultural Cinema, Embodiment, and the Senses*. Durham, NC: Duke University Press.

Mukii, Ng'endo (2018) "Yellow Fever Film by Ng'endo Mukii," *Shades of Noir* (5 November). Available online: http://shadesofnoir.org.uk/yellow-fever-film-by-ngendo-mukii/ [Accessed December 2018].

Mulvey, Laura (1975) "Visual pleasure and narrative cinema," *Screen* 16(3), pp. 6–18.

Ohito, Esther O. and Shenila Khoja-Moolji (2018) "Reparative readings: Re-claiming the black feminised bodies as sites of pleasures and possibilities," in *Gender and Education*, 30(3), pp. 277–294.

Parkinson, Justin (2016) "The significance of Sarah Baartman," *BBC News Magazine* (7 January). Available online: www.bbc.co.uk/news/magazine-35240987 [Accessed January 2019].

Peterson, Carla L. (2001), "Foreword: Eccentric bodies." In M. Bennet and V. Dickerson (eds) *Recovering the Black Female Body: Self-representations by African American Women*. New Brunswick, NJ: Rutgers University Press, pp. ix–xvi.

Price, Janet and Margrit Shildrick (1999) *Feminist Theory and the Body: A Reader*. Oxford: Taylor and Francis.

Puechguirbal, Nadine (2003) "Gender training for peacekeepers: Lessons from the DRC," *International Peacekeeping*, 10(4), pp. 113–128.

Sambou, Régina (2018) "Cinéma: Maki'la dans la section forum de la Berlinale 2018," *Africulturelle* (9 February). Available online: https://africulturelle.com/2018/02/09/cinema-makila-dans-la-section-forum-de-la-berlinale-2018/ [Accessed October 2018].

Sekayi, Dia (2003), "Aesthetic resistance to commercial influences: The impact of the eurocentric beauty standard on black college women," *Journal of Negro Education*, 72(4), pp. 467–477.

Shohat, E. (2003) "Post-Third-Worldist culture: Gender, nation, and the cinema." In Guneratne, A.R. and Dissanayake, W. (eds) *Rethinking Third Cinema*. London: Routledge. pp. 51–78.

Simmonds, Felly Nkweto (1999) "My body, myself: How does a black woman do sociology?" In Janet Price and Margrit Shildrick (eds) *Feminist Theory and the Body: A Reader*. New York: Routledge, pp. 50–63.

Vourlias, Christopher (2018a) "Berlin: Director Bahango hopes to inspire Congolese women to pick up cameras," *Variety* (16 February). Available online: https://variety.com/2018/film/spotlight/berlin-film-festival-2018-bahango-makila-berlinale-1202696635/ [Accessed October 2018].

Vourlias, Christopher (2018b) "South Africa's Jenna Bass Explores race, class and gender in 'High Fantasy'," *Variety* (21 July). Available online: https://variety.com/2018/film/news/south-africa-jenna-bass-race-class-gender-high-fantasy-1202696614/ [Accessed January 2019].

Walker, Speshal T. (2014) *Black Beauty, White Standards: Impacts on Black Women and Resources for Resistance and Resilience*. Graduate Doctoral Dissertations. Boston: University of Massachusetts.

Young, R. (1995) *Colonial Desire: Hybridity in Theory, Culture and Race*. London: Routledge.

Filmography

A Gentle Magic, Dir. Lerato Mbangeni and Tseliso Monaheng, South Africa, 2017

Aji-Bi: Under the Clock Tower, Dir. Raja Saddiki, Morocco, 2016

Bezness, Dir. Nouri Bouzid, France/Tunisia/Germany, 1992

Black Barbie, Dir. Comfort Arthur, Ghana, 2016

Body Beautiful, Dir. Omelga Mthiyane, South Africa, 2004

Fantacoca, Dir. Agnes Ndibi, Cameroon, 2001

Félicité, Dir. Alain Gomis, France/DRC, 2017

Hedi, Dir. Mohamed Ben Attia, Tunisia/Belgium/France, 2016

High Fantasy, Dir. Jenna Bass, South Africa, 2017

Les Silences du palais / The Silences of the Palace, Dir. Moufida Tlatli, Tunisia/France, 1994

Love the One You Love, Dir. Jenna Bass, South Africa, 2014

Maki'la, Dir. Machérie Ekwa Bahango, Democratic Republic of the Congo, 2018

Me broni ba, Dir. Akosua Adoma Owusu, Ghana, 2009

Vénus noire / Black Venus, Dir. Abdellatif Kechiche, France/Belgium, 2010

Yellow Fever, Dir. Ng'endo Mukii, UK/Kenya, 2012

7

(RE)DEFINING FEMALE SEXUALITY THROUGH FILM

In 2018, *Rafiki*, directed by the award-winning filmmaker Wanuri Kahiu, was the first Kenyan film to be selected for Cannes in the Un Certain Regard section. A gentle love story of the blossoming romance between two young Kenyan women, the film was celebrated and admired for tackling a subject that remains controversial and taboo in many African societies but was also condemned for the same reasons. It was banned upon its release by the Kenya Film Classification Board (KFCB), because of its queer narrative that supposedly promotes homosexuality/lesbianism. Kahiu successfully sued the KFCB at the Kenyan High Court, thus managing to temporarily lift the ban for seven days in the last week of September 2018. This allowed the film to be screened in cinemas across Kenya, to adults only, enabling its eligibility for the Best Foreign Language Film category at the Academy Awards, which requires a film to have a theatrical release in its home country.

At the time the KFCB issued a press release that lamented the temporary lifting of the ban as "a sad moment and a great insult, not only to the film industry, but to all Kenyans who stand for morality, that a film that glorifies homosexuality is allowed to be the country's branding tool abroad."[1] The KFCB reiterated its position that films should reflect the "dominant values" of the Kenyan people, and that "[h]omosexuality does not qualify as such." Homosexuality is still illegal in Kenya at the time of writing, and punishable by 14 years in prison. Despite this legal context, and the KFCB setting itself up as the moral compass of the Kenyan nation, thousands of people flocked to cinemas to see the film, which has received glowing reviews worldwide since its premiere at Cannes.

While homophobia is certainly widespread, it is of course not limited to the African continent, and the popularity of the film revealed that Kenyans are keen to engage with non-heteronormative expressions of sexuality and LGBTQI+ issues. For some, reactions to the film confirmed the dominant voice of homophobia in Kenya, for others it might have affirmed their belief, or even convinced them, that queer people exist in Kenya as they do anywhere else in the world, and that the film can contribute to creating a society where tolerance and understanding override prejudice and hatred. Whatever the case may be, the worldwide interest in, and popularity of, *Rafiki* underscore two main points: that there is an urgent need to tell more stories about female sexualities that overcome and subvert patriarchal, heteronormative and narrow-minded cultural views; and that audiences in Africa and elsewhere want and need to see these representations. The film broke taboos on several levels, not only in its courageous, albeit non-explicit display of female sexuality, but in its representation of *queer* female sexuality in particular. A detailed analysis of *Rafiki* follows in the case studies at the end of this chapter, in which the focus is on the expression of female sexualities in film. We start with an exploration of theoretical writing on female sexualities and its presence in African cinema, followed by an outline of scholarship on lesbian and queer identities in sub-Saharan and North Africa, again with a focus on film. The chapter concludes with two case studies, from Kenya and Tunisia respectively.

Female sexualities, feminism and film

African cultures are often perceived as more conservative than Western cultures when it comes to public displays of a sexual or erotic nature, as a result of different cultural norms and perspectives on intimacy and privacy. While we have to beware of generalisations that reinforce stereotypes, sexuality and sexual expression is undeniably a taboo subject in many cultures globally. Female sexuality in particular is often a topic not to be discussed or represented openly, regarded as a subject of shame or something to be hidden. The sexuality of the female Black and Arab African body has been misrepresented, eroticised, exoticised, and simultaneously abhorred and desired in the White colonial imaginary, through processes of enslavement and oppression. Reclaiming and celebrating African female sexuality can be an emancipatory and liberatory act for women, and is increasingly enacted by female African cultural practitioners, including writers and filmmakers. The aim of this chapter is to consider female African sexualities in a contemporary context, and representations thereof in African film. As the analyses of the films *Rafiki* (2018) and *Foreign Body* (2016) in this chapter indicate, our interest here is also to consider multiple configurations of sexuality beyond the heteronormative, as filmic representations of queer African sexualities are proliferating.

Sylvia Tamale, a Ugandan feminist scholar and human rights activist and one of the most important contemporary writers on African sexualities[2], warns against the oversimplification and essentialisation of practices and discourses of sexualities in Africa, advocating instead for sexualities to be understood within their multiplicity of contextual meanings (Tamale 2011, 11–12). Given the complex and heterogeneous manifestations of sexuality in any cultural context, a simplistic view of African sexualities originating from notions of male domination and female subordination is insufficient, and researchers in this area thus argue for a conceptual reframing of sexualities in Africa. Too many neo-colonialist viewpoints reinforce notions of a "'world-wide patriarchy' and 'universal female subordination'" (Arnfred 2004, 11). The gender-and-development (GAD) discourse is one of these as it serves the interests of international charities and NGOs that construct African women purely as victims, justifying their intervention into issues such as HIV/AIDS, FGM, polygamy, pregnancy and infant mortality. In fact, these interventions curb and control African women's sexualities and bodies and deny them agency. It is artists and creative practitioners who often challenge stereotypical and stagnant notions of sexuality, creating complex and audacious representations of female sexualities in Africa.

Recognising the importance of including female sexualities in public discourse should not lead to an uncritical or romanticised celebration of the power of female sexuality, since it remains the case that women everywhere continue to struggle against patriarchal oppression that affects their private and public lives and the expression of their sexualities. Despite progress, customs persist in cultures, traditions and religions across the world that contribute to suppressing women's sexual expression, in the form of traditions like female genital mutilation, forced marriages, child brides, non-consensual sex in marriage and others (Segoete 2015). While most of these traditions are long-standing, more recent phenomena such as the HIV/AIDS crisis have been used to reinforce the subjugation of female sexuality. Certain cultural, traditional and religious norms coalesce to consign women into subservient roles that prevent sexual agency. As evidenced by *Rafiki* and *Foreign Body*, the agents and institutions of religion and culture still forcefully prevent any challenge to the hegemonic status quo of heteronormative patriarchy. Where the Transatlantic slave trade and colonisation perpetuated the suppression of female sexuality, historians and cultural scholars point out that sexuality was inherent to African cultural expression long before Western intervention. Modern monotheistic religions, including Christianity and Islam, are predominantly patriarchal, with women's rights and bodily ownership being curtailed and a premium placed on female virginity, chasteness and modesty. The importance of marriage, in both Christianity and Islam, indicates a shared heteronormativity between these two religions (Arnfred 2004, 20). It is within these historical and contemporary socio-cultural contexts that African women are still negotiating and reclaiming their sexualities.

African scholars and researchers writing about African women's sexualities today include Sylvie Tamale, Charmaine Pereira, Kopano Ratele, Desiree Lewis, Elizabeth Khaxas, Patricia McFadden, Pumla Gqola, Zanele Muholi and Akosua Ampofo. Their work intertwines theory and activism, "with the urgency of writing which tackles the politics of gender and sexualities within African contexts and with an eye attuned to the fact that researching these politics has often been done in the name of 'culture', the exotic and the sub-human" (Bennett 2011). Amina Mama claims that "the historical legacy of racist fascination with African's allegedly profligate sexuality has deterred researchers" (Mama 1995, 39). Where Arnfred argued that female sexuality is a neglected topic (2004, 7), she revised this in a later publication, arguing that, in comparison to Western feminists, African feminists might not have felt a similar need for analysing sexualities because sexuality in Africa has been, and to some extent still is, a site of female capacity and power (Amfred 2015, 150). While sexuality might previously not have been discussed as widely or explicitly within African feminism, this is certainly changing, with a number of vibrant movements across the continent challenging and destabilising imposed notions of morality (Tamale 2011, 2). What is clear, is that African sexualities are complex and diverse, and shaped by myriad historical and recent experiences including colonialism, globalisation, patriarchy, tradition, class, religion and culture.

Historically, African cinema has at times been described as "prudish" due to the relative rarity of depictions of overt or explicit sexuality. Film scholar Françoise Pfaff ascribed this to conservative norms within African cultures, associating sex with procreation rather than pleasure (1996, 259). She shows how filmmakers explore other ways of depicting romance and passion, for example in verbal rather than visual expressions of sexual desire. This is perhaps most clearly so in francophone West African cinema. Alexie Tcheuyap confirmed that "[s]ex is more often mentioned than seen in African films. What is displayed on screen is a kind of *trompe-l'oeil*" (2005, 145). It is within this cinematic context that Ivorian Desiré Ecaré's *Visages de femmes/Faces of Women* (1985) or Burkinabe Fanta Régina Nacro's short films *Puk Nini* (1996) and *Le truc de Konaté/Konaté's Gift* (2001) – films that celebrate female sexual freedom and choice – were regarded as controversial when they were released. While cultural and aesthetic norms led to the relative absence, at least historically, of explicit displays of sexuality and nudity in African film, this could also be the result of African filmmakers' awareness of the neocolonialist and/ or voyeuristic implications of displaying eroticism, in particular with regard to the orientalist White male gaze onto the "exotic" or "erotic" black female body. Nevertheless, our research shows that sexuality and sexual identity have been explored by many African directors, male and female, often in subversive and courageous ways. For women, depictions of female sexuality can be an act of reclaiming ownership and agency of sexuality. As Bakare-Yusuf urges: "Telling stories about female sexual pleasure, agency and power allows us to uncover a tradition and community of powerful, feisty, indomitable women who will not be cowed by oppression or violation" (2013, 37).

Taboo desires: lesbian and other queer African identities

Several African countries have extremely strict legislation regarding homosexual acts and relations. Even in countries without overt anti-gay legislation, persistent prejudices view people that identify as LGBTQI+ as deviant and the expression or discussion of homosexuality in public as a social taboo. Many African politicians and heads of state have made homophobic pronouncements promulgated by the media, in civil society, and by public institutions like churches and schools.[3] With the exception of South Africa and Cape Verde, LGBTQI+ rights in Africa are very limited, and at the time of writing, homosexuality is outlawed in 34 African countries.[4] As such, in parts of Africa, it is dangerous for people who identify as LGBTQI+, homosexual or queer, to be open about their sexual orientation or to express their sexuality publicly. It is not surprising then that queer representations in film have been few and far between until very recently.

South Africa is an exception in relation to the rest of the continent, with a liberal attitude towards gays and lesbians, inscribed in its Bill of Rights. The Constitution of South Africa, adopted in 1996 after the end of apartheid, prohibits discrimination and disadvantage on the basis of race, gender, sex, religion, age, disability, sexual orientation and many other criteria. In fact, South Africa has one of the most progressive constitutions in the world regarding gay and lesbian equality (Botha 2011). Though these rights are underscored legally, in reality things are still very different: like in other African countries, homosexuality is viewed as an "un-African" Western perversion. Homosexual identities have been shaped in South Africa by a long history of racial struggles against an oppressive system. Botha states:

> Apartheid legislated who people were, where they could live, with whom they could associate, and even what kind of sex they could have. Asserting a lesbian and gay identity in South Africa became a defiance of the fixed identities – of race, ethnicity, class, gender and sexuality – that the apartheid system attempted to impose upon the whole society.
>
> *(ibid.)*

The complete silence on lesbian issues in particular was compounded by the fact that women's organisations, such as the ANC Women's League, did not address issues of sexuality in their meetings and discussions. Indeed, homophobia was not at all addressed at the height of the anti-apartheid and other African liberation movements, as the national liberation project packaged concepts of the patriarchal family and heterosexual relations as central to its ideals (Campbell 2003, 159). Indeed, mediatised discussions of homosexuality in Africa at large show how both homosexuality and homophobia are variously seen as Western imports. With the advancement of African feminist scholarship across the continent, we now understand that issues of national identity, gender, sexuality, class and race are historically complexly intersectional.

African leaders who speak out against homosexuality often claim that it is a Western import and deeply un-African, thereby maintaining a myth that homosexuality is absent or incidental to African societies and that it was introduced by European colonisers and Arab slave traders. In proclaiming African culture as heterosexual and thereby condoning homophobia, these leaders in fact reveal their ignorance of cultural traditions. There is little dispute that same-sex relationships existed in pre-colonial societies. A growing number of ethnographic publications explore same-sex patterns and relations across Africa, historically and contemporarily, including work by Murray and Roscoe (1998), Amadiume (1998), Morgan and Wieringa (2005), Ekine and Abbas (2013), Munro (2012), Epprecht

(2013), Nyeck and Epprecht (2013), Van Klinken and Chitando (2016), and Matebeni, Monro and Reddy (2018). Although same-sex relationships did occur in pre-colonial Africa, most researchers conclude that the meaning behind traditional and historical same-sex relationships is not clear-cut, as it cannot be compared to the homosexual and queer identities of contemporary society. Homosexuality as it is expressed today is far removed from the life of, for example, the Lovedu Rain Queen in northern South Africa with her hundreds of wives, or that of an early twentieth century female-husband among the Nuer in Sudan, the Nandi in Kenya, the Igbo in Nigeria or Fon in Dahomey (present-day Benin) (Morgan and Wieringa 2005, 281).

Researchers have also revealed the contradiction in the fact that homophobic African leaders, in their roles as defenders of African culture, in effect absorb conservative European Christian or Arab Muslim morals into presumed African values in their denouncements of homosexuality. It was in fact colonialists, and in particular missionaries, who instilled homophobic attitudes in African societies. Existing homophobia is part of a conservative tradition that became prominent in the context of imperial expansion and the spread of Victorian ideas on sex, sexuality and same-sex relationships (Murray and Roscoe 1998; Morgan and Wieringa 2005). A growing body of research, activism and art has unequivocally demonstrated the fallacy of Africa's exclusive "heterosexuality" and the view that it is a "Western perversion" (Ossome in Ekine and Abbas 2013, 34). Part of this misconception is a highly moralised imagined African past and an insistence on an "authentic" African identity, implicating in fact those decolonising movements that are invested in pan-Africanism and African feminism, both of which are complicit in a particular identity politics that has excluded LGBTQI+ people by normalising heterosexuality (ibid., 42). In 2018 British Prime Minister Theresa May, lobbied by UK activists, issued an official apology to citizens of the Commonwealth for historically inflicting anti-gay laws upon their countries. These "sodomy laws" from the colonial era were still in place in 36 out of 53 Commonwealth nations in 2018. As such, the taboo on homosexuality and the resulting homophobia in African societies is actually based on non-African moralities.

Two separate but interlinked narratives dominate discussions of queer African sexualities, "one claims queer sexualities are 'un-African' and the other treats Africa as a site of obsessive homophobia" (Ekine 2013, 78). The first grew out of religious fundamentalism that regards homosexuality as abnormal and denies the existence of queerness on the continent. The second position is embedded in colonial discourses of divergent and anomalous African sexualities and contemporary discourses of a neoliberal LGBTQI+ activist agenda "which seeks to universalise white Euro-American sexual norms and gender expressions" (ibid.). The challenge for queer activists in Africa is to balance the "meta-narratives of LGBT imperialism and homophobic religious fundamentalism on the one hand, and indigenous contemporary constructions of sexuality and gender on the other" (ibid.).

The term *queer* has been adopted by some African writers and activists in order to denote a political position rather than a gender identity or sexual behaviour

(Ekine and Abbas 2013, 3). The use of this term underscores a perspective that embraces gender and sexual plurality and seeks to transform and subvert sexuality in Africa rather than assimilate it into oppressive "hetero-patriarchal-capitalist frameworks" (ibid.). Given this chapter's interest in female sexualities, including lesbian representations and queer female identities, we need to consider the relationship between queer African sexualities and African feminism. Awino Okech argues that it is possible for queer politics and activism to be part of mainstream African feminist spaces (in Ekine and Abbas 2013, 9). African women's movements have been accused of homophobia, as was evident in the aftermath of the UN Fourth World Conference on Women in Beijing, with many female African activists proclaiming that sexual matters were not the priority of African women. Sex and sexuality were only prioritised insofar as they impacted on issues of health, mobility, employment and so on. Issues around corporeal autonomy and sexual identity remain contentious issues within legislation and activism in many African countries (ibid., 10). Despite the tensions between feminism, women's rights and queer activism, Okech maintains that LGBTQI+ work has historically drawn on a large body of feminist theory: "Queer and feminism converge insofar as both question the inevitability and naturalness of heterosexuality and both, to some extent at least, link the binary divide of gender with that between heterosexuality and homosexuality" (Jackson quoted by Okech in Ekine and Abbas 2013, 10).

The debates around homosexuality, LGBTQI+ and queer issues and expressions in Africa are complex, with an urgent need for the acknowledgement of diversity, plurality and contextual specificity. More and more African activists are speaking out against homophobia and against the persecution of people who express non-heteronormative sexual identities. This is also evident in the proliferation of fiction films and documentaries on the subject, made by African as well as foreign filmmakers. A film that should be mentioned as exemplary in its representation of many of the issues that queer Africans deal with, is *Stories of Our Lives*, directed by Jim Chuchu (Kenya, 2014) and created by The Nest Collective, a Nairobi-based arts collective. This anthology film consists of five short films that dramatise the real-life stories of LGBTQI+ people in Kenya, constructed through interviews with people identifying as LGBTQI+ that formed the basis of the short narratives. Because of the legal status of homosexuality in Kenya, the film was banned in the country by the Kenya Film Classification Board, and the individual members of the collective initially remained anonymous in the film's credits. The number of African films with queer topics has grown exponentially in recent years, and as they relate to women in particular we could identify themes such as lesbian relationships and love stories, for example *Quest for Love* (Helena Nogueira, South Africa, 1988), *Karmen Geï* (Joseph Gaï Ramaka, Senegal, 2001), *The World Unseen* (Shamim Sarif, South Africa/UK, 2007), *Difficult Love* (Zanele Muholi and Peter Goldsmid, South Africa, 2010). *L'autre femme*, (Marie Kâ, Senegal, 2013), *While You Weren't Looking* (Catherine Stewart, South Africa 2015), *uNomalanga and the Witch* (Palesa Shongwe, South Africa, 2014) and *Rafiki* (Wanuri Kahiu, 2018), as well as the persecution of lesbians, including the practice of corrective or curative rape, in

Rape for Who I Am, (Lovinsa Kavuma, South Africa, 2006), and *Lost in the World* (\h Xolelwa "Ollie"Nhlabatsi, South Africa, 2015).

Lindsey Green-Simms (2018) has argued that filmmakers in Ghana, Nigeria, and Tanzania, making melodramas with wide popular appeal, "have been quite eager to take on the salacious topic of homosexuality" (655). She claims that Nollywood films have addressed homosexuality perhaps more than any other African film industry, but because these films are mostly rather homophobic, ending with punishment of the gay characters through Christian salvation and morality, it is problematic to place these films under a category of queer cinema (Green-Simms and Azuah 2012). While a film such as *Men in Love* (Moses Ebere, Nigeria, 2010) adheres to this description, Nollywood films that deal with the topic of male homosexuality in an activist and affirmative way are also emerging, including *Rag Tag* (Adaora Nwandu, UK/Nigeria, 2006) and *We Don't Live Here Anymore* (Tope Oshin, Nigeria, 2018), which was sponsored by The Initiative for Equal Rights.

Critical and theoretical writing on queer African cinema is still in the process of catching up with the fast-growing filmic output: Schoonover and Galt's *Queer Cinema in the World* (2016) refers to a number of African films, placing queer African cinema within a broader category of world cinema. In addition to the work of Green-Simms and Azuah referenced above, Claudia Böhme has written about homosexuality in Tanzanian video-films (2015). In terms of the distribution and exhibition of queer films in Africa, many of these remain unseen on the continent due to strict censorship laws bolstered by homophobic attitudes and legislation. South Africa is, again, an exception, as home of the first queer film festival on the continent: the now discontinued Out in Africa South African Gay and Lesbian Film Festival, which ran from 1994 until 2015. The Durban Gay and Lesbian Film Festival was founded in 2011. Also in 2011, the organisation Gay Kenya announced the OUT Film Festival in Nairobi, aiming to showcase films, documentaries, features and plays about LGBT people in Africa. Batho Ba Lorato (People of Love) Film Festival in Gaborone was founded in 2013 by Lesbians, Gays and Bisexuals of Botswana, and the Queer Kampala International Film Festival was founded in 2016 in Uganda. Despite these promising recent developments, with the exception of South Africa, there are very few openly queer-identified African filmmakers, nor any coherent queer film movement on the continent (Green-Simms 2018, 653). Given the fate of *Rafiki* outlined above, one can only hope that queer activism on the continent will eventually lead to a more tolerant environment which would allow for queer African films to be more widely seen in Africa.

Lesbianism in North Africa

Where homophobia in sub-Saharan Africa is often justified through Christian fundamentalist beliefs and in particular evangelical churches, in Islamic states and in countries with substantial Muslim populations, the perspective on homosexuality is somewhat ambiguous. While we need to consider nuances and differences between terms such as "Arab" and "Muslim" for the region's populations, we can make generalised assumptions regarding North Africa, since the percentage of Muslims is so dominant. As such, Sharia law forms the basis of most legislation and criminal courts in North Africa, except in Tunisia. In scholarship on Islam and sexualities, there is an equally ambiguous dialogue between both discourses. On the one hand, a growing number of scholars argue that historical evidence shows a very lenient approach to people who engage in same-sex acts. On the other hand, the increased politicisation of conservative Islam over the past few decades, has pointedly impacted same-sex relationships. More and more, we need to consider individual nations' legislation when it comes to the institutionalisation of religion and the criminalisation of sexuality.

As the case studies in this chapter contain an in-depth analysis of a Tunisian film by Raja Amari, the vision of sexualities in these films is dependent on a legislative system in a state that at least portrays itself as secular, even though the practice and moral prejudices are often still inspired by Islamic law. As Kaya Davies Hayon (2018) illustrates, for example, same-sex acts between men are punishable by imprisonment in most Islamic societies, and death in some Islamic states (including in Mauritania and some parts of Northern Nigeria). While many Islamic states explicitly prohibit sexual interaction between men, there are no explicit official restrictions on lesbian relationships, as they are not perceived to be disruptive of the authority of the dominant patriarchal order: "In Shi'ism [...] lesbianism was not a matter of juristic focus at all" (Hamoudi 2015, 71). This means that women who participate in same-sex acts are doubly marginalised, as their desires are either seen as negligible or they are curtailed in patriarchal society. Despite the severity of such laws, a kind of "situational bisexuality" is widespread in many Islamic societies (Kugle 2010, 10). These acts are tolerated in some societies so long as they remain clandestine and do not disrupt quintessentially patriarchal institutions like marriage or the family.

Likewise, scholarship has contained a polemical dialogue on homosexuality in majority-Muslim states. The historical approach as described above is problematised by scholars like Habib (2007), who argue that an identitarian homosexuality is not only evident in Islamic history and culture but can be understood through models of sexuality that emphasise its inherent or "essential" nature. Opposed to this is a strand of scholarly work that criticises or denies the existence of the category or word "homosexuality" in the Arab world altogether. These scholars emphasise the need to move away from a Western tendency to homogenise the Muslim (woman) to critique the internalisation of orientalist perceptions from the colonial era. As elsewhere, the internalised Victorian social and sexual mores need to be rejected in the Muslim world, so that instead "indigenous processes to empower the sexually 'marginalized' populations in Muslim states" can be created (Ahmed-Ghosh 2012, 378). As Ahmadi (2012) argues,

> Islam, as a religion of peace and as a religion that stands against oppression, has the ability to ameliorate this perceived repression by providing a forum of acceptance for Muslims and voices of dissent against the punitive and over-bearing historical perspectives on homosexuality.

Where sexuality was "historically viewed as fluid, with rare public strictures, today we are seeing harsh laws dictated by conservative Islamic regimes and courts challenging this sexual fluidity and replacing it with harsher sentences to ensure heterosexual conformity" (Ahmed-Ghosh 2012, 378). The rich and empowering indigenous heritage needs to be used to protest against state policing of sexualities and ensure respect and consideration for the lived experience of those with same-sex desires or in same-sex relationships.

Despite the conservatism surrounding the candid expression of non-normative desires in Muslim societies today, Habib argues "[f]ilms from the decades preceding the mid-1970s tend to be engaged in a rather open and positive dialogue with [their] audience as regards sexual deviation" (2007, 95). As Walter Armbrust has shown, before the eighties Egyptian cinema in particular was characterised by a sense of freedom of expression. Part of that was a small minority of films that offered far more transgressive representations of female and male (homo)sexuality than it does today. With the privatisation of Egyptian cinema under president Anwar Sadat, the figure of the homosexual was "relegated to a dark closet" (Habib 2007, 113). Nowadays, homosexuality is seldom featured openly in Arab cinema.

However, a glance over film history in Tunisia shows a particularly daring sense of identity, independence and aesthetic accomplishments. The Golden Age of the late eighties and nineties – with the success of filmmakers such as Nouri Bouzid, Férid Boughedir and Moufida Tlatli – showed a proclivity for liberal sexual values and morals on the screen. Male filmmakers like Nouri Bouzid pushed the boundaries of expectation with a couple of highly sexualised gay protagonists in *Man of Ashes* (1986) and *Bezness* (1992). Boughedir's sensuous young women in *Halfaouine* (1990) or *A Summer in La Goulette* (1996) learn very early on how to use their sexualities to their advantage and teach their male lovers how to please them. Yet these films often feel like voyeuristic documents playfully but problematically privileging the male gaze upon the woman's sexualised body. In Tlatli's work these slanted views of women's sexuality were addressed through a more politicised and emancipated representation of women's gendered struggles. See for example *The Silences of the Palace* (1994), where Alia decides she can live without a man to raise her child alone, or *The Season of Men* (2000), in which the women on Djerba form a cheerful, hardworking and talkative community, and where some decide they are better off without their man in order to be free, raise their children and enjoy their lives.

Sexuality and sensuality in Tunisian cinema however often seem to have served as a smokescreen hiding other contentious issues from view. Indeed, Tunisia has been described as a hypocritical or even schizophrenic cinematic country, where the government is concerned with its image abroad. Thought to be among the more liberal nations in the Arab world, since 2011 it has become clear that it was actually one of the most repressive regimes under President Ben Ali. One example is the censorship and subsequent banning of *Fatma 75* by Selma Baccar, a film that highlights women's roles in the history of Tunisia, in particular the liberation struggle and in contemporary protests against the government. Officially, the film was banned for containing an extended scene of sexual education but in reality, Baccar told us, it was because of its political content.

In the Maghreb, outsiders may expect to encounter historical and contemporary censorship more readily than elsewhere, because of its perceived conservative societies. While this cannot be wholly denied in general terms, when we look more closely at the details of individual nation's censorship rules, we notice a wide variety of sensibilities and sensitivities across the Maghreb and the rest of (North) Africa, especially where Islam is the dominant religion. Likewise, taboos and the resultant censorship rules are in constant flux throughout history, and one particularly interesting element in a government's hold over its country's reputation is how one of the main preoccupations is the depiction of women's bodies, in particular their sexualities. Often in traditional societies but also elsewhere, women and their behaviours, dress sense and language are most often the subject of censorious tendencies. Women's bodies all too often are the battlefields of institutions and reputations.

These difficulties notwithstanding, a handful of films have emerged that feature queer characters. As one of the authors found out while curating a programme of queer Arab films, most do not deal explicitly with the theme of female same-sex desire. Tunisian science-fiction thriller *Bedwin Hacker* by Nadia El Fani (2003) is, to the best of our knowledge, the only film by a woman that has foregrounded a queer female character, but El Fani's position in Tunisian cinema is controversial and contested. Also in Tunisia, Selma Baccar's *Khochkhach/Flower of Oblivion* (2006) focuses on a woman whose husband is attracted to young men, with her sexual frustration leading her to an asylum. Very recently, Sonia Chamkhi's debut film *Narcisse* (2018) also carefully touches on gay desire in the context of a theatre production in Tunis. In Moroccan Narjiss Nejjar's *L'Amante du Rif* (2011) a subplot is dedicated to two lesbians who can find love and peace only in prison. Both the asylum in *Khochkhach* and the prison in *L'Amante du Rif* serve as loci where, paradoxically, women can be free and resist the power of the patriarchy from within its quintessential institutions.

Case study: *Rafiki*, (Wanuri Kahiu, Kenya/South Africa/Germany/Netherlands/France/Norway/Lebanon, 2018)

As we outlined in Chapter 1, Kenya has an increasingly prolific film industry with more well-known female than male filmmakers. Of this group of women directors, Wanuri Kahiu is one of the best-known internationally, having directed a number of award-winning features, documentaries and short films. Kahiu initially studied a BSc in Management Science in the UK, and then completed a Masters degree in film production and directing at the University of California. Her first fiction feature film, *From a Whisper* (2008) tells the story of a young woman in search of her missing mother, in the chaotic aftermath of the twin bombings of the US Embassies in Nairobi and Dar es Salaam in 1998. It received 12 nominations and won five awards at the African Movie Academy Awards in 2009. In 2009, Kahiu directed *Pumzi*, a female-centred sci fi short film about a young African woman's attempt to escape the controlled subterranean compound she is restricted to after World War III, the "Water Wars," has rendered much of the world a barren and desolate post-apocalyptic landscape. *Pumzi* was hailed as the first Kenyan sci fi film and remains important and much-celebrated given the growing awareness and popularity of the genre of Afrofuturism. It is particularly significant as an example of a nascent genre of African feminist science fiction film. There have been various reports of collaborations between Kahiu and Nigerian feminist sci-fi writer Nnedi Okorafor, and the result of such a collaboration is certainly much-anticipated by fans of African sci fi literature and film.

Kahiu is the founder of Afrobubblegum, a media company based in Nairobi that supports, creates and commissions "fun, fierce and frivolous" African art. Afro-bubblegum is, in fact, a form of artistic expression that Kahiu wants to create through her work. Given its subject matter and the dangerous prevalence of homophobia in Kenya, it might seem as if *Rafiki* is anything but "fun and frivolous." However, the film's feminine aesthetic and the innocence, honesty and naivety of the developing relationship between its two young protagonists, retain a playfulness and lightness that belies its serious subject matter. The script, based on an award-winning short story entitled *Jambula Tree* by Ugandan writer Monica Arac de Nyeko, was co-written by Kahiu and South African filmmaker Jenna Cato Bass. Such creative collaborations between female cultural practitioners in Africa, as in the example of Kahiu and Okorafor above, are significant and propitious, as they contribute to creating a fertile environment for more female-centred African stories and voices to be heard.

Rafiki opens with scenes of everyday life in Nairobi, representing the city as a bustling and vibrant urban hub. The city has received similar representations in other Kenyan films, including Kahiu's own *From a Whisper*, in *Togetherness Supreme* (Nathan Collett, 2010), and in *Nairobi Half Life* (David "Tosh" Gitonga, 2012), its effervescence depicted in bright colours and soundscapes. We hear the sounds of the city – vehicles, car horns, lively chatter and shouting – and see slice-of-life scenes of its inhabitants, including tailors, butchers, skateboarders, animals, children playing games, and people cooking, shaving, selling and buying food and other products at street stalls, and dancing or making music on the spot. In a city like Nairobi, much of life takes place outside in full view of everyone. As such, the city represents freedom, opportunity, diversity and modernity, but also immorality, crime and greed. Nairobi, and in particular the neighbourhood in which the two protagonists, Kena and Ziki, live, functions as a character rather than a mere backdrop to the story.

We are first introduced to the tomboyish and androgynous Kena (Samantha Mugatsia), a skateboarder who plays football with her male friends and regularly catches rides on the back of her friend Blacksta's motorbike. The film's main theme is foreshadowed in a homophobic remark about gay men by two of Kena's male friends. Tellingly, the film's title means "friend" in Kiswahili, a word that hints at the necessity to disguise a same-sex romance as platonic friendship in an intolerant environment. The first encounter between Kena and Ziki (Sheila Munyiva) is their meeting of eyes across the road, both are conspicuous in their individualism and style: Ziki's radiant pink and purple braids, youthful bubble skirts and wittily sloganed t-shirts are hard to miss even in an environment saturated with colour. The film's representations of modern urban youth culture and femininity – in the characters' individual styles expressed through their clothing, hair and jewellery – are significant, and there is a freshness in its depictions of individualism and identity. This is a female-centred "Afropop" style which is further underlined by the film's soundtrack of hip hop and pop music exclusively featuring young female African musicians.

Kena and Ziki's first encounter stands in stark contrast to the male-dominated public environment. The film immediately cuts to a shot of political campaign posters, and an outside restaurant with two women, Mama Atim and her daughter, chatting and gossiping. We learn that Kena's father, a small-business owner who is running in the forthcoming local elections, has divorced her mother to marry a much younger woman who is now pregnant. Kena's mother is very religious – the first time the viewer encounters her she is praying in her house – and she is also embittered by her failed marriage and her ex-husband's new relationship. The viewer is rapidly introduced to a complex and multifaceted societal context inflected and shaped by romantic, familial and platonic relationships, politics, religion, prejudice, intolerance and little distinction between the public and the private, reinforced by the intimate camerawork and tight framing of faces. Politics and religion, represented by the state and the church, bastions of patriarchy, are indeed major obstacles in Kena and Ziki's blossoming romance, as Ziki's father is a high-profile politician running against Kena's father, and the church is led by an evangelical minister who preaches against homosexuality. The film draws on the very familiar star-crossed lovers' trope, a universal theme set in a very specific socio-cultural context. While the development of their romantic relationship is natural and gentle, the unlikeliness of their relationship is observed by everyone around them: "Today the sun will rain," declares Mama Atim as she witnesses the daughters of the two politically-opposed fathers together.

It is clear that societal norms conspire against their relationship in different ways – they are both young women, from families on different sides of a political divide and different social backgrounds: while Kena is from a modest working-class background, Ziki is from a wealthier and politically prominent family. As the attraction between them develops, they need to find a private space where they are undisturbed by the prying eyes of the community. Their first private meeting is on the rooftop of a building from where they can see the world but remain undetected. The first moments between them are unsure, shy and apprehensive, but they gradually learn more about each other. Both are on the verge of finishing high school and Kena has aspirations to become a nurse. Ziki tells her off, demanding that she aims higher to become a doctor or surgeon. Ziki wants to travel and see the world, she is unconventional and non-conformist and regularly clashes with her parents who want her to follow a traditional career and domestic path. The girls make a pact, promising each other that they will never be "like any of them down there," but instead strive to be "something real." Their other private space is a disused and abandoned Volkswagen minibus draped in pink bougainvillea. The colour palette of the film remains significant and symbolic throughout: when Kena and Ziki are alone together their surroundings are bathed in soft hues and delicate pastels, a momentary respite from the oppressive and claustrophobic colours and sounds of the city. The dominance of pink could of course be read as significant as a colour traditionally associated with femininity and with gay culture. Kahiu has cited Marcel Camus' *Black Orpheus* (1959) and Mélanie Laurent's *Breathe* (2014) as stylistic influences in the making of the film, as well as the work of African American visual artist Mickalene Thomas, South African photographer Zanele Muholi and Kenyan-born visual artist Wangechi Mutu. The influences of these Black female artists, and their feminist/feminine aesthetics that celebrate female sexuality, beauty and power are certainly evident in the stylistic choices of *Rafiki*.

Kena's mother notices a difference in her daughter but assumes that the change is due to a boy, perhaps Blacksta. She tells her daughter to "choose wisely" and not be weighed down by people who keep her stuck, but of course her mother could not know that taking this advice to heart would play out very differently for Kena. In an intimate scene Ziki is braiding Kena's hair and persuades her to wear a dress to which Kena's mother remarks that she now looks like "a proper woman." She states: "All we need is a nice rich doctor," reinforcing the societal norms and conventions that Kena and Ziki so desperately want to escape, and also inadvertently suggesting that Kena couldn't be that doctor herself. Alternating with their private spaces and moments they also embrace the bustle of the city as they start exploring their environment and each other. Their relationship slowly and gently develops through glances, brief touches and little dialogue. Their first kiss is tender and soft, and when they eventually consummate their relationship during a night spent together in the minibus, the sensual moments between them are modest and subdued, with no nudity on display. This depiction of a lesbian sexual encounter is markedly different from other recent films about lesbian relationships, including *Blue is the Warmest Colour* (Abdellatif Kechiche, France, 2013) and *The Miseducation of Cameron Post* (Desiree Akhavan, US, 2018). While some critics have interpreted this non-explicit depiction of a sexual encounter as censorship-compliant and not daring enough for international audiences, we would like to argue that it instead avoids any sensationalism and gratuitous sex or nudity – subverting and denying a heteronormative or patriarchal gaze rather than challenging it. The notion of a "safe space" becomes significant here, both idealistically, in the film's setting, and also in the medium of film itself as capable of providing a safe space to tell potentially contentious stories.

As we outlined, religion has colluded with patriarchy to propagate homophobia, and this is also challenged in *Rafiki*. In a church scene the minister preaches against same sex marriage and proclaims that it is not a human right: "What is a human right?" "Isn't it God who decides what is right and what isn't? God's laws don't change like human laws," he declares, supporting his argument with a verse from the Bible. This increasingly perilous and intolerant environment puts a strain on Kena and Ziki's relationship, exacerbated by the community's snooping and Ziki's mother catching the two girls kissing. They escape to their safe haven, the minibus, where they dream about having their own place and living together. But Mama Atim and her daughter find them there, followed by a mob who drag them out of the vehicle and violently attack them. These scenes are shocking and potentially triggering for viewers who have experienced homophobic violence. Defeated and injured at a police station, they are not offered support or safety, but are mocked by police. Their parents come to fetch them; Ziki's father angrily slaps his daughter, while Kena's father is loving and comforting. In a subsequent scene Kena's mother has taken her to church in an attempt for her to be absolved from her "sins" through prayer. As a result of the violent public outing of the girls' relationship, Kena's father's campaign posters have been vandalised and his shop has lost customers. But he drops out of the election race willingly as he refuses to reject his daughter, thus providing a beacon of understanding and acceptance in an otherwise cruel and intolerant world. In a heart-breaking scene Kena visits Ziki at home but Ziki rejects her, broken, hurt and disillusioned: "Are you planning to marry me, are we going to have this beautiful family?" she sneers bitterly, alluding to the impossibility of their relationship. She is busy packing as her parents are sending her to London.

Time passes, and we next see Kena working in a hospital. Mama Atim has been admitted as a patient but will not allow Kena to touch her. She informs her that Ziki is back and there is a shot of Kena's hospital locker with a postcard from Ziki carrying the words: "I miss you." The film ends with the two young women meeting on a hilltop, again a safe space removed from the hostility and judgement of the public. In the final shot, Ziki softly calls out Kena's name, who looks back and smiles, with Ziki's hand on her shoulder. This open and auspicious ending, suggesting the possibility of the two women reuniting, is one of the reasons why the Kenya Film Classification Board banned the film. The censors wanted Kahiu to change the ending as it was not remorseful enough, but when she refused the KFCB concluded that the hopeful ending was promoting homosexuality.

It took Kahiu and her producers seven years to put together the financing for the film, resulting in a co-production between seven countries: Kenya, South Africa, Germany, Netherlands, France, Norway and Lebanon. Kahiu has speculated in interviews that the struggle to find production money might have been due to a fear of potential funders to offend African governments. Her perseverance in spite of these financial difficulties are testament to Kahiu's labour of love in the service of a story she was desperate to tell. She wanted to make this film in the context of Kenya's new constitution voted for by the majority of the population in 2010; under this constitution your identity and however you identify yourself is protected, regardless of race, religion or gender. Acts of "unnatural sex" are still criminalised but these would be very difficult to prove as it would require a violation of an individual's privacy, which is protected. Kahiu has argued that homophobia, rather than homosexuality, is un-African, and goes against the tolerance and unity embedded in the African concept of *ubuntu*. Kahiu wants to contribute to creating hope for a more tolerant, safe and just society, in which a marginalised minority would also have the right to community and belonging. This, she has argued, is entirely in keeping with the spirit of the Kenyan constitution and national anthem that promote peace, love and unity (Bacon 2018). *Rafiki* should be seen as a hugely significant film for Kenyan and African youth; a film that advocates individualism, difference, tolerance and understanding, a love story that has not been told or heard enough in Africa, presenting characters that African youth can identify with. "To see young people in love from the continent is so glorious, and it's so needed," Kahiu has said (Vourlias 2018).

It was perhaps a bitter irony, if not surprising, that despite its temporary unbanning in Kenya to make it eligible for Oscar submission, *Rafiki* was in the end not selected as Kenya's entry for Best Foreign Language Film. That honour went to *Supa Modo* (Likarion Wainaina, 2018), a wholly deserving but uncontroversial choice in its universally affecting story of a young girl with a terminal illness dreaming of being a superhero. Important recognition from the continent came in the form of main actor Samantha Mugatsia winning the Best Actress Award at FESPACO 2019. Kahiu has also spoken in interviews about the tremendous response the film received from Kenyans, with young Kenyan women sharing their stories on social media of coming out to friends and family as a result of watching *Rafiki*. This underscores the fact that *Rafiki* is an African story made in and for an African context, despite the fact that it might not be seen as widely on the continent as Kahiu would have hoped. It is a story of liberated female sexuality that presents a different narrative to the dangerous, dogmatic and imaginary notion of an exclusively heterosexual Africa.

Case study: *Corps étranger/Foreign Body* (Raja Amari, France/Tunisia, 2016)

Foreign Body (2016) by Tunisian Raja Amari is not only part of a dominant theme in North African cinema, films about refugees crossing the Mediterranean, it is also unique – indeed, almost auteurist – in its treatment of three protagonists' sexualities. While the story is framed by the politics of migration, dealing with both hope and desperation, and balancing the politics of historical colonialism and contemporary legal and illegal migration in France, it also digs deep into the psychological and physical bonds among North Africans in France. Amari makes a film that is simultaneously politically relevant and highly personal. In this story, the individual comes first, and is confused by his or her relationships with other "Others" in France. *Foreign Body* is a visceral, immersive film experience, with a unique approach with a handheld camera and extreme close-ups that encourage the spectator to experience the foreign body alternately in pain and full of desire. Female sexuality in this film is explored in all its physicalities and used in the struggle for survival at all costs.

Perhaps the most famous film about female sexuality/sensuality coming out of Tunisia is Raja Amari's *Satin rouge* (2002) with Palestinian superstar Hiam Abbass. It outlines the emotional and physical changes Lilia, a widow, undergoes as she starts to assert herself and her sexuality as a belly dancer in a cabaret. She discovers her body and gains confidence, as she embarks upon a love affair with a much younger man, whom – she discovers later on – is her daughter's boyfriend. This debut feature has been analysed in much academic work for its emancipatory and taboo-busting view of a lower-class middle-aged Tunisian woman. Indeed, it has heralded the rest of Amari's work as a director interested mainly in embodiment and in discovering the individual woman's sexuality. As such, we witness Lilia escaping her mundane existence through the embodied practice of belly dance (Davies Hayon 2018). Her newly discovered sexuality is the means by which she is able to transcend the (restrictive) roles of widow, housewife and mother imposed upon her by dominant Tunisian society.

Satin rouge set the tone for Amari's career, as returning themes in her films are the exploration of the female body through dance and self-expression, developing a narrative of independence and increasing self-confidence. Another recurring theme that is intertwined with the limits and possibilities for female self-expression is how women from the lower social class are often alone and lonely in their struggle to come to terms with their desires. Finally, a trope that is becoming quite typical for a Raja Amari film is the love triangles she creates between two women and one man: in *Satin rouge* between a mother, daughter and their lover; in *Buried Secrets* (2009) Aicha (Hafsia Herzi), the younger of two daughters, sexually obsesses over a young couple she spies on; and in *Foreign Body* an intense love triangle develops between an older woman, a younger daughter figure and a young man. These three tropes are inherent to all Amari's films, and all contribute to the assertion that the female body and its blossoming confidence through sensuous movement (dance or sex) is a site of power. Claiming ownership of the female body then leads to an empowering, desiring physicality.

While these aspects of her filmmaking practice show a will to deconstruct both the exoticising colonial gaze onto the Arab woman's body and the eroticising patriarchal version of gendered division in Tunisia, Amari's power to make such sexualised films is at least also partly down to her ability to cast transnational, non-Tunisian star actresses such as Hiam Abbass (*Satin rouge* and *Foreign Body*) and Hafsia Herzi (*Buried Secrets*) in the main roles. Likewise, having attended the FEMIS film school in Paris, she is one of a group of young female filmmakers returning to their home countries to make films that are able to offer searing critiques on "hypocritical sensibilities" (Khélil, 2007; Schultz 2002) by approaching subjects like women's bodies and sexualities.

In *Foreign Body*, Samia (Sarra Hannachi) is a newly arrived Tunisian illegal immigrant in France. The film opens on a sequence of Samia nearly drowning in the Mediterranean as she arrives on the coast of Southern France. She ends up in Lyon, looks up Imed (Salim Kechiouche) – an old friend from her village who works in a café, who takes her in and helps her on her way – and ends up working for a bourgeois lady, Leila (Hiam Abbass). These three characters form the crux of the story. Their gender, age, class and backgrounds define them as their situations turn life into an intense, desperate and stressfully lonely struggle to survive. It becomes clear that Samia is fleeing her extremist brother's impending release from prison in Tunisia and looking for a better life in France. Leila's husband has passed away, and she looks for house help to cope with life as a lonely widow who is lost in a world where her husband no longer fills her daily life and gives it meaning. Her nationality is left ambiguous, although she is Arab and identifies with Samia's ordeal once she knows her situation. Imed's intentions are equally left ambiguous as he seems to care for Samia, but his obvious attraction to her is hampered by his troubled association with a group of extremist young men, both in Tunisia and in France.

These men threaten and intimidate Samia, which not only leads her to flee Imed's flat, it also foreshadows the rest of the film in which young men always serve as intimidating figures. They define her sexuality by her gender, suspicious when she is in the company of men, not so when she is in very intimate contact with a woman. Because she is a beautiful young woman travelling alone, they are suspicious of her and overhearing their conversations fills Samia with fear and paranoia. Being in France these poor, insecure conservative young men have specific expectations about how modernity and liberal behaviour impact on women and they expect her to clean up and do the dishes. They talk loudly about her behind her back, bump into her on purpose, and ask Imed loudly who she is and why she is there. According to a few of them she should not be left alone, because "some girls these days are really…," referring to Samia's independence interpreted as loose morals – the ellipsis revealing an unspoken but prejudiced attitude.

This exclusionary attitude and the schism between men and women sets the tone for her meeting with Mme. Berteau, Leila. There is an instant attraction for Samia, as she admires the style, language and gestures of the *bourgeois française*. From Mme. Berteau's first coffee to Samia's wheedling her way into her apartment and life, there is a sense of Samia's admiration for and aspiration to be like her. As Leila's affinity for Samia grows as well, the development of their relationship highlights the fine line between wanting to *be* the other or wanting to be *with* the other. When Leila starts to guide Samia on how to behave in the upper classes, and how to dress, echoes of Imed's instructions on how to be French clarify a sense of integration into a society or a class, but also give a sense of the Pygmalion nature of the relationship between Samia and Leila. From opportunism (the women need one another: Leila needs companionship to combat her loneliness and Samia needs a job where she does not have to be known to the authorities) the relationship grows into a co-dependency that, at times, borders on the sinister. It is presumed that Samia seeks refuge, safety, protection with a mother figure: outside the flat, e.g. when they go shopping, Samia sticks so close to Leila that she is in her shadow. Inside the flat the physical closeness is further emphasised by the two women constantly gazing at and imitating one another. Their mutual interest becomes obsessive, and ambiguously sexual in nature. The tension throughout the film is sexual but suggested rather than enacted. In a hammam scene, for example, the two women mirror one another's poses and gazes.

Leila revels in Samia's touch as she massages the older woman, and offers to return the favour. Leila notices Samia's scars, and says she admires Samia's beautiful skin. In return, a little bit later Samia compliments Leila on her beauty, wealth and style.

Samia's very physical presence in her acquaintance's life is emphasised when she goes back to Imed's bar to return his keys and stays to dance. She drinks alcohol although Imed does not approve, and she dances provocatively, lifting her shirt to reveal her belly in a belly dancing moment. One wonders whether this is an emancipatory act, where she is rejecting his authority over her, dancing alone and looking at him with a challenging gaze; or whether she is seducing him. The constant challenge from Samia is very complex. Imed's returned gaze is one of worry and hatred: is he feeling protective over her or rather possessive and over-bearing? Later on, his judgment is clarified as fed by conservative morals when he accuses her of "whoring yourself out," to which she reacts by slapping him across the face, rejecting his role in her life. As he starts following Samia, Leila meets Imed and after drinking in his bar and flirting with him, impressing him with her stylish, bourgeois performance, she goes home with him. Instead of sleeping with him, as we expect, she sleeps where Samia slept, in the exact same position, sym-bolically and sexually linking her to her protégée in Imed's eyes. And when Samia angrily asks Leila "did you sleep with him," she gets no answer – again giving the film and the relationships in the film a sense of ambiguity and tension. Imed and Leila continue their flirtation, and after Leila starts dressing him, teaching him manners as well, in another Pygmalion trope, they do eventually have sex.

But Imed is forced to accept that he is a tool in the relationship between the two women. He is not an object of affection but rather an instrument of jea-lousy: in an awkward visit to Leila's house, he initially thinks he is the object of desire of both women, but as Leila and Samia flirt, drink and dance toge-ther, the confusion about his exclusion reaches a climax. His gaze upon the dancing women is refused. The corporeal sameness and attraction between Leila and Samia excludes his presence and confirms his alterity. The camera remains extremely close to Samia's dancing body, and observes his admiring, possessive gaze from a distance, excluding him physically, while Leila joins the dance and the intimacy between the two women becomes blatantly obvious. In a jealous rage, he hurts Leila and Samia throws him out. Leila and Samia then console one another in a desiring embrace. Leila later mirrors this protective act when Imed, on an unannounced visit, violently pushes Samia and repeats she is a whore. Leila throws him out, and she and Samia finally sleep together. In an act of revenge, the women decide to inform on Imed in order to guarantee Samia's safety and the survival of their relationship. Indeed, images of the sea bed at the very end of the film close the framing of the love triangle in the context of the refugee crisis, as we see Imed's scarf drifting in the undercurrent, confirming he did not survive the crossing of the Mediterranean, problematis-ing the women's selfish act of survival at all costs. When we see the couple visiting Samia's mother in Tunisia, we finally see Samia smile and relax, sur-rounded by the two women she loves and needs the most.

★★★★

Differently than *Rafiki* then, in *Foreign Body* there is an internal and external struggle with physical attraction, which is not innocent nor based on love, but based on a very complex identity, class and generational struggle. Nevertheless, the lesbian relationship is still empowering: the ambiguity of the relationship and the avoidance of any simple explanation or refusal to define it within clearly set boundaries makes this relationship a transitional one: from opportunism it goes through co-dependency to a peaceful and mutually respectful, protective bond. Perhaps due to its framing within a reference to Mediterranean deaths through migration, and coloured by a conservative religious perspective, *Foreign Body* is much darker than *Rafiki,* even if the violence is not as externally devastating and physical as in the Kenyan film: here the violence is slow, internal, psychological, thriller material. Despite the film's darker ambience, *Foreign Body* is still indicative of how women can utilise their sexuality in a deliberately powerful way to disrupt heteronormative patriarchy.

Both *Rafiki* and *Foreign Body* explore the complexities but also affirmative aspects of female African sexualities, with sexuality becoming a site of female capacity and power. These African narrative constructions of sexuality and gender are crucial, in particular in queer representations, as Sokari Ekine states:

> Western interventions which seek to impose a Western narrative on the queer African struggle are part of an uninterrupted history of suppressing the needs and experiences of Africans dating back to colonisation. The African struggle is not only directed at changing existing legislation; it is a struggle in which we seek to reassert our own narrative and reclaim our humanity.
>
> *(Ekine and Abbas 2013, 87)*

This is exactly what films such as *Rafiki* and *Foreign Body* do.

Notes

1 Taken from a press release published on the KFCB's websitekfcb.co.ke.
2 She was also named "Worst Woman of the Year" by a conservative group in Uganda in 2003: www.awid.org/news-and-analysis/worst-woman-year-sylvia-tamale-publishes-african-sexualities-reader
3 Ex-presidents Robert Mugabe from Zimbabwe and Sam Nujoma from Namibia have been two of the most prominent anti-gay voices; ex-president of Nigeria, Goodluck Jonathan, signed a law in 2014 making it illegal for gay people to hold a meeting; Ugandan President Yoweri Museveni signed an anti-gay bill in 2014; in 2018 a senior Tanzanian politician, Paul Makonda, commissioner for the commercial capital Dar es Salaam, called on the public to report suspected gay men to the police.
4 To put this in context and avoid any assumption that homophobia and intolerance of homosexuality is an exclusively "African" problem, at the time of writing homosexual relationships are still criminalised in 72 countries around the world.

Bibliography

Ahmadi, Shafiqa (2012) "Islam and homosexuality: Religious dogma, colonial rule, and the quest for belonging," *Journal of Civil Rights and Economic Development*, 26(3), pp. 537–563.

Ahmed-Ghosh, Huma (2012) "Introduction: Lesbians, sexuality, and Islam," *Journal of Lesbian Studies*, 16(4), pp. 377–380.

Amadiume, Ifi (1998) *Male Daughters, Female Husbands: Gender and Sex in an African Society*. London: Zed Books Ltd.

Arnfred, Signe (2004) *Re-thinking Sexualities in Africa*. Uppsala: Nordic Africa Institute.

Arnfred, S. (2015) "Female sexuality as capacity and power?: Reconceptualizing sexualities in Africa," *African Studies Review*, 58(3), pp. 149–170.

Bacon, Redmond (2018) "'We truly love our country' – An interview with 'Rafiki' director Wanuri Kahiu." Available online: https://muchadoaboutcinema.com/2018/05/24/we-truly-love-our-country-an-interview-with-rafiki-director-wanuri-kahiu/ [Accessed November 2018].

Bakare-Yusuf, Bibi (2013) "Thinking with pleasure: Gender, sexuality and agency." In Susie Jolly et al. (eds) *Women, Sexuality and the Political Power of Pleasure*. London: Zed Books, pp. 28–41.

Bennett, Jane (2011) "'Worst woman of the year': Sylvia Tamale publishes African sexualities: a reader." Available online: www.awid.org/news-and-analysis/worst-woman-year-sylvia-tamale-publishes-african-sexualities-reader [Accessed November 2018].

Böhme, Claudia (2015) "Showing the unshowable: The negotiation of homosexuality through video films in Tanzania," *Africa Today*, 61(4), pp. 62–82.

Botha, Martin P. (2011) "Post-apartheid cinema: a thematic and aesthetic exploration of selected short and feature films," *Ilha do Desterro* (October), pp. 225–267. Available online: https://periodicos.ufsc.br/index.php/desterro/article/view/2175-8026.2011n61p225 [Accessed January 2019].

Campbell, Horace (2003) *Reclaiming Zimbabwe: The Exhaustion of the Patriarchal Model of Liberation*. Claremont: David Philip Publishers.

Davies Hayon, K. (2018) *Sensuous Cinema. The Body in Contemporary Maghrebi Film*. London: Bloomsbury.

Ekine, Sokari and Hakima Abbas (eds) (2013) *Queer African Reader*. Cape Town: Pambazuka Press.

Epprecht, Marc (2013) *Sexuality and Social Justice in Africa: Rethinking Homophobia and Forging Resistance*. London: Zed Books.

Green-Simms, Lindsay (2018) "Queer African cinema, queer world cinema," *College Literature*, 45(4), pp. 652–658.

Green-Simms, Lindsey and Unoma Azuah (2012) "The video closet: Nollywood's gay-themed movies," *Transition* 107(1), pp. 32–49.

Habib, S. (2007) *Female Homosexuality in the Middle East: Histories and Representations*. London: Routledge.

Hamoudi, Haider Ala (2015) "Sex and the Shari'a: Defining gender norms and sexual deviancy in Shi'i Islam," *Fordham International Law Journal*, 39(1), pp. 25–99.

Khélil, H. (2007) *Abécédaire du Cinéma Tunisien*. Tunis: Simpact.

Kugle, Scott Siraj al-Haqq (2010) *Homosexuality in Islam: Critical Reflection on Gay, Lesbian, and Transgender Muslims*. London: OneWorld Publications.

Mama, Amina (1995) *Beyond the Masks: Race, Gender and Subjectivity*. London and New York: Routledge.

Matebeni, Zethu, Surya Munro and Vasu Reddy (eds) (2018) *Queer in Africa: LGBTQI Identities, Citizenship, and Activism*. London: Routledge.

Morgan, Ruth and Saskia Wieringa (2005) *Tommy Boys, Lesbian Men and Ancestral Wives: Female Same-Sex Practices in Africa*. Johannesburg: Jacana Media.

Munro, Brenna M. (2012) *South Africa and the Dream of Love to Come: Queer Sexuality and the Struggle for Freedom*. Minneapolis, MN: University of Minnesota Press.

Murray, Stephen O. and Will Roscoe (eds) (1998) *Boy-wives and Female Husbands: Studies in African Homosexualities*. Basingstoke: Macmillan.

Nyeck, S.N. and Marc Epprecht (2013) *Sexual Diversity in Africa: Politics, Theory, and Citizenship*. Montreal: McGill-Queen's University Press.

Pfaff, F. (1996) "Eroticism and Sub-Saharan African films." In I. Bakari and M. Cham (eds) *African Experiences of Cinema*. London: British Film Institute.

Segoete, Lineo (2015) "African female sexuality is past taboo." Available online: https://thisisafrica.me/sexuality-taboo/ [Accessed November 2018].

Schoonover, Karl and Rosalind Galt (2016) *Queer Cinema in the World*. Durham: Duke University Press.

Schultz, Kate (2002) "Interview: Self-empowerment by way of the midriff; Raja Amari's 'Satin Rouge'," *Indiewire* (20 August). Available online: www.indiewire.com/2002/08/interview-self-empowerment-by-way-of-the-midriff-raja-amaris-satin-rouge-80248/ [Accessed December 2018].

Tamale, Sylvie (ed.) (2011) *African Sexualities: A Reader*. Cape Town: Pambazuka Press.

Tcheuyap, Alexie (2005) "African cinema and representations of (homo)sexuality." In Flora Veit-Wild and Dirk Naguschewski (eds) *Body, Sexuality, and Gender: Versions and Subversions in African Literatures*. Amsterdam and Union, NJ: Rodopi, pp. 143–156.

Van Klinken, Adriaan and Ezra Chitando (eds) (2016) *Public Religion and the Politics of Homosexuality in Africa*. London: Routledge.

Vourlias, Christopher (2018) "Wanuri Kahiu on banned LGBT love story 'Rafiki': 'It's time we had fun'," *Variety*. Available online: https://variety.com/2018/film/festivals/wanuri-kahiu-rafiki-banned-kenya-1202802850 [Accessed November 2018].

Filmography

Anonymes / Buried Secrets, Dir. Raja Amari, Tunisia/Switzerland/France, 2009

Asfour Stah/Halfaouine: Boy of the Terraces, Dir. Férid Boughedir, Tunisia/France/Italy, 1990

Aziz Rouhou / Narcissus, Dir. Sonia Chamkhi, Tunisia, 2015

Bedwin Hacker, Dir. Nadia El Fani, France/Morocco/Tunisia, 2003

Bezness, Dir. Nouri Bouzid, France/Tunisia/Germany, 1992

Black Orpheus, Dir. Marcel Camus, Brazil/France/Italy, 1959

Corps étranger / Foreign Body, Dir. Raja Amari, France/Tunisia, 2016

Difficult Love, Dir. Zanele Muholi and Peter Goldsmid, South Africa, 2010

Fatma 75, Dir. Selma Baccar, Tunisia, 1975

From a Whisper, Dir. Wanuri Kahiu, Kenya, 2008

Karmen Geï, Dir. Joseph Gaï Ramaka, Senegal/France/Canada, 2001

Khochkhach / Flower of Oblivion, Dir. Selma Baccar, Tunisia, 2006

L'amante du rif / Rif Lover, Dir. Narjiss Nejjar, Morocco, 2011

L'autre femme / The Other Woman, Dir. Marie Kâ, Senegal, 2013

La saison des hommes/The Season of Men, Dir. Moufida Tlatli, Tunisia/France, 2000

La vie d'Adèle / Blue is the Warmest Colour, Dir. Abdellatif Kechiche, France/Belgium/Spain, 2013

Le truc de Konaté / Konaté's Gift, Dir. Fanta Régina Nacro, Burkina Faso, 2001

Les Silences du palais / The Silences of the Palace, Dir. Moufida Tlatli, Tunisia/France, 1994

Lost in the World, Dir. Xolelwa "Ollie"Nhlabatsi, South Africa, 2015

Man of Ashes, dir. Nouri Bouzid, Tunisia, 1986

Men in Love, Dir. Moses Ebere, Nigeria, 2010

Nairobi Half Life, Dir. David "Tosh" Gitonga, Kenya/Germany, 2012

Puk Nini, Dir. Fanta Régina Nacro, France/Burkina Faso, 1996

Pumzi, Dir. Wanuri Kahiu, South Africa/Kenya, 2009

Quest for Love, Dir. Helena Nogueira, South Africa, 1988

Rafiki, Dir. Wanuri Kahiu, Kenya/South Africa/Germany/Netherlands/France/Norway/ Lebanon, 2018

Rag Tag, Dir. Adaora Nwandu, UK/Nigeria, 2006

Rape for Who I Am, Dir. Lovinsa Kavuma, South Africa, 2006

Respire / Breathe, Dir. Mélanie Laurent, France, 2014

Satin rouge / Red Satin, Dir. Raja Amari, France/Tunisia, 2002

Stories of Our Lives, Dir. Jim Chuchu, Kenya/South Africa, 2014

Supa Modo, Dir. Likarion Wainaina, Germany/Kenya, 2018

The Miseducation of Cameron Post, Dir. Desiree Akhavan, US, 2018

The World Unseen, Dir. Shamim Sarif, South Africa/UK, 2007

Togetherness Supreme, Dir. Nathan Collett, Kenya/Venezuela, 2010

Un été à La Goulette / A Summer in La Goulette, Dir. Férid Boughedir, Tunisia/France/Belgium, 1996

uNomalanga and the Witch, Dir. Palesa Shongwe, South Africa, 2014

Visages de femmes / Faces of Women, Dir. Desiré Ecaré, France/Ivory Coast, 1985

We Don't Live Here Anymore, Dir. Tope Oshin, Nigeria, 2018

While You Weren't Looking, Dir. Catherine Stewart, South Africa 2015

8

SPIRITUAL PATHWAYS TO EMANCIPATION

One of the first feature films by a Moroccan woman dealt with women's complex emancipation in Islam: Farida Benlyazid's *Bab Al-Sama Maftuh/A Door to the Sky* (1988) looks at a specifically feminist process of emancipation for a young woman, Nadia (Zakia Tahri), who returns from France to Morocco for the funeral of her father. The film is about the rediscovery of a Moroccan Sufi cultural and spiritual heritage, along with inheritance issues in women's personal status laws and a feminist awakening. Nadia sets up a Zawiya, a shelter for women based on the principles of Sufi spirituality, a space where women find new agency through their spiritual journeys. The film "proposes Sufism as a path that undoes binaries and contests views that Islam [oppresses] women" (Gauch 2009, 109). Benlyazid's film focuses on the ambiguities in Islamic feminism, its pluralism, and highlights the Sufi interest in the power of visual manifestations of spirituality. Its feminist spirit is evident in the inscription of women's consciousness in Islamic culture. The film references historical Islamic feminist figures such as Fatima al-Fihriya, founder of the Karaouine Mosque and university in the ninth and tenth centuries; it also foregrounds the specific veil Nadia choses to wear and her "embodied behaviour" looking beyond surface meanings, emphasising the veil's capacity to signify choices and beliefs (Mahmoud 2005, 15); and the setting of the film in the architecturally beautiful city of Fez, a centuries old centre of spiritual learning, is equally conspicuous. The recent documentary *New Moon* (2018) by Kenyan Philippa Ndisi-Herrmann looks at the story of religious self-discovery. This multi-layered film, about the development of a big port on the tiny island of Lamu and the impact of the building site on its locals, turns into a personal exploration of Sufism in Eastern Africa. Ndisi-Herrmann turns the camera on herself in order to confront her struggle with being a modern, liberal woman embracing Islam. Like *A Door to the Sky*, this intimate film depicts not the challenges between modern life and traditional Islam, but the personal spiritual path of a young woman. Her struggle with the complexities of her chosen faith turns into an emancipatory process that enables the director to grow in consciousness and confidence.

Cinema can *depict* spirituality, and it can *perform* spirituality. Both Benlyazid and Ndisi-Herrmann depict the spiritual journey of a young, modern woman and enact the ambiguity within Islam towards feminism and emancipation. By negotiating both Sufi Islamic sensibilities and modern, Westernised, secular values, these films show how spirituality is an act of increasing consciousness and visual performance. These diverse elements of spirituality have fed cinema since its early days. From the very beginning, spirituality has played a central role in both the narratives, characterisations and storytelling in film and in its sacramental quality. Wright shows how "religion has colonised [cinema] and has found itself challenged and altered in the course of the encounter," both in a productive and in a destructive manner (Wright 2006, 2). Spirituality can be used in a cinematic narrative for personal and communal self-discovery, both in spite of spiritual practices or because of them, as our case studies will show. At times spiritual and religious beliefs could be central to feminist narratives in a positive and productive way, and at other times they are questioned when they contribute to the oppression and subjugation of women. Film's multiple relationships with spirituality is evident in its aesthetic aspects, religion being a narrative-producing mechanism that continues to tackle grand themes like forgiveness, redemption, sacrifice and tradition. However, religious powers are also among the harshest critics of, and censorial hindrances, to cinema. Indeed, Lyden's historical overview of the role of religion in world cinema shows that "there have always been conflicts between religious and filmic perspectives, but there has [also] been appreciation of shared interests and values" (Lyden 2009, 3). Wright further emphasises how "film can be perceived and used as a means of reflection and spiritual experience" (Wright 2006, 3), in other words, how film can assume a sacramental quality in and of itself. Plate delineates the parallels between film and religion, showing how both "function by re-creating the known world and then presenting that alternative version to their viewers or worshippers" (Plate 2017, 3). Both cinema and religion make manifest the unrepresentable: they bring audiences close to the ineffable, invisible and unknowable.

African thinkers extol the expressive and intellectual vitality of African art and its interactive relationship and interplay with spirituality. While most studies on spirituality and film engage with Western religions and presume the universality of such monotheistic religions, we need to give space to the tensions between and blending of precolonial, indigenous or alternative religious practices and new spiritualities. Congolese philosopher Mudiji Malamba Gilombe says that art and religion are intimately and uniquely related in the African context in that they evoke and manifest depths of existence that cannot otherwise be expressed, through a synthesis of the imaginary and the real (Gilombe 1988, 256). Art is the privileged voice by which humans express beauty and excellence. As Rosalind Hackett illustrates, spiritualities combine metaphysical and philosophical systems of thought (1998). She emphasises that spiritualities are concerned with art and that the ritual significance of artistic objects is mirrored in the artistic value of spirituality. But cultural critics need to diffuse the centrality of performed rituals in faith, and recognise religion's implicitness in everyday life in people's lived experience. In this chapter, we examine the context of spiritual phenomena and religious expressions as they are engaged with in films from the African continent, and we take into account historical changes and multiple, contested perspectives. As art and spirituality are both systems of communication, we must continue to re-examine them "in specific historical contexts and relations of power," with a multi-dimensional perspective (Hackett 1998, 12).

Women, film and spirituality in Africa

When considering the relationship between African film and religion we need to think through its complex history as well as its contemporary consciousness. Women's roles in religion are as diverse as culture and society are on the continent. In this book we are bound to limit ourselves to a manageable number of the countless spiritual denominations and experiences on the continent. Still, we look at both monotheistic and the more traditional "indigenous" spiritualities. In this chapter, we engage with a wide variety of spiritual practices on the African continent, ranging from pre-colonial and traditional belief systems, to Christianity, Islam and Judaism, as well as the lasting influence of indigenous spiritualities on the post-colonial realities. We are especially interested in how women filmmakers have engaged with these in their films. We have opted to use the term "spiritualities," as we do not want to limit ourselves to any presumed or received general understanding of what "religion" might be, and rather want to engage with tools that express faiths or belief systems in diverse cultural contexts. We emphasise that spiritualities, in particular their plurality, is an inclusive term that embraces all forms of belief systems or convictions that go beyond and include the humanistic. We stress the role of women in these spiritualities: how women have experienced or expressed their faith, which roles they are ascribed in films that touch on spiritual topics. Women filmmakers simultaneously accentuate the importance and increasing relevance of the interrelationships between the different faiths on the one hand, and between faith and culture on the other. This interplay is of central importance to historical cinema as well as the manifestation of a postcolonial spiritual lived experience of women's lives and cultural expressions.

African spirituality and the feminine

Spiritual beliefs and practices are often central to, or given a prominent place, in African films, considering that the African worldview is intrinsically "religio-centric," as spirituality permeates all realms of life to the extent that life is perceived holistically with no separation between the "sacred" and the "profane" (Mbiti 1990). African Traditional Religions (ATRs) and their various engagements with the material and the spiritual world should be understood as a constellation of different worldviews, beliefs in gods and deities, uses of symbols, traditions and practices. These are manifested in an array of rites and rituals (including sacrifices and offerings), ceremonies, festivals, healings practices, celebrations of the human life cycle, and a constant interplay between the material world and the metaphysical and invisible world. Indigenous African beliefs include impersonal mystical powers, spirit beings, divinities or gods, and a Supreme being (Turaki 2000). The importance of community, represented by the concept of *ubuntu*, is often central to these belief systems, as is the significance of ancestral spirits. Historical events and processes, like the Transatlantic Slave Trade, colonisation, the incursions of Christian missionaries and Islamisation have left an indelible mark on traditional spiritual beliefs, at times fusing to create the syncretism of present day African spiritualities.

Whereas movements of colonisation and religious conversion in Africa were mostly violent and oppressive (missionaries demolishing indigenous art and symbols and colonisers suppressing or outright banning traditional beliefs and rituals) traditional spiritualities have survived in various guises. In fact, African spiritualities have been integral to struggles for independence and resistance against oppression. Diverse spiritual African worldviews include the belief in a world governed by the law of the spirit, in which the whole of creation is filled with the ubiquitous presence of impersonal powers and forces, spirit beings, and a host of divinities and gods (Turaki 2000). Animism, the spiritual belief that all objects, places and living beings possess a distinct spiritual essence, is central to this worldview. Steyne describes it as follows:

> Everything in life can be influenced by and responds to the world of spirits. Whatever happens in the physical realm has a spiritual coordinate and, likewise, whatever transpires in the spiritual realm has direct bearing on the physical world. Man is related to and dependent upon the unseen. For this reason all of life is to be understood spiritually. The correct response to any situation is spiritual, whether the matter is a family affair, sickness, or ceremonial practice.
>
> *(Steyne 1990, 59)*

Nigerian poet and philosopher Harry Garuba (2003) has critiqued Western misunderstandings of this fundamentally spiritual worldview prevalent in Africa and its diaspora, which involves the continuous evolution of indigenous wisdom through an acceptance of the malleable and fluid nature of knowledge. Cultural practices in post-independence Africa have assimilated the machineries of modernity – science, technology and models of governance – "into the matric of traditional ritual and culture" (Garuba 2003, 263–264). Garuba observes in the syncretism of different belief systems the "re-traditionalisation of Africa" in different aspects of life when, for example, African presidents include praise singers into the protocols for their inaugurations, or ancestor worship is practiced in Christian churches. Scholars of African culture have examined the incorporation of traditional cultural forms such as the Yoruba *oriki* (praise poetry), ritual performances and practices, and motifs from folktales into the context of modern social and political life.

The divine and the worldly, the traditional and the modern, the metaphysical and the scientific exist side-by-side in different societal and cultural contexts, mostly in harmony but at times also in conflict. Garuba terms these processes of re-traditionalisation a manifestation of an animist unconscious, which operates through a practice that he describes as "a continual re-enchantment of the world." Metaphysical or magical elements of thought are not displaced or rejected in modern Africa, but continually assimilate new developments in science and technology to lead not to a disenchantment with modernity, but to a perpetual re-enchantment in which "the rational and scientific are appropriated and transformed into the mystical and magical" (ibid., 267). Garuba's re-appropriation of animism in a modern, contemporary African context prompts us to discard the unproductive binaries of tradition versus modernity, magical versus rational, spiritual versus secular. Instead, the simultaneity of these ideas in fact makes spirituality an inherent aspect of everyday life. The animistic mode of thought is embedded within the processes of common social, material and economic activities and "subverts the authority of Western science by reinscribing the authority of magic within the interstices of the rational/secular/modern" (ibid., 271). In film, such "magical," supernatural or metaphysical elements offer audiences the opportunity to suspend their rational or scientific disbelief, and challenge viewers to accept the centrality of metaphysical spirituality without prejudice. Audiences are invited to open themselves up to systems of knowledge that challenge the foundations of scientific rationality, and to do this without exoticising or othering what they see on screen.

Of great interest to our study is the widely held claim that African spirituality is essentially feminist. Almost all African creation myths present the female and male elements as equal, with no overarching supreme (male) God (Salami 2017). In African Traditional Religions, a union of male and female forces operate in harmony. There is a balance between the masculine and feminine and for every male deity there is a female counterpart. There are many female deities in indigenous beliefs, of which the best-known is Mami Wata, a female water spirit venerated in many parts of Africa. Sexuality and gender are complexly intertwined with spirituality, through for examples the rites of passage in various African cultures that mark different stages of development, growth and sexual maturation. Whereas socialisation practices do at times subordinate women's sexual lives to men's, spirituality can be a form of empowerment that lifts women into positions of divine authority (Moyo 2004). Indeed, African women have, since the advent of the Transatlantic Slave Trade 400 years ago, fought against oppression, colonialism and racism through various spiritual belief systems. For example, Nehanda Charwe Nyakasikana (c. 1840–1898) was a *svikiro*, a spirit medium of the Shona people of Zimbabwe. As one of the spiritual leaders of the Shona, she inspired the revolt against the British South Africa Company's colonisation of Mashonaland and Matabeleland (Kamba 2017). Even long after her execution by the British, freedom fighters sought out the spirit of Nehanda for guidance in the independence struggle.

Today, in Africa and in its diasporas, we observe a return to ancestral traditional spiritualities. Spiritual practices that have been denigrated by colonisers are decolonised through the assertion that a return to indigenous faiths is empowering (Adegoke 2016). African spirituality is re-appropriated in popular culture, for example in Beyoncé's pastiche of the Yoruba pantheon of Orishas, in particular her interpretation of the Goddess Oshun, a deity of the river often clad in yellow, associated with female sexuality and pleasure. For Black people across the diaspora, an embrace of African spirituality becomes a medium for self-definition and understanding of Black identity, gender roles and sexuality beyond and outside of the confines of the White gaze (Rutledge 2017). Spiritual belief systems offer proto-feminist examples of gender equality – indigenous forms of feminism embraced in contemporary processes of emancipation. Examples of feminist and feminine African spiritual beliefs and practices can be found in many of the films we reference in this book, for example in the depictions of the pangools, the ancestral spirits in Safi Faye's *Mossane*, or in the spiritually feminine importance of water and the mystical existence of Mossane herself. In Fanta Nacro's film *The Night of Truth* one of the main female characters pours a libation on the ground as an appeal to the ancestral spirits. In Rahmatou Keïta's *The Wedding Ring*, Tiyaa's quest to be reunited with the love of her life is guided by the symbolic meanings of celestial movements. In these films, such metaphysical beliefs and rituals are not seen as antithetical to contemporary life but integrated into African modernity through "a continual re-enchantment of the world" (Garuba 2003, 265).

Islam and women in African cinema

On the African continent, diverse regions showcase widely varied practices of Islam. Here we focus on the North African region and South Africa. In global cinema the discourse on Islam and Muslims is imbued with negative stereotypes and often conflated with the Middle East at large, particularly in cinema from the Global North (Shaheen 2001). What we see instead in African cinema is historical and contemporary visions of an Islam that has brought civilisation, wealth and learning to the world. In fact, Africa was one of the first continents Islamic scholars travelled to in pre-colonial times, and since the seventh century, Islam has spread all over the continent.

Like any other major religion, Islam has an ambivalent relationship with cinema. Where modernity and the impact of popular culture on daily life increased the appeal of cinema, "traditional and religious circles remain[ed] strongly against cinema, which they believe[d] advocates Western values and secularism, if not impiety" (Dönmez-Colin 2004, 9). The depiction of Muslim women in film is entirely dependent on the time and place, and on interpretations of, or adherence to, Islamic law. Egyptian scholar Viola Shafik delineates the influence of religion, specifically Islam, on censorship in the Arab countries, including North Africa. She shows how from the earliest days of cinema, majority-Muslim governments decided that "heavenly religions should not be criticised," that "heresy and magic may not be positively portrayed" and that "immoral actions and vices on screen are not justified and will even be punished" (Shafik 2016, 34). At the same time, there are hardly any Christians on screen in Arab cinema and if there are they have minor roles in which they are usually mocked. Portrayals of Jews are likewise frowned upon and Jews (still) feature as stereotypical caricatures or as evil powers that need to be thwarted. In Laïla Marrakchi's *Marock* (2005), the neutral depiction of a young Jewish man was cause for some critics to call the filmmaker a Zionist. But even when it comes to depictions of Islam there are severe restrictions: orthodox versions of Islam are to be avoided and a depiction of the prophet himself is absolutely off-limits (Shafik 2016, 49). All these moral concerns for cinema in majority-Muslim countries, on top of the further diversity within Islam, make religion in cinema a very complex theme, subject to severe restrictions. And yet, Nacim Pak-Shiraz (2018) shows how even strict forms of Islam can have creative relationships with film. She shows how religion is both a text and a ritual, and that both need cultural approaches rather than literal ones. A beautiful example of this can be found in the film *Inch'Allah Dimanche* by Algerian Yamina Benguigui (2001), in which the preparations and the rituals of Eid al-Adha (sacrificing the sheep) is an opportunity for Zouina to emancipate herself and her daughters by ensuring their education and her own independence and friendships with other women. Her agency is developed through a ritual and consumed against the conservative, patriarchal Islamic rules of her husband.

Islamic feminists advocate women's rights, gender equality, and social justice grounded in a spiritual framework. Pioneering Arab scholars recognise the role of Islam in a global feminist movement, in for example Fatema Mernissi's or Nawal El Saadawi's work. These Moroccan and Egyptian intellectuals have very different approaches: Mernissi looks at the history of women in Islam from the starting point of the scripture of the Quran, whereas El Saadawi looks at contemporary cultural practices and strongly opposes any religious obstacles to women's emancipation. Advocates of feminist movements in the majority-Muslim world seek to highlight the equality deeply rooted in the Quran and encourage a questioning of the patriarchal interpretation of Quranic teachings through diverse personal status laws, working towards the creation of more equal and just societies. Thus, Islamic feminism does not support the contention that discrimination against women is religiously based. On the contrary, it sees the oppression of women as a deviation from the original spirit of Islam. That this oppression may appear most dramatic in the domestic sphere is the result of the tendency in some Islamic states towards secularisation in the public sphere, while at the same time leaving the private realm to regulation by Islamic law (Samiuddin and Khanam 2002). The recognition and protection of human rights, and constitutions guaranteeing equal rights to all citizens, may set up a conflict with the personal status codes that often privilege men over women. As a result, one of the major areas of scholarship and campaigning for Islamic feminists in various parts of the world are these personal status laws and their variants in diverse countries. Although some personal status laws are in clear conflict with the principle of gender equality, progressive Arab scholars maintain that it would be wrong to conclude that Islam itself is opposed to equality between the sexes.

Muslim feminism in South Africa likewise asserts the belief that the Quran prescribes the equality and identical spiritual and moral obligations placed on all individuals, regardless of their sex. Shamima Shaikh was one of South Africa's best-known Muslim women's rights activists who used her public platform to convey this message. Islamic feminist scholar Sa'diyya Shaikh (2004) foregrounds her position as a South African Muslim woman whose existential, spiritual and ethical universe is based on an Islamic world-view, and whose coming of age was formulated within the socio-political context of apartheid. For her, Islam transcends boundaries of race and demands human agency in the quest for social justice. Her own experiences of patriarchy urge her to contest received ideas of Islam. She understands the term "feminism" as

> a critical awareness of the structural marginalisation of women in society and engaging in activities directed at transforming gender power relations in order to strive for a society that facilitates human wholeness for all based on principles of gender justice, human equality, and freedom from structures of oppression.
>
> *(Shaikh 2004, 148)*

Shaikh focuses her scholarship primarily on Islam's inherent plurality, encompassing realities from varying socio-cultural and political positions. For Shaikh, the realities of the gender dynamics in Islam are as complex and diverse as the realities of women in any other spiritual, social or political context.

The South African Islamic cultural and intellectual feminist community of which Sa'diyya Shaikh and Shamima Shaikh are part also includes a number of filmmakers, like Zulfah Otto-Sallies and Rayda Jacobs. Their films imagine and represent an Islamic modernity through a female identity that is both Islamic and modern. These two directors are part of a loose affiliation of female Muslim filmmakers that emerged in the early noughties. Their work is of interest particularly because the directors draw on their experiences as Muslim women in a secular society. They present progressive and thoughtful interpretations of the role of women in a Muslim community in post-apartheid South Africa. Zulfah Otto-Sallies' short film *Raya* (2001), documentary *Through the Eyes of My Daughter* (2004), and feature film *Don't Touch* (2006) all deal with the attempts of a rebellious Muslim youth to find ways to reconcile their spiritual tradition with a modern, secular society. Otto-Sallies, whose untimely death in 2016 led to the outpouring of tributes from the South African film industry, believed that film can change perspectives on women's rights and their roles in society. Rayda Jacobs' *Confessions of a Gambler* (2007) is based on her own novel of the same title, which she converted into a screenplay, co-directed and acted the leading role. It depicts the myriad challenges faced by a Muslim woman in Cape Town, whose life spins out of control when she becomes addicted to gambling. More recently, Sara Blecher's *Mayfair* (2018) is a gangster tale set in the multicultural Islamic community of Johannesburg's Mayfair district. All these contexts in which Muslim women are represented and voice their concerns, show how diverse Muslim spiritualities and realities are, and how spirituality is an inherent part of women's lived realities on the continent.

Christianity and women in African cinema

A condensed history of the colonial and postcolonial impact of the Christian faith on the African continent would highlight the appearance of Christianity in 1AD, with Mark the Evangelist's arrival in Egypt. Christianity remained dominant in North Africa until the Roman Emperor Constantine's rule. Both were gradually pushed out of the region when Islam arrived in the seventh century. In sub-Saharan Africa Christianity arrived with the Portuguese colonists in the fifteenth century. In the seventeenth century, in the Kingdom of Kongo (modern-day Angola), the female prophet Kimpa Vita took her place in Christian history (Thornton 1998). She and her followers saw in the united Kongo the origin of Christ's true birthplace. She is now seen as an antislavery figure and an inspiration to modern African democracy movements, as well as the protector of children and mothers.[1]

Dutch Christians arrived in South Africa in the seventeenth century but by and large indigenous spiritualities remained undisturbed until the nineteenth century missionaries came to Africa as part of the antislavery crusades. With these missions came Western education, literacy and healthcare. However, the spread of Christianity also paved the way for further oppression, colonisation and commercial speculation or expropriation of land. Moreover, in its original rigid European form, Christianity denied people pride in indigenous cultures and traditions (BBC World Service n.d.). Missionaries disapproved of the manner in which Africans worshipped, for example through the worship of figurines and animal sacrifices. Demanding monogamy, disapproving of traditions, dances and dress, Christianity persisted for a long time and indeed some of the most excessive forms of Christianity can now be found on the African continent and indeed in televangelism. In other areas, the Christian religion evolved in its own way, specific to the geographical and cultural context, with people practising their own Africanised forms of Christianity.

Just like any other religious practice, Christianity has its activists and feminists. Christian feminists argue that, in order to fully understand Christian values, believers need to recognise the contributions of women to Christian history. Similar to Islamic feminists, Christian feminists believe in a God who sees all human beings as equal, regardless of sex or race, having created all humans in His (or Her) image. Indeed, some feminist theologians believe that God is a woman. A distinction needs to be made between Christian feminists and Christian leaders who advocate women's rights. In areas where the term feminism is seen as an all-too White privilege, there are still those women leaders who take women's issues as their priority. One such example is Mercy Amba Oduyoye from Ghana. She is called the "mother of African women's theologies" (Pui-lan) and is the director of the Institute of Women in Religion and Culture at Trinity Theological Seminary in Legon, Ghana. She champions the fight against women's poverty, against gendered violence and against global injustice, and dedicates her life to promoting women's rights, education and health. Ghana was Christianised during colonial times. This missionary movement strictly guided the learning away from indigenous customs and values. Oduyoye's powerful message, echoing other feminist advocates, is one of realistically blending indigenous with Christian spirituality. As such, Oduyoye shows, African Christians can draw upon their own ancestors' wisdom and customs in the practice of their faith.

Like Oduyoye, Kenyan Teresia Mbari Hinga (2017) looks at women's rights and feminism from the perspective of "what matters" in the lives of African women. She shows that "what matters" has been co-opted by other causes, often expressed either by men or outsiders. As Oredein writes in her review of Mbari Hinga's work, "an African Christian feminist perspective interrogates cultural formations and communal concerns that both arise from within and are imposed upon African contexts" (Oredein 2018). This confirms the concern with African women's specific issues being spoken about and their voices being heard elsewhere. These African Christian feminists not only juxtapose their work with the feminist theological movement in the West, they also express the urgency with which Western feminism is required to consider "different" concerns such as communities' lived experiences and women's physical and mental health. Indeed, African Christian feminists foreground African women's daily concerns such as economic independence, identity narratives, health and educational standards, and the socio-political priorities of communities. Moving the experience and interpretation of Christianity away from a privileged European context and background enables African Christian feminists to focus on the powers and rights of African women, including relevant cultural practices rather than "imported" ones.

Expressions of the Christian faith are present in many women's films from predominantly Christian African countries, even if they are not always central to the films' narratives. Christianity is depicted variously as an affirmative force or as a restrictive societal imposition. We observe this, for example, in some of the case studies discussed previously: in *Something Necessary* Anne's Christian faith provides solace to the PTSD she is experiencing, and numerous scenes depict her in prayer; in *Rafiki*, Kena's pious mother is not accepting of her daughter's sexuality and the church is a space of intolerance and homophobia. Indeed, certain manifestations of the Christian faith on the African continent are rather extreme in nature, and in some of these, film has become a tool in the spreading of a particular Christian message. Christianity is for example often depicted in Nollywood films, usually pitted against supernatural beliefs, with the films' narrative conclusions generally restoring the hegemony of Christian beliefs.

A more sinister manifestation of Christianity can be found in evangelical Nigerian videos. While the number of women directing films in the Nollywood industry is limited, a few powerful women act as producers or funders for such evangelical films. However, some of the videos and production companies, attached to specific preachers and churches, are highly problematic, as their specific preachings use spirituality as a tool for propaganda that terrorises its audiences, using indoctrination or indeed brainwashing techniques. The phenomenon of witchcraft accusations against children is part of this dangerous manifestation of

Christian practices on the continent, and occurs not only in Nigeria but also in countries like Zambia, as our case study of *I Am Not a Witch* will show. These corrupted aspects of Christianity have been called out, as Oha states: "Pastors in Nigeria (and elsewhere) have been constantly exposed and attacked in the media for living scandalous lives, and particularly for their involvement in sexual immorality" (2000, 194). The rhetoric of these videos centres on the conflict between God and Satan, and while "especially Pentecostalism has points of intersection with indigenous religious systems in the idea of the potency and operation of evil spiritual forces [...] the former still regards the latter as the site and domain of demonic operations" (ibid., 192). The simplistic binary between good and evil at the source of these films is also the narrative source of spiritual warfare, which offers ready-made narratives and explanations of human problems. As such these Christian videos have yet to deconstruct the simplistic binary and colonial semiotic. At the same time, they may benefit from more acceptance of "spiritism." A positive and productive hybridity of a spirituality that employs native spirits as well as Christian elements is something that would benefit a liberated evangelical video industry and bring the production into contact once more with the lived experience of its audiences.

Judaism and women in African cinema

Sizeable Jewish communities, such as the Beta Israel in the Horn of Africa and Ashkenazi Jews in South Africa, have been present on the African continent for centuries, each with their own particular history and rich cultural heritage. While all these communities and especially their historical significance in the spiritual development of regions, tribes and nations are interesting in their own right, very few films have been made by or about their presence. More recently, the interest in these Jewish communities is growing, and specifically in North Africa an opening up towards different cultural and spiritual expressions can be observed. As Albert Memmi points out in *The Colonizer and the Colonized*, the Jew in North Africa is positioned in between the colonised and the coloniser. The Jewish person represents a portion of the population that is always perceived as an outsider: liberal, rich and therefore not like the majority of the Arab or African populations but also not ethnically White. Likewise, in cinema, depictions of Jewish religious life have often been negative. This is not only because some films tend to cater to Christian or Muslim antisemitism, but also because Jewish filmmakers are themselves highly secularised and have a very critical view of traditional Jewish religious life (Lyden 2009, 4). While Jewish people have in many cases been at the forefront of the development and commercialisation of cinema in the world, historically, the depiction of the Jew in narrative cinema in North Africa has been that of an outsider.

In the context of our study, it is worthwhile outlining some of the basic discourses in Jewish feminism, precisely because they remain so hidden from cinema.

Jewish women have been at the forefront of feminist movements around the world, even if, stereotypically, most Jews come from the secular middle or upper classes of society. As Joyce Antler describes, the "women's movement allowed Jewish women to escape their suburban, parochial, confined environments" (2018, 18) to become rebels from materialism and conformity. She describes how the Jewish feminist movement started growing in the seventies to address both religious and secular life.

Whereas feminism's embrace of radical individualism was usually rejected in Orthodox Jewish feminism, more liberal religious Jewish feminists did successfully critique ancient patriarchal customs (ibid., 9). Their resistance to assimilation asserted the need for Jewish women to proclaim their distinctiveness as Jews rather than to blend into the mainstream, while problems with Zionism and anti-Semitism grew in importance in the global politics of nationhood and post-colonial identities. As such, a smaller group of Jewish women allied themselves with Third World anti-colonialist and anti-racist struggles, opposing Zionism as a project of military occupation and state force, and intersectionality became increasingly important in the fight against patriarchal institutions and masculinist systems in Jewish religious and community life (ibid., 16). At the UN International Women's Conference in 1985 in Nairobi, harsh condemnations of Israel and anti-Zionist rhetoric raised awareness among Jewish attendees and colleagues, resulting in some cases in a splitting apart and in other cases an alignment of African and Jewish feminist organisations. Likewise, some White Jewish South Africans, including prominent women like politician and activist Helen Suzman, were involved in the struggle against apartheid. It is estimated that Jews were disproportionately represented (by as much as 2,500%) among Whites involved in the anti-apartheid movement.

North African Jews are, for the most part, descendants from the Spanish Jewish communities who fled to North Africa in the seventh and again in the fifteenth centuries. The assimilations between the Berber and Jewish communities in North Africa have resulted in a rich, complex history represented especially in Berber heritage. Pioneering Moroccan Izza Génini specialises in safeguarding this Berber-Jewish heritage in music documentaries. Her films celebrate national diversity as a subtle critique of the compulsive effort to achieve national unity. She emphasises Morocco's multicultural heritage through music and ritual performances and celebrates her transnational identity, defined by a personal and subjective point of view. She has made over twenty non-fiction films, most of which deal with Moroccan-Jewish contributions to Morocco's multicultural identity, and the intercultural exchange that defined Jewish-Arab relationships in Morocco. A large number of her documentaries deal with female performers, and the very particular role these performers take up in the wider societal context. Our first case study focuses on the large Sephardic Jewish communities in North Africa, specifically because in a culture perceived as conservative and Muslim, the presence of Jewish cultures and spiritualities is increasingly acknowledged in contemporary Moroccan cinema.

Case study: *Marock* (Morocco, Laïla Marrakchi, 2005)

The Moroccan government has held tight reins over public discourse on Jews in Morocco, and has controlled how, where and to what end Jews were represented in public media. More recently, we suggest that in Maghrebi cinema Jewish culture is perceived as being entirely secularised, and more culturally relevant than spiritually. In post-colonial Moroccan cinema, the discourse on the Jewish presence in Morocco has changed. After Moroccan independence in 1956, "Jews were granted citizenship and there were some efforts to include them in the new national administration, but they were not easily assimilated into public visions of a national Moroccan future in the Arab world" (Kosansky and Boum 2012, 423). In the process of establishing a solid national identity, efforts were made for general Arabisation and Islamisation of culture and politics. Slowly but surely, since the reign of King Mohammed VI, the Jewish figure has become used furtively to demonstrate the liberal virtues of the independent Moroccan state, as Jews represent a vehicle for testing the limits of free expression in a cinema where previously taboo topics are gradually allowed. In film, the "recent treatments of Jewish themes and histories reflect the shifting relationship between state and civil society in the postcolonial period" (ibid., 423), which is all part of a "larger trend in which institutionally entrenched Moroccans [...] have been reconsidering the Jewish component of the Moroccan national narrative over the course of the twentieth century" (ibid., 429). Increasingly there is a recognition of internal social diversities and recuperation of a repressed history. The earliest film to do so was *Marock* by Laïla Marrakchi (2005). It was part of a sudden surge of Jewish characters in Moroccan cinema in 2006–2007. Three films usually discussed together in this context are *Marock* (2005) *Où vas -tu Moshé* (Hassan Benjelloun, 2007) and *Goodbye Mothers* (Mohamed Ismaïl, 2007). But *Marock* was criticised ardently by Moroccan Muslims for addressing the relationship between a Jewish man and a Muslim woman, and by Moroccan Jews for its disregard of a long-term vision of the Jewish presence in Morocco. However, in our analysis of the film we show how the intimate relationship between Muslim and Jewish adolescents in bourgeois Casablanca not only offers a pathway towards emancipation for the protagonists, the depiction of the relationship also goes beyond caricature and indeed reveals how the Moroccan youth becomes increasingly politicised and critical of the *status quo* in Jewish-Muslim relations.

In *Marock*, Marrakchi portrays the wealthy Westernised youth of Casablanca. Rita (Morjana Alaoui) is a carefree 17-year-old student who kisses boys in parking lots, goes clubbing with a wide circle of friends and smokes marijuana on her roof top while her parents and nanny think she is studying with her girlfriends. Western music features very prominently in her life: she dances around the house and at school, and the soundtrack of the film is dominated by David Bowie's "Rock 'n' Roll Suicide," subtly foreshadowing the tragedy of the film. She comes from a very wealthy Muslim family and as the film starts, Ramadan starts as well. She spots Youri (Matthieu Boujenah) at one of the nightclubs she frequents and falls for his macho good looks, not knowing or caring that he is Jewish. Youri drives a fast car and lives in a grand mansion where he regularly entertains friends. Rita and Youri's love affair starts out based on outward looks and behaviour but quickly develops into a love they say will conquer any religious limitations they face. However, they avoid the confrontation with society, seemingly being subconsciously aware of their own naivety.

Spirituality is central to the narrative, in the sense that the two young protagonists seem to live carefree and easy lives oblivious to the realities of their intercultural, interreligious relationship in a country that struggles with heterogeneity. Muslim Rita for example ignores the rules of Ramadan and says she has her period so that she does not have to partake in the fast. Likewise, she finds her brother's increasingly pious nature annoying, because she wants to talk to him at the moment he is praying. Moreover, her parents hardly feature in her life, whereas the nannies and drivers have a much more direct impact. As such, even when they notice her impious nature, they still submit to their role of serving rather than guiding her. While they warn her of the complex consequences of having a Jew in her life, they still indulge her every whim. Her parents gain authority only when they find out she is having a relationship with a Jew, and they forbid her to engage in the leisure activities to which she is accustomed.

Like Rita, Youri comes from a very rich family, but he is portrayed as completely independent. The difference between being a girl and a boy, even in these wealthy and liberal communities, is highlighted in the film. At no point is there any reference to his Jewishness coming from himself, rather it is Rita's surroundings that point out to her that she needs to be careful about associating with him. The physical attraction between them however is so strong that their spiritual identities lose all relevance. And it is only when their love is consummated for the first time that Rita finds the Star of David necklace around Youri's neck, touches it and pauses. He takes it off but instead of putting it away, he places it around Rita's neck. She keeps it on, and they proceed to make love. This image in the film is doubly controversial. Not only are a Moroccan Muslim and Jew making love, the Jew symbolically "claims" the Muslim woman by putting a quintessentially Jewish symbol around her neck. Her brother spots the necklace and tells their parents.

So, it is *in spite of* their religious surroundings and their having to face one another's integrity in their respective spiritual communities that Rita and Youri love one another. We argue, in fact, that their love is their new spirituality that will eventually kill one of them and emancipate the other. Rita turns her back completely on the failed heterogeneity of Morocco, and go to France. But France only offers another replacement for a failed spirituality, namely the continued privilege of a neoliberal and secular lifestyle. However, Rita's spiritual heritage will follow her there even more than in Morocco, as she will be marked as a Muslim outsider in France's prejudiced culture against its Arab citizens.

The heterogeneity of Moroccan society is something that has been noted and acknowledged in the arts since the end of the 1990s. Even still, the postcolonial wish for homogeneity in national unity remains stronger and continues to undermine the celebration of spiritual or ethnic diversity. Contemporary women filmmakers contribute significantly to the subversion of this homogeneity in order to celebrate the complexity of historical diversity while also promoting new forms of cultural transnationalism. For example, Marrakchi engages with the lived experience of diversity in Morocco, using young love across spiritual borders – a universal *Romeo and Juliet* type love story – to illustrate alternative spaces for an awakening consciousness, through both personal and communal self-discovery. The film "alludes to the failure of the nation-state ideology to recognize the ethnic, religious and class diversity that characterizes modern Morocco" (Hirchi 2011, 105) and instead challenges the protagonists and the audience to open up to the possibility of mixing a materialistic, pragmatic culture in the wealthy suburbs of Casablanca with the greater ideological struggles between spiritual and identitarian philosophies.

When the film was released in Morocco in 2005, it "generated passionate and conflicting reactions from its audiences" (Hirchi 2011, 90; Elkabas 2016, 75). It was a time of substantive social, economic and political reforms as politicians were preparing for legislative elections in 2007. As such, the reception of the film was determined by the ideological positions of its critics, defined by, on the one hand, an appreciation for the courage to embrace freedom of expression and on the other hand a castigating of Marrakchi for showing "disrespect" to Islamic values that allegedly bind Moroccans together. In a society struggling to bridge tradition and modernity at this crucial time before elections, the film – as the first to engage with interfaith relationships – undermined the legitimacy of conservative discourses about interpersonal relations. It laid bare the "hypocrisies in Moroccan society" and the wide divergence between official positions and actual practices related to daily prayer, alcohol consumption, fasting in Ramadan, abortion, virginity, homosexuality and mixed marriage (Hirchi 2011, 91). Indeed, *Marock* opened a space for dialogue on the freedom of speech, women's place in society, and ethnic and religious relations. It criticises Muslim fundamentalism and religious hypocrisy, exemplified by Mao, Rita's brother, and by displaying growing love between two Moroccans regardless of their religion. When Youri says to Rita that "we are all Moroccans first and Muslims and Jews second" he addresses a very sensitive ideological issue, where this discourse might refer to the unity that a postcolonial nation aspires to but where the lived experience still deals with complex taboos in a conservative society.

Capturing the heterogeneous nature of contemporary Morocco, Marrakchi not only deals with the love between a Jew and a Muslim, but also explores the diversity of spiritual experience within the same demographic. Youri's seemingly uncomplicated belonging to Casablanca's neoliberal community shows an engagement with the centuries' old presence of Jews in Morocco. Morocco is their ancestral home. However, *Marock's* sympathy for its Jewish protagonists "triggered anger from members of the Party of Justice and Development, who interpret any association with Judaism as anti-Arab" (Hirchi 2011, 92). Likewise, the presence of an Islamist in Rita's family, who criticises her decadent lifestyle, shows a society struggling to reconcile spirituality and secularism and facing increased extremism in the face of increasing secularism. As with the daring portrayal of sexuality between lovers of different denominations, this polarisation within spiritual communities discloses the precedence of an urban bourgeoisie that controls the country's wealth. Within this maelstrom of identities, Rita symbolises the rebellion against the constraints of any spiritual traditionalism.

Feminist issues are addressed passionately by Marrakchi, inspired by the revision of the Moroccan Family Code – the Mudawana – during the making of the film in 2004. Still rooted entirely in Muslim Sharia law, the new Mudawana now ensured women's rights within the family. It delineated that women share responsibility for the family with their husbands; that women cannot be married against their will; that the minimum age of marriage for men and women is 18; that a wife can object to her husband taking a second wife; that a woman can petition for divorce; and that a daughter has the same inheritance rights as a son (Errazzouki 2018). In *Marock*, Rita certainly claims her rights as a woman to choose her own partner, as a daughter she does not allow her brother to take privileges and in her relationship with Youri she does not allow him to look at other women. Her friends though fail to do so, perhaps indicating that it is Rita's family wealth as well as her feisty nature that allows her to act on her privilege. Rita emerges as an agent of change determined to live up to her secular cultural ideals by rejecting the *status quo* in society. And yet, escaping to France at the end of the film also feels like a defeat: the update of the Mudawana may not have been enough for a feminist like Rita, and Morocco still fails its women, even the privileged ones. While Rita has faith in her secular ideals, exploring all the possibilities of self-liberation, she is still limited by a conservative society. The film shows that Morocco is not yet what Rita aspires to: a secular ideology that promotes diversity, cultural tolerance and social and political change.

These social and political changes are also reflected in the soundtrack. It is a fusion of Western and Arab songs that serve as a contextualisation of the spiritual focus of Rita and Youri's love and life. If love replaces spirituality, then the lyrics emphasise how love is the only ideology. David Bowie's lyrics in "Rock 'n' Roll Suicide" for example emphasise the excitement but mostly the tragedy of living fast and dying young. The other song that appears on the soundtrack three times is "L.O.V.E. Love" by Orange Juice, a song whose lyrics really stress the importance of love as a spiritual experience, something that is impossible to explain but that guides all decisions beyond reason, with lines like: "it's all in the heavens" and "love is something that is so divine."

The only non-Western song in the film is the Arabic "Sidi'h'bibi" by Mano Negra. Again, it is a love song that celebrates the spiritual nature of love's experience: "My darling here he is/He bewitched me, here he is/He comes with grace/ The one who makes me suffer, he is there." The significance of the song's origins and the band's politics cannot be overstated. Mano Negra are pioneers of world fusion and a band that embodies heterogeneity, cultural pluralism and freedom of expression. "Sidi'h'bibi," a huge hit in the nineties, was their only song in Arabic –

a cover of an originally Algerian song by Salim Halali, of Jewish-Arab heritage. As such, the song sums up the film's struggles and strengths: modern young people are trying to embrace the heterogeneity of, and in, Morocco. But being (neo-)liberal in a country still struggling with its colonial past and a contemporary struggle between modernism and conservatism is complicated. Love offers an opportunity to escape the worries of such a complex society. At the same time, love also complicates things further as it crosses boundaries. Young people in this film come across stringent boundaries and attempt to emancipate themselves from these limits. Youri's death is a symbol of the impossibility of a reconciliation between all the heterogeneous ideologies coexisting in Morocco's urban centres, whereas Rita has to leave Morocco because (as opposed to *Française* in Chapter 2) she is unable to reconcile her liberal modern values with the tragedy of Youri's death in a nation struggling with increasingly conservative powers.

Case study: *I Am Not a Witch* (Rungano Nyoni, UK/France/Germany/Zambia, 2017)

A belief in witchcraft exists in traditional spiritual belief systems everywhere, as does the belief in witch doctors or *sangomas* (as they are called in Southern Africa) – traditional healers who treat illnesses believed to be caused by witchcraft through spiritual rites and rituals. Feminist cultural theorists have argued that the witch is the ultimate personification of the patriarchy's fear of powerful women, because they embody the potential for self-directed feminine power, and sexual and intellectual freedom (Solle 2017). The symbol of the witch has been appropriated by feminists, starting with the suffragettes and later re-emerging in the women's liberation movements of the sixties. This symbol likewise exists in African popular culture, for example in Nigerian writer Nnedi Okorafor's short story "Hello, Moto" (2011), adapted into a sci fi short film by Nigerian director C. J. Obasi as *Hello, Rain* in 2018. "There is witchcraft to science and a science to witchcraft," declares the witch, Rain, in Okorafor's narrative, as this female character is associated not only with technological expertise but also with environmental and spiritual knowledge (Jeffreys, 2018). Okorafor's story affirms the recent resurgence of interest in the complex figure of the witch in contemporary popular culture. Witchcraft has its roots in histories of oppression and times of uncertainty and the contemporary manifestations of witchcraft accusations in Africa could likewise be linked to societal instability and insecurity in times of war, economic decline, disastrous environmental change and other phenomena. Witches' magic could therefore be interpreted as the wisdom and practice of oppressed peoples, and as such the witch has become an important motif for feminist, environmentalist and postcolonial reinterpretation (Federici, 2017).

Whilst the witch has become an affirmative symbol in contemporary feminism, in Africa accusations of witchcraft are altogether more ominous and oppressive, with real witch-hunts arising in countries like Gambia, Ghana, Nigeria, Tanzania and Zambia. NGOs have defined poverty, urban migration and the collapse of traditional communities as root causes, while superstitious societal fears are further exploited by unscrupulous Christian preachers. Older women are often accused of witchcraft and ostracised by their communities, as for example in Ghanaian documentary filmmaker Yaba Badoe's *The Witches of Gambaga* (2010), which depicts the plight of women expelled from their communities and forced to take refuge in "witches' camps" in northern Ghana. Witchcraft accusations against older women also often have a more cynical motive, as it offers families a convenient way of getting rid of elderly female relatives who have become a financial burden. Child witchcraft accusations are now on the rise, as children are blamed for any misfortune that befalls a family or community.

Often these children are forced via persecution and torture to confess to being witches, with preachers performing exorcisms and deliverance ceremonies in churches, at a hefty price demanded from the families of the accused. Many African countries have instituted national laws against child witchcraft accusations, but often these are not observed on a local level. Pentecostal churches, which portray the world as a literal battleground between Godly forces and demonic spirits, encourage their congregations to blame witchcraft for their members' misfortunes or personal failures (Ellison n.d.). It is important to note that these church leaders are not enacting any traditional belief but are rather emulating American televangelist counterparts. This has led to a religious hybridisation where indigenous beliefs have merged with an extreme form of Christianity, which has brought great wealth to church leaders. As we outlined above, Nollywood has been complicit in negatively portraying children as witches, but we have elected to focus here on a more critical representation of child witchcraft accusations, analysing Zambian filmmaker Rungano Nyoni's debut feature *I Am Not a Witch* (2017).

Nyoni was born in Zambia and moved to Wales as a child. She graduated from Central Saint Martins – University of the Arts London with an MA in Acting and has directed several award-winning short films, notably the multiple award-winning children-focused *Mwansa the Great* (2011). *I Am Not a Witch* (2017) tells the story of an eight-year-old girl accused of witchcraft and sent to a witches' camp. The film was shot over six weeks around Lusaka, the capital of Zambia, and features a cast of non-professional actors from across the country, including the main actress, Margaret Mulubwa. In researching the film, Nyoni spent a month at a witch camp in Ghana, which she describes in interviews as a village of around 80 older women who have all been accused of witchcraft and exiled from their homes. While the women are sometimes subjected to a trial, often an accusation is enough to stigmatise them. To be allowed into a witch camps, the women have to admit to being a witch, thus performing a false identity for the sake of personal safety. *I Am Not a Witch* premiered in the Director's Fortnight section at the 2017 Cannes Film Festival and has won numerous awards worldwide, including a BAFTA (British Academy for Film and Television Arts) award for Outstanding Debut. The Zambian president Edgar Lungu publicly congratulated the film and filmmaker when it was selected for Cannes and its success has raised hopes for the development of a fledgling Zambian film industry. Nyoni, however, has expressed her discomfort with the film being viewed as central to an emerging Zambian film industry, given that it is a British-produced and funded film.

I Am Not a Witch is a feminist satire told through a generic mix of farce, fable, magical realism and arthouse aesthetics. Nyoni envisioned the film as an absurdist dark comedy, an exaggeration of real life, that would call out her country's history of misogyny and condemn the ludicrousness of witchcraft accusations against older women and children. We are introduced to this innovative narrative and aesthetic approach right at the start of the film, which opens with Italian composer Vivaldi's famous "The Four Seasons" concerto as a bus of tourists approaches a witch camp. The White tourists gawk at African women with white face paint, dressed in identical blue overalls, sitting motionless behind a fence in a row facing the tourists. All the women are tethered to white ribbons attached to their shoulder blades – the film's main ingenious magical realist conceit – which the tour guide explains is to prevent the women from flying away; they are witches after all. The scene builds up to a climax as the music reaches a crescendo and the women start shouting and waving their arms around as if possessed. It is a surreal and alienating opening, made all the more strange by the presence of the baroque music soundtrack, which serves to set up a Western versus African dichotomy, implicating the neo-colonial complicity in perpetuating the super-stitions that creates such oppression and incarceration.

After this introduction, the film cuts to a young girl, the protagonist, who observes a woman falling over while carrying a bucket of water on her head. This unfortunate incident is used as grounds for the young girl to be accused of witch-craft. As the woman claims to a policewoman that the young girl is a witch, other witnesses come forward as well, including a man claiming that the girl hit him with an axe which caused his arm to fall off (although his arm has been magically reat-tached to his body). The policewoman attempts to show sympathy for the girl and to humanise her by asking her name, but the baying mob prevents her from answering. In fact, we never learn her real name. This minor incident escalates to a full-blown witch trial, in which the young girl is found guilty and sent off to a witch camp, where she too is tethered to a long white ribbon and informed that she will transform into a goat if she tries to escape. Each ribbon is attached to an enormous spool, and the spools sit on the bed of an orange 18-wheeler truck, restricting the freedom of movement of the women in a rather grotesque way.

The corrupt and portly Mr Banda, a government official, becomes the girl's guardian. He is a comical character who is lying in the bath when we are introduced to him, being scrubbed by his dutiful wife. He receives a phone call from the policewoman informing him of the young girl who has just been accused of being a witch. On his way to see her, Banda visits a witchdoctor who performs a ceremony involving a chicken in order to determine whether or not she is a witch. The witchdoctor performs a ritualistic dance to a soundtrack of improvisational and dis-sonant jazz music. As with the baroque music, the film's musical choices are often incongruous and disconcerting. Banda, in a pompous display of self-importance, tells the witches what the government has done for them – a new truck, longer ribbons –

as he presents to them the newest and youngest member of their community. The women are shocked that such a young girl has been accused of witchcraft. Frightened and mute, she tries to run away but is thwarted by her restrictive ribbon. The young girl gradually settles into her new community and is named "Shula" by the older women, which means "to be uprooted."

Shula does not say much, muted by the shock of what is happening to her, and her inscrutable expression carries the incomprehension of her situation. The older women take her into their care and offer a sense of community and protection. They present Shula with a blue horn through which she can listen to the distant chatter and laughter of schoolchildren carried on the wind – another magical realist detail, and an attempt to reconnect Shula with the life of a child from which she was severed. Witch camps often serve as exploitative sources for free labour, and each morning the women of the camps are driven to a corn field or a quarry to work.

Banda sees in Shula an opportunity for power and profit, and he takes her around on official government errands, exploiting her alleged witch's power to bolster his own standing. Shula is presented with a line-up of suspects and asked to pick out the culprit who stole a villager's money, and she is expected to take part in rainmaking ceremonies in the drought-stricken region. Banda even accompanies Shula onto a television chat show, where viewers get to call in to ask her questions, and which presents an opportunity for Banda to advertise special Shula-branded eggs that allegedly "bring back the life in your breakfast." When a caller questions whether Shula is actually a witch rather than just a normal child, the camera lingers on her state guardian, silent, uncertain and dumbfounded. We learn that Banda's wife was also accused of witchcraft and still has a ribbon attached to her shoulder blades; she advises Shula that it is marriage and respectability that absolved her.

When Shula is expected by the queen to bring rain if she really is a witch, the narrative gradually builds up to its climax as Shula starts dancing in the dust and is carried off roughly when she urinates on the dry earth. That evening Shula informs the older women that she should have chosen to become a goat, to be free, and she gets up at night and leaves the large white tent with sleeping women. A cut to the next morning shows two men transporting Shula's body on a cart drawn by oxen and laying her down on the dry earth, covered by a sack. The women, now dressed in striking red, mourn her death as they gather around her body, carrying out a final celebratory song for Shula as clouds gather, thunder is heard, and it finally starts to rain. The rainstorm washes the screen to white, fading gradually into the final scene of the film that comprises a slow zoom into the truck with the enormous spools and cut ribbons billowing in the wind.

There are many elements in *I Am Not a Witch* that link with African spiritual beliefs, such as the magical properties of inanimate objects evoking animism, the rituals conducted by a witch doctor, and rainmaking ceremonies linked to feminine power. Nyoni takes some creative licence when depicting rather complex belief systems, and although the film's satirical and caustic tone is unmistakable, it is not repudiating mystical or supernatural belief systems altogether. Rather it is interrogating beliefs that could be harmful or oppressive, especially society's misogynistic tendency to curb the power of women seen as nonconformist, rebellious or dangerous. It is calling out the corruption of adults like Banda and the queen, who exploit innocent women and children by capitalising on societal fears and superstitions in the way that Pentecostal churches and other state apparatuses have done in real-world examples in Africa. Shula's death, similar to the ending of Safi Faye's *Mossane*, another film about a magical young girl, is perhaps inevitable, as it serves as the catalyst for the women's emancipation. In spite of the societal restrictions they are subjected to, created by a dangerous mix of metaphysical beliefs, modernity and capitalism, the women undertake the emancipatory act of cutting their ribbons.

★★★★

Spirituality and cinema have a longstanding relationship, and in Africa, spirituality is central to the arrival of cinema, both as a censorship tool and in the development into an Africanised performance on screen. In the films discussed here, spirituality – whether this is Islam or an indigenous system – serves as a pathway to emancipation not so much as an aid but as a system against which to assert one's individual identity. In both films a young person dies because of spiritually-inspired frustrations. In *Marock*, Youri's death inspires Rita to turn her back on majority-Muslim Morocco and its intolerance for diversity. In *I Am Not a Witch*, inspired by stories and myths, Shula chooses death over a lifetime in captivity. Both young women make devastating choices, because their experience of spirituality is one that holds them back. And yet, in making these decisions, they emancipate themselves from an old, inflexible spirituality to take the path of freedom, channelling their inner agency. They know that spirituality is meant to embrace all people as equals, and because of society's failure to enact this, young women are forced to assert their agency in spite of spiritual constraints, setting an example for those less able to express themselves. An individual and more tolerant path is taken, away from a spirituality that is imposed by human forces that retain conservative power structures. It is Shula and Rita's forceful act *against* spirituality and the way they *enact* this process that shapes their pathway to emancipation.

Note

1 There are several documentaries about Kimpa Vita, one recent example being the Ne Kunda Nlaba biopic *Kimpa Vita: The Mother of African Revolution* (2016).

Bibliography

Adegoke, Yomi (2016) "'Jesus hasn't saved us': The young black women returning to ancestral religions," *Broadly Blog*. Available online: https://broadly.vice.com/en_us/a rticle/bjgxx4/jesus-hasnt-saved-us-young-black-women-returning-ancestral-religions [Accessed February 2019].

Antler, Joyce (2018) *Jewish Radical Feminism: Voices from the Women's Liberation Movement*. New York: NYU Press.

BBC World Service (n.d.) "Christianity," *The Story of Africa*. Available online: www.bbc.co. uk/worldservice/africa/features/storyofafrica/index_section8.shtml [Accessed January 2019].

Bortolot, Alexander Ives (2003) "Women leaders in African history: Dona Beatriz, Kongo Prophet," *The MET Museum* website. Available online: www.metmuseum.org/toah/hd/p wmn_4/hd_pwmn_4.htm [Accessed January 2019].

Dönmez-Colin, Gönül (2004) *Women, Islam and Cinema*. London: Reaktion Books

Elkabas, Charles (2016) "Religion and individual civil rights: Moroccan Jewish citizens in Where Are You Going Moshe?" *Journal of African Cinemas* 8(1), pp. 75–86.

Ellison, Marc (n.d.) "Branded and beaten: The children accused of witchcraft and murder," *BBC News Resource*. Available online: www.bbc.co.uk/news/resources/idt-sh/nigeria_ children_witchcraft [Accessed February 2019].

Errazzouki, Samia (2018) "Ten years after Morocco's Mudawwana: The rhetoric and reality of women's rights," *Mediterranean Politics* 23(4), pp. 539–545.

Federici, Silvia (2017) *Caliban and The Witch: Women, the Body and Primitive Accumulation*. New York, NY: Autonomedia.

Garuba, Harry (2003) "Explorations in animist materialism: Notes on reading/writing African literature, culture, and society," *Public Culture*, 15(2), pp. 261–285.

Gauch, Suzanne (2009) "Now you see it, now you don't: Transnational feminist spectatorship and Farida Benlyazid's *A Door to the Sky*," *Camera Obscura*, 24(2), pp. 107–137.

Gilombe, Mudiji Malamba (1988) *Culture et art africain au défi de l'acculturation*, Kinshasa: Revue africaine de théologie.

Hackett, Rosalind (1998) *Art and Religion in Africa*. London: A&C Black.

Hirchi, Mohammed (2011) "The ethics and politics of Laila Marrakchi's *Marock*," *South Central Review* 28(1), pp. 90–108.

Jeffreys, Tom (2018) "The return of the witch in contemporary culture," *Frieze*. Available online: https://frieze.com/article/return-witch-contemporary-culture?fbclid=IwAR0enNn Ommo-qSATM4vr1I9EZsUEEXL6c7Ka-W34PH_5FW2lLTuF3wuu0wU [Accessed February 2019].

Kamba, Donald (2017) "Women's role in African spirituality," *The Sunday Mail* (5 March). Available online: www.sundaymail.co.zw/womens-role-in-african-spirituality/ [Accessed February 2019].

Kosansky, Oren and Aomar Boum (2012) "The 'Jewish question' in postcolonial Moroccan cinema," *International Journal of Middle East Studies*, 44(3), pp. 421–442.

Lusungu Moyo, Fulata (2004) "Religion, spirituality and being a woman in Africa: Gender construction within the African religio-cultural experiences," *Agenda, Empowering Women for Gender Equity*, 61, pp. 72–78.

Lyden, John (2009) *The Routledge Companion to Religion and Film*. London and New York: Routledge.

Mahmood, S. (2005) *Politics of Piety: The Islamic Revival and the Feminist Subject*. Princeton: Princeton University Press.

Mbari Hinga, Teresia (2017) *African, Christian, Feminist: The Enduring Search for What Matters*. Maryknoll, NY: Orbis Books.

Mbiti, John S. (1990) *African Religions and Philosophy*, 2nd edition. London: Heinemann.

Oha, Obododimma (2000), "The rhetoric of Nigerian Christian videos." In J. Haynes (ed.) *Nigerian Video Films*. Ohio University Center, pp. 192–199.

Okorafor, Nnedi (2011) *Hello, Moto*. New York, NY: Tor Books.

Oredein, Oluwatomisin (2018) "Review of African, Christian, feminist," *Reading Religion* (April 27). Available online: http://readingreligion.org/books/african-christian-feminist [Accessed January 2019].

Pak-Shiraz, Nacim (2011/2018) *Shi'i Islam in Iranian Cinema. Religion and Spirituality in Film.* London: IB Tauris.

Plate, S. Brent (2017) *Religion and Film. Cinema and the Re-Creation of the World.* New York: Columbia University Press.

Pui-lan, Kwok (2004) "Mercy Amba Oduyoye and African women's theology," *Journal of Feminist Studies in Religion,* 20(1), pp. 7–22.

Rutledge, Emerald (2017) "African spirituality and the power of religious reclamation." Available online: www.aaihs.org/african-spirituality-and-the-power-of-religious-reclamation/ [Accessed February 2019].

Salami, Mini (2017) "What most people don't know about African spirituality," *MSA Afropolitan.* Available online: www.msafropolitan.com/2017/10/what-most-people-dont-know-about-african-spirituality.html [Accessed February 2019].

Samiuddin, Abida and Khanam, R. (2002) *Muslim Feminism and Feminist Movement.* New Delhi: Global Vision Publishing House.

Shafik, Viola (2016) *Arab Cinema. History and Cultural Identity.* Cairo: AUC Press.

Shaheen, Jack G. (2001) *Reel Bad Arabs: How Hollywood Vilifies a People.* Northampton: Olive Branch Press.

Shaikh, S. (2004) "Transforming feminisms: Islam, women, and gender justice." In Omid Safi (ed.) *Progressive Muslims: On Justice, Gender and Pluralism.* Oxford: Oneworld.

Solle, Kristen J. (2017) *Witches, Sluts, Feminists: Conjuring the Sex Positive.* Berkeley, CA: ThreeL Media.

Steyne, Philip M. (1990) *Gods of Power: A Study of the Beliefs and Practices of Animists.* Houston: Touch.

Turaki, Yusufu (2000) 'Africa traditional religious system as basis of understanding Christian spiritual warfare.' Available online: www.lausanne.org/content/west-african-case-study [Accessed February 2019].

Thornton, Pr. John K. (1998) "Kimpa Vita of Kongo." In *The Kongolese Saint Anthony: Dona Beatriz Kimpa Vita and the Antonian Movement, 1684–1706.* Available online: https://africaheritages.wordpress.com/african-leaders-and-empires/african-women-leaders/kimpa-vita-of-kongo/ [Accessed January 2019].

Wright, Melanie (2006) *Religion and Film: An Introduction.* London: IB Tauris.

Filmography

Bab Al-Sama Maftuh / A Door to the Sky, Dir. Farida Benlyazid, Morocco, 1989

Confessions of a Gambler, Dir. Rayda Jacobs, South Africa, 2007

Don't Touch, Dir. Zulfah Otto-Sallies, South Africa, 2006

Goodbye Mothers, Dir Mohamed Ismaïl, Morocco, 2007

Hello, Rain, Dir. C. J. Obasi, Nigeria, 2018

I Am Not a Witch, Dir. Rungano Nyoni, UK/France/Germany/Zambia, 2017

Inch'Allah Dimanche, Dir. Yamina Benguigui, France/Algeria, 2001

Kimpa Vita: The Mother of African Revolution, Dir. Ne Kunda Nlaba, DRC, 2016.

La nuit de la vérité / The Night of Truth, Dir. Fanta Régina Nacro, Burkina Faso/France, 2004

Marock, Dir. Laila Marrakchi, Morocco/France, 2005

Mayfair, Dir. Sara Blecher, South Africa, 2018

Mossane, Dir Safi Faye, Germany/Senegal, 1996

Mwanza the Great, Dir. Rungano Nyoni, UK/Zambia, 2011

New Moon, Dir. Philippa Ndisi-Herrmann, Kenya, 2018

Où vas -tu Moshé, Dir. Hassan Benjelloun, Morocco, 2007

Rafiki, Dir. Wanuri Kahiu, Kenya/South Africa/Germany/Netherlands/France/Norway/
   Lebanon, 2018
Raya, Dir. Zulfah Otto-Sallies, South Africa, 2000
Something Necessary, Dir. Judy Kibinge, Germany/Kenya, 2013
The Witches of Gambaga, Dir. Yaba Badoe, Ghana, 2010
Through the Eyes of My Daughter, Dir. Zulfah Otto-Sallies, South Africa, 2004
Zin'naariya! / *The Wedding Ring*, Dir. Rahmatou Keïta, Burkina Faso/Niger/France, 2016

EPILOGUE

The lack of access to African cinema has been decried by scholars, critics, curators and cinephiles for decades. As film festival curators and researchers, we – the authors of this book – have privileged access to films, whereas this is not the case for most audiences as cinemas and film festivals worldwide continue to neglect African film. Very few African films receive theatrical releases in the UK, where this book has been published. The five African film festivals in the UK – a consortium called TANO[1] (meaning "five" in Swahili) – have attempted to address this lacuna. Each of these UK-based festivals also collaborates with other internationally located African film festivals, to share resources and best practice.

One of the initiatives to combat the limited access to African cinema came from the Africa in Motion Film Festival, an African film festival launched in Scotland in 2006, with which both authors have been closely involved (Bisschoff as founder and director until 2012, and Van de Peer as director for a number of years). Africa in Motion launched a searchable African film database in 2016, where information on African films is stored (including titles, directors, year of production, production countries, themes, genres and synopses) and users can find details on distributors and rights holders, thus enabling others to get access to the films (www.africanfilm database.com). Previously, the MNet African Film Library, managed by the South African broadcaster MNet, and the Médiathèque des Trois Mondes in Paris were two of the central databases and catalogues for information on African cinema, but these have disappeared due to a lack of funding.

Lack of funding is less of an issue in the US. Some initiatives that specifically support the distribution of African women's films, within a broader remit, are Arab Film Distribution (www.arabfilm.com/) (Seattle), California Newsreel (http://newsreel.org) (San Francisco), Women Make Movies (www.wmm.com) (New York) and Array Now (www.arraynow.com) (Los Angeles). Perhaps one of the reasons these distribution initiatives dedicate part of their remit to African films by women, is precisely that they are American. By and large, feminism and racism are both very urgently debated issues in the US, while film is big business, and so is activism, as exemplified by movements such as Black Lives Matter and #MeToo. In the UK, it is still very difficult to find distributors dedicated to African cinema (the community interest company Aya Distribution (www.ayadistribution.org/) being a lone exception), as distributors and cinemas are overwhelmingly interested in films that they are certain would yield a substantial financial return. There is still a lack of belief or interest in films from Africa, due to ingrained prejudice. Theatrical distribution of African films is much more extensive in countries such as France and Belgium, with many European distributors specialising in the distribution of African cinema, although still marginal within a diverse menu of world cinema. As such, very often, film festivals are the only places where one can see classic or new African films.

When it comes to the exhibition of African films at film festivals around the world, there is a gaping hole in the programmes of most of the prominent festivals where women's films are concerned. While the major players such as Cannes and Berlinale do occasionally recognise the quality of African cinema, they tend to stick to certain individual favourite directors (or male auteurs) rather than acknowledging a solid basic knowledge of the diversity of African cinema. The Toronto International Film Festival is one A-list film festival which has been demonstrably dedicated to promoting the diversity of African cinema, in particular championing young and emerging voices. As Lindiwe Dovey superbly shows in her book *Curating Africa* (2015), the politics of screening specific African films at specific film festivals are subject to intricate, complex and often hidden agendas.

The most "important" festivals on the African continent are geographically very well spread out: there is the hub of West African cinema at FESPACO in Burkina Faso. The International Cinema Days in Carthage in Tunisia and the Cairo International Film Festival in Egypt represent the north of the continent. The East of the continent is represented by the Zanzibar International Film Festival in Tanzania, while the Durban International Film Festival takes place annually in South Africa. Chronologically, Carthage was the first to be established in 1966. FESPACO followed suit in 1969. The Cairo Festival was founded in 1976 while Durban was founded in 1979 and ZIFF in 1997. There are also an increasing number of film festivals on the continent specifically dedicated to women (see Table 9A.1 in the Appendix).

There are many festivals dedicated to African cinema globally – in many European countries and in the Americas, to Japan, Australia and New Zealand. Some of these regularly dedicate entire programmes to women's films, or ensure fair representation of African women both in front of, and behind, the camera. Besides film festivals, there are a few other avenues to explore in order to see African films, including digital distribution through an increasing number of video-on-demand and online streaming platforms such as Mubi, Netflix, Amazon Prime Video and Google Play, and other, more specifically Africa-oriented ones – in particular for Nollywood films – such as the Africa Movie Channel, The Africa Channel,

TracePlay, Iroko TV, Millennium TV, AfroStream, Ibaka TV, AfriNolly, and many others. African films are also increasingly available on DVD (including restorations and re-releases of classic films) which could be purchased online from outlets such as Amazon and specialist distributors such as those mentioned above, or from street vendors in African cities.

Note

1 TANO consists of Africa in Motion in Scotland, Afrika Eye in Bristol, Film Africa in London, Watch-Africa in Wales and the Cambridge African Film Festival.

Appendix

TABLE 9A.1 African women's film festivals

Festival	City	Country	Founder/ Director	Year	Month
International Images Film Festival for Women	Harare and Bulawayo	Zimbabwe	Tsitsi Dangarembga	2002	August
Films Femmes Afrique/African Women's Film Festival	Dakar	Senegal	Amayel Ndiaye and Stéphanie Maurin	2003 (second edition in 2016)	February
Festival International du Film de Femmes de Salé	Salé	Morocco	Hassania Raho	2004	September
Cairo International Women Film Festival	Cairo	Egypt	Amal Ramsis	2007	March
Mis Me Binga Festival	Yaoundé	Cameroon	Narcisse Wandji	2010	March
Women of the Sun Film Festival	Johannesburg	South Africa	Eve Rantseli	2010 (not currently active)	September
Journées cinématographiques de la femme africaine (JCFA)/The Film Festival of African Women	Ouagadougou	Burkina Faso	Michel Ouedraogo	2012	March
Udada International Women's Film Festival	Nairobi	Kenya	Matrid Nyagah	2014	October
Festival du cinéma au féminin/ Women's Film Festival	Kinshasa	Democratic Republic of the Congo	Clarisse Muruba	2014	June
Mzansi Women's Film Festival	Johannesburg	South Africa	Ntokozo Mahlalela	2014	August
Tazama African Women Film Festival	Brazzaville	Republic of the Congo	Claudia Haidara-Yoka	2014	January

Festival	City	Country	Founder/Director	Year	Month
Urusaro International Women Film Festival	Kigali	Rwanda	Poupoun Sesonga Kamikazi	2016	March
Ndiva Women's Film Festival	Accra	Ghana	Aseye Tamakloe	2017	November
Mama Afrika Film Festival	Nairobi	Kenya	Matrid Nyagah	2018	September
African Women Arts and Film Festival (AWAF)	Dar es Salaam	Tanzania	Unknown	2019	March
Cotonou International Women's Film Festival	Cotonou	Benin	Unknown	2019	September

INDEX

Note: Film titles are in *italic* followed by the year in parentheses; titles of other works are in *italic*; the page span for the table is in **bold**.